WESLEYAN THEOLOGY
A SOURCEBOOK

WESLEYAN THEOLOGY
A SOURCEBOOK

Thomas A. Langford

THE LABYRINTH PRESS

Durham, North Carolina

Library of Congress Cataloging in Publication Data

Main entry under title:

Wesleyan theology.

    1. Methodist Church—Doctrines—Addresses, essays,
lectures. 2. Theology, Doctrinal—Addresses, essays, lectures.
I. Langford, Thomas A.
    BX8332.W45   1984   230'.7   84-7170
    ISBN 0-939464-40-3 (lib. bdg.)
    ISBN 0-939464-41-1 (pbk.)

Printed in the United States of America

This book was published with the assistance of a grant
from the Center for Studies in the Wesleyan Tradition
of the Duke University Divinity School.

CONTENTS

Preface   vii

Introduction: John Wesley   1

PART I

EARLY DEVELOPMENTS

John Fletcher, "First Check to Antinomianism"   23

Adam Clarke, "Justification"   35
    "The Holy Spirit"   39

Nathan Bangs, "On Election"   45
    "On Christian Perfection"   50

Richard Watson, "Man a Moral Agent"   56
    "The Justice and Grace of God"   62

PART II

DEVELOPING DISTINCTIVENESS

Francis Asbury, "Valedictory Address"   67

Phoebe Palmer, "The Way of Holiness"   86

Daniel D. Whedon, "Doctrines of Methodism"   91

William Burt Pope, "Methodist Doctrine"   105

Thomas N. Ralston, "Christian Baptism"   115
    "The Lord's Supper"   122

John Miley, "Theism"   127

       "Sufficiency of the Atonement"   132

Milton S. Terry, "Methodism and Biblical Criticism"   137

PART III

CHANGING DIRECTION

Borden Parker Bowne, "The Immanence of God"   151

Albert C. Knudson, "Henry Clay Sheldon—Theologian"   162

Olin A. Curtis, "The Church of Our Lord"   174

Edgar Sheffield Brightman, "The Resultant Idea of God"   182

Harris Franklin Rall, "The Finality of the Christian Religion"   194

Georgia Harkness, "The Work of the Holy Spirit"   204

L. Harold DeWolf, "The God Who Speaks"   212

PART IV

RESTATING DOCTRINES

Edwin Lewis, "A Christian Manifesto"   221

Edward T. Ramsdell, "The Rational Predicament"   230

Albert C. Outler, "Holiness of Heart and Life"   240

Robert E. Cushman, "The Shape of Christian Faith—A Platform"   250

Carl Michalson, "Jesus of Nazareth and the Word of Faith"   259

PART V

DOCTRINE AND DOCTRINAL STATEMENTS

Albert C. Outler, "Introduction of the Disciplinary Statement"   273

Robert E. Cushman, "Church Doctrinal Standards Today"   279

Bi-Lateral Dialogues with Lutherans and Roman Catholics   291

Index   307

PREFACE

The Methodist theological tradition is being freshly discovered and this discovery now needs to be explored in depth. Primary source materials provide opportunity for a first-hand encounter with this tradition, yet much important material is not readily available. Consequently, the selections included in this collection make accessible characteristic writings of important thinkers, and discussion of critical issues that have been significant in the formation of Methodist theology.

The Wesleyan tradition is broader than United Methodism, but in order to keep clear focus and to provide enough material for adequate interpretation of historical developments, the concentration is on United Methodism, the dominant stream of the tradition. Only a limited number of particularly important readings have been chosen. This has been done to allow the authors to speak for themselves with some fullness. Short introductions are provided but the conviction underlying this book of readings is that primary sources are of basic historical importance, and these must be presented in such a way that they will be carefully read for their own value.

The principles of selection for this volume need to be set forth. Major authors and themes that have played a critical role in the development of Wesleyan theology have been chosen. Where the author is primary, the selection attempts to present both individual distinctiveness and an issue that is important for the ongoing tradition. Where the theme has primary importance, a representative writer on that theme has been chosen. To balance these interests in limited space has forced difficult decisions of inclusion and exclusion, but an effort has been made to represent the tradition in accurate ways. Greater weight has been placed on the earlier part of the tradition because of the difficulty of obtaining primary documents and the general lack of familiarity with these materials. The selections of individual theologians stops with the generation which is now retired from active appointment; this decision speaks to the overabundance not paucity of current activity and important theological statements. It is assumed that contemporary materials are more readily available and that teachers or groups can make their own choice among current writers and directions. In order to provide more primary content, footnotes in the selections have been excluded.

To survey the Wesleyan theological tradition, to assume responsibility for selecting its leading spokespersons and ideas, and to indicate its historical development constitute a heavy responsibility. It must be emphasized that the Wesleyan tradition is open for interpretation of both its achieved character and its future prospects. This book of readings represents an attempt to open a door through which others may enter and look and learn.

The selections are arranged in chronological order with a minimal historical framework provided. For a study of these theologians and issues that sets them into an interpretative context, reference may be made to my book *PRACTICAL DIVINITY: THEOLOGY IN THE WESLEYAN TRADITION* (Abingdon, 1983).

My hope in providing these resources is that they will excite interest in Wesleyan theology and lead to a more thorough understanding and appreciation of the Wesleyan tradition.

TAL

INTRODUCTION

JOHN WESLEY

John Wesley (1703–1791), the founder of Methodism, left a rich deposit of writings. His works cover a number of areas, including sermons, biblical interpretation, and theological treatises; journals, diaries, letters and biographies; hymns and a manual on practical medicine. He published more than any other theologian in the Methodist tradition and any small group of selections cannot do adequate justice to the numerous facets of his thought. Nevertheless, the following selections provide an introduction to his major themes of salvation, the Christian life, and the Lord's Supper. In these selections both the breadth of Wesley's indebtedness to the ecumenical Christian tradition and his distinctive interpretation of the Christian message are evident. In Wesley's holistic presentation of the Christian gospel, theology and preaching, new birth and nurture, sacraments and service are tightly interwoven. We begin our study of major thinkers and themes in the Wesleyan tradition with John Wesley whose stewardship of his spiritual, intellectual, and organizational gifts inaugurated the Methodist movement. The sermon, article, and hymns that follow (both of which are by Charles Wesley [1707–1788], John's brother and close associate who set Methodist theology in verse) illustrate Wesley's development of central themes and provide a brief introductory context for the study of Wesley's theological descendents.

1

SALVATION BY FAITH

preached at
ST. MARY'S OXFORD, BEFORE THE UNIVERSITY,
on June 18, 1738.

"By grace are ye saved through faith." Eph. ii. 8.

1. All the blessings which God hath bestowed upon man, are of his mere grace, bounty, or favour; his free, undeserved favour; favour altogether undeserved; man having no claim to the least of his mercies. It was free grace that "formed man of the dust of the ground, and breathed into him a living soul," and stamped on that soul the image of God, and "put all things under his feet." The same free grace continues to us, at this day, life, and breath, and all things. For there is nothing we are, or have, or do, which can deserve the least thing at God's hand. "All our works, thou, O God! hast wrought in us." These, therefore, are so many more instances of free mercy: And whatever righteousness may be found in man, this is also the gift of God.

2. Wherewithal then shall a sinful man atone for any the least of his sins? with his own works? No. Were they ever so many, or holy, they are not his own, but God's. But indeed they are all unholy and sinful themselves, so that every one of them needs a fresh atonement. Only corrupt fruit grows on a corrupt tree. And his heart is altogether corrupt and abominable; being "come short of the glory of God," the glorious righteousness at first impressed on his soul, after the image of his great Creator. Therefore, having nothing, neither righteousness nor works, to plead, his mouth is utterly stopped before God.

3. If then sinful men find favour with God, it is "grace upon grace!" If God vouchsafe still to pour fresh blessings upon us, yea, the greatest of all blessings, salvation; what can we say to these things, but, "Thanks be unto God for his unspeakable gift!" And thus it is. Herein "God commendeth his love toward us, in that, while we were yet sinners, Christ died" to save us. "By grace," then, "are ye saved through faith." Grace is the source, faith the condition, of salvation.

Now, that we fall not short of the grace of God, it concerns us carefully to inquire,

I. What faith it is through which we are saved.
II. What is the salvation which is through faith.
III. How we may answer some objections.

I. What faith it is through which we are saved.

1. And, First, it is not barely the faith of a Heathen.

2

Now, God requireth of a Heathen to believe, "that God is; that he is a rewarder of them that diligently seek him;" and that he is to be sought by glorifying him as God, by giving him thanks for all things, and by a careful practice of moral virtue, of justice, mercy, and truth, toward their fellow-creatures. A Greek or Roman, therefore, yea, a Scythian or Indian, was without excuse if he did not believe thus much: The being and attributes of God, a future state of reward and punishment, and the obligatory nature of moral virtue. For this is barely the faith of a Heathen.

2. Nor, Secondly, is it the faith of a devil, though this goes much farther than that of a Heathen. For the devil believes, not only that there is a wise and powerful God, gracious to reward, and just to punish; but also, that Jesus is the Son of God, the Christ, the Saviour of the world. So we find him declaring, in express terms, (Luke iv. 34,) "I know thee who thou art; the Holy One of God." Nor can we doubt but that unhappy spirit believes all those words which came out of the mouth of the Holy One; yea, and whatsoever else was written by those holy men of old, of two of whom he was compelled to give that glorious testimony, "These men are the servants of the Most High God, who show unto you the way of salvation." Thus much, then, the great enemy of God and man believes and trembles in believing, —that God was made manifest in the flesh; that he will"tread all enemies under his feet;" and that "all Scripture was given by inspiration of God." Thus far goeth the faith of a devil.

3. Thirdly. The faith through which we are saved, in that sense of the word which will hereafter be explained, is not barely that which the Apostles themselves had while Christ was yet upon earth; though they so believed on him as to "leave all and follow him;" although they had then power to work miracles, to "heal all manner of sickness, and all manner of disease;" yea, they had then "power and authority over all devils;" and, which is beyond all this, were sent by their Master to "preach the kingdom of God."

4. What faith is it then through which we are saved? It may be answered, First, in general, it is a faith in Christ: Christ, and God through Christ, are the proper objects of it. Herein, therefore, it is sufficiently, absolutely distinguished from the faith either of ancient or modern Heathens. And from the faith of a devil it is fully distinguished by this, —it is not barely a speculative, rational thing, a cold, lifeless assent, a train of ideas in the head; but also a disposition of the heart. For thus saith the Scripture, "With the heart man believeth unto righteousness;" and, "If thou shalt confess with thy mouth the Lord Jesus, and shalt believe with thy heart, that God hath raised him from the dead, thou shalt be saved."

3

5. And herein does it differ from that faith which the Apostles themselves had while our Lord was on earth, that it acknowledges the necessity and merit of his death, and the power of his resurrection. It acknowledges his death as the only sufficient means of redeeming man from death eternal, and his resurrection as the restoration of us all to life and immortality; inasmuch as he "was delivered for our sins, and rose again for our justification." Christian faith is then, not only an assent to the whole gospel of Christ, but also a full reliance on the blood of Christ; a trust in the merits of his life, death, and resurrection; a recumbency upon him as our atonement and our life, *as given for us*, and *living in us*; and, in consequence hereof, a closing with him, and cleaving to him, as our "wisdom, righteousness, sanctification, and redemption," or, in one word, our salvation.

II. What salvation it is, which is through this faith, is the Second thing to be considered

1. And, First, whatsoever else it imply, it is a present salvation. It is something attainable, yea, actually attained, on earth, by those who are partakers of this faith. For thus saith the Apostle to the believers at Ephesus, and in them to the believers of all ages, not *Ye shall be*, (though that also is true,) but, "*Ye are saved* through faith."

2. *Ye are saved* (to comprise all in one word) from sin. This is the salvation which is through faith. This is that great salvation foretold by the angel, before God brought his First-begotten into the world: "Thou shalt call his name JESUS. For he shall save his people from their sins." And neither here, nor in other parts of holy writ, is there any limitation or restriction. All his people, or, as it is elsewhere expressed, "all that believe in him," he will save from all their sins; from original and actual, past and present sin, "of the flesh and of the spirit." Through faith that is in him, they are saved both from the guilt and from the power of it.

3. First. From the guilt of all past sin: For, whereas all the world is guilty before God, insomuch that should he "be extreme to mark what is done amiss, there is none that could abide it;" and whereas, "by the law is" only "the knowledge of sin," but no deliverance from it, so that, "by fulfilling the deeds of the law, no flesh can be justified in his sight;" now 'the righteousness of God, which is by faith of Jesus Christ, is manifested unto all that believe." Now "they are justified freely by his grace, through the redemption that is in Jesus Christ." Him God hath set forth to be a propitiation through faith in his blood, to declare his righteousness for (or by) the remission of the sins that are past." Now hath Christ taken away "the curse of the law, being made a curse for us." He hath "blotted out the handwriting that was against us, taking it out of the way, nailing

4

it to his cross." There is, therefore, no condemnation now, to them which" believe "in Christ Jesus."

4. And being saved from guilt, they are saved from fear. Not indeed from a filial fear of offending; but from all servile fear; from that fear which hath torment; from fear of punishment; from fear of the wrath of God, whom they now no longer regard as a severe Master, but as an indulgent Father."They have not received again the spirit of bondage, but the Spirit of adoption, whereby they cry, Abba, Father: The Spirit itself also bearing witness with their spirits, that they are the children of God." They are also saved from the fear, though not from the possibility, of falling away from the grace of God, and coming short of the great and precious promises. Thus have they"peace with God through our Lord Jesus Christ. They rejoice in hope of the glory of God. And the love of God is shed abroad in their hearts, through the Holy Ghost which is given unto them." And hereby they are persuaded, (though perhaps not at all times, nor with the same fulness of persuasion,) that "neither death, nor life, nor things present, nor things to come, nor height, nor depth, nor any other creature, shall be able to separate them from the love of God, which is in Christ Jesus our Lord."

5. Again, through this faith they are saved from the power of sin, as well as from the guilt of it. So the Apostle declares, "Ye know that he was manifested to take away our sins; and in him is no sin. Whosoever abideth in him, sinneth not." (1 John iii. 5, &c.) Again, "little children, let no man deceive you. He that committeth sin is of the devil. Whosoever believeth, is born of God. And whosoever is born of God doth not commit sin, for his seed remaineth in him: And he cannot sin, because he is born of God." Once more, "We know, that whosoever is born of God sinneth not: But he that is begotten of God, keepeth himself, and that wicked one toucheth him not." (1 John v.18.)

6. He that is, by faith, born of God, sinneth not (1.) By any habitual sin; for all habitual sin is sin reigning: But sin cannot reign in any that believeth. Nor (2.) By any wilful sin; for his will, while he abideth in the faith, is utterly set against all sin, and abhorreth it as deadly poison. Nor (3.) By any sinful desire; for he continually desireth the holy and perfect will of God; and any tendency to an unholy desire, he, by the grace of God, stifleth in the birth. Nor (4.) Doth he sin by infirmities, whether in act, word, or thought; for his infirmities have no concurrence of his will; and without this they are not properly sins. Thus, "he that is born of God doth not commit sin:" And though he cannot say, he hath not sinned, yet now "he sinneth not."

7. This then is the salvation which is through faith, even in the present

world: A salvation from sin, and the consequences of sin, both often expressed in the word *justification*; which, taken in the largest sense, implies a deliverance from guilt and punishment, by the atonement of Christ actually applied to the soul of the sinner now believing on him, and a deliverance from the power of sin, through Christ *formed in his heart*. So that he who is thus justified, or saved by faith, is indeed *born again*. He is *born again of the Spirit* unto a new life, which "is hid with Christ in God." And as a new-born babe he gladly receives the *adolon,* "*sincere* milk of the word, and grows thereby;" going on in the might of the Lord his God, from faith to faith, from grace to grace, until, at length, he come unto "a perfect man, unto the measure of the stature of the fulness of Christ."

III. The First usual objection to this is,

1. That "to preach salvation, or justification, by faith only, is to preach against holiness and good works." To which a short answer might be given: "It would be so, if we spake, as some do, of a faith which was separate from these: But we speak of a faith which is not so, but productive of all good works, and all holiness."

2. But it may be of use to consider it more at large; especially since it is no new objection, but as old as St. Paul's time. For even then it was asked, "Do we not make void the law through faith?" We answer, First, all who preach not faith, do manifestly make void the law; either directly and grossly, by limitations and comments that eat out all the spirit of the text; or, indirectly, by not pointing out the only means whereby it is possible to perform it. Whereas, Secondly, "we establish the law," both by showing its full extent and spiritual meaning; and by calling all to that living way, whereby "the righteousness of the law may be fulfilled in them." These, while they trust in the blood of Christ alone, use all the ordinances which he hath appointed, do all the "good works which he had before prepared that they should walk therein," and enjoy and manifest all holy and heavenly tempers, even the same mind that was in Christ Jesus.

3. "But does not preaching this faith lead men into pride?" We answer, Accidentally it may: Therefore ought every believer to be earnestly cautioned, in the words of the great Apostle, "Because of unbelief" the first branches "were broken off; and thou standest by faith. Be not high-minded, but fear. If God spared not the natural branches, take heed lest he spare not thee. Behold, therefore, the goodness and severity of God! On them which fell severity; otherwise thou also shalt be cut off." and while he continues therein, he will remember those words of St. Paul, foreseeing and answering this very objection, (Rom iii. 27,) "Where is

boasting then? It is excluded. By what law? of works? Nay: But by the law of faith." If a man were justified by his works, he would have whereof to glory. But there is no glorying for him "that worketh not, but believeth on him that justifieth the ungodly." (Rom. iv. 5.) To the same effect are the words both preceding and following the text. (Eph. ii. 4, &c.:) "God, who is rich in mercy, even when we were dead in sins, hath quickened us together with Christ, (by grace ye are saved,) that he might show the exceeding riches of his grace in his kindness toward us through Christ Jesus. For, by grace are ye saved through faith; and that not of your-selves." Of yourselves cometh neither your faith nor your salvation. "It is the gift of God;" the free, undeserved gift; the faith through which ye are saved, as well as the salvation, which he of his own good pleasure, his mere favour, annexes thereto. That ye believe, is one instance of his grace; that, believing, ye are saved, another. "Not of works, lest any man should boast." For all our works, all our righteousness, which were before our believing, merited nothing of God but condemnation: So far were they from deserving faith, which therefore, whenever given, is not of works. Neither is salvation of the works we do when we believe: For it is then God that worketh in us: And, therefore, that he giveth us a reward for what he himself worketh, only commendeth the riches of his mercy, but leaveth us nothing whereof to glory.

4. "However, may not the speaking thus of the mercy of God, as saving or justifying freely by faith only, encourage men in sin?" Indeed it may and will: Many will "continue in sin that grace may abound:" But their blood is upon their own head. The goodness of God ought to lead them to repentance; and so it will those who are sincere of heart. When they know there is yet forgiveness with him, they will cry aloud that he would blot out their sins also, through faith which is in Jesus. And if they earnestly cry, and faint not; if they seek him in all the means he hath appointed; if they refuse to be comforted till he come; "he will come, and will not tarry." And he can do much work in a short time. Many are the examples, in the Acts of the Apostles, of God's working this faith in men's hearts, even like lightning falling from heaven. So in the same hour that Paul and Silas began to preach, the jailor repented, believed, and was baptized; as were three thousand, by St. Peter, on the day of Pentecost, who all repented and believed at his first preaching. And, blessed be God, there are now many living proofs that he is still "mighty to save."

5. Yet to the same truth, placed in another view, a quite contrary objection is made: "If a man cannot be saved by all that he can do, this will drive men to despair." True, to despair of being saved by their own

works, their own merits, or righteousness. And so it ought; for none can trust in the merits of Christ, till he has utterly renounced his own. He that"goeth about to establish his own righteousness," cannot receive the righteousness of God. The righteousness which is of faith cannot be given him while he trusteth in that which is of the law.

6. "But this," it is said, "is an uncomfortable doctrine." The devil spoke like himself, that is, without either truth or shame, when he dared to suggest to men that it is such. It is the only comfortable one, it is "very full of comfort," to all self-destroyed, self-condemned sinners. That "whosoever believeth on him shall not be ashamed. That the same Lord over all is rich unto all that call upon him:" Here is comfort, high as heaven, stronger than death! What! Mercy for all? for Zaccheus, a public robber? for Mary Magdalene, a common harlot? Methinks I hear one say, "Then I, even I, may hope for mercy!" And so thou mayest, thou afflicted one, whom none hath comforted! God will not cast out thy prayer. Nay, perhaps, he may say the next hour, "Be of good cheer, thy sins are forgiven thee;" so forgiven, that they shall reign over thee no more; yea, and that "the Holy Spirit shall bear witness with thy spirit that thou art a child of God." O glad tidings! Tidings of great joy, which are sent unto all people! "Ho, every one that thirsteth, come ye to the waters: Come ye, and buy, without money and without price." Whatsoever your sins be, "though red, like crimson," though more than the hairs of your head, "return ye unto the Lord, and he will have mercy upon you; and to our God, for he will abundantly pardon."

7. When no more objections occur, then we are simply told, that "salvation by faith only ought not to be preached as the first doctrine, or, at least, not to be preached at all." But what saith the Holy Ghost? "Other foundation can no man lay than that which is laid, even Jesus Christ." So then, that "whosoever believeth on him shall be saved," is, and must be, the foundation of all our preaching; that is, must be preached first. "Well, but not to all." To whom, then, are we not to preach it? Whom shall we except? the poor? Nay; they have a peculiar right to have the gospel preached unto them. The unlearned? No. God hath revealed these things unto unlearned and ignorant men from the beginning. The young? By no means. "Suffer these," in anywise, to come unto Christ, "and forbid them not." The sinners? Least of all. "He came not to call the righteous, but sinners to repentance." Why then, if any, we are to except the rich, the learned, the reputable, the moral men. And, it is true, they too often except themselves from hearing; yet we must speak the words of our Lord. For thus the tenor of our commission runs, "Go and preach the gospel to every creature." If any man wrest it,

8

or any part of it, to his destruction, he must bear his own burden. But still, "as the Lord liveth, whatsoever the Lord saith unto us, that we will speak."

8. At this time, more especially, will we speak, that "by grace are ye saved through faith:" Because, never was the maintaining of this doctrine more seasonable than it is at this day. Nothing but this can effectually prevent the increase of the Romish delusion among us. It is endless to attack, one by one, all the errors of that Church. But salvation by faith strikes at the root, and all fall at once where this is established. It was this doctrine, which our Church justly calls *the strong rock and foundation of the Christian religion,* that first drove Popery out of these kingdoms; and it is this alone can keep it out. Nothing but this can give a check to that immorality which hath "overspread the land as a flood." Can you empty the great deep, drop by drop? Then you may reform us by dissuasives from particular vices. But let the "righteousness which is of God by faith" be brought in, and so shall its proud waves be stayed. Nothing but this can stop the mouths of those who "glory in their shame, and openly deny the Lord that bought them." They can talk as sublimely of the law, as he that hath it written, by God in his heart. To hear them speak on this head might incline one to think they were not far from the kingdom of God: But take them out of the law into the gospel; begin with the righteousness of faith; with Christ, "the end of the law to every one that believeth;" and those who but now appeared almost, if not altogether Christians, stand confessed the sons of perdition; as far from life and salvation (God be merciful unto them!) as the depth of hell from the height of heaven.

9. For this reason the adversary so rages whenever "salvation by faith" is declared to the world: For this reason did he stir up earth and hell, to destroy those who first preached it. And for the same reason, knowing that faith alone could overturn the foundations of his kingdom, did he call forth all his forces, and employ all his arts of lies and calumny, to affright Martin Luther from reviving it. Nor can we wonder thereat; for, as that man of God observes, "How would it enrage a proud strong man armed, to be stopped and set at nought by a little child coming against him with a reed in his hand!" especially, when he knew that little child would surely overthrow him, and tread him under foot. Even so, Lord Jesus! Thus hath thy strength been ever "made perfect in weakness!" Go forth, then, thou little child that believest in him, and his "right hand shall teach thee terrible things!" Though thou be as helpless and weak as an infant of days, the strong man shall not be able to stand before thee. Thou shalt prevail over him, and subdue him, and overthrow him, and

9

trample him under thy feet. Thou shalt march on, under the great Captain of thy salvation, "conquering and to conquer," until all thine enemies are destroyed, and "death is swallowed up in victory."

Now, "thanks be to God, which giveth us the victory through our Lord Jesus Christ;" to whom, with the Father and the Holy Ghost, be blessing, and glory, and wisdom, and thanksgiving, and honour and power and might, for ever and ever. Amen.

THE PROMISE OF SANCTIFICATION
(Exek. xxxvi. 25, &c.)
BY THE REV. CHARLES WESLEY

1 God of all power, and truth, and grace,
    Which shall from age to age endure;
  Whose word, when heaven and earth shall pass,
    Remains, and stands for ever sure:

2 Calmly to thee my soul looks up,
    And waits thy promises to prove;
  The object of my steadfast hope,
    The seal of thine eternal love.

3 That I thy mercy may proclaim,
    That all mankind thy truth may see,
  Hallow thy great and glorious name,
    And perfect holiness in me.

4 Chose from the world, if now I stand
    Adorn'd in righteousness divine;
  If, brought unto the promised land,
    I justly call the Saviour mine;

5 Perform the work thou hast begun,
    My inmost soul to thee convert:
  Love me, for ever love thine own,
    And sprinkle with thy blood my heart.

6 Thy sanctifying Spirit pour,
    To quench my thirst and wash me clean;
  Now, Father, let the gracious shower
    Descend and make me pure from sin.

7 Purge me from every sinful blot;
     My idols all be cast aside:
  Cleanse me from every evil thought,
     From all the filth of self and pride.

8 Give me a new, a perfect heart,
     From doubt, and fear, and sorrow free:
  The mind which was in Christ impart,
     And let my spirit cleave to thee.

9 O take this heart of stone away!
     (Thy rule it doth not, cannot own;)
  In me no longer let it stay:
     O take away this heart of stone!

10 The hatred of my carnal mind
      Out of my flesh at once remove;
   Give me a tender heart, resign'd
      And pure, and fill'd with faith and love.

11 Within me thy good Spirit place,
      Spirit of health, and love, and power;
   Plant in me thy victorious grace,
      And sin shall never enter more.

12 Cause me to walk in Christ my Way,
      And I thy statutes shall fulfil;
   In every point thy law obey,
      And perfectly perform thy will.

13 Hast thou not said, who canst not lie,
      That I thy law shall keep and do?
   Lord, I believe, though men deny;
      They all are false, but thou art true.

14 O that I now, from sin released,
      Thy word might to the utmost prove!
   Enter into the promised rest,
      The Canaan of thy perfect love!

15 There let me ever, ever dwell;
      Be thou my God, and I will be
   Thy servant: O set to thy seal!
      Give me eternal life in thee.

16 From all remaining filth within
      Let me in thee salvation have:

From actual and from inbred sin
 My ransom'd soul persist to save.

17 Wash out my old orig'nal stain:
  Tell me no more it cannot be,
 Demons or men! The Lamb was slain,
  His blood was all pour'd out for me!

18 Sprinkle it, Jesu, on my heart:
  One drop of thy all-cleansing blood
 Shall make my sinfulness depart,
  And fill me with the life of God.

19 Father, supply my every need;
  Sustain the life thyself hast given;
 Call for the corn, the living bread,
  The manna that comes down from heaven.

20 The gracious fruits of righteousness,
  Thy blessings' unexhausted store,
 In me abundantly increase;
  Nor let me ever hunger more.

21 Let me no more, in deep complaint,
  "My leanness, O my leanness!" cry;
 Alone consumed with pining want,
  Of all my Father's children I!

22 The painful thirst, the fond desire,
  Thy joyous presence shall remove;
 While my full soul doth still require
  The whole eternity of love.

23 Holy and true, and righteous Lord,
  I wait to prove thy perfect will;
 Be mindful of thy gracious word,
  And stamp me with thy Spirit's seal!

24 Thy faithful mercies let me find,
  In which thou causest me trust;
 Give me thy meek and lowly mind,
  And lay my spirit in the dust.

25 Show me how foul my heart hath been,
  When all renew'd by grace I am:
 When thou hast emptied me of sin,
  Show me the fulness of my shame.

26   Open my faith's interior eye,
      Display thy glory from above;
    And all I am shall sink and die,
      Lost in astonishment and love.

27   Confound, o'erpower me with thy grace,
      I would be by myself abhorr'd;
    (All might, all majesty, all praise,
      All glory be to Christ my Lord!)

28   Now let me gain perfection's height!
      Now let me into nothing fall!
    Be less than nothing in my sight,
      And feel that Christ is all in all!

THE CHARACTER OF A METHODIST

1. The distinguishing marks of a Methodist are not his opinions of any sort. His assenting to this or that scheme of religion, his embracing any particular set of notions, his espousing the judgment of one man or of another, are all quite wide of the point. Whosoever, therefore, imagines that a Methodist is a man of such or such an opinion, is grossly ignorant of the whole affair; he mistakes the truth totally. We believe, indeed, that "all Scripture is given by the inspiration of God;" and herein we are distinguished from Jews, Turks, and Infidels. We believe the written word of God to be the only and sufficient rule both of Christian faith and practice; and herein we are fundamentally distinguished from those of the Romish Church. We believe Christ to be the eternal, supreme God; and herein we are distinguished from the Socinians and Arians. But as to all opinions which do not strike at the root of Christianity, we think and let think. So that whatsoever they are, whether right or wrong, they are no distinguishing marks of a Methodist.

2. Neither are words or phrases of any sort. We do not place our religion, or any part of it, in being attached to any peculiar mode of speaking, any quaint or uncommon set of expressions. The most obvious, easy, common words, wherein our meaning can be conveyed, we prefer before others, both on ordinary occasions, and when we speak of the things of God. We never, therefore, willingly or designedly, deviate from the most usual way of speaking; unless when we express scripture truths in scripture words, which, we presume, no Christian will condemn. Neither do we affect to use any particular expressions of Scripture more frequently than others, unless they are such as are more frequently

used by the inspired writers themselves. So that it is as gross an error, to place the marks of a Methodist in his words, as in opinions of any sort.

3. Nor do we desire to be distinguished by actions, customs, or usages, of an indifferent nature. Our religion does not lie in doing what God has not enjoined, or abstaining from what he hath not forbidden. It does not lie in the form of our apparel, in the posture of our body, or the covering of our heads; nor yet in abstaining from marriage, or from meats and drinks, which are all good if received with thanksgiving. Therefore, neither will any man, who knows whereof he affirms, fix the mark of a Methodist here, — in any actions or customs purely indifferent, undetermined by the word of God.

4. Nor, lastly, is he distinguished by laying the whole stress of religion on any single part of it. If you say, "Yes, he is; for he thinks 'we are saved by faith alone:'" I answer, You do not understand the terms. By salvation he means holiness of heart and life. And this he affirms to spring from true faith alone. Can even a nominal Christian deny it? Is this placing a part of religion for the whole? "Do we then make void the law through faith? God forbid! Yea, we establish the law." We do not place the whole of religion (as too many do, God knoweth) either in doing no harm, or in doing good, or in using the ordinances of God. No, not in all of them together; wherein we know by experience a man may labour many years, and at the end have no religion at all, no more than he had at the beginning. Much less in any one of these; or, it may be, in a scrap of one of them: Like her who fancies herself a virtuous woman, only because she is not a prostitute; or him who dreams he is an honest man, merely because he does not rob or steal. May the Lord God of my fathers preserve me from such a poor, starved religion as this! Were this the mark of a Methodist, I would sooner choose to be a sincere Jew, Turk, or Pagan.

5. "What then is the mark? Who is a Methodist, according to your own account?" I answer: A Methodist is one who has "the love of God shed abroad in his heart by the Holy Ghost given unto him;" one who "loves the Lord his God with all his heart, and with all his soul, and with all his mind, and with all his strength." God is the joy of his heart, and the desire of his soul; which is constantly crying out, "Whom have I in heaven but thee? and there is none upon earth that I desire beside thee! My God and my all! Thou art the strength of my heart, and my portion for ever!"

6. He is therefore happy in God, yea, always happy, as having in him "a well of water springing up into everlasting life," and overflowing his soul with peace and joy. "Perfect love" having now "cast out fear," he

"rejoices evermore." He "rejoices in the Lord always," even "in God his Saviour;" and in the Father,"through our Lord Jesus Christ, by whom he hath now received the atonement." "Having" found "redemption through his blood, the forgiveness of his sins," he cannot but rejoice, whenever he looks back on the horrible pit out of which he is delivered; when he sees "all his transgressions blotted out as a cloud, and his iniquities as a thick cloud." He cannot but rejoice, whenever he looks on the state wherein he now is; "being justified freely, and having peace with God through our Lord Jesus Christ." For "he that believeth, hath the witness" of this"in himself;" being now the son of God by faith. "Because he is a son, God hath sent forth the Spirit of his Son into his heart, crying, Abba, Father!" And "the Spirit itself beareth witness with his spirit, that he is a child of God." He rejoiceth also, whenever he looks forward, "in hope of the glory that shall be revealed;" yea, this his joy is full, and all his bones cry out, "Blessed be the God and Father of our Lord Jesus Christ, who, according to his abundant mercy, hath begotten me again to a living hope—of an inheritance incorruptible, undefiled, and that fadeth not away, reserved in heaven for me!"

7. And he who hath this hope, thus "full of immortality, in every-thing giveth thanks;" as knowing that this (whatsoever it is) "is the will of God in Christ Jesus concerning him." From him, therefore, he cheer-fully receives all, saying, "Good is the will of the Lord;" and whether the Lord giveth or taketh away, equally "blessing the name of the Lord." For he hath "learned, in whatsoever state he is, therewith to be content." He knoweth "both how to be abased and how to abound. Everywhere and in all things he is instructed both to be full and to be hungry, both to abound and suffer need." Whether in ease or pain, whether in sickness or health, whether in life or death, he giveth thanks from the ground of his heart to Him who orders it for good; knowing that as "every good gift cometh from above," so none but good can come from the Father of Lights, into whose hand he has wholly committed his body and soul, as into the hands of a faithful Creator. He is therefore "careful" (anxiously or uneasily) "for nothing;" as having "cast all his care on Him that careth for him," and "in all things" resting on him, after"making his request known to him with thanksgiving."

8. For indeed he "prays without ceasing." It is given him"always to pray, and not to faint." Not that he is always in the house of prayer; though he neglects no opportunity of being there. Neither is he always on his knees, although he often is, or on his face, before the Lord his God. Nor yet is he always crying aloud to God, or calling upon him in words: For many times "the Spirit maketh intercession for him with

15

groans that cannot be uttered." But at all times the language of his heart is this: "Thou brightness of the eternal glory, unto thee is my heart, though without a voice, and my silence speaketh unto thee." And this is true prayer, and this alone. But his heart is ever lifted up to God, at all times and in all places. In this he is never hindered, much less interrupted, by any person or thing. In retirement or company, in leisure, business, or conversation, his heart is ever with the Lord. Whether he lie down or rise up, God is in all his thoughts; he walks with God continually, having the loving eye of his mind still fixed upon him, and everywhere "seeing Him that is invisible."

9. And while he thus always exercises his love to God, by praying without ceasing, rejoicing evermore, and in everything giving thanks, this commandment is written in his heart, "That he who loveth God, love his brother also." And he accordingly loves his neighbour as himself; he loves every man as his own soul. His heart is full of love to all mankind, to every child of "the Father of the spirits of all flesh." That a man is not personally known to him, is no bar to his love; no, nor that he is known to be such as he approves not, that he repays hatred for his good-will. For he "loves his enemies;" yea, and the enemies of God, "the evil and the unthankful." And if it be not in his power to "do good to them that hate him," yet he ceases not to pray for them, though they continue to spurn his love, and still "despitefully use him and persecute him."

10. For he is "pure in heart." The love of God has purified his heart from all revengeful passions, from envy, malice, and wrath, from every unkind temper or malign affection. It hath cleansed him from pride and haughtiness of spirit, whereof alone cometh contention. And he hath now "put on bowels of mercies, kindness, humbleness of mind, meekness, longsuffering:" So that he "forbears and forgives, if he had a quarrel against any; even as God in Christ hath forgiven him." And indeed all possible ground for contention, on his part, is utterly cut off. For none can take from him what he desires; seeing he "loves not the world, nor" any of "the things of the world;" being now "crucified to the world, and the world crucified to him;" being dead to all that is in the world, both to "the lust of the flesh, the lust of the eye, and the pride of life." For "all his desire is unto God, and to the remembrance of his name."

11. Agreeable to this his one desire, is the one design of his life, namely, "not to do his own will, but the will of Him that sent him." His one intention at all times and in all things is, not to please himself, but Him whom his soul loveth. He has a single eye. And because "his eye is single, his whole body is full of light." Indeed, where the loving eye of

the soul is continually fixed upon God, there can be no darkness at all, "but the whole is light; as when the bright shining of a candle doth enlighten the house." God then reigns alone. All that is in the soul is holiness to the Lord. There is not a motion in his heart, but is according to his will. Every thought that arises points to Him, and is in obedience to the law of Christ.

12. And the tree is known by its fruits. For as he loves God, so he keeps his commandments; not only some, or most of them, but all, from the least to the greatest. he is not content to "keep the whole law, and offend in one point;" but has, in all points, "a conscience void of offence towards God and towards man." Whatever God has forbidden, he avoids; whatever God hath enjoined, he doeth; and that whether it be little or great, hard or easy, joyous or grievous to the flesh. He "runs the way of God's commandments," now he hath set his heart at liberty. It is his glory so to do; it is his daily crown of rejoicing, "to do the will of God on earth, as it is done in heaven;" knowing it is the highest privilege of "the angels of God, of those that excel in strength, to fulfil his commandments, and hearken to the voice of his word."

13. All the commandments of God he accordingly keeps, and that with all his might. For his obedience is in proportion to his love, the source from whence it flows. And therefore, loving God will all his heart, he serves him with all his strength. He continually presents his soul and body a living sacrifice, holy, acceptable to God; entirely and without reserve devoting himself, all he has, and all he is, to his glory. All the talents he has received, he constantly employs according to his Master's will; every power and faculty of his soul, every member of his body. Once he "yielded" them "unto sin" and the devil, "as instruments of unrighteousness;" but now, "being alive from the dead, he yields" them all "as instruments of righteousness unto God."

14. By consequence, whatsoever he doeth, it is all to the glory of God. In all his employments of every kind, he not only aims at this, (which is implied in having a single eye,) but actually attains it. His business and refreshments, as well as his prayers, all serve this great end. Whether he sit in his house or walk by the way, whether he lie down or rise up, he is promoting, in all he speaks or does, the one business of his life; whether he put on his apparel, or labour, or eat and drink, or divert himself from too wasting labour, it all tends to advance the glory of God, by peace and good-will among men. His one invariable rule is this, "Whatsoever ye do, in word or deed, do it all in the name of the Lord Jesus, giving thanks to God and the Father by him."

15. Nor do the customs of the world at all hinder his "running the race

that is set before him." He knows that vice does not lose its nature, though it becomes ever so fashionable; and remembers, that "every man is to give an account of himself to God." He cannot, therefore, "follow" even "a multitude to do evil." he cannot "fare sumptuously every day," or "make provision for the flesh to fulfill the lusts thereof." He cannot "lay up treasures upon earth," any more than he can take fire into his bosom. He cannot "adorn himself," on any pretence, "with gold or costly apparel." He cannot join in or countenance any diversion which has the least tendency to vice of any kind. He cannot "speak evil" of his neighbour, any more than he can lie either for God or man. He cannot utter an unkind word of any one; for love keeps the door of his lips. He cannot speak "idle words;" "no corrupt communication" ever "comes out of his mouth," as is all that "which is" not "good to the use of edifying," not "fit to minister grace to the hearers." But "whatsoever things are pure, whatsoever things are lovely, whatsoever things are" justly "of good report," he thinks and speaks, and acts, "adorning the Gospel of our Lord Jesus Christ in all things."

16. Lastly. As he has time, he "does good unto all men;" unto neighbours and strangers, friends and enemies: And that in every possible kind; not only to their bodies, by "feeding the hungry, clothing the naked, visiting those that are sick or in prison;" but much more does he labour to do good to their souls, as of the ability which God giveth; to awaken those that sleep in death; to bring those who are awakened to the atoning blood, that, "being justified by faith, they may have peace with God;" and to provoke those who have peace with God to abound more in love and in good works. And he is willing to "spend and be spent herein," even "to be offered up on the sacrifice and service of their faith," so they may "all come unto the measure of the stature of the fulness of Christ."

17. These are the principles and practices of our sect; these are the marks of a true Methodist. By these alone do those who are in derision so called, desire to be distinguished from other men. If any man say, "Why, these are only the common fundamental principles of Christianity!" thou hast said; so I mean; this is the very truth; I know they are no other; and I would to God both thou and all men knew, that I, and all who follow my judgment, do vehemently refuse to be distinguished from other men, by any but the common principles of Christianity, — the plain, old Christianity that I teach, renouncing and detesting all other marks of distinction. And whosoever is what I preach, (let him be called what he will, for names change not the nature of things,) he is a Christian, not in name only, but in heart and in life. He is inwardly and

outwardly conformed to the will of God, as revealed in the written word. He thinks, speaks, and lives, according to the method laid down in the revelation of Jesus Christ. His soul is renewed after the image of God, in righteousness and in all true holiness. And having the mind that was in Christ, he so walks as Christ also walked.

18. By these marks, by these fruits of a living faith, do we labour to distinguish ourselves from the unbelieving world, from all those whose minds or lives are not according to the Gospel of Christ. But from real Christians, of whatsoever denomination they be, we earnestly desire not to be distinguished at all, not from any who sincerely follow after what they know they have not yet attained. No: "Whosoever doeth the will of my Father which is in heaven, the same is my brother, and sister, and mother." And I beseech you, brethren, by the mercies of God, that we be in no wise divided among ourselves. Is thy heart right, as my heart is with thine? I ask no farther question. If it be, give me thy hand. For opinions, or terms, let us not destroy the work of God. Dost thou love and serve God? It is enough. I give thee the right hand of fellowship. If there be any consolation in Christ, if any comfort of love, if any fellowship of the Spirit, if any bowels and mercies; let us strive together for the faith of the Gospel; walking worthy of the vocation wherewith we are called; with all lowliness and meekness, with long-suffering, forbearing one another in love, endeavouring to keep the unity of the Spirit in the bond of peace; remembering, there is one body, and one Spirit, even as we are called with one hope of our calling; "one Lord, one faith, one baptism; one God and Father of all, who is above all, and through all, and in you all."

O THE DEPTH OF LOVE DIVINE

1   O the depth of love divine,
Th'unfathomable grace!
Who shall say how bread and wine
God into man conveys!
How the bread his flesh imparts,
How the wine transmits his blood,
Fills his faithful people's hearts
With all the life of God!

2   Let the wisest mortal show
How we the grace receive;
Feeble elements bestow

A power not theirs to give.
Who explains the wondrous way,
How through these the virtue came?
These the virtue did convey,
Yet still remain the same.

3   How can heavenly spirits rise,
By earthly matter fed,
Drink herewith divine supplies,
And eat immortal bread?
Ask the Father's wisdom how;
Him that did the means ordain!
Angels round our altars bow
To search it out in vain.

4   Sure and real is the grace,
The manner be unknown;
Only meet us in thy ways
And perfect us in one.
Let us taste the heavenly powers;
Lord, we ask for nothing more.
Thine to bless, 'tis only ours
To wonder and adore.

CHARLES WESLEY

PART I

EARLY DEVELOPMENTS

The immediate successors to John Wesley were characterized by their efforts to reassert major themes of Wesley's thought. While the desire was to be faithful, there was little effort simply to repeat what Wesley had said. Rather, the dominant intention was to continue the spirit of Wesley's thought, especially his full-orbed Christian affirmation, his biblical foundations, his sense of the primacy and sufficiency of grace, and his special emphasis on the work of the Holy Spirit. Over time, however, particular challenges evoked some shift of emphasis.

Yet, the primary theological themes found continual expression in the theologians who are represented in these initial selections. John Fletcher, Adam Clarke, Nathan Bangs, and Richard Watson were the leaders and typified the character of early Methodist theology. In all of these writers salvation was central: it was rooted in prevenient grace, was dependent upon God's justifying forgiveness, and reached toward Christian perfection or sanctification. The affirmation of Methodist positions was cast against the backdrop of challenge from other theological positions. Consequently, both the themes addressed and the running dialogue, especially with Calvinism, are prominent. These early Methodists were establishing theological principles, foundations upon which later theology would be constructed.

JOHN FLETCHER

After Wesley, John Fletcher (1729–1785) was the first significant theologian in the Methodist tradition. Born in Nyon, Switzerland, he was christened Jean Guillaume de la Flechere. After joining a Methodist Society he sought ordination in the Church of England and served as vicar of Madeley, Shropshire. Fletcher was distinguished by his piety as well as his theological ability. In the tempestuous decade of the 1770s, his was a clear, balanced, compelling voice. Fletcher became a theological writer when tensions increased between Methodists and Calvinists. In the Conference of 1770, John Wesley had been unclear about the relation of faith and works. Fletcher's carefully wrought theological statement of the contested issues helped clarify Wesley's thought. The selection included in this text comes from his *Checks to Antinomianism*: in this major work Fletcher intended to defend Wesley's commanding interest in morally responsible and mature Christian life. Fletcher was an important progenitor of distinctive Methodist theological emphases because he set the directions for future Methodist theological developments. The "First Check to Antinomianism" is selected from *The Works of the Reverend John Fletcher* (New York: B. Waugh and T. Mason, 1935), I, pp.11–39.

FIRST CHECK TO ANTINOMIANISM

Honoured and Reverend Sir,—Before a judge passes sentence upon a person accused of theft, he hears what his neighbours have to say for his character. Mr. Wesley, I grant, is accused of what is worse than theft, *dreadful heresy*; and I know that whosoever maintains a dreadful heresy is a *dreadful heretic*; and that the Church of Rome shows no mercy to such. But may not "real Protestants" indulge, with the privilege of a felon, one whom they so lately respected as a brother? And may not I, an old friend and acquaintance of his, be permitted to speak a word in his favour, before he is branded in the forehead, as he has already been on the back?

This step, I fear, will cost me my reputation, (if I have any,) and involve me in the same condemnation with him whose cause, together with that of truth, I design to plead. But when humanity prompts, when gratitude calls, when friendship excites, when reason invites, when justice demands, when truth requires, and conscience summons, he does not deserve the name of a *Christian friend*, who, for any consideration, hesitates to vindicate what he esteems truth, and to stand by an aggrieved friend, brother, and father. Were I not, sir, on such an occasion as this to step out of my beloved obscurity, you might deservedly reproach me as a *dastardly wretch*: nay, you have already done it in general terms, in your excellent sermon on the fear of man. "How often," say you, "do men sneakingly forsake their friends, instead of gloriously supporting them against a powerful adversary, even when their cause is just, for reasons hastily prudential, for fear of giving umbrage to a superior party or interest?"

These generous words of yours, Rev. sir, together with the leave you give both Churchmen and Dissenters to direct to *you* their answers to your circular letter, are my excuse for intruding upon you by this epistle, and my apology for begging your candid attention, while I attempt to convince you that my friend's principles and Minutes are not heretical. In order to this, I shall lay before you, and the principal persons, both clergy and laity, whom you have, from all parts of England and Wales, convened at Bristol, by printed letters, —

I. A general view of the Rev. Mr. Wesley's doctrine.

II. An account of the commendable design of his Minutes.

III. A vindication of the propositions which they contain, by arguments taken from Scripture, reason, and experience; and by quotations from eminent Calvinist divines, who have said the same things in different words.

And suppose you yourself, sir, in particular, should appear to be a strong assertor of the doctrines which you call a *dreadful heresy* in Mr. Wesley, I hope you will not refuse me leave to conclude, by expostulating with you upon your conduct in this affair, and recommending to you, and our other Christian friends, the forbearance which you recommend to others, in one of your sermons: "Why doth the narrow heart of man pursue with malice or rashness those who presume to differ from him?" Yea, and what is more extraordinary, those who agree with him in all essential points?

I. When, in an intricate case, a prudent judge is afraid to pass an unjust sentence, he inquires, as I observed, into the general conduct of the person accused, and by that means frequently finds out the truth which he investigates. As that method may be of service in the present case, permit me, sir, to lay before you a general view of Mr. Wesley's doctrine.

1. For above these sixteen years I have heard him frequently in his chapels, and sometimes in my church: I have familiarly conversed and corresponded with him, and I have often perused his numerous works in verse and prose: and I can truly say that, during all that time, I have heard him, upon every proper occasion, steadily maintain *the total fall of man in Adam*, and his utter inability to recover himself, or take any one step toward his recovery, "without the grace of God preventing him, that he may have a good will, and working with him when he has that good will."

The deepest expressions that ever struck my ears on the melancholy subject of our natural depravity and helplessness, are those which dropped from his lips: and I have ever observed that he constantly ascribes to Divine grace, not only the good works and holy tempers of believers, but all the good thoughts of upright heathens, and the good desires of those professors whom he sees "begin in the Spirit and end in the flesh:" when, to my great surprise, some of those who accuse him of "robbing God of the glory of his grace, and ascribing too much to man's power," directly or indirectly maintain that Demas and his fellow apostates never had any grace; and that if once they went on far in the ways of God, it was merely by the force of fallen nature; a sentiment which Mr. Wesley looks upon as diametrically opposite to the humbling assertion of our Lord, "Without me ye can do nothing;" and which he can no more admit than the rankest Pelagianism.

2. I must likewise testify, that he faithfully points out *Christ as the only way of salvation*; and strongly recommends faith as the only mean of receiving him, and all the benefits of his righteous life and meritorious death: and truth obliges me to declare, that he frequently expresses his detestation of the errors of modern Pharisees, who laugh at original sin, set up the powers of fallen man, cry down the operation of God's Spirit, deny the absolute necessity of the blood and righteousness of Christ, and refuse him the glory of all the good that may be found in Jew or Gentile. And you will not without difficulty, sir, find in England, and perhaps in all the world, a minister who hath borne more frequent testimonies, either from the pulpit or the press, against those dangerous errors. All his works confirm my assertion, especially his sermons on Original Sin,

and Salvation by Faith, and his masterly Refutation of Dr. Taylor, the wisest Pelagian and Socinian of our age. Nor am I afraid to have this testimony confronted with his Minutes, being fully persuaded that, when they are candidly explained, they rather confirm than overthrow it.

His manner of preaching the fall and the recovery of man is attended with a peculiar advantage: it is close and experimental. He not only points out the truth of those doctrines, but presses his hearers to cry to God that they may feel their weight upon their hearts. Some open those great truths very clearly, but let their congregations rest, like the stony ground hearers, in the first emotions of sorrow and joy which the word frequently excites. Not so Mr. Wesley: he will have true penitents "feel the plague of their own hearts, travail, be heavy laden," and receive "the sentence of death in themselves," according to the glorious "ministration of condemnation:" and according to "the ministration of righteousness and of the Spirit which exceeds in glory," he insists upon true believers knowing for themselves, that Jesus "hath power on earth to forgive sins;" and asserts, that they "taste the good word of God, and the powers of the world to come," and that they "are made partakers of the Holy Ghost and the Divine nature; the Spirit itself bearing witness with their spirits that they are children of God."

3. The next fundamental doctrine in Christianity is that of *holiness of heart and life*; and no one can here accuse Mr. Wesley of leaning to the Antinomian delusion, which "makes void the law through" a speculative and barren "faith:" on the contrary, he appears to be peculiarly set for the defence of practical religion: for, instead of representing Christ "as the minister of sin," with Ranters, to the great grief and offence of many, he sets him forth as a complete *Saviour from sin*. Not satisfied to preach holiness begun, he preaches finished holiness, and calls believers to such a degree of heart-purifying faith, as may enable them to triumph in Christ, as "being made to them of God, sanctification as well as righteousness."

It is, I grant, his misfortune (if indeed it be one) to preach a fuller salvation than most professors expect to enjoy here; for he asserts that Jesus can "make clean" *the inside* as well as *the outside* of his vessels unto honour; that he hath power on earth "to save his people from their sins;" and that his blood "cleanses from all sin," from the guilt and defilement both of original and actual corruption. He is bold enough to declare, with St. John, that "if we say we have no sin, *either by nature or practice*, we deceive ourselves, and the truth is not in us: but if we confess our sins, God is faithful and just to forgive us our sins, and to cleanse us from all unrighteousness." He is legal enough not to be ashamed of these words of Moses: "The Lord thy God will circumcise thine heart, and the heart of thy seed, to love the Lord thy God with all thine heart, and with all thy soul, that thou mayest live." And he dares to believe that the Lord can perform the words which he spoke by Ezekiel: "I will sprinkle clean water upon you, and you shall be clean: from ALL your filthiness and from ALL your idols will I cleanse you. A new heart also will I give you: I will take away the stony heart out of your flesh, and I will give you a heart of flesh; and I will put my Spirit within you, and cause you to walk in my statutes; and ye shall keep my judgments, and do them. I will also save you from *all* your uncleannesses." Hence it is that he constantly exhorts his hearers "to grow in grace, and in the knowledge of our Saviour;" till by a strong and lively faith they can continually "reckon themselves to be dead indeed unto sin, but alive unto God through Jesus Christ our Lord." He tells them, that "he who committeth sin, is the servant of sin;"—that "our old man is crucified with Christ, that the body of sin might be destroyed, that henceforth we should not serve sin;"—that "if the Son shall make us free, we shall be free indeed;"—and that although "*the* law of the Spirit of life in Christ Jesus" will not deliver us from the innocent infirmities incident to flesh and blood, it will nevertheless make us "free from the law of sin and death," and enable us to say with holy triumph, "How shall we, that are dead to sin, live any longer therein?" In a word, he thinks that God can so "shed abroad his love in our hearts, by the Holy Ghost given unto us," as to "sanctify us wholly, soul, body, and spirit;" and enable us to "rejoice evermore, pray without ceasing, and in every thing give thanks." And he is persuaded, that He who "can do far exceeding abundantly above all that we can ask or think," is able to fill us with the "perfect love which casts out fear; that we, being delivered out of the hands of our enemies," may have "the mind which was in Christ;" be righteous as the *man*Jesus was righteous; "walk as he also walked," and be in our measure, "as he was in the world:" he as the stock of the tree of righteousness, and we as the branches, "having our fruit" from him "unto holiness," and "serving God without fear in true holiness and righteousness all the days of our life."

This he sometimes calls *full sanctification*, the state of "fathers in Christ," or the "glorious liberty of the children of God;" sometimes "a being strengthened, stablished, and settled;" or "being rooted and grounded in love;" but most commonly he calls it *Christian perfection*: a word which, though used by the apostles in the same sense, cannot be used by him without raising the pity or indignation of one half of the religious world; some making it the subject of their pious sneers and godly lampoons; while others tell you roundly "they abhor it above every thing in the creation.."

On account of this doctrine it is that he is traduced as a Pharisee, a papist, an antichrist; some of his opposers taking it for granted that he makes void the priestly office of Christ, by affirming that his blood can so completely wash us here from our sins, that at death we shall "be found of him in peace, without spot, wrinkle, or any such thing;" while others, to colour their opposition to the many scriptures which he brings to support this unfashionable doctrine, give it out, that he only wants the old man to be so refined in all his tempers, and regulated in all his outward behaviour, as to appear perfect in the flesh; or, in other terms, that he sets up Pharisaic SELF, instead of "Christ *completely* formed in us *as the full* hope of glory." But I must (for one) do him the justice to say he is misapprehended, and that what he calls perfection is nothing but the rich cluster of all the spiritual blessings promised to believers in the Gospel; and, among the rest, a continual sense of the virtue of Christ's atoning and purifying blood, preventing both old guilt from returning and new guilt from fastening upon the conscience; together with the deepest consciousness of our helplessness and nothingness in our best estate, the most endearing discoveries of the Redeemer's love, and the most humbling and yet ravishing views of his glorious fulness. Witness one of his favourite hymns on that subject:—

> Confound, o'erpower me with thy grace;
>   I would be my myself abhorr'd:
> (All might, all majesty, all praise,
>   All glory be to Christ my Lord!)
> Now let me gain perfection's height,
>   Now let me into nothing fall;
> Be less than nothing in my sight,
>   And feel that *Christ is all in all*.

4. But this is not all: he holds also *general redemption*, and its necessary consequences, which some account *dreadful heresies*. He asserts with St. Paul, that "Christ, by the grace of God, tasted death for every man;" and this grace he calls *free*, as extending itself *freely* to all. Nor can he help expressing his surprise at those pious ministers who maintain that the Saviour keeps his grace, as they suppose he kept his blood, from the greatest part of mankind, and yet engross to themselves the title of *preachers of FREE grace!*

He frequently observes, with the same apostle, that "Christ is the Saviour of *all* men, but especially of them that believe;" and that "God will have *all* men to be saved," consistently with their moral agency, and the tenor of his Gospel.

With St. John he maintains that "God is love," and that "Christ is the propitiation not only for our sins, but also for the sins of the *whole world.*" With David he affirms that "God's mercy is over *all* his works:" and with St. Peter, that "the Lord is not willing that any should perish, but that *all* should come to repentance;" yea, that God, without hypocrisy, "commandeth *all* men, *every where*, to repent." Accordingly he says with the Son of God, "Whosoever will, let him come and take of the water of life freely;" and after his blessed example, as well as by his gracious command, he "preaches the Gospel TO *every creature;*" which he apprehends would be inconsistent with common honesty, if there were not a Gospel FOR *every creature.* Nor can he doubt of it in the least, when he considers that Christ is a king as well as a priest; that we are under a law to him; that those men who "will not have him to reign over them, shall be brought and slain before him;" yea, that he will "judge the secrets of men," according to St. Paul's Gospel, and take vengeance on all them that obey not his *own* Gospel, *and* be the author of eternal salvation to *none but* them that obey him. With this principle, as with a key given us by God himself, he opens those things which are "hard to be understood," in the Epistles of St. Paul, and "which they that are unlearned and unstable wrest, as they do some other scriptures, *if not* to their own destruction, *at least to* the overthrowing of the faith of some" weak Christians, and the hardening of many, very many infidels.

As a true son of the Church of England, he believes that "Christ redeemed him and all mankind;" that "for us men," and not merely for the *elect*, "he came down from heaven, and made upon the cross a full, perfect, and sufficient sacrifice, oblation, and satisfaction, for the sins of the *whole* world." Like an honest man, and yet a man of sense, he so subscribed the seventeenth article as not to reject the thirty-first, which he thinks of equal force, and much more explicit; and, therefore, as the seventeenth article authorizes him, he "receives God's promises in suchwise as they are generally set forth in holy Scripture;" rejecting, after the example of our governors in Church and state, the Lambeth articles, in which the doctrine of *absolute unconditional* election and reprobation was maintained, and which some Calvinistic divines, in the days of Queen Elizabeth, vainly attempted to impose upon these kingdoms, by adding them to the thirty-nine articles. Far, therefore, from thinking he does not act a fair part in rejecting the doctrine of particular redemption, he cannot conceive by what salvo the consciences of those ministers, who embrace it, can permit them to say to each of their communicants,

"The blood of Christ was shed for *thee;*" and to baptize promiscuously *all* children within their respective parishes, "in the name of the Father, and of the Son, and of the Holy Ghost," when all that are unredeemed have no more right to the *blood, name,* and *Spirit* of Christ, than Lucifer himself.

Thus far Mr. Wesley agrees with Arminius, because he thinks that illustrious divine agreed thus far with the Scriptures, and all the early fathers of the Church. But if Arminius, (as the author of *Pietas Oxoniensis* affirms, in his letter to Dr. Adams,) "denied, that man's nature is totally corrupt; and asserted, that he hath still a freedom of will to turn to God, but not without the assistance of grace," Mr. Wesley is no Arminian; for he strongly asserts the *total* fall of man, and constantly maintains that by nature man's will is only free to evil, and that Divine grace must first prevent, and then continually farther him, to make him willing and able to turn to God.

I must, however, confess, that he does not, as some *real Protestants,* continually harp upon the words FREE grace, and FREE will; but he gives reasons of considerable weight for this. (1.) Christ and his apostles never did so. (2.) He knows the word *grace* necessarily implies the *freeness* of a favour; and the word *will,* the *freedom* of our choice: and he has too much sense to delight in perpetual tautology. (3.) He finds, by blessed experience, that when the will is touched by Divine grace, and yields to the touch, it is as free to good, as it was before to evil. He dares not, therefore, make the maintaining *free will,* any more than *free breath,* the criterion of an unconverted man. On the contrary, he believes none are converted but those who have a *free will* to follow Jesus; and, far from being ashamed to be called a "free-willer," he affirms it as essential to all men to be "free-willing creatures," as to be "rational animals;" and he supposes he can as soon find a diamond or a flint without gravity, as a good or bad man without free will.

Nor will I conceal that I never heard him use that favourite expression of some good men, *Why me? Why me?* though he is not at all against their using it, if they can do it to edification. But as he does not see that any of the saints, either of the Old or New Testament ever used it, he is afraid to be humble and "wise above what is written," lest "voluntary humility" should introduce refined pride before he is aware. Doubting, therefore, whether he could say, *Why me? Why me?* without the self-pleasing idea of his being preferred to thousands, or without a touch of the secret self applause that tickles the Pharisee's heart, when he "thanks God he is not as other men," he leaves the fashionable exclamation to others, with all the refinements of modern divinity; and chooses to keep to St. Paul's expression, "He loved me," which implies no exclusion of his poor fellow sinners; or to that of the royal psalmist, "Lord, what is *man*, that thou art mindful of him; and the *son of man*, that thou visitest him."

5. As a consequence of the doctrine of general redemption, Mr. Wesley lays down two axioms, of which he never loses sight in his preaching. *The first* is, that ALL OUR SALVATION IS OF GOD IN CHRIST, and therefore of GRACE;—all opportunities, invitations, inclination, and power to believe being bestowed upon us of mere grace;—grace most absolutely free: and so far, I hope, that all who are called Gospel ministers agree with him. But he proceeds farther; for, *secondly*, he asserts with equal confidence, that according to the Gospel dispensation, ALL OUR DAMNATION IS OF OURSELVES, by our obstinate unbelief and avoidable unfaithfulness; as we may "neglect so great salvation," desire to "be excused" from coming to the feast of the Lamb, "make light of" God's gracious offers, refuse to "occupy," bury our talent, and act the part of the "slothful servant;" or, in other words, "resist, grieve, do despite to," and "quench the Spirit of grace," *by our moral agency*.

The first of these evangelical axioms he builds upon such scriptures as these:—"In me is thy help. Look unto me and be saved. No man cometh unto me except the Father draw him. What hast thou that thou hast not received? We are not sufficient to think aright of ourselves, all our sufficiency is of God. Christ is exalted to give repentance. Faith is the gift of God. Without me ye can do nothing," &c, &c.

And *the second* he founds upon such passages as these: "This is the condemnation, that light is come into the world, and men loved darkness rather than light. Ye always resist the Holy Ghost. They rejected the counsel of God toward themselves. Grieve not the Spirit. Quench not the Spirit. My Spirit shall not always strive with man. Turn, why will ye die? Kiss the Son, lest ye perish. I gave Jezebel time to repent, and she repented not. The goodness of God leads [not *drags*,] thee to repentance, who after thy hardness and impenitent heart treasurest up wrath unto thyself. Their eyes have they closed, lest they should see, and be converted, and I should heal them. See that ye refuse not him that speaketh from heaven. I set before you life and death, choose life! Ye will not come unto me that ye might have life. I *would* have gathered you, and ye *would not*," &c, &c.

As to the *moral agency* of man, Mr. Wesley thinks it cannot be denied upon the principles of common and civil government; much less upon those of natural and revealed religion; as nothing would be more absurd than to bind us by laws of a civil or spiritual nature; nothing more foolish than to propose to us punishments and rewards; and nothing more capricious than to inflict the one or bestow the other upon us; if we were not *moral agents*.

He is therefore persuaded, the most complete system of divinity is that in which neither of those two axioms is superseded: He thinks it is bold and unscriptural to set up the one at the expense of the other, convinced that the prophets, the apostles, and Jesus Christ left us no such precedent; and that, to avoid what is termed *legality*, we must not run into refinements which they knew nothing of, and make them perpetually contradict themselves: nor can we, he believes, without an open violation of the laws of candour and criticism, lay a greater stress upon a few obscure and controverted passages, than upon a hundred plain and irrefragable Scripture proofs. He therefore supposes that those persons are under a capital mistake who maintain only the first Gospel axiom, and under pretence of securing to God *all* the glory of the salvation of *one* elect, give to perhaps *twenty* reprobates full room to lay *all* the blame of their damnation either upon their first parents, or their Creator. This way of making twenty *real* holes, in order to stop a *supposed* one, he cannot see consistent either with wisdom or Scripture.

Thinking it therefore safest not to "put asunder" the truths which "God has joined together," he makes all extremes meet in one blessed Scriptural medium. With the Antinomian he preaches, "God worketh in you both to will and to do of his good pleasure;" and with the Legalist he cries, "Work out, therefore, your own salvation with fear and trembling;" and thus he has all St. Paul's doctrine. With the Ranter he says, "God has chosen you, you are elect;" but, as it is "through sanctification of the Spirit and belief of the truth," with the disciples of Moses he infers, "make your calling and election sure, for if ye do these things ye shall never fall." Thus he presents his hearers with all St. Peter's system of truth, which the others had rent to pieces.

Again, according to the *first* axiom, he says with the perfect Preacher, "All things are now ready;" but with him he adds also, according to the *second*, "Come, lest you never taste the Gospel feast." Thinking it extremely dangerous not to divide the word of God aright, he endeavours to give to every one the portion of it that suits him, cutting, according to times, persons, and circumstances, either with the smooth or the rough edge of his two-edged sword. Therefore, when he addresses those that are steady, and "partakers of the Gospel grace from the first day until now," as the Philippians, he makes use of the *first* principle, and testifies his confidence, "that he who hath begun a good work in them, will perform it until the day of Christ." But when he expostulates with persons, "that ran well, and do not now obey the truth," according to his *second* axiom, he says to them, as St. Paul did to the Galatians, "I stand in doubt of you; ye are fallen from grace."

In short, he would think that he mangled the Gospel, and forgot part of his awful commission, if, when he has declared that "he who believeth shall be saved," he did not also add, that he "who believeth not shall be damned;" or, which is the same, that none perish merely for Adam's sin, but for their own unbelief, and wilful rejection of the Saviour's grace. Thus he advances God's glory every way, entirely ascribing to his mercy and grace all the salvation of the elect, and completely freeing him from the blame of directly or indirectly hanging the millstone of damnation about the neck of the reprobate. And this he effectually does, by showing that the former owe all they are, and all they have, to creating, preserving, and redeeming love, whose innumerable bounties they freely and continually receive; and that the rejection of the latter has absolutely no cause but their obstinate rejecting of that astonishing mercy which wept over Jerusalem; and prayed, and bled even for those that shed the atoning blood—the blood that expiated all sin but that of final unbelief.

I have now finished my sketch of Mr. Wesley's doctrine, so far as it has fallen under my observation during above sixteen years' particular acquaintance with him and his works. It is not my design, sir, to inquire into the truth of his sentiments, much less shall I attempt to prove them orthodox, according to the ideas that some *real Protestants* entertain of orthodoxy. This only I beg leave to observe: Suppose he is mistaken in all the scriptures on which he founds his doctrine of Christian perfection and general redemption, yet his mistakes seem rather to arise from a regard for Christ's glory, than from enmity to his offices; and all together do not amount to any heresy at all; the fundamental doctrines of Christianity, namely, *the fall of man, justification by the merits of Christ, sanctification by the agency of the Holy Spirit,* and *the worship of the one true God in the mysterious distinction of Father, Son, and Holy Spirit,* as it is maintained in the three creeds, not being at all affected by any of his peculiar sentiments.

But you possibly imagine, sir, that he has lately changed his doctrine, and adopted a new system. If you do, you are under a very great mistake; and to convince you of it, permit me to conclude this letter by a paragraph of one which I received from him last spring:—

"I always did (for between these thirty and forty years) clearly assert the total fall of man, and his utter inability to do any good of himself: the absolute necessity of the grace and Spirit of God to raise even a good thought or desire in our hearts: the Lord's rewarding no works, and accepting of none, but so far as they proceed from his preventing, convincing, and converting grace, through the Beloved; the blood and righteousness of Christ being the sole meritorious cause of our salvation. And who is there in England that has asserted these things more strongly and steadily than I have done?"

Leaving you to answer this question, I remain, with due respect, Hon. and Rev. sir, your obedient servant, in the bond of a peaceful Gospel,

Madeley July 29, 1771   J. Fletcher

ADAM CLARKE

Adam Clarke (1760?–1832), a native of Ireland who became a Methodist preacher in his early twenties, was a scholar of the first order and one of the most important theologians of early Methodism. In a remarkable way he combined a life of energetic preaching with serious scholarship and careful textual work with a broad vision of Christian mission. Known especially for his classical commentaries and linguistic accomplishments (he deciphered the Coptic language on the Rosetta Stone), he was also a significant theological voice. His *magnum opus* was his *Commentary on the Bible* on which he worked for forty years. He also published sermons and essays on theology such as *The Doctrine of Salvation by Faith* (1816) and *Christian Theology* (1835). The selections included in this collection illustrate, in title and content, characteristic emphases of both Clarke and Methodism in the early nineteenth century. "Justification" and "The Holy Spirit" are taken from *Christian Theology* (London: Thomas Tegg and Son, 1835), pp.154–160, 167–172, 176–177.

JUSTIFICATION

The following are a few of the leading acceptations of the verb, which we translate "to justify:"—

1. It signifies to declare or pronounce one just or righteous; or, in other words, to declare him to be what he really is: "He was justified in the Spirit," 1 Tim. iii.16. 2. To esteem a thing properly, Matt. xi.19. 3. It signifies to approve, praise, and commend, Luke vii.29; xvi.15. 4. To clear from all sin, 1 Cor. iv.4. 5. A judge is said to justify, not only when he condemns and punishes, but also when he defends the cause of the innocent. Hence it is taken in a forensic sense, and signifies to be found or declared righteous, innocent, &c., Matt. xii.37. 6. It signifies to set

free, or escape from, Acts xiii.39. 7. It signifies, also, to receive one into favour, to pardon sin, Rom. viii.30; Luke xviii.14; Rom. iii.20; iv.2; 1 Cor. vi.11, &c. In all these texts, the word "justify" is taken in the sense of remission of sins through faith in Christ Jesus; and does not mean making the person just or righteous, but treating him as if he were so, having already forgiven him his sins.

Justification, or the pardon of sin, must precede sanctification; the conscience must be purged or purified from guilt, from all guilt, and from all guilt at once; for in no part of the Scripture are we directed to seek remission of sins *seriatim;* one now, another then; and so on.

The doctrine of justification by faith is one of the grandest displays of the mercy of God to mankind. It is so very plain that all may comprehend it; and so free that all may attain it. What more simple than this? Thou art a sinner, in consequence condemned to perdition, and utterly unable to save thy own soul. All are in the same state with thyself, and no man can give a ransom for the soul of his neighbour. God, in his mercy, has provided a Saviour for thee. As thy life was forfeited to death because of thy transgressions, Jesus Christ has redeemed thy life by giving up his own; He died in thy stead, and has made atonement to God for thy transgression; and offers thee the pardon He has thus purchased, on the simple condition, that thou believe that his death is a sufficient sacrifice, ransom, and oblation for thy sin; and that thou bring it, as such, by confident faith to the throne of God, and plead it in thy own behalf there. When thou dost so, thy faith in that sacrifice shall be imputed to thee for righteousness; that is, it shall be the means of receiving that salvation which Christ has bought by his blood.

The doctrine of the imputed righteousness of Christ, as held by many, will not be readily found in Rom. iv., where it has been supposed to exist in all its proofs. It is repeatedly said, that faith is imputed for righteousness; but in no place here, that Christ's obedience to the moral law is imputed to any man. The truth is, the moral law was broken, and did not now require obedience; it required this before it was broken; but, after it was broken, it required death. Either the sinner must die, or some one in his stead; but there was none whose death could have been an equivalent for the transgressions of the world but Jesus Christ. Jesus, therefore, died for man; and it is through his blood, the merit of his passion and death, that we have redemption; and not by his obedience to the moral law in our stead: Our salvation was obtained at a much higher price. Jesus could not but be righteous and obedient; this is consequent on the immaculate purity of his nature; but his death was not a necessary consequent. As the law of God can claim only the death of a transgressor

—for such only forfeit their right to life—it is the greatest miracle of all that Christ could die, whose life was never forfeited. Here we see the indescribable demerit of sin, that it required such a death; and here we see the stupendous mercy of God, in providing the sacrifice required. It is therefore by Jesus Christ's death, or obedience unto death, that we are saved, and not by his fulfilling any moral law. That he fulfilled the moral law, we know; without which he could not have been qualified to be our Mediator; but we must take heed lest we attribute that to obedience (which was the necessary consequence of his immaculate nature) which belongs to his passion and death. These were free-will offerings of Eternal Goodness, and not even a necessary consequence of His incarnation.

This doctrine of the imputed righteousness of Christ is capable of great abuse. To say that Christ's personal righteousness is imputed to every true believer, is not scriptural: To say that he has fulfilled all righteousness for us, in our stead, if by this is meant his fulfilment of all moral duties, is neither scriptural nor true; that he has died in our stead, is a great, glorious, and scriptural truth; that there is no redemption but through his blood is asserted beyond all contradiction in the oracles of God. But there are a multitude of duties which the moral law requires, which Christ never fulfilled in our stead, and never could. We have various duties of a domestic kind which belong solely to ourselves, in the relation of parents, husbands, wives, servants, &c., in which relations Christ never stood. He has fulfilled none of these duties for us, but he furnishes grace to every true believer to fulfil them to God's glory, the edification of his neighbour, and his own eternal profit. The salvation which we receive from God's free mercy, through Christ, binds us to live in a strict conformity to the moral law; that law which prescribes our manners, and the spirit by which they should be regulated, and in which they should be performed. He who lives not in the due performance of every Christian duty, whatever faith he may profess, is either a vile hypocrite or a scandalous antinomian.

God is said to be "no respecter of persons" for this reason among many others, that, being infinitely righteous, he must be infinitely impartial. He cannot prefer one to another, because he has nothing to hope or fear from any of his creatures. All partialities among men spring from one or other of these two principles, hope or fear; God can feel neither of them, and therefore God can be no respecter of persons. He approves or disapproves of men according to their moral character. He pities all, and provides salvation for all, but he loves those who resemble him in his holiness; and he loves them in proportion to that resemblance, that is, the more of his image he sees in any the more he loves him, and *e contra.* And every man's work will be the evidence of his conformity or nonconformity to God; and according to this evidence will God judge him. Here, then, is no respect of persons. God's judgment will be according to a man's work, and a man's work or conduct will be according to the moral state of his mind. No favouritism can prevail in the day of judgment; nothing will pass there but holiness of heart and life. A righteousness imputed, and not possessed and practised, will not avail where God judgeth according to every man's work. It would be well if those sinners and spurious believers, who fancy themselves safe and complete in the righteousness of Christ, while impure and unholy in themselves, would think of this testimony of the apostle.

As eternal life is given IN the Son of God, it follows it cannot be enjoyed WITHOUT him. No man can have it without having Christ; therefore "he that hath the Son hath life," and "he that hath not the Son hath not life." It is in vain to expect eternal glory if we have not Christ in our heart. The indwelling Christ gives both a title to it and a meetness for it. This is God's record. Let no man deceive himself here. An indwelling Christ, and glory; no indwelling Christ, no glory. God's record must stand.

Who are Christ's flock? All real penitents; all true believers; all who obediently follow his example, abstaining from every appearance of evil, and in a holy life and conversation show forth the virtues of Him who called them from darkness into His marvellous light. "My sheep hear my voice and follow me." But who are not his flock? Neither the backslider in heart; nor the vile antinomian, who thinks the more he sins the more the grace of God shall be magnified in saving him; nor those who fondly suppose they are covered with the righteousness of Christ while living in sin; nor the crowd of the indifferent and the careless; nor the immense herd of Laodicean loiterers; nor the fiery bigots, who would exclude all from heaven but themselves, and the party who believe as they do. These the Scripture resembles to swine, dogs, goats, wandering stars, foxes, lions, wells without water, &c., &c. Let not any of these come forward to eat of this pasture, or take of the children's bread. Jesus Christ is the Good Shepherd; the Shepherd who, to save his flock, laid down his own life.

To forsake all, without following Christ, is the virtue of a philosopher. To follow Christ in profession, without forsaking all, is the state of the generality of Christians. But to follow Christ, and forsake all, is the perfection of a Christian.

Talking about Christ, his righteousness, merits, and atonement, while the person is not conformed to his word and Spirit, is no other than solemn deception.

The white robes of the saints cannot mean the righteousness of Christ, for this cannot be washed and made white in his own blood. This white linen is said to be the righteousness of the saints, Rev. xix.8; and this is the righteousness in which they stand before the throne; therefore it is not Christ's righteousness, but it is a righteousness wrought in them by the merit of his blood and the power of his Spirit.

We must beware of Antinomianism, that is, of supposing that, because Christ has been obedient unto death, there is no necessity for our obedience to his righteous commandments. If this were so, the grace of Christ would tend to the destruction of the law, and not to its establishment. He only is saved from his sins who has the law of God written in his heart, who lives an innocent, holy, and useful life. Wherever Christ lives he works; and his work of righteousness will appear to his servants, and its effect will be quietness and assurance for ever. The life of God in the soul of man is the principle which saves and preserves eternally. . . .

THE HOLY SPIRIT

The Witness of the Spirit. — As every pious soul that believed in the coming Messiah, through the medium of the sacrifices offered up under the law, was made a partaker of the merit of his death, so every pious soul that believes in Christ crucified is made a partaker of the Holy Spirit. It is by this Spirit that sin is made known, and by it the blood of the covenant is applied; and, indeed, without this the want of salvation cannot be discovered, nor the value of the blood of the covenant duly estimated.

From the foundation of the church of God it was ever believed by his followers, that there were certain infallible tokens by which he discovered to genuine believers his acceptance of them and of their services. This was sometimes done by a fire from heaven consuming the sacrifice; sometimes by an oracular communication to the priest or prophet; and at other times, according to the Jewish account, by changing the fillet or cloth on the head of the scape-goat from scarlet to white: But most commonly, and especially under the Gospel dispensation, he gives this assurance to true believers by the testimony of his Spirit in their consciences, that he has forgiven their iniquities, transgressions, and sins, for His sake who has carried their griefs and borne their sorrows.

"The Spirit itself"—That same Spirit, the Spirit of adoption; that is, the Spirit who witnesses this adoption; which can be no other than the Holy Ghost himself, and certainly cannot mean any disposition or affection of mind which the adopted person may feel; for such a disposition must arise from a knowledge of this adoption, and the knowledge of this adoption cannot be known by any human or earthly means; it must come from God himself. "With our spirit"—In our understanding, the place or recipient of light and information; and the place or faculty to which such information can properly be brought. This is done, that we may have the highest possible evidence of the work which God has wrought. As the window is the proper medium to let the light of the sun into our apartments, so the understanding is the proper medium of conveying the Spirit's influence to the soul. We therefore have the utmost evidence of the fact of our adoption which we can possibly have; we have the word and Spirit of God, and the word sealed on our spirit by the Spirit of God. And this is not a momentary influx: If we take care to walk with God, and not grieve the Holy Spirit, we shall have an abiding testimony; and while we continue faithful to our adopting Father, the Spirit that witnesses that adoption will continue to witness it; and hereby we shall know that we are of God by the Spirit which he giveth us.

"The same Spirit," viz., the Spirit that witnesses of our adoption and sonship, makes intercession for us. Surely, if the apostle had designed to teach us that he meant our own sense and understanding by the Spirit, he never could have spoken in a manner in which plain common sense was never likely to comprehend his meaning. Besides, how can it be said that our own spirit, our filial disposition, bears witness with our own spirit; that our own spirit helps the infirmities of our own spirit; that our own spirit teaches our own spirit that of which it is ignorant; and that our own spirit maketh intercession for our spirit, with groanings unutterable? This would have been both incongruous and absurd. We must, therefore, understand these places of that help and influence which the followers of God receive from the Holy Ghost; and consequently, of the fulfilment of the various promises relative to this point which our Lord made to his disciples.

This Holy Spirit is sent forth to witness with their spirit. He is to bear His testimony where it is absolutely necessary,— where it can be properly discovered,—where it can be fully understood, and where it cannot be mistaken:—viz., in their hearts; or, as St. Paul says, "the Spirit itself beareth witness with our spirit:" The Spirit of God with the spirit of man— Spirit with spirit—intelligence with intelligence; the testimony given and received by the same kind of agency: A spiritual agent in a spiritual substance.

This witness is not borne in their passions, nor in impressions made upon their imagination; for this must be from its very nature doubtful and evanescent: But it is borne in their understanding, not by a transitory manifestation, but continually—unless a man by sins of omission or commission grieve that Divine Spirit, and cause Him to withdraw His testimony—which is the same thing as the Divine approbation. And God cannot continue to the soul a sense of His approbation, when it has departed from the holy commandment that was given to it: But, even in this case, the man may return by repentance and faith to God, through Christ, when pardon will be granted and the witness restored.

Wherever this Spirit comes, it bears a testimony to itself. It shows that it is the Divine Spirit, by its own light; and he who receives it is perfectly satisfied of this. It brings a light, a power, and conviction, more full, more clear, and more convincing to the understanding and judgment, than they ever had, or ever can have, of any circumstance or fact brought before the intellect. The man knows that it is the Divine Spirit, and he knows and feels that it bears testimony to the state of grace in which he stands.

So convincing and satisfactory is this testimony that a man receiving it is enabled to call God his Father, with the utmost filial confidence. Surprised and convinced, he cries out at once, "Abba, Father! My Father! My Father!" having as full a consciousness that he is a child of God, as the most tenderly beloved child has of his filiation to his natural parent. He has the full assurance of faith; the meridian evidence that puts all doubts to flight.

And this, as was observed above, continues; for it is the very voice of the indwelling Spirit: For "crying" is not only the participle of the present tense, denoting the continuation of the action; but, being neuter, it agrees with the Spirit of his Son; so it is the Divine Spirit which continues to cry, "Abba, Father!" in the heart of the true believer. And it is ever worthy to be remarked, that when a man has been unfaithful to the grace given, or has fallen into any kind of sin, he has no power to utter this cry. The Spirit is grieved and has departed, and the cry is lost! No power of the man's reason, fancy, or imagination, can restore this cry. Were he to utter the words with his lips, his heart would disown them. But, on the other hand, while he continues faithful, the witness is continued; the light and conviction, and the cry, are maintained. It is the glory of this grace that no man can command this cry; and none can assume it.

Where it is, it is the faithful and true witness: Where it is not, all is uncertainty and doubt.

The persons mentioned, Rom. viii. 15, 16, had the strongest evidence of the excellence of the state in which they stood; they knew that they were thus adopted; and they knew this by the Spirit of God, which was given them on their adoption; and, let me say, they could know it by no other means. The Father who had adopted them could be seen by no mortal eye; and the transaction, being of a purely spiritual nature, and transacted in heaven, can be known only by God's supernatural testimony of it upon earth. It is a matter of such solemn importance to every Christian soul, that God in his mercy has been pleased not to leave it to conjecture, assumption, or inductive reasoning; but attests it by his own Spirit in the soul of the person whom he adopts through Christ Jesus. It is the grand and most observable case in which the intercourse is kept up between heaven and earth; and the genuine believer in Christ Jesus is not left to the quibbles or casuistry of polemic divines or critics, but receives the thing, and the testimony of it, immediately from God himself. And were not the testimony of the state thus given, no man could possibly have any assurance of his salvation which would beget confidence and love. If to any man his acceptance with God be hypothetical, then his confidence must be so too. His love to God must be hypothetical, his gratitude hypothetical, and his obedience also. If God had forgiven me my sins, then I should love him, and I should be grateful, and I should testify this gratitude by obedience. But who does not see that these must necessarily depend on the "if" in the first case? All this uncertainty, and the perplexities necessarily resulting from it, God has precluded by sending the Spirit of his Son into our hearts, by which we cry, "Abba, Father;" and thus our adoption into the heavenly family is testified and ascertained to us in the only way in which it can possibly be done, by the direct influence of the Spirit of God. Remove this from Christianity and it is a dead letter.

The fact to be witnessed is beyond the knowledge of man: No human power or cunning can acquire it: If obtained at all, it must come from above. In this, human wit and ingenuity can do nothing. It is to tell us, that we are reconciled to God; that our sins are blotted out; that we are adopted into the family of heaven. The apostle tells us, that this is witnessed by the Spirit of God. God alone can tell whom he has accepted; whose sins he has blotted out; whom he has put among his children:— This he makes known by his Spirit in our Spirit; so that we have (not by induction or inference) a thorough conviction and mental feeling, that we are his children.

There is as great a difference between this, and knowledge gained by logical argument, as there is between hypothesis and experiment. Hypothesis states that a thing may be so: Experience alone proves the hypothesis to be true or false. By the first, we think the thing to be possible or likely; by the latter we know, experience, or prove, by practical trial, that the matter is true, or is false, as the case may be.

I should never have looked for the "witness of the Spirit," had I not found numerous scriptures which most positively assert it, or hold it out by necessary induction; and had I not found, that all the truly godly, of every sect and party, possessed the blessing,—a blessing which is the common birth-right of all the sons and daughters of God. Wherever I went amongst deeply religious people, I found this blessing. All who had turned from unrighteousness to the living God, and sought redemption by faith in the blood of the cross, exulted in this grace. It was never looked on by them as a privilege with which some peculiarly favoured souls were blessed: It was known from Scripture and experience to be the common lot of the people of God. It was not persons of a peculiar temperament who possessed it; all the truly religious had it, whether in their natural dispositions sanguine, melancholy, or mixed. I met with it everywhere, and met with it among the most simple and illiterate, as well as among those who had every advantage, which high cultivation and deep learning could bestow. Perhaps I might, with the strictest truth, say, that, during the forty years I have been in the ministry, I have met with at least forty thousand who have had a clear and full evidence that God, for Christ's sake, had forgiven their sins, the Spirit himself bearing witness with their spirit that they were the sons and daughters of God....

The Holy Spirit in the soul of a believer is God's seal, set on his heart to testify that he is God's property, and that he should be wholly employed in God's service.

As Christ is represented as the ambassador of the Father, so the Holy Spirit is represented the ambassador of the Son, coming vested with his authority, as the interpreter and executor of His will.

We know by the Spirit which he hath given us, that we dwell in God, and God in us. It was not by conjecture or inference that Christians of old knew they were in the favour of God; it was by the testimony of God's own Spirit in their hearts; and this Spirit was not given in a transient manner, but was constant and abiding, while they continued under the influence of that faith which worketh by love. Every good man is a temple of the Holy Ghost; and wherever He is, He is both light and power. By his power He works; by his light He makes both Himself and his work known. Peace of conscience and joy in the Holy Ghost must proceed from the indwelling of that Holy Spirit; and those who have these blessings must know that they have them, for we cannot have heavenly peace and heavenly joy without knowing that we have them. But this Spirit in the soul of a believer is not only manifest by its effects, but it bears its own witness to its own indwelling. So that a man not only knows that he has the Spirit from the fruits of the Spirit, but he knows that he has it from its own direct witness. It may be said, "How can these things be?" And it may be answered, "By the power, light, and mercy of God." But that such things are, the Scriptures uniformly attest; and the experience of the whole genuine church of Christ, and of every truly converted soul, sufficiently proves. "As the wind bloweth where it listeth," and we "cannot tell whence it cometh and whither it goeth, so is every one that is born of the Spirit:" The thing is certain, and fully known by its effects; but how this testimony is given and confirmed, is inexplicable. Every good man feels it, and knows he is of God by the Spirit God has given him. . . .

NATHAN BANGS

Nathan Bangs (1778–1862) was the first major theological voice of North American Methodism. Born in Stratford, Connecticut, and self-educated, he participated in the intellectual discussions of his time and wrote extensively on theological issues. He was licensed to preach in 1801 and spent six years in Canada as a Methodist itinerant missionary. In 1820 he was appointed head of the Methodist Publishing Concern in New York and editor of *The Methodist Magazine* (later *The Methodist Quarterly Review*) from 1820–1836. He was also one of the founders of the Methodist Missionary Society. Among his more important publications are: *Predestination Examined* (1817), *Methodist Episcopacy* (1820), *Essay on Emancipation*(1840), and *Letters on Sanctification* (1851). As a writer, editor, and denominational spokesman, Bangs provided leadership for the emerging North American church and set trends of theological interest and development. The selections from Bangs' writings indicate two of his central interests: the work of the Holy Spirit and the grace of God in human volitional activity. The selections "On Election" and "On Christian Perfection" are taken from *The Errors of Hopkinsianism* (New York: D. Hitt and T. Mare, 1815), pp.97–115, 153–158, 183–187; 195–197.

ON ELECTION

Rev. Sir,

1. On entering upon the doctrine of election, it is proper to notice the tendency of some of your remarks upon this important point. Your labouring to prove that election is not founded upon works foreseen, is calculated to impress the reader with an idea that we believe it is. This sentiment *you* know was not advocated in the debate; and you also know

that the "disputant on the" Hopkinsian "side," laboured to force me to assert and defend the doctrine, that election to eternal life depends on our works. His efforts, however, were unavailing. So far from believing this sentiment, we continually maintain that the election of souls to eternal life, is predicated of the goodness of God; and that, if it depended wholly upon works, no one would see life. It was pure love that moved God to give his Son, and that moved the Son to suffer and die for man. It is pure love that moves the Holy Trinity to begin, carry on, and perfect the work of salvation in the hearts of sinners. But such is the order of God, and the economy of grace, that this work of salvation is not effected without the co-operation of the free volitions of man. *Work out your own salvation with fear and trembling, for it is God that worketh in you, both to will and to do of his good pleasure.* Neither are we justified here as penitent sinners by works, but by faith. *With the heart man believeth unto righteousness. He that believeth and is baptized, shall be saved.* Nor does it follow by consequence from our doctrine, that election to eternal life depends upon our works as its *cause.* It is true, we believe, from the undeviating testimony of scripture, that by the *evidence* of our *good works*, which are the fruits of justifying faith, we are justified in the sight of men here, and in the sight of God at the great day. . . .

6. You only beat the air in your first section, where you say, "It is to be shown that election is not founded on works," p.58. Here you suppose that our doctrine, either by principle or consequence, makes election to eternal life, depend solely on our works. But this supposition arises from a mistaken apprehension of our doctrine. If a beggar were to receive from the hand of a wealthy benevolent man, something to supply his wants, does it follow that the act of the beggar in receiving the gratuitous donation from his benefactor, is the *foundation*, or *meritorious cause* of his subsistence? By no means. The *benevolence* of the donor, and not the *act* of the beggar, is the source of the poor man's subsistence. Mankind may be fitly compared to beggars, as they stand related to God. He offers them grace: if any comply with the condition of the gospel, and receive the gift of pardon by faith, does it follow that their act of receiving is the foundation of their pardon? It does not. The source of all the favours bestowed on fallen men, is in the plenitude of divine goodness. It was infinite condescension in God that caused him to provide a Saviour for sinners, and to accommodate the terms of acceptance and salvation to the weakness of man. The question is not therefore, as your readers might infer, whether our election to eternal life be predicated of *works* or *grace*; but whether grace, the grace of eternal life, be unconditionally bestowed on some, and whether all the rest be unconditionally reprobated to eternal

death, without any respect to their wicked works. All the scriptures therefore which you have quoted to prove that *grace* is the *first* and *moving* cause of our salvation, makes nothing against us; and all you say against works being the *foundation* of our election, is wide of the point, as we never held they were. Nevertheless, that *believing* in the Lord Jesus, is the condition of our justification here, as penitent sinners, and that those *good works* which spring from a living, justifying faith, are the evidences both of our justification here and hereafter, is abundantly manifest from scripture. *By grace are ye* (not shall be) *saved, through faith, and that not of yourselves; it is the gift of God*, Eph. ii.8. *And by him, all that believe are justified from all things*, Acts xiii.39. *He that believeth on him is not condemned; but he that believeth not is condemned already*, BECAUSE *he hath not believed on the name of the only begotten Son of God*, John iii.18. Who that reads these scriptures can doubt but that faith in Christ is a *condition* on the performance of which our justification is suspended? Any man who can doubt it, with such plain and positive testimony before his eyes, may turn sceptic and doubt of every thing. If this be so, that our justification is suspended on our believing, that believing is the expressed *condition* of justification, then your doctrine of *unconditional* election to eternal life, is erroneous. And if this part of your system be erroneous, so also must the dreadful counterpart of it be, namely, *unconditional reprobation to eternal death*. In regard to this part of your system, I believe you have quoted no scripture to support it—and you are quite excusable; for indeed there are none to be found.

The word which the translators of our bible have rendered *reprobate*, is *adokimos*, and this comes from *dokimos*, which signifies to *try*, *prove*, as metals are tried and proved in the fire. It is applied figuratively to man —Previous to justification all men are *adokimos*, reprobates; that is, such as will not bear the test, when their characters are examined by the standard of Christianity. They must first be cast into the refining fire of God's Spirit, until the dross of sin be separated from them, and then they are *dokimos*, elect, or *approved*. This word occurs but eight times in all the New Testament. In 1 Cor. ix. 27. Paul saith, *Lest that by any means, when I have preached to others, I myself should be adokimos, a cast-away*, or *reprobate*; one that will not bear the test of examination at the great day; or one that will not be *approved* by his judge. In 2 Cor. xiii. 5,6,7. —Rom. i. 28. —2 Tim. iii. 8. and Tit. i. 16. it is rendered *reprobate*;—in Heb. vi. 8. *rejected*. Any person who will consult the places where this word occurs, will be convinced that it is used to designate a person whose conduct is disapproved in the sight of God—Those who have so much of the *dross of sin* about them, that, when weighed in the scale of truth, they *are found wanting*. But the *dokimoi*, the *elect*, it appears, are those of whom God approves. They having been refined in the fire of God's Spirit, and still enduring all the severe trials which come upon them, are found *pure* and *good*, and shall be found unto praise and glory, if they become not, by departing from God, *reprobates*, or cast aways, 1 Cor. ix. 27. It appears therefore, that the *reprobates* may become *elect*, and the *elect* may become *reprobates*. Here is no foundation for the doctrine of *eternal* and *unconditional* election and reprobation.

Allowing the accuracy of the above remarks, that the reprobates are such as are *disapproved*, after being *tried*, how can they be reprobated from all eternity, seeing they could not be *tried* before they had an opportunity of *acting*? Can gold be tried before it exists? To say that God *knew* who would stand the test of examination, is no argument in favour of Hopkinsianism. This declares that God's determination respecting the final estates of men, was antecedent to his *knowledge* of them; so that prescience itself is dependent for its existence upon preordination. See Letter I. p. 34, 35.

God saith concerning the Israelites, *I have chosen you in the furnace of affliction*. Were they in the furnace of affliction before they were born? If not, this *choice* could not have been from all eternity.

8. In Eph. v. 6. the Apostle Paul assigns a reason why impenitent sinners are finally damned. — "Let no man deceive you with vain words, for *because of these things* cometh the wrath of God upon the children of disobedience." The things to which the Apostle alludes, are mentioned in the preceding verse—*For this ye know, that no whoremonger, nor unclean person, nor covetous man, who is an idolater, hath any inheritance in the kingdom of Christ and of God*. How different the opinion of this Apostle from yours! "It is not," say you, "assigning a sufficient reason for their reprobation, to say they were wicked, and would not accept of mercy," p.63. Now sir, either you, or Jesus Christ and the Apostle Paul, are mistaken. Paul saith in the above passage, "The wrath of God cometh on the children of disobedience, *because* of their wickedness." You say, "This is not a sufficient reason." Paul saith, 2 Thess. ii. 10,11,12. That sinners are damned *because* they received not the love of the truth *that they might be saved*—and for this *cause* God shall send them strong delusions, that they should believe a lie, that they all might be damned who believe not the truth, but had pleasure in unrighteousness. But you say, this is not a sufficient reason. If the Apostle had believed your doctrine, would he not have said, *they are damned on account* of an *eternal decree of reprobation*, which immutably secured their wickedness, that they might be vessels of wrath and "suitable objects" of eternal indignation? Jesus Christ said,

Luke xiii. 34. How oft would I have gathered you together, and ye would not? Behold your house is left unto you desolate. *Ye would not* accept of mercy, and therefore ye shall be rejected, i.e. reprobated. You reply, "This is not assigning a sufficient reason for their reprobation." Are then Dr. Hopkins and yourself wiser than Jesus Christ, and his servant Paul! Surely this is being wise above what is written. Were I to quote all the scriptures which assign the wickedness of sinners, and their refusal to accept of mercy as the *cause* of their final condemnation, I should transcribe a great part of the bible. They are fitted, it is true, for destruction; but they fit themselves by abusing the goodness of God, by an obstinate refusal of mercy; in a word, by *not receiving the truth that they might be saved.*

9. Although you strongly assert your belief in unconditional predestination, you seem ashamed of it in the discussion of your subject. For in p.59 you very modestly say, "But why did the Lord of Angels *suffer* them to rebel?"—and p.60, "Why were such a part of the Angels suffered to apostatize?" This language, sir, ill becomes the lips of such a rigid predestinarian as you have avowed yourself to be. To hold that God *absolutely decreed*, before the foundation of the world, that precisely so many intelligent beings should apostatize, and that every particular sin of their lives were not only unalterably fixed in the mind of God, but also "brought to pass" by him: and then talk about *suffering* their apostacy, is truly ridiculous. Why not speak out, and ask, Why did God *decree* and *foreordain* that Angels should rebel, and that precisely so many of the human family should apostatize, and remain in their apostacy, and finally be damned. And why not give a categorical answer to these questions, in conformity to your unscriptural doctrine? *Because he would.* Does the absurdity of your doctrine appear so glaringly horrid at some times, that you wish to draw a veil over it?

10. Page 64, "Paul mentions the greatness of his sin, as one reason why he obtained mercy." Is this correct? He is so far from assigning the "greatness of his sin" as a reason why he obtained mercy, that he says, 1 Tim. i. 13. But I obtained mercy *because* I did it *ignorantly* and in *unbelief.* These words seem to suppose, that if he had *believed* Christ was the promised *Messiah*, and if he had *known* him to be the person against whom he acted so violently, he should not have obtained mercy. He says indeed, in v. 14, *And the grace of our Lord Jesus was exceeding abundant with faith and love.* And in v. 16, "Howbeit, for this *cause* I obtained mercy, (not because he had been a great sinner, but *because of the abundance of the grace of Jesus Christ) that in me first Jesus Christ might shew forth all long-suffering, for a pattern to them who should hereafter believe in him to life everlasting."* The

cause of which he here speaks, is not that he had been a great sinner, (although he had been even a blasphemer, and a persecutor, and injurious, v. 13.) but that Christ's long-suffering might be manifest, — and that the Apostle might be a pattern to others, not of "indwelling sin," but of faith and purity. — In the whole passage, I cannot discover that the Apostle had the remotest allusion to sin, as a *reason* why he obtained mercy. O sir, what a dangerous sentiment you have advanced! Paul obtained mercy because of the greatness of his sin: Let us *sin* then, may all blasphemers say, that grace may abound. Do not say that this objection was brought against the Apostle's doctrine, as well as against yours; and therefore you teach the same thing. It is a legitimate consequence from your sentiment; but was an unjust reflection upon the Apostle. Paul obtained mercy *because* he was a great sinner. "Well then," says a correct reasoner, "the same *cause* under the same circumstances, will produce the same *effect*; I will therefore be a great sinner, that I also may obtain mercy." Will you undertake to prove that his reasoning is not conclusive?

ON CHRISTIAN PERFECTION

Rev. Sir,

Having shewn in my former letter, the inconsistency of your doctrine of personal election, I come now to examine what you say respecting "sinful imperfection." It is matter of some surprise, that, after all which has been said and written to the contrary, you should strive to impose upon the public a belief, that we hold, "that saints in this life are as perfect as they will be in heaven." p.103, note. O sir, is it fair, is it consistent with that *charity which hopeth all things*, thus to misrepresent a body of people! And how do you attempt to prove your assertion? Why, "By the argument which they use in their book of Discipline against the power of death to sanctify," *ibid*. And pray sir, do you really believe in the *power of death* to sanctify? It would seem so by this observation of yours, as also from what you say about Paul's desiring to *die*, because death would put an end to that body of sin under which he groaned. — But from what part of the scriptures do you prove this strange doctrine? Does not John say, 1 John i. 7. *The blood of Jesus Christ his Son, cleanseth us from all sin*? Does not the apostle Paul ask, Heb. ix. 14. *How much more shall the blood of Christ, who through the eternal Spirit, offered himself without spot to God, purge your conscience from dead works to serve the living God*? In this passage they are said to be purged from dead works, *by the blood of Christ*, that they might serve the living God. — But if they do not serve the living God until purified, and if *death* acts as a purifier, then we do not serve the living God until after death. It is seriously doubted whether a solitary passage of scripture can be found in all the Bible to support the idea, that *death* is the *destroyer* of sin. On the contrary, death is all along represented as a *consequence of sin*, and the last enemy. Shall the effect destroy its cause? And shall the enemy of mankind do the most friendly and beneficial act towards them? — The "arguments," therefore "which we use against the power of death to sanctify," do not necessarily suppose, that we are as sinless in this life, as are the *spirits of just men made perfect*. It is true, we wish to ascribe the glory of our salvation, from the foundation to the top-stone, to Jesus Christ, and not to death; and in this respect we accord with the holy scriptures, which teach us to ascribe honour and glory *unto him that loved us, and washed us in his own blood*.

As the *consequence* which you endeavour to infer from our doctrine, has no connexion with it, so neither do we hold it in *principle*. And you might have convinced yourself of this, if you had taken the trouble of looking in our discipline, instead of quoting merely from recollection, and perhaps from hearsay. To convince you of your mistake, I will transcribe some passages from the discipline, published in 1803. P. 120, After having shewn the difference between the Mosaic economy, comprehending the political, moral, and ceremonial laws, and the Adamic law of innocence; and also shewing the reason why men cannot fulfil the requirements of the latter, the author concludes thus, — "Consequently, no man is able to perform the service, which the Adamic law requires." Compare this with p. 106. "To explain myself a little farther on this head; 1. Not only *sin, properly* so called, that is, a voluntary transgression of a known law, but sin, improperly so called, that is, an involuntary transgression of a divine law, known or unknown, needs the atoning blood. 2. I believe there is no such perfection *in this life*, as excludes these involuntary transgressions, which I apprehend to be naturally consequent on the ignorance and mistakes inseparable from mortality. 3. Therefore *sinless perfection* is a phrase I never use, lest I should seem to contradict myself. 4. I believe a person filled with the love of God, is still liable to these involuntary transgressions. 5. Such transgressions you may call sins, if you please; I do not for the reasons above mentioned." Take another instance from page 123, "But the best of men may say, Thou art my light, my holiness, my heaven. — Through my union with thee, I am full of light, of holiness, and happiness. And if I were left to myself, I should be nothing but sin, darkness, and hell." "The best of men need

Christ as their priest, their atonement, their advocate with the Father; not only, as the continuance of their every blessing depends on his death and intercession, but on account of their coming short of the law of love."

From these quotations, all of which are taken from our *discipline*, it is undeniably plain, 1. That we believe that a *perfect christian*, when considered in relation to the Adamic law, falls far short of its requirements; and therefore, on this account, may be denominated a transgressor. 2. But that no man since the fall is under that law, because it is, properly speaking, a law of works; whereas we are under the dispensation of grace. And will you undertake to prove, that the glorified saints in heaven do not perfectly fulfil this law? Are they not perfectly freed not only from sin, but also from all its consequences? At least at the resurrection, when their glorified bodies shall become like unto *Christ's most glorious body*. If you cannot prove this, neither can you prove that we hold to as great perfection *in this life*, as the saints in heaven possess. 3. That such is our situation, surrounded with temptations, the spirit shrouded in a corruptible body, our reasoning powers impaired, that we frequently *involuntarily* transgress the law of love, under which we are; but that these are not *sins*, "properly so called." 4. That therefore we continually need the atoning merits of Christ to wash us, and the Holy Spirit to help our infirmities. — After reading these remarks, it is possible you may think, that, among other sins, which you suppose you momentarily commit, you have been guilty, I hope unintentionally, of the sin of misrepresentation. Having made these observations to remove the misapprehension which may have arisen in the minds of your readers, respecting our ideas of christian perfection, I proceed to examine, in the first place, those texts of scripture with which you attempt to support your doctrine of "sinful imperfection.". . .

II. 1. Having thus cleared the way, by rescuing the sacred scriptures from the "unholy service (to borrow the words of an eminent author) into which they were pressed against their will," I shall attempt to prove our doctrine of evangelical perfection, by an appeal to "unequivocal" texts of holy writ. And let it be remembered, that the point in debate is not whether we are as perfect in this life, as are the glorified spirits; nor whether we may be so perfect as to keep the Adamic law; but whether a *Christian* may arrive to such a state of perfection as to keep the gracious law under which the gospel of Christ places him, so as, in this sense to be delivered from sin. It ought furthermore to be observed, that no man since the introduction of moral evil into our world, is under the Adamic law, (which was a law of works) for justification and salvation. Neither is it a rule of life or of judgment: This point is so clear that it is needless to spend time to prove it. Taking it for granted, therefore, that we are under the *law of liberty*, established by Jesus Christ, I undertake to prove that a Christian, whose heart is thoroughly changed by the Spirit of God, does and must, in order to enter into life, keep it.

2. *But Noah found grace in the eyes of the Lord. Noah was a* JUST *man, and* PERFECT *in his generation, and Noah walked with God*, Gen. vi. 8,9. It may be asked, Why was Noah *just* and *perfect*? Because he found *grace* in the sight of God. It was not therefore from obedience to the Adamic, nor ceremonial law, that he was made perfect, but because he believed God, and faithfully improved the light of the dispensation of grace, under which he lived. He walked with God, like Enoch before him, who walked with God three hundred years, and did not *see death*, for God *translated him*; and before his translation, he had this testimony that he pleased God, Heb. xi. 5. If death be necessary to cleanse the heart from sin, and if none can enter heaven without being previously cleansed, what becomes of *Enoch*, who did not *see death*. Here is at least one exception to your doctrine— Is not the prophet Elijah another?

3. You have frequently alluded to Isaiah vi. 5. Woe is me, &c. If you had read on to the 7th verse, you would have discovered the doctrine for which we contend. *Then flew one of the seraphims unto me, having a live coal in his hand, which he had taken with the tongs from the altar. And he laid it upon my mouth and said, Lo this hath touched thy lips; and thine* INIQUITY IS TAKEN AWAY, *and thy* SIN IS PURGED. Does not this text undeniably prove the doctrine of a deliverance from sin?— Equally in point are the words of the Psalmist, Psa. ciii. 12. *As far as the east is from the west, so far hath he removed our transgressions from us*. Observe that this is not spoken in anticipation of what shall be done at *death*; but it asserts what had already been accomplished.

4. Turn we our attention to the New Testament writers. *What shall we say then, shall we* CONTINUE *in* SIN *that grace may abound? God forbid: how shall we that are dead to sin*, LIVE *any longer therein?* Rom. vi. 1,2. How shall we that are *dead to sin*, consistently with that character we are called to support, as the servants of God, live any longer in sin!

V. 6. *Knowing this that our old man* IS CRUCIFIED (not shall be crucified at death) *with him, that the body of sin might be destroyed, that henceforth we should not serve sin. V. 7, For he that is dead is freed from sin. V. 11. Likewise reckon ye yourselves to be dead indeed unto* SIN, *but alive unto God through Jesus Christ our Lord.* V. 12. Let not sin therefore reign in your mortal bodies, that ye should obey it in the lusts thereof. V. 14. For SIN SHALL NOT HAVE DOMINION OVER YOU. No language can be more express, to denote the total destruction of sin from the human heart. "Observe the confidence with which he speaks"— Knowing this—what? Why, *that the old man is crucified, that the body of sin might be destroyed—that they were freed from sin— that they should reckon themselves dead to sin—that sin should not have dominion over them.* How diametrically opposite were the sentiments of this holy Apostle, in regard to deliverance from sin, and your's, sir, who so strenuously plead for its continuance through life! The man who can read the above passages of sacred scripture, and then deny the necessity and possibility of the destruction of sin from the heart in this life, may, with equal propriety, deny every doctrine of the Bible. See also from ver. 18–22, in the last of which it is said, *But now being made* FREE *from* SIN, *and become servants to God, ye have your fruit unto holiness, and the end everlasting life.*

5. The Apostle John bears testimony to the same truth, 1 John i, 6. *If we say that we have fellowship with him, and walk in darkness* (to walk in *sin* is the same as to walk in *darkness*) *we* LIE, *and do not the truth.* Do you not, sir, profess to have fellowship with Jesus Christ? and do you not also profess to live in sin every moment? In which particular are you mistaken? You think you ought not to have the "least mite of charity" for a Christian who professes to be delivered from sin! How different the judgment of St. John. It would seem that he had so little charity for those professors of his day, who said they had fellowship with God, and yet walked in darkness, that with his apostolic plainness, he called them liars. V. 7. *But if we walk in the light as he is in the light, we have fellowship one with another, and the blood of Jesus Christ his Son cleanseth us from* ALL SIN. How much sin is there left when *all* is taken away? And it ought to be observed that the Apostle does not speak of a *future* cleansing, but the blood of Christ *now cleanseth.* Ch. iii. 8. *He that committeth sin is of the Devil; for the Devil sinneth from the beginning.* If your doctrine be true, that all must "always sin in thought, word, and deed," then, according to John, all are children of the Devil. Who represents Christ as "vanquished" now? *For this purpose the Son of God was manifested, that he might destroy the works of the devil.* Will you say, that the *very purpose* for which the Son of God was manifested, shall not be accomplished? He came, according to the language of the Apostle Paul, *to redeem us from* ALL INIQUITY, *and to purify to himself a peculiar people, zealous of good works.* If therefore none are *purified,* if none are redeemed from *all iniquity* in this life, the benevolent design for which the Lord Jesus came into the world is not answered. And is it not highly dishonourable to God, to suppose that the express *design* for which he gave his Son; and equally dishonourable to the Son who came to accomplish the same *end,* to say that this desirable end is not, in any instance, obtained? . . .

10. You will, without doubt, acknowledge that conviction, justification and sanctification, are all the work of God. And Moses saith, *His work is perfect*, Deut. xxxiii. 4. When therefore a sinner is convicted, justified and sanctified, he is *perfectly* convicted, justified and sanctified; for all the *works of God are perfect*. Any thing is perfect, which answers its END. Thus when God finished his work of creation, he pronounced it all *very good*, that is, *perfect*; because each and every part was fitted for the place it was designed to occupy, and to discharge the duties resulting from its relative situation. When souls are born into the kingdom of God, they are said to be *created anew unto good works, which God ordained that ye should walk in them*. To say therefore that adult christians do not walk in good works, but in sin, is to pronounce them *imperfect*; and to pronounce them in this sense imperfect, is to say that God's work is *defective* — that he has not so wrought believers, as to answer the *end* of their new creation. Again, the end for which Christ died for us is, *That he might redeem us from all iniquity, and purify to himself a peculiar people, zealous of good works*. This then is the *end*, the manifest *design* of God in the work of redemption and salvation. To accomplish this *end*, and fit man for this *design*, God works in the hearts of those who believe in Jesus Christ. To say, therefore, that obedient believers are not redeemed from all iniquity, and purified from all sin, "properly so called," is to say that the gracious design of God is frustrated, even towards those who are given to Christ. And that the Apostle in the above passage spoke of being *redeemed from all iniquity in this life*, is undeniably certain, from his adding, *a peculiar people zealous of good works*; unless you absurdly suppose that he meant they should not be *zealous of good works* until after death. — Now, as it is impious to insinuate that the *perfect work of God* is *defective*, that his benevolent designs to the world never take effect, so it is absurd to say that believers are not saved from sin. If indeed we were left to ourselves in the work of salvation, we might well despair of an exemption from the curse of the law, and an emancipation from the thraldom of sin. But when we take into consideration that he who is omnipotent in *power* and unbounded in wisdom and goodness, has undertaken to accomplish this glorious and desirable work, all our fears of its *complete* accomplishment are dissipated. He who worketh in us to *will* and to *do* of his own *good pleasure*, is fully able and abundantly willing to work in us *perfect* faith and love, *perfect* humility and patience, *perfect* meekness and temperance, goodness and forbearance, which are some of the perfect graces which adorn the soul of a christian. *Faithful is he that calleth you, who also will do it*, says Paul, 1 Thess. v. 24.

RICHARD WATSON

R ichard Watson (1781–1833), a British Methodist, was the first systematic theologian in Methodism and its most influential spokesman for the first half of the nineteenth century. His *Theological Institutes* (1833) was not only important in British Methodism but was the primary theological text of the North American Methodist ministerial course of study. Watson solidified Methodist theology and set it forth in well-organized detail. The selections included in these readings present an increasingly pervasive theme in Methodist thought: human moral agency. It is necessary to see this theme in relation to the discussion of grace in Fletcher and of the Holy Spirit in Clarke and Bangs and as it is worked out by later writers such as Whedon. The interaction of prevenient grace and human agency is one of the distinctive issues of the Wesleyan theological tradition. Among Watson's more important writings are: *An Apology for the Bible* (1796), *A Biblical and Theological Dictionary* (1831), and *Life of John Wesley* (1831). Watson served as secretary to the Wesleyan Missionary Society (1821–25) and as President of the Conference (1826). The selections, "Man a Moral Agent" and "The Justice and Grace of God" are from *Theological Institutes* (London: John Mason, 1858), I, pp.1–9, 15–16, and IV, p.132, 134–138.

MAN A MORAL AGENT

The theological system of the holy Scriptures being the subject of our inquiries, it is essential to our undertaking to establish their divine authority. But before the direct evidence which the case admits is adduced, our attention may be profitably engaged by several considerations, which afford presumptive evidence in favour of the revelations of the Old and

New Testaments. These are of so much weight that they ought not, in fairness, to be overlooked; nor can their force be easily resisted by the impartial inquirer.

The moral agency of man is a principle on which much depends in such an investigation; and, from its bearing upon the question at issue, requires our first notice.

He is a moral agent who is capable of performing moral actions; and an action is rendered moral by two circumstances, — that it is voluntary, and that it has respect to some rule which determines it to be good or evil. "Moral good and evil," says Locke, "is the conformity or disagreement of our voluntary actions to some law, whereby good or evil is drawn upon us from the will or power of the law-maker."

The terms found in all languages, and the laws which have been enacted in all states, with accompanying penalties, as well as the praise or dispraise which men, in all ages, have expressed respecting the conduct of each other, sufficiently show that man has always been considered as an agent actually performing, or capable of performing, moral actions; for as such he has been treated. No one ever thought of making laws to regulate the conduct of the inferior animals, or of holding them up to public censure or approbation.

The rules by which the moral quality of actions has been determined are, however, not those only which have been embodied in the legislation of civil communities. Many actions would be judged good or evil were all civil codes abolished; and others are daily condemned or approved in the judgment of mankind which are not of a kind to be recognised by public laws. Of the moral nature of human actions there must have been a perception in the minds of men previous to the enactment of laws. Upon this common perception all law is founded, and claims the consent and support of society; for in all human legislative codes there is an express or tacit appeal to principles previously acknowledged, as reasons for their enactment.

This distinction in the moral quality of actions previous to the establishment of civil regulations, and independent of them, may, in part, be traced to its having been observed, that certain actions are injurious to society, and that to abstain from them is essential to its well-being. Murder and theft may be given as instances. It has also been perceived, that such actions result from certain afflictions of the mind; and the indulgence or restraint of such affections has, therefore, been also regarded as a moral act. Anger, revenge, and cupidity, have been deemed evils, as the sources of injuries of various kinds; and humanity, self-government, and integrity, have been ranked among the virtues; and thus, both certain actions, and the principles from which they spring, have, from their effect upon society, been determined to be good or evil.

But it has likewise been observed, by every man, that individual happiness, as truly as social order and interests, is materially affected by particular acts, and by those feelings of the heart which give rise to them; as, for instance, by anger, malice, envy, impatience, cupidity, &c.; and that whatever civilized men, in all places, and in all ages, have agreed to call vice, is inimical to health of body, or to peace of mind, or to both. This, it is true, has had little influence upon human conduct; but it has been acknowledged by the poets, sages, and satirists of all countries, and is adverted to as matter of universal experience. Whilst, therefore, there is, in the moral condition and habits of man, something which propels him to vice, uncorrected by the miseries which it never fails to inflict, there is also something in the constitution of the human soul which renders vice subversive of its happiness, and something in the established law and nature of things which renders vice incompatible with the collective interests of men in the social state.

Let that, then, be granted by the Theist which he cannot consistently deny,—the existence of a supreme Creator, of infinite power, wisdom, goodness, and justice, who has both made men and continues to govern them; and the strongest presumption is afforded,—by the very constitution of the nature of man, and the relations established among human affairs, which, with so much constancy, dissociate happiness from vicious passions, health from intemperance, the peace, security, and improvement of society from violence and injustice,—that the course of action which best secures human happiness has the sanction of his will; or, in other words, that He, by these circumstances, has given his authority in favour of the practice of virtue, and opposed it to the practice of vice.

But though that perception of the difference of moral actions which is antecedent to human laws, must have been strongly confirmed by these facts of experience, and by such observations, we have no reason to conclude that those rules by which the moral quality of actions has, in all ages, been determined, were formed solely from a course of observation on their tendency to promote or obstruct human happiness; because we cannot collect, either from history or tradition, that the world was ever without such rules, though they were often warped and corrupted. The evidence of both, on the contrary, shows, that so far from these rules having originated from observing what was injurious and what beneficial to mankind, there has been, almost among all nations, a constant reference to a declared will of the supreme God, or of supposed deities, as the rule which determines the good or the evil of the conduct of men; which will was considered by them as a law, prescribing the one and restraining the other under the sanction, not only of our being left to the natural injurious consequences of vicious habit and practice in the present life, or of continuing to enjoy the benefits of obedience in personal and social happiness here; but also of positive reward and positive punishment in a future life.

Whoever speculated on the subject of morals and moral obligation, in any age, was previously furnished with these general notions and distinctions; they were in the world before him; and if all tradition be not a fable, if the testimony of all antiquity, whether found in poets or historians, be not delusive, they were in the world in those early periods when the great body of the human race remained near the original seat of the parent families of all the modern and now widely-extended nations of the earth; and, in those early periods, they were not regarded as distinctions of mere human opinion and consent, but were invested with a divine authority.

We have, then, before us two presumptions, each of great weight. First, that those actions which, among men, have almost universally been judged good, have the implied sanction of the will of our wise and good Creator, being found in experience, and by the constitution of our nature and of human society, most conducive to human happiness. And, second, that they were originally, in some mode or other, prescribed and enjoined as his law, and their contraries prohibited.

If, therefore, there is presumptive evidence, of only ordinary strength, that the rule by which our actions are determined to be good or evil is primarily a law of the Creator, we are all deeply interested in ascertaining where that law exists in its clearest manifestation. For ignorance of the law, in whole or in part, will be no excuse for disobedience, if we have the opportunity of acquainting ourselves with it; and an accurate acquaintance with the rule may assist our practice in cases of which human laws take no cognizance, and which the wilfully corrupted general judgment of mankind may have darkened. And should it appear either that in many things we have offended more deeply than we suspect, whether wilfully or from an evitable ignorance; or that, from some common accident which has befallen our nature, we have lost the power of entire obedience without the use of new and extraordinary means, the knowledge of the rule is of the utmost consequence to us, because by it we may be enabled to ascertain the precise relation in which we stand to God our Maker; the dangers we have incurred; and the means of escape, if any have been placed within our reach.

It is well observed by a judicious writer, that "all the distinctions of good and evil refer to some principle above ourselves; for, were there no supreme Governor and Judge to reward and punish, the very notions of good and evil would vanish away; they could not exist in the minds of men, if there were not a supreme Director to give laws for the measure thereof."

If we deny the existence of a divine law obligatory upon man, we must deny that the world is under divine government; for government without rule or law is a solecism; and to deny the divine government, would leave it impossible for us to account for that peculiar nature which has been given to man, and those relations among human concerns and interests to which we have adverted, and which are so powerfully affected by our conduct;—certain actions and habits which almost all mankind have agreed to call good, being connected with the happiness of the individual, and the well-being of society; and so on the contrary. This, too, has been matter of uniform and constant experience from the earliest ages; and warrants, therefore, the conclusion, that the effect arises from original principles and a constitution of things which the Creator has established. Nor can any reason be offered why such a nature should be given to man, and such a law impressed on the circumstances and beings with which he is surrounded, except that both had an intended relation to certain courses of action as the sources of order and happiness, as truly as there was an intended relation between the light, and the eye which is formed to receive its rays.

But as man is not carried to this course of action by physical impulse or necessity; as moral conduct supposes choice, and therefore instruction, and the persuasion of motives arising out of it; the benevolent intention of the Creator as to our happiness could not be accomplished without instruction, warning, reward, and punishment; all of which necessarily imply superintendence and control, or, in other words, a moral government. The creation, therefore, of a being of such a nature as man, implies divine government, and that government a divine law.

Such a law must be the subject of revelation. Law is the will of a superior power; but the will of a superior visible power cannot be known without some indication by words or signs, in other terms, without a revelation; and much less the will of an invisible power, of an order superior to our own, and confessedly mysterious in his mode of existence, and the attributes of his nature.

Again: The will of a superior is not in justice binding until, in some mode, it is sufficiently declared; and the presumption, therefore, that God wills the practice of any particular course of action, on the part of his creatures, establishes the farther presumption, that of that will there has been a manifestation; and the more so if there is reason to suppose, that any penalty of a serious nature has been attached to disobedience.

The revelation of this will or law of God may be made either by action, from which it is to be inferred; or by direct communication in language. Any indication of the moral perfections of God, or of his design in forming moral beings, which the visible creation presents to the mind; or any instance of his favour or displeasure towards his creatures clearly and frequently connected in his administration with any particular course of conduct; may be considered as a revelation of his will by action; and is not at all inconsistent with a further revelation by the direct means of language.

The Theist admits that a revelation of the will of God has been made by significant actions, from which the duty of creatures is to be inferred; and he contends that this is sufficient. "They who never heard of any external revelation, yet if they knew, from the nature of things, what is fit for them to do, they know all that God will or can require of them."

They who believe that the holy Scriptures contain a revelation of God's will do not deny that indications of his will have been made by action; but they contend that they are in themselves imperfect and insufficient, and that they were not designed to supersede a direct revelation. They hold, also, that a direct communication of the divine will was made to the progenitors of the human race, which received additions at subsequent periods, and that the whole was at length embodied in the book called, by way of eminence, "The Bible." . . .

Now it is not necessary to prove at length, what is so obvious, that if we had no method of knowing the will and purposes of God, but by inferring them from his works and his government, we could have no information as to any purpose in the divine Mind to forgive his sinning creatures. The Theist, in order to support this hope, dwells upon the proofs of the goodness of God with which this world abounds, but shuts his eyes upon the demonstrations of his severity: yet these surround him as well as the other; and the argument from the severity of God is as forcible against pardon, as the argument from his goodness is in its favour. At the best, it is left entirely uncertain; a ground is laid for heart-rending doubts, and fearful anticipations; and, for any thing he can show to the contrary, the goodness which God has displayed in nature and providence may only render the offence of man more aggravated, and serve to strengthen the presumption against the forgiveness of a wilful offender, rather than afford him any reason for hope.

The whole of this argument is designed to prove, that had we been left, for the regulation of our conduct, to infer the will and purposes of the supreme Being from his natural works, and his administration of the affairs of the world, our knowledge of both would have been essentially deficient; and it establishes a strong presumption in favour of a direct revelation from God to his creatures, that neither his will concerning us, nor the hope of forgiveness, might be left to dark and uncertain inference, but be the subjects of an express declaration.

THE JUSTICE AND GRACE OF GOD

If all knowledge of right and wrong, and all gracious influence of the Holy Spirit, and all objects of faith have passed away from the Heathen, through the fault of their ancestors not liking to "retain God in their knowledge," and without the present race having been parties to this wilful abandonment of truth, then they would appear no longer to be accountable creatures, being neither under law not under grace; but as we find it a doctrine of Scripture that all men are responsible to God, and that the whole world will be judged at the last day, we are bound to admit the accountability of all, and, with that, the remains of law and the existence of a merciful government towards the Heathen on the part of God. . . .

It is allowed, and all scriptural advocates of the universal redemption of mankind will join with the Calvinists in maintaining the doctrine, that every disposition and inclination to good which originally existed in the nature of man is lost by the fall; that all men, in their simply natural state, are "dead in trespasses and sins," and have neither the will nor the power to turn to God; and that no one is sufficient of himself to think or do anything of a saving tendency. But as all men are required to do those things which have a saving tendency, we contend that the grace to do them has been bestowed upon all. Equally sacred is the doctrine to be held, that no person can repent or truly believe except under the influence of the Spirit of God; and that we have no ground of boasting in ourselves, but that all the glory of our salvation, commenced and consummated, is to be given to God alone, as the result of the freeness and riches of his grace.

It will also be freely allowed, that the visitations of the gracious influences of the Holy Spirit are vouchsafed in the first instance, and in numberless other subsequent cases, quite independent of our seeking them or desire for them; and that when our thoughts are thus turned to serious considerations, and various exciting and quickening feelings are produced within us, we are often wholly passive; and also, that men are sometimes suddenly and irresistibly awakened to a sense of their guilt and danger by the Spirit of God, either through the preaching of the word instrumentally or through other means, and sometimes, even, independent of any external means at all; and are thus constrained to cry out, "What must I do to be saved?" All this is confirmed by plain verity of holy writ; and is also as certain a matter of experience as that the motions of the Holy Spirit do often silently intermingle themselves with our thoughts, reasonings, and consciences, and breathe their milder persuasions upon our affections.

From these premises the conclusions which legitimately flow are in direct opposition to the Calvinistic hypothesis. They establish,

1. The justice of God in the condemnation of men, which their doctrine leaves under a dark and impenetrable cloud. More or less of these influences from on high visit the finally impenitent, so as to render their destruction their own act by resisting them. This is proved, from the Spirit having striven with those who were finally destroyed by the flood of Noah; from the case of the finally impenitent Jews and their ancestors, who are charged with always resisting the Holy Ghost; from the case of the apostates mentioned in the Epistle to the Hebrews, who are said to have done despite to the Spirit of grace; and from the solemn warnings given to men in the New Testament, not to grieve and quench the Holy Spirit. If, therefore, it appears that the destruction of men is attributed to their resistance of those influences of the Holy Spirit, which, but for that resistance, would have been saving, according to the design of God in imparting them, then is the justice of God manifested in their punishment; and it follows, also, that his grace so works in men, as to be both sufficient to lead them into a state of salvation, and even often actually to place them in this state, and yet so as to be capable of being finally and fatally frustrated.

2. These premises, also, secure the glory of our salvation to the grace of God; but not by implying the Calvinistic notion of the continued and uninterrupted irresistibility of the influence of grace and the passiveness of man, so as to deprive him of his agency; but by showing that his agency, even when rightly directed, is upheld and influenced by the superior power of God, and yet so as to be still his own. For, in the instance of the mightiest visitation we can produce from Scripture, that of St. Paul, we see where the irresistible influence terminated, and where his own agency recommenced. Under the impulse of the conviction struck into his mind, as well as under the dazzling brightness which fell upon his eyes, he was passive, and the effect produced for the time

necessarily followed; but all the actions consequent upon this were the results of deliberation and personal choice. He submits to be taught in the doctrine of Christ; he confers not with flesh and blood; he is not disobedient to the heavenly vision; he faints not under the burdensome ministry he had received; and he keeps his body under subjection, lest after having preached to others he should himself become a castaway. All these expressions, so descriptive of consideration, choice, and effort, show that the irresistible impulse was not permanent, and that he was subsequently left to improve it or not, though under a powerful but still a resistible motive operating upon him to remain faithful.

For the gentler emotions produced by the Spirit, these are, as the experience of all Christians testifies, the ordinary and general manner in which the Holy Spirit carries on his work in man; and if all good desires, resolves, and aspirations are from him, and not from our own nature, (and, if we are utterly fallen, from our own nature they cannot be,) then, if any man is conscious of having ever checked good desires, and of having opposed his own convictions and better feelings, he has in himself abundant proof of the resistibility of grace, and of the superability of those good inclinations which the Spirit is pleased to impart. He is equally conscious of the power of complying with them, though still in the strength of grace; which yet, whilst it works in him to will and to do, neither wills nor acts for him, nor even by him, as a passive instrument. For if men were wholly and at all times passive under divine influence; not merely in the reception of it, (for all are, in that respect, passive,) but in the actings of it to practical ends; then would there be nothing to mark the difference between the righteous and the wicked but an act of God, —which is utterly irreconcilable to the Scriptures. They call the former "obedient," the latter "disobedient;" one "willing," the other "unwilling;" and promise or threaten accordingly. They attribute the destruction of the one to their refusal of the grace of God, and the salvation of the other, as the instrumental cause, to their acceptance of it; and to urge that that personal act by which we embrace the grace of Christ, detracts from his glory as our Saviour by attributing our salvation to ourselves, is to speak as absurdly as if we should say that the act of obedience and faith required of the man who was commanded to stretch out his withered arm, detracted from the glory of Christ's healing virtue, by which, indeed, the power of complying with the command and condition of his being healed was imparted.

PART II

DEVELOPING DISTINCTIVENESS

Methodism's efforts to express a distinctive theology became increasingly self-conscious as the nineteenth century progressed. What were the Wesleyan movement's dominant themes? A number of theologians attempted to express their understanding of the movement's characteristic emphases. Francis Asbury discussed the theological foundations of Methodist polity. Phoebe Palmer renewed stress upon sanctification, although with new nuances. Daniel D. Whedon set forth a full range of Methodist doctrines emphasizing their distinctive character. William Burt Pope discussed Methodist doctrine stressing its kinship with catholic Christianity. John Miley structured his understanding of Methodist Episcopal theology by establishing theism as his base, and Milton Terry stressed a Methodist understanding of biblical study. In their efforts to clarify the Methodist position, these writers not only reaffirmed their inheritance, but also felt free to set new directions. All of these theologians were vigorous champions for their new emphases as means of continuing the vitality of the Methodist tradition.

FRANCIS ASBURY

F rancis Asbury (1745–1816) was the most important leader in establishing Methodism on the North American continent. An untiring worker, an example of disciplined living, an organizer of genius, and a spokesman for the new movement, Asbury molded Episcopal Methodism and imparted to it a sense of mission. Asbury was not a technical theologian, and most of his writings are short and directed toward a specific situation. Among the more important statements that he made was his Valedictory Address to Bishop William McKendree. When asked on his deathbed if he wanted to convey any special message, he replied that he had already expressed his mind in his communication to Bishop McKendree. In this address Asbury discusses the nature of the Methodist Episcopal Church, the development of its distinctive life, and its special mission. The selection is taken from *The Journal and Letters of Francis Asbury*, eds. J. Manning Potts, Elmer T. Clark, and Jacob S. Patton (London and New York: Epworth Press and Abingdon Press, 1958), vol. III, pp.475–92.

LANCASTER, PENNSYLVANIA
August 5, 1813

A Valedictory Address to William McKendree, Bishop of the Methodist Episcopal Church in the United States of America. By Francis Asbury.

Speaking to the Genessee Annual Conference in your presence on the subject of apostolical, missionary, Methodist Episcopal Church government, I was desired to commit my thoughts to writing. I feel the more disposed to do this, that I may leave a written testimony which may be seen, read, and known when your friend and father is taken from the evil to come.

Sir: My advice is that there be only three effective bishops, as from the beginning, traveling through the whole continent, each one to preside alternately in all the Annual Conferences, one to preside during the sitting of the same Conference, the other two to have charge of and plan the stations and perform ordinations, assisted by the elders in both branches. The plan of stations should be submitted to the President of the Conferences, in triune order, to give a final decision before it is read out. I wish to warn you against the growing evil of locality in bishops, elders, preachers, or Conferences. Locality is essential to cities and towns, but traveling is as essential to the country. Were I to name cities, such as Jerusalem, Antioch, and Rome, with all the great cities, both ancient and modern, what havoc have these made in the Churches! Alas for us! out of seven hundred traveling preachers, we have about one hundred located in towns and cities and small rich circuits. Guard particularly against two orders of preachers: the one of the country, the other for the cities; the latter generally settle themselves to purchase ministers, and too often men of gifts and learning intend to set themselves to sale.

I am bold to say that the apostolic order of things was lost in the first century, when Church governments were adulterated and had much corruption attached to them. At the Reformation, the reformers only beat off a part of the rubbish, which put a stop to the rapid increase of absurdities at that time; but how they have increased since! Recollect the state of the different Churches, as it respects government and discipline, in the seventeenth century when the Lord raised up that great and good man, John Wesley, who formed an evangelical society in England. In 1784, an apostolical form of Church government was formed in the United States of America at the first General Conference of the Methodist Episcopal Church held at Baltimore, in the State of Maryland.

You know, my brother, that the present ministerial cant is that we cannot now, as in former apostolical days, have such doctrines, such discipline, such convictions, such conversions, such witnesses of sanctification, and such holy men. But I say that we can; I say we must; yea, I say we have. And can men claim the rights and privileges of apostles if they are impostors and not true ministers of the holy sanctuary? Instead of going to preach, they stay to preach. Hence it is that schools, colleges, and universities undertake to make men ministers that the Lord Jesus Christ never commanded to be made. The present Episcopal Churches are greatly independent of each other. All the numerous orders of Presbyterians, Independents, and Baptists are also local. If we wish to see pure and unadulterated Church history, let us go to the Acts of the Apostles and mark the characters of those ministers in the time of persecution—such as Paul, Timothy, Titus, Tychicus, Archippus, Trophimus, Artemas, Luke, Epaphroditus, etc.—men who did honor to themselves as ministers of Christ. But there are too many the opposite of these, whom we can view in no other light, at present, than as men going into the ministry by their learning, sent by their parents or moved by pride, the love of ease, money or honor. Are not such moved by Satan more than by the Holy Ghost to assume the sacred office of the holy ministry? Mark well what a situation the apostles were in. If unfaithful in the discharge of their duty, God would condemn and punish them the most severely. On the other hand, the people were ready to starve, stone, or beat them to death. Modern priests will please the people, that they may not be starved or beaten; but will not God condemn such teachers to everlasting destruction? We lay no claim to the Latin, Greek, English, Lutheran, Swedish, or Protestant Episcopal Church order. It will be seen that we are so unlike them that we could not stand as related to them. Would their bishops ride five or six thousand miles in nine months for eighty dollars a year, with their traveling expense less or more, preach daily when opportunity serves, meet a number of camp meetings in the year, make arrangements for stationing seven hundred preachers, ordain a hundred more annually, ride through all kinds of weather, and along roads in the worst state at our time of life—the one sixty-nine, the other in his fifty-sixth year?

When the Methodist preachers came first to this country, one-half of the continent was overspread with different names and orders of Presbyterians, Independents, Baptists, English, French, German, Holland, Scotch, and Irish, with many Quakers. In the Southern part were Episcopalians. They had but few churches and no bishops. At this time the Methodists were, among others, not organized and had not the ordinances among us. As some in pleasantry said: "We were a Church, and no Church." In some places we communed with the Episcopalians. In 1779, some of our brethren in Virginia attempted to organize themselves into a Church; but in 1780, the writer of this address visited them, when they agreed to suspend their administration, and with united voice call upon Mr. Wesley to make some provision for them. Accordingly, in 1784, our faithful father, Mr. Wesley, ordained Thomas Coke, bishop, or general superintendent, and Francis Asbury was elected by the General Conference held in Baltimore, Md., December, 1784, general superintendent; was first ordained deacon and elder; on December 27, bishop, or general superintendent; Richard Whatcoat in May, 1800; and William

McKendree in May, 1808. Dr. Coke was ordained deacon and elder by two scriptural English bishops, and so was John Wesley. Do any ancient or modern Churches stand on any better ground than we do with respect to ordination, with John Wesley's apostolic right? Probably Paul was ordained with Barnabas. (Acts xiii, 1–3.)

Should any ask why we did not seek ordination from other Churches, we answer them by asking if we should go to local men to be ordained traveling bishops. Should we go to Presbyterians to be ordained Episcopal Methodist? or to Episcopalians, who at that time had no bishop or power of ordination in the United States till application was made to the British Parliament, and that legislative body passed a law for the express purpose authorizing their bishops to consecrate and ordain bishops for the thirteen States of America, in 1785? Here let it be observed, that the Methodist was the first Church organized after the establishment of peace in 1783, and that the Protestant Episcopalians were not organized as a Church until after there was a law passed by the British Parliament. Or could we subscribe to Calvinian articles? Surely, no. Or could we submit to locality? By no means. Let local men ordain local men, baptize, or rebaptize local men; we must shape our course otherwise and prepare to meet the different Annual Conferences from Maine to Georgia and the Mississippi, and to retain all the ancient essential branches of Methodism in all its parts and try sacredly to maintain our traveling plan and support a true missionary, apostolic Church. And suppose this excellent constitution and order of things should be broken, what shall the present or future bishops do? Let them do as your noble countryman did — resign and retire to private life.

It is a serious thing for a bishop to be stripped of any constitutional rights chartered to him at his ordination, without which he could not and would not have entered into that sacred office, he being conscious at the same time he had never violated those sacred rights. Comparing human Church history with the Acts of the Apostles, it will manifestly appear that the apostolic order of things ended in about fifty years. With the preachers and people of that day, the golden order was lost. But we must restore and retain primitive order; we must, we will, have the same doctrine, the same spirituality, the same power in ordinances, in ordination, and in spirit.

Joseph Pilmoor had been but a short time on his mission to this country before he saw that it would not be proper for the Methodists to continue an Episcopal society. He was for forming an independent Church of England. Mr. Wesley was called for near twelve or thirteen years, repeatedly, to do something for his people in America. Dr. Whitehead reproached Mr. Wesley, in writing his "Life," for ordaining preachers in America, unless he had the voice of preachers and people in America; yet, if my memory serves me right, the Doctor grants Mr. Wesley's right so to do if he had had their voice; and this he most assuredly had, and it had been communicated to him by word and letter; or why did every heart leap with joy and the members of society and the congregations in America embrace our Church form and order and by thousands giving up themselves to the ordinances and presenting their children for baptism for nearly thirty years last past?

You have often heard me say that Church governments changed with the Church into strange, incredible forms—as monarchy, aristocracy, democracy, and legal establishments—when scholars, lawyers, doctors, and peers became bishops and bishops became kings, temporal princes, and peers, and presbyters became assemblymen and senators; in this country they become chaplains to Congress; yes, members of Congress! It will come to this conclusion, that ours is the apostolic plan. But say you, Are all apostles? Are all that we have ordained holy men? They might have been. Were Judas, Simon Magus, and Demas faithful unto death? Ministers may fall from grace and office; and no wonder if we, on ordaining four thousand local and nearly two thousand traveling preachers, should find some to turn out apostates.

Thus I have traced regular order and succession in John Wesley, Thomas Coke, Francis Asbury, Richard Whatcoat, and William McKendree. Let any other Church trace its succession as direct and as pure, if they can. Does any one doubt the experience, piety, or labors of these men, so long tried, known, and read of all men, both friends and enemies, for so many years?

William P. Otterbein, of Baltimore, a regular Presbyterian— the German apostle to America—whose piety, labors, and learning were great, this man of God assisted T. Coke, R. Whatcoat, and T. Vasey in the ordination of Francis Asbury. You will say if our Church were as pure as the primitive Church, will it not, may it not, like other modern, decline? I answer, We live in a purer age and in a free country. If discipline be maintained, men that carry sand instead of salt for the sheep will be constrained soon to leave us, to join some more honorable, but perhaps fallen, Church where they can have more ease and greater emoluments. We have lived to see the end of such persons who left us and set up for themselves—witness Hammett and O'Kelly.

Thomas Haweis, a moderate Episcopalian, fifty years a beneficed minister, is one of the most impartial historians on the subject of episcopacy. I shall close this address with several quotations from his work, wherein you will see that he, without knowledge or design, has given the order of Episcopal Methodism the plume of honor above all others:

"From the morning spread upon the mountains to the meridian splendor of the Sun of righteousness, I wish to trace the progress of his gospel amidst the storms of persecution, till his glory shall be finally revealed, and all flesh shall see it together, for the mouth of the Lord hath spoken it. Contemptuous infidelity, proud philosophy, bigoted superstition, atheistical immorality, heretical and schismatical depravity, may unite their powers against the child Jesus and his everlasting gospel, but the gates of hell shall never prevail. His persecuted Church shall rise. I have continued to prefer an episcopal mode of Church government, unless I can find a better. I am satisfied that the Methodist mode of episcopal government is more apostolic than the Church of England ever was, will, or can be, without a radical reformation from its essential form of locality, written sermons and prayers, State laws, and human policy." (Vol. I, p.12, of his Introduction.)

"When I speak of episcopacy as most correspondents in my poor idea to the apostolic practice and general usage of the Church in the first and generally esteemed purer ages, let no man imagine I plead for that episcopacy which, rising very early on the stilts of practical pride and worldly-mindedness, has since overspread the earth with its baneful shadow; or suppose those to be true successors of the apostles who, grasping at power and preeminence over Churches which their labors never planted nor watered, claiming dominion over districts, provinces, and kingdoms beyond all power of individual superintendency." (P.14.)

Here, Bishop, mark: "Planted or watered." We have planted and watered; although our continent is three thousand miles in length, we have measured it year after year, embracing fifty-one or two districts, about six hundred circuits, and nine Annual Conferences, all which, with very few exceptions, we have visited. Then, according to our author, we are apostolic bishops; for we have both planted and watered, and do water still. As to temporal power, what have we to do with that in this country? We are not senators, congressmen, or chaplains; neither do we hold any civil offices. We neither have, nor wish to have, anything to do with the government of the States, nor, as I conceive, do the States fear us. Our kingdom is not of this world. For near half a century we have never grasped at power.

"All united in one Church fellowship [so the Methodists] under the superintendency of apostolic men at first and on their decease, the most distinguished for zeal, wisdom, sufferings, influence, or respectability of any kind, was called by the suffrage of the elders and people to be their superintendent, president, *praeses; hegoumenos*, a leader; and thus the name of bishop *(kat' exochen)*, on account of preeminence, became very early appropriate to one who was *primus inter pares*; and, as Archbishop Usher says, differed only in degree of advantagement and not in order. These were, I apprehend, always from the apostolic days raised to their station by the voice of the people and their fellows. They preside in the deliberations of their several Churches, with the presbyters, their assessors. They were deputed to all synods which treated of ecclesiastical matters; and whilst every congregation judged its own members, they received the accusations against elders who were charged with offenses and censured or removed them. They examined the chosen candidates for the ministry, and, with the presbyter, ordained them by imposition of hands. This dangerous eminence marked them as peculiar victims in days of persecution. Far, therefore, from being an enviable or desirable situation, no man dare to aspire after or occupy it but such as counted their lives not dear unto themselves, that they 'might finish their course with joy, and the ministry which they had received from the Lord to fulfill it,' whether as confessors or martyrs." (P.16.)

"The sudden ability of illiterate men of so great a number in a moment, and with perfection, to speak in all languages, to express themselves with such propriety and force as not only to be clearly understood, but impressive on the consciences of the numerous foreigners then at Jerusalem from every nation under heaven, such a phenomenon could not but strike the hearers with astonishment and afford an evidence of divine agency too incontestible to admit of a rational doubt." (P.28.)

Now, Bishop McKendree, I will make this remark, that to take this transaction of the Divine Spirit prophetically, it saith to every minister, "Go ye into all the world, and preach the gospel to every creature"; and that in all ages to come, unlettered men should be raised up to preach the gospel with the power of the Holy Ghost sent down from heaven. One may say, This man speaks well!—ah, he is a college-taught man! Again it may be said, This man speaks well; he is a scholar! But you are mistaken. He has only a common education—a plowman, a tailor, a carpenter, or a shoemaker! Then he must be taught of God, if he is not taught of man. Then we may rationally conclude that learning is not an essential qualification to preach the gospel. It may be said no man but a fool will speak against learning. I have not spoken against learning. I have only said that it cannot be said to be an essential qualification to preach the gospel. It was once reported that two impostors (Roman priests) came to England, entered themselves as porters or draymen, but said they had received the gift of tongues and were called to preach. But

Dr. Doddridge, being in the city, was requested to examine them and found they were scholars; but when he examined them in Welsh, the cheat was found out. And too often the learned priests deceive the people by their learning, or professing so to be; because the first preachers were blest with the gift of tongues immediately from heaven; so that a man must spend four or seven years in learning languages before he is permitted to preach the gospel. And who is to decide the question? Their practice and that of our Lord does not strictly agree....

"A Church without evidence of the influence and experience of the operation of the Holy Ghost hath but a name to live and is dead, and whatever may be its forms, or however sound its confession of faith, it hath no more title to be reckoned a Christian Church than a statue or corpse to be esteemed a living man. The form in which the Church appeared in the best, the primitive age, under the immediate inspection of the apostles and disciples of the Lord, deserves our consideration. And here, drawing around me the sacred circle, I wish to confine myself to the words of the Holy Ghost without any regard to the traditions of men. And I shall begin at Jerusalem. This was the fruitful womb from whence issued the noble army of martyrs, confessors, and evangelists, who, holding up the word of light, diffused the blessings of the glory of God the Saviour to the ends of the earth. These were the fruits of our Lord's ministry during his labors in Judea and the adjacent countries. They consisted of twelve men, first chosen, called apostles, or *persons sent*. To these were added seventy others, who were sent out to preach and teach. They were all endowed with miraculous powers; and on their return from their itinerancy through the nation, reported with triumph the wonders they had wrought. About five hundred brethren were summoned to behold our Lord's ascension into heaven." (P.52.)

"Three thousand believed on the first day (Pentecost), and myriads followed them. The immensity of this number affords us two views of their Church order: First, as necessarily distributed into various congregations, no one place being capable of containing such myriads or any one bishop or elder sufficient to administer the ordinances among them. We accordingly find them breaking bread from house to house (Acts ii, 46), preaching and teaching in every house (Acts v, 42), which seems to describe the Church at Jerusalem. Second, these several *house Churches* formed one united Church body under the presidency of James, and not Peter. (Acts xv, 13.) He was at the head of the first council. To him Paul addressed himself (Acts xxi, 18) when all the elders or presbyters being assembled by him he reported to them the happy success of his ministry among the Gentiles. The necessity of a president where so great a

74

number of elders resided and so many congregations were formed seems as natural for the preservation of order as it appears actually the case in this mother of all the Churches." (Pp.54,55.)

"The care of the poor widows led to the institution of the order of deacons. This originated in a complaint of real or supposed partiality in the distribution of the alms of the faithful to the native Jewish widows, in preference to the Hellenists. (Acts vi, 1.) The apostles themselves being too much engaged to attend to these temporal concerns, recommended it to the Church to elect seven persons for the discharge of this office. These were accordingly chosen by general suffrage, not for each separate congregation, but for the whole body, and were set apart by the apostles after solemn prayer and imposition of hands, to this service. Though the care of the widows was immediately intrusted to them, it prevented them not from being employed in other labors of love. Philip was an evangelist and Stephen a like zealous advocate of Christ and his cause. In consequence of his boldness in the synagogue of the Libertines, the blood of this first martyr was shed by the fury of his enemies, and a great and general persecution following, all the principal disciples were dispersed except the apostles who remained at Jerusalem. (Acts viii, 1.) These, flying in different directions, everywhere preached the gospel and with great success through Judea, Galilee, and Samaria, and some as far as Antioch, Damascus, Phenice, and Cypress. They were village preachers, highway preachers, and were not ashamed of the gospel of Christ. Paul (Acts xxiv, 23), in revisiting the Churches which had been planted principally by himself, edifies, comforts, and establishes them by ordaining elders in every Church with prayers and fasting." (P.56.)

"Returning through Pisidia and Attalia, they arrived happily at Antioch, communicating the glad tidings of their success and of the Gentile Churches which they had planted. I can only observe here that I find in all these widely dispersed and numerous congregations no mention made of any appointment but that of presbyters, all cemented in one bond of union under the supervisal of the great *itinerant evangelists."* (P.62.)

And so it should have continued, and would have continued, if there had been a succession of a faithful seed of holy men to follow apostolic order, but as early as the second century they must have their *local* bishops or local apostles.

"Though James was not superior to Peter or the other apostles at Jerusalem [he may mean he was not superior as to age, gifts, or standing; but certainly he was superior, inasmuch as he had never so publicly denied his Lord], he had been evidently appointed to fill the place of

75

president, or *primus inter pares*. Yet neither he nor any of his apostolic associates assumed to themselves authority to decide but by the suffrage of the whole body of the Church under immediate divine direction." (P.63.)

Our Annual, or more particularly our General Conference resembles this grand council at Jerusalem, where James presided and all the other apostles, elders, and brethren solemnly discussed the cause or causes before them, and James pronounced sentence according to the unanimous suffrage of the assembly, and the definitive decree was in favor of Gentile liberty.

Paul and Barnabas separated for a while (Acts xv, 39); but probably God overruled this for good, and perhaps the Churches were more profited by their distinct labors than if they had traveled in company.

Dr. Haweis continues: "It is evident that Timothy was still but a youth (ch. iv, 14), and whatever office he sustained or with whatever gifts he was endued he received them by the laying on of Paul's hands and of the presbytery. (1 Tim. iv, 14.) Did presbyters then ordain bishops, or were the terms synonymous?" Query, Had there not been two distinct acts in his ordination? Compare 1 Timothy iv, 14, and 2 Timothy i, 6: "The laying on the hands of the presbytery, stir up the gift of God, which is in thee, by the putting on of my hands." That Timothy was left at Ephesus with *superintending* authority, where there were many bishops, is evident. (1 Tim. i, 3.) He was enjoined to encourage and honor those who presided over the congregations well, and especially such as were more actively laborious in preaching and catechising. (V. 18.) Respecting hands, he was to lay hands suddenly on no man; and, without partiality or personal respect, he was to admit none into the ministry but after proper examination and conviction of their call and qualifications. He was also cautiously to receive and weigh all accusations against elders who should give offense and pronounce the sentence due to their unfaithfulness, acts strongly marking superior jurisdiction, and I hence infer that particular Churches neither ordained nor censured their own ministers, although they elected and recommended; and, if faulty, accused them by two or three witnesses before the great itinerant evangelists." (P.76.)

Mark well the similarity of apostolic order and government and the Methodist Episcopal form of things!

In the Second Epistle to Timothy, Paul appears to have "returned again to the house of his prison at Rome, and ready to be offered up on the altar of martyrdom. He had detached his faithful itinerant helpers to a variety of services [although a prisoner, yet clothed with the authority of Christ, he appointed men of God their work], Cresens, to Galatia; Titus, to Dalmatia; while Timothy himself had been left in Asia, from whence he was shortly to proceed to Rome with Mark, who had once departed from the work, but had now returned to the labors and dangers of itinerancy. The principal subject of the Epistle is the dying charge of the great apostle to his beloved son respecting his own teaching and conduct and worthy the attentive consideration of every bishop or presbyter upon earth." (See p.77.)

Paul's two favored sons, Timothy and Titus, were his chief companions, and greatly employed in the regulation of the congregations which had been raised by his labors. The postscript of his first Epistle calls Timothy the first bishop of the Church of the Ephesians; but there is no such title given him by Paul or any intimation of his being at Ephesus but as one of the great *itinerant evangelists*, the companion of Paul and deputed by him to assist in bringing the congregations into a regular order of worship and discipline.

"It nowhere appears that Titus was more the Bishop of Crete than of Dalmatia (2 Tim. iv, 10) or of Nicopolis (Titus iii, 2) or had any fixed residence or diocese, he being one of the great itinerant evangelists who went about preaching everywhere in season, out of season. And therefore as soon as he had settled the Cretan Church in the most edifying manner, he was ordered to come and winter with Paul at Nicopolis, and Artemas or Tychicus should be dispatched to fill his place in the Cretan congregations.

"A general superiority in all the Churches which they visited appears to have been exercised by these great evangelists, though none appears stationary in any one place. They ordained, censured, regulated, were the cementing bond of union to the different Churches [so should the Methodist bishops be], maintaining a unity of order and procedure through the whole. They all bore the name of apostles (2 Cor. viii, 23), were everywhere received with reverence and obeyed with filial affection. ['Whether any do enquire of Titus, he is my partner and fellowhelper concerning you: or our brethren be enquired of, they are the messengers of the churches, and the glory of Christ.'] They assumed no domain over their faith, but were helpers of the joy of the faithful wherever they went. The gifts, abilities, and zeal which they displayed, with every divine temper which adorns the Christian ministry, could not but give them weight and procure them influence by whatever name they might be distinguished, and in every Christian Church, in the very nature of things, such men must possess superiority, whatever be its constitution. Even where the most absolute parity is established, to these their fellows naturally give place. They are the presidents in all associations; heard with respect, commanding obedience; capable of swaying the decisions of their brethren; consulted in all difficult cases, and placed foremost in the hour of danger. To them is intrusted the care of eleemosynary distributions for the benefit of the body to which they belong, and in private and public all concede to them the seal of honor." (P.78.)

If the elders that rule well are worthy of double honor, then the bishops that rule well must be worthy of triple honor, especially when they do so large a part of ruling, preaching and presiding in Conferences.

"In the primitive Church [in speaking or writing it was common to consolidate the first churches into one, although they consisted of many societies, so we say the Methodist Episcopal Church], this superiority, was vested in the apostles and their companions, the great itinerant evangelists, Barnabas, Silas, Artemas, Tychicus, Titus, Timothy, and many others, *chief men among the brethren.*" (P.79.)

Notwithstanding all these were great men in the Church of God, yet, as we have seen, none of them were writers. The Epistle to Titus bears some resemblance to that to Timothy. Men placed in similar situations were called to act under the same principles and to employ the same means. If we are willing, here we may see the propriety of our superintendency, presiding elders, as in the second part of the primitive Church, which order was lost in the first and not found again until the seventeenth century, partially in Europe but more perfectly in America in the organization and establishment of the Methodist Episcopal Church.

"I conclude, as soon as a little society was formed of Christians, a room was opened for their assembling and the most apt to teach appointed to minister to them in holy things [perhaps not unlike a class leader and local preacher in one]. He was a man of gravity, generally of the more aged, approved by his fellows and willing to devote himself to their service. His appointment was signified by prayer and imposition of hands by the Apostle Paul or some of the itinerant evangelists and the presbytery, and without this I meet no ordination. Every Church that is, every society exercised discipline over its own members, to admit, admonish, or expel. Before these itinerating evangelists all accusations against offending presbyters were brought. [These evangelists seem not to have been stationary, but to have gone about everywhere, chiefly under the direction of the apostle Paul.]

"These evangelists were usually supported by the Churches or societies but often, like Paul, maintained themselves by their own labors. During the first ages, the ministry was not appropriated to gentlemen or scholars. No man was bred to it as a profession or went into it for a maintenance. They were pastors of a different stamp. The stationary presbyters, or bishops, during the lives of the apostle and his associate evangelists, were under their superintendency. But it will appear very early in the second century, when the first race of great itinerants departed [or were slain for the testimony of Jesus], that one among the ministers in every place began to have the name of bishop (*kat' exochen*) on account of preeminency, with presbyters, his coadjutors, acting with him as one body." (Pp.86,87.)

This leads me to conclude that there were no local bishops until the second century; that the apostles, in service, were bishops, and that those who were ordained in the second century mistook their calling when they became local and should have followed those bright examples in the apostolic age. I am not under the difficulties that some are respecting the same men who were ordained elders being called sometimes bishops, I am not sure that what was written to Timothy and Titus, that *they themselves must be blameless as bishops, or overseers,* excluded them from being evangelists. As to those at Ephesus who were elders in office, they were in charge and duty overseers. In some sense among us every leader of a class, every local preacher, traveling preacher, and every officer in the Church may be called an overseer. Bishops, presbyters, and deacons, seem to have been the established form in all the Asiatic Churches in the second century.

"Hitherto not a man eminent for science or letters had appeared in the Church. All those whose works have come down to us bear a stamp of simplicity divested of human attainments. Yet by these the gospel had been supported in its purity, afforded a noble army of martyrs, and been spread to the ends of the earth, from the Pillars of Hercules to the Parthians, from the savage nations of the North to the Indies and Abyssinia." (P.146.)

"Considering the time and regarding the persons called to be saints, a learned ministry cannot be supposed in the primitive Church. The presbyters have been, in general, men simple and unlettered, though full of faith and the Holy Ghost, the qualifications which then determined the suffrage of the several flocks. And after all the fine things so elegantly written (by the heathen philosophers) about virtue and morals, their own conduct afforded a pregnant example of the impotence of the doctrines which they taught, whilst the Christian bishops not only lived what they professed to teach, but were every day ready to go to prison and to death for the name of the Lord Jesus." (P.126.) No man counting his life dear who stood for Jesus, "bold to seal the truth with blood."

"A learned and ingenuous age prides itself on its superiority in defense of revealed religion and apologizes for the Bible, but what hath (this mode) of arguing proved? The plain story of a plain unlettered man telling of the sufferings of Christ and the glory which hath followed with their consequences hath done more in the way of conversion to real and vital Christianity than all these great polemics put together. [The learned may smile in Saul's armor, but give me the sling and the stone, and the gigantic Goliath falls.] I see the smile on the wise academician and the contemptuous infidel, but I am not ashamed of that gospel of Christ which is the power of God unto salvation to every one that believeth, nor of the sound though unlearned teacher who, having diligently read his Bible and then taught of God himself, is blessed with their conversation." (P.148.)

O my son, by *diligence, discipline*, and *faithfulness*, God hath made us a blessing to hundreds and thousands of those who have died within these last thirty years! Thus our work and reward have gone before us and more work and reward are given to us daily. Let the Annual Conferences, the quarterly meeting Conferences, let the presiding elders, deacons, and preachers, all feel their dignity, do their duty, and especially guard against every danger and innovation. Alas for us, if ever our excellent constitution and order of things be changed or corrupted! (It is said that a good old bishop prayed that he might be taken away if Arius were restored, but the heretic himself was taken away.) I believe that those who would divide the body of Christ will be "divided in Jacob and scattered in Israel." Thirty years' labor and experience have taught us something.

Be diligent to see and know how the different charitable contributions are disposed of. Sign no journals of an Annual Conference till everything is recorded, everything appears correctly and fairly. Should there be at any time failures in any department such as you cannot cure or restore, *appeal to the General Conference*. Be rigidly strict in all things. Examine well those who come as candidates for the ministry. It is ours to plead, protest, and oppose designing men from getting into the ministry. It is the peculiar excellence of our Church and the superintendents' glory and stronghold that the character of every minister among us must undergo a strict examination once a year. Put men into office in whom you can confide. If they betray your trust and confidence, let them do it but once. Of all wickedness, spiritual wickedness is the greatest; and of all deceptions, religious deception is the worst. Beware of men who have a constitutional cast to deception. Let every office, grade, and station among us know his place, keep his place, and do his duty; then you need not fear for the ark of God. The Lord Jesus will take care of and support his own cause.

If we have not men of great talents, we have men of good hearts. Endeavor to obtain and preserve a noble independence of soul, the willing servant of all, but the slave of none. Put full confidence in men who merit your confidence. Never be afraid to trust young men; they are able, and you will find enough willing to endure the toils and go through the greatest labors; neither are they so likely to fail as old men are.

"The simplicity of gospel truth ill accords with a *farrago* of rites and ceremonies. Nothing could be more unadorned than the primitive worship. A plain man, chosen from among his fellows, in his common garb, stood up to speak, or sat down to read the Scriptures, to as many as chose to assemble in the house appointed. A back room, and that probably a mean one, or a garret, to be out of the way of observation, was their temple. Hymns sung to Christ, as their God, appeared to the heathens a prominent and striking feature of the Christian worship. The Holy Scriptures were read in portions; and the presbyter, or bishop, or two or three of the congregation who were endued with talents, spoke a word of exhortation to the people agreeably to the scripture which had been read. Prayer from the heart, without a prompter, followed, to which the people replied with a loud and audible *amen*. He that led the worship prayed from his heart, and out of its abundance. I have no doubt the Lord's Prayer always made a part of their public services. The Supper of the Lord closed the devotions of his day. I think it was as constant as the return of that day, and every member of the Churches as constantly participant. A friendly feast, or meal, called *agape*, from the love and union with which they kept it, served at one as an opportunity of ministering an act of charity to the poor, where all distinctions of rich and poor were laid aside and no man took before others his own supper, but all with humble equality acknowledged themselves members of the living head, Christ, and of one another." (P.150.)

"Then, also, I apprehend every man produced, according to his ability, weekly what he had laid by for charitable purposes, which formed a fund of obligations under the control of the Church, through the ministration of the bishop, presbyter, and deacon, for all the various purposes of general good such as purchasing the elements for the Lord's Supper, the provisions for the table of the *agape*, for the necessaries of the poor, the support of evangelists, the relief of the persecuted, and for the welfare of such Churches and persons whose indigence called for the help of their richer brethren. As yet I can perceive no part of this fund appropriated to pay the salaries of any minister of the sanctuary, unless he came under the title of an itinerant evangelist, and, being incapable of providing his own maintenance and wholly occupied in the gospel work, was justly entitled, as preaching the gospel, to live by the gospel. I very much doubt if the bishop or presbyter and deacons received anything for their labors of love. I am persuaded they thought their work their best wages.

"Amid the flames of persecution kindled without and the corruptions and errors broached within the Church continued to raise her scarred head, encircled with glory, and to enlarge her borders farther and wider. After the departure of the great itinerant evangelists to their rest in glory and on the increasing extent of the Christian Church in every place the desirableness of a *stationary president* seems to have introduced a change in the government of several evangelical cities and churches. The very learned Chancellor King endeavors to prove that in the largest cities there was but one Church and one bishop. I have already given my reasons for differing from him and for supposing the necessity of many house congregations where the body of Christian professors was so great, and as they sought to avoid observation and to attract as little as possible the attention of the rulers, they would not, assuredly, in such immense multitudes, have assembled in one place. That about the beginning of the second century a bishop appears at the head of a presbytery, can hardly be doubted, and the name became appropriate to one which before all the presbyters had equally borne. Being now no longer under the superintending care of the great apostolic evangelists, who went about everywhere to establish, to preserve the unity of the Church, and be the cementing bond of the whole body, the several presbyters and Churches seem to have chosen one of their own body to supply the precedence these had before exercised. Whether the largest cities, as King argues, formed only one congregation with many presbyters, or rather, as I think, consisted of many congregations with presbyters in each of them, the whole seems now to have formed one body under a superintendent (or *episcopus*, overseer) chosen by themselves. Every Church exercised discipline over its own members, in which the whole assemblage of the faithful gave their suffrage. Their reverence for their pastors was great; but clerical dominion had, as yet, found no place." (P.126.)

We have a few more thoughts to add. It is my confirmed opinion that the apostles acted both as bishops and traveling superintendents in planting and watering, ruling and ordering the whole connection; and that they did not ordain any local bishops, but that they ordained local deacons and elders. I feel satisfied we should do the same. I found my opinion on Acts xiv, 23: *'And when they had ordained them elders in every Church, and had fasted and prayed with them, they commended them to the*

Lord." "For this cause left I thee in Crete, that thou should set in order things that are wanting, and ordain elders in every city, as I have appointed thee." (Titus i, 5.) That is, do what Paul has left undone. Mark! it was in the *second* visit that Paul and Barnabas established order; and why was Timothy or Titus sent if elders could ordain elders? And why had the apostles to go or send, if it was not held as the divine right of the apostles to ordain? I shall not unchristian any Church or Churches that have the truth of the gospel and the power of God among them, as I have already said.

The Presbyterian Churches, at the first, should have established a moderate episcopacy and apostolic form from whence they came, one from the high steeples of the Church of Rome and the other from the high steeples of the Church of England. An elective, easy government, and a traveling and local ministry, with a judicious discipline, would have been better than steeples, bells, schools, colleges, and universities to make men ministers whom the Lord never called. The ninth century appears to have been the time of midnight darkness. The light of the Reformation began to dawn in the eleventh and twelfth centuries. The reformers were great men; but such was the state of affairs that no doubt there was yet much darkness mingled with the light; hence, it might be said: "All heads, and no heads." And I should be more afraid of a many-headed monster than of a single-headed one.

You know that for four years past I have, with pleasure, resigned to you the presidency of the nine Annual Conferences. This has removed a great burden of care from me and given me much ease. You have my letters addressed to you on the subject. It may be objected by some that our form of Church government partakes too much of the government of the nation. It does not partake of its nature; but there are some similitudes of form, but not of nature. The one is civil, the other spiritual and entirely disunited. Our government being spiritual, one election to office is sufficient during life, unless in cases of debility, a voluntary resignation of the office, corruption in principle, or immorality in practice.

The great diversity of gifts, both among our traveling and local ministry, is happily diffused abroad by our mode of circulation, to the benefit of hundreds and thousands. Many of our local ministers are men of approved abilities, with grace and gifts worthy to fill any pulpit. Many of them travel hundreds of miles in the year, are gladly received, and readily employed to preach by their traveling brethren, and feel themselves at perfect ease and completely at home on the different circuits and at camp meetings where they visit, having no fear they will be considered as intruders.

Further, it may be asked, Is it proper to have no learned men among us? Answer: Men who are well read I call learned men; and we have men of learning among us, both traveling and local. Where are our young men who are bred to the law? and some are doctors; and many others who are very studious and making great progress in Latin and Greek; and many have competent knowledge of the English language. Particularly, see in the British connection such men as Drs. Coke and Clarke; a Benson, Creighton, and others. And in many instances men who profess the least know the most.

A venerable German divine once wrote in Latin to the English doctors; but he had to complain that they answered him in English. But you may say, Would we not derive great advantages from reading the Scripture in their original tongues and judging of the correctness of the translations? Undoubtedly; but these advantages are in the margins of the best editions of the Bible. As to our translation, it is, perhaps, one of the best and most correct upon earth. To attain to a proper knowledge of the etymology of all the words used, even in the Septuagint, I know not how many languages you must know besides the Latin, Greek, and Hebrew. If you suggest anything more, I will maturely consider it.

My dear Bishop, it is the traveling apostolic order and ministry that is found in our very constitution. No man among us can locate without order, or forfeit his official standing. No preacher is stationary more than two years; no presiding elder more than four years; and the constitution will remove them; and all are movable at the pleasure of the superintendent whenever he may find it necessary for the good of the cause. It is the privilege of every traveling minister with us to say: "I am not obliged to serve you another year; I will speak to the superintendent who will not impose on you a second year." We must conclude that all the ancient, imperial, Latin, and Greek Churches were episcopal from their foundation to this very day, though in a crooked, muddy succession; perhaps all corrupted in ordinances, and many of them in doctrines; and, in too many instances, the vilest of men have filled the most sacred offices in the Church. The Reformed English, Scotch, Danish, Swede, Episcopal Churches, have all corrupted their ways before the Lord. Let Presbyterians say and write what they may, as if episcopacy never existed, it must be granted that in the first, second, and third centuries many of the bishops were holy men, who traveled and labored in the ministry very extensively, not unlike their grand pattern, St. Paul, and the other holy apostolical men, of which we have good historical evidence, which is all the evidence that can now be given. To the people of our day we give ocular demonstration, and the generations to come may read our Church records and Conference journals, where they shall see what vast tracts of country we traveled over in visiting the nine Conferences annually. As to the doctrines of the Reformation, we have said, in a second reformation they were the real gospel. They have been well introduced and complete forms of Church government established. Presbyterians and Independents were formed too about the sixteenth century.

Finally, farewell in the Lord!

Yours,
Francis Asbury

PHOEBE PALMER

Phoebe Palmer (1807–1874) was a lay evangelist who played an important role in the renewal of Methodist interest in Christian perfection. With her sister, Sara Lankford, she held Tuesday meetings for the promotion of holiness in New York City beginning in 1835. The response to these meetings was immediate and their influence extended quickly. The message that Phoebe Palmer taught was that Christian holiness is a promise of the Scriptures and that acceptance of the biblical promises is the event which brings sanctification to an individual's life. She intended to be more explicit about the method which leads to sanctification, to reduce the role of emotionalism, and reinforce assurance of holiness. She found her answer in a "short way," an explicit method which conveyed certainty. Holiness, Phoebe Palmer believed, carries ethical implications, so she became involved in an inner city rescue mission and in societal moral concerns and she encouraged responsible action. After the Civil War she was a leader in the National Camp Meeting Association for the Promotion of Holiness and continued to be a prominent spokeswoman for entire sanctification. She wrote a number of books, among them are *Pioneer Experiences* (1868) and *Four Years in the Old World* (1866). *The Way of Holiness* (1850) is her most important publication; the section that follows introduces her "short way" to the experience of Christian perfection. The selection is taken from *The Way of Holiness* (New York: Lang and Scott, 1851), pp. 17–24.

THE WAY OF HOLINESS
IS THERE NOT A SHORTER WAY?
SECTION I

"Be always ready to give an answer to every man that asketh you a reason of the hope that is within you, with meekness and fear." —Peter.

"I have thought," said one of the children of Zion to the other, as in love they journeyed onward in the way cast up for the ransomed of the Lord to walk in; "I have thought," said he, "whether there is not a *shorter way* of getting into this way of holiness than some of our... brethren apprehend?"

"Yes," said the sister addressed, who was a member of the denomination alluded to; "Yes, brother, THERE IS A SHORTER WAY! O! I am sure this long waiting and struggling with the powers of darkness is not necessary. There is a shorter way." And then, with a solemn feeling of responsibility, and with a realizing conviction of the truth uttered, she added, "But, brother, there is but one way."

Days and even weeks elapsed, and yet the question, with solemn bearing, rested upon the mind of that sister. She thought of the affirmative given in answer to the inquiry of the brother—examined yet more closely the Scriptural foundation upon which the truth of the affirmation rested—and the result of the investigation tended to add still greater confirmation to the belief, that many sincere disciples of Jesus, by various needless perplexities, consume much time in endeavoring to get into this way, which might, more advantageously to themselves and others, be employed in making progress in it, and testifying, from experimental knowledge, of its blessedness.

How many, whom Infinite Love would long since have brought into this state, instead of seeking to be brought into the possession of the blessing at once, are seeking a preparation for the reception of it! They feel that their *convictions* are not deep enough to warrant an approach to the throne of grace, with the confident expectation of receiving the blessing *now*. Just at this point some may have been lingering months and years. Thus did the sister, who so confidently affirmed "there is a shorter way." And here, dear child of Jesus, permit the writer to tell you just how that sister found the "shorter way."

On looking at the requirements of the word of God, she beheld the command, "Be ye holy." She then began to say in her heart, "Whatever my former deficiencies may have been, God requires that I should *now* be holy. Whether *convicted*, or otherwise, *duty is plain*. God requires *present* holiness." On coming to this point, she at once apprehended a simple truth before unthought of, i.e., *Knowledge is conviction*. She well knew that, for a long time, she had been assured that God required holiness. But she had never deemed this knowledge a sufficient plea to take to God—and because of present need, to ask a present bestowment of the gift.

Convinced that in this respect she had mistaken the path, she now, with renewed energy, began to make use of the knowledge already received, and to discern a "shorter way."

Another difficulty by which her course had been delayed she found to be here. She had been accustomed to look at the blessing of holiness as such a high attainment, that her general habit of soul inclined her to think it almost beyond her reach. This erroneous impression rather influenced her to rest the matter thus:—"I will let every high state of grace, in name, alone, and seek only to be *fully conformed to the will of God, as recorded in his written word*. My chief endeavors shall be centred in the aim to be an humble *Bible Christian*. By the grace of God, all my energies shall be directed to this one point. With this single aim, I will journey onward, even though my faith may be tried to the uttermost by those manifestations being withheld, which have previously been regarded as essential for the establishment of faith."

On arriving at this point, she was enabled to gain yet clearer insight into the simplicity of the way. And it was by this process. After having taken the Bible as the rule of life, instead of the opinions and experience of professors, she found, on taking the blessed word more closely to the companionship of her heart, that no one declaration spoke more appealingly to her understanding than this: "Ye are not your own, ye are bought with a price, therefore glorify God in your body and spirit which are his."

By this she perceived the duty of *entire consecration* in a stronger light, and as more sacredly binding, than ever before. Here she saw God as her Redeemer, claiming, by virtue of the great price paid for the redemption of body, soul, and spirit, the *present and entire service* of all these redeemed powers.

By this she saw that if she lived constantly in the entire surrender of all that had been thus dearly purchased unto God, she was but an unprofitable servant; and that, if less than all was rendered, she was worse than unprofitable, inasmuch as she would be guilty of keeping back part of that price which had been purchased unto God: "Not with corruptible things, such as silver and gold, but by the precious blood of Jesus." And after so clearly discerning the will of God concerning her, she felt that the sin of Ananias and Sapphira would be less culpable in the sight of Heaven than her own, should she not at once resolve on living in the *entire* consecration of all her redeemed powers to God.

Deeply conscious of past unfaithfulness, she now determined that the time past should suffice; and with a humility of spirit, induced by a consciousness of not having lived in the performance of such a "reasonable service," she was enabled, through grace, to resolve, with firmness of purpose, that entire devotion of heart and life to God should be the absorbing subject of the succeeding pilgrimage of life.

SECTION II

"We by his Spirit prove,
And know the things of God,
The things which freely of his love
He hath on us bestow'd."

After having thus resolved on devoting the entire service of her heart and life to God, the following questions occasioned much serious solicitude:— How shall I know when I have consecrated all to God? And how ascertain whether God *accepts* the sacrifice — and how know the manner of its acceptance? Here again the blessed Bible, which she had now taken as her counselor, said to her heart, "We have received not the spirit of the world, but the Spirit which is of God, that we might know the things freely given to us of God."

It was thus she became assured that it was her privilege to *know when she* had consecrated all to God, and also to know that the sacrifice was *accepted,* and the resolve was solemnly made that the subject should not cease to be absorbing, until this knowledge was obtained.

Feeling it a matter of no small importance to stand thus solemnly pledged to God, conscious that sacred responsibilities were included in these engagements, a *realization* of the fact, that neither body, soul, nor spirit, time, talent, nor influence, were, even for one moment, at her own disposal, began to assume the tangibility of living truth to her mind, in a manner not before apprehended.

From a sense of responsibility thus imposed, she began to be more abundant in labors, "instant in season and out of season."

While thus engaged in active service, another difficulty presented itself. How much of self in these performances? said the accuser. For a moment, almost bewildered at being thus withstood, her heart began to sink. She felt most keenly that she had no certain standard to raise up against this accusation?

It was here again that the blessed word sweetly communed with her heart, presenting the marks of the way, by a reference to the admonition of Paul: "Therefore, my beloved brethren, be ye steadfast and unmovable, always abounding in the work of the Lord, forasmuch as ye know that your labor is not in vain in the Lord."

These blessed communings continued thus: If the primitive Christians had the assurance that their labors were in the Lord; and thus enjoyed the heart-inspiring *confidence* that their labors were *not in vain,* because performed in the might of the Spirit, then it is also your privilege to *know* that your labor is in the Lord. It was at this point in her experience that she first perceived the *necessity,* and also the *attainableness* of the witness of *purity of intention*—which, in her petition to God, as most expressive of her peculiar need, she denominated, "The witness that the spring of every motive is pure."

It was by the word of the Lord she became fully convinced that she needed this heart-encouraging confidence in order to insure success in her labors of love. The next step taken was to resolve, as in the presence of the Lord, not to cease importuning the throne of grace until the witness was given "that the spring of every motive was pure."

On coming to this decision, the blessed Word, most encouragingly, yea, and also assuringly, said to her heart, "Stand still, and see the salvation of God!"

DANIEL D. WHEDON

Daniel D. Whedon (1808–1885) was an American preacher, theologian, author and editor. Born in Onondaga, New York, he graduated from Hamilton College and served on the faculty of Wesleyan University, Connecticut, and the University of Michigan. Intellectually able and morally sensitive, Whedon originally trained for law and then became a Methodist minister. He was a theological spokesman for the Methodist Episcopal Church as editor of the *Methodist Quarterly Review* (1856–1884) and wrote a major study, *The Freedom of Will* (1864), in which he challenged Jonathan Edwards' interpretation of human free agency. He also edited commentaries on the Old and New Testaments (12 vols.). Whedon was instrumental in reshaping Wesleyan theology in North America by placing more emphasis upon human capability and giving less weight to the grounding of this ability in prevenient grace. Utilizing philosophical tools to discuss distinctive qualities of human life, Whedon attempted to reinforce the integrity of human personhood with responsibility for choice and action. In his synoptic treatment, Whedon indicates the distinctiveness of Methodist theological positions. Whedon's "Doctrines of Methodism" needs to be read in connection with the next selection, "Methodist Doctrine," from William Burt Pope which emphasizes Methodism's relation to catholic Christianity. These articles together represent nineteenth century Methodism's effort to gain clear self-understanding. "Doctrines of Methodism" is chosen from *Essays, Reviews, and Discourses* (New York: Phillips and Hunt, 1887), pp. 109–146.

DOCTRINES OF METHODISM

It is our purpose in the present article to furnish a brief statement of the doctrines of the Methodist Episcopal Church, especially those points in which there exists an issue with Calvinism. As a receiver of those doctrines, it will, of course, be expected, and probably desired, that the writer should present them favorably, and as they are viewed by their advocates. Occasional argumentative issues may be stated, in order that the points of collision may be more easily understood; but it forms no part of our province to *prove* the doctrines presented. It is believed that such a statement, at the present time, may tend to remove misunderstanding, and serve the cause of Christian unity.

In regard to the issue, it may be generally remarked that in those points which more immediately concern the divine government Calvinism affirms more than Arminianism, and that more the latter declines to accept. Both sides, for instance, affirm foreknowledge, free-will, and the necessity of divine grace to salvation; Calvinism superadds to these respectively, foreordination, necessity, and irresistibleness, to which Arminianism declines assent. On points less central, as final apostasy, entire sanctification, and witness of the Spirit, our Arminianism affirms, and Calvinism rejects.

FUNDAMENTAL MAXIM OF DIVINE GOVERNMENT

The fundamental maxim upon which the issue above named is primarily grounded, and from which, if we mistake not, most of the other issues logically result, is the Edwardean maxim, that it is no matter how we come by our evil volitions, dispositions, or nature, in order to responsibility, provided we really possess them. Or we may state the maxim thus: God judges us as he finds us to be, good or evil, and holds us responsible without regard to the means by which we became so. We do not say that all who are considered Calvinists hold this maxim. But upon the acceptance or rejection of this proposition it logically depends, as it appears to us, whether the man *should be* a Calvinist or Arminian. From our rejection of this maxim it is that we differ from some or all the classes of Calvinists on the subject of *free-will, divine sovereignty, predestination, election, primary responsibility for inborn depravity, partial atonement,* and *final perseverance.* To this maxim, that *it is no matter how we come by volitional state in order to its being responsible,* we oppose the counter maxim

92

that *in order to responsibility for a given act or state, power in the agent for a contrary act or state is requisite.* In other words: *"no man is to blame for what he cannot help." Power underlies responsibility.* Non-existence of power is non-existence of responsibility. The only limitation of this principle is the maxim that *self-superinduced inability does not exclude responsiblity.* The agent who abdicates his powers we hold to be responsible for his impotence, and for all the non-performances which legitimately result. Our entire axiom, then, is: *all inability to an act or state, not self-superinduced, excludes responsibility.* The man who maintains, counter to this our position, the above-specified Edwardean maxim must, we think, if a logical reasoner, support all the Calvinistic views above enumerated. The man who adopts our maxim is as logically bound to reject them.

FREE-WILL

When a man transgresses a divine requirement by a wrong volition, the question arises: *Could he have willed otherwise?* He is held by the law penally responsible for the act. If, now, the maxim be true that God regards not the way in which he became possessed of the volition, then no power to the contrary is required. God may create him without power for other volition; may create him in fixed and necessitated possession of the volition, yet may still hold him responsible, and consign him to endless penalty. If, on the other hand, adequate power for a contrary volition must underlie obligation for a contrary volition, and so for responsibility for the actual volition, then there must have existed in the given agent power for a volition contrary to the volition actually put forth.

Methodism has, in accordance with this view, from the beginning maintained this doctrine of free-will. We have ever maintained that it imputes injustice to God to suppose that he holds us responsible for a necessitated act or condition; or that he ever requires an act or condition for which he does not furnish the adequate power. It is the apparent making of this imputation in the various doctrines of Calvinism with which Methodism has taken issue.

Our view of free-will is tolerably well expressed by the formula: "the power of contrary choice." It would, perhaps, be more accurately expressed by the formula furnished and condemned by Edwards (p.419, Andover Edition, 1840): *"The power of choosing differently in given cases."* The question proposed by Fletcher to Toplady was: *"Is the will at liberty to choose otherwise than it does, or is it not?"* The man who affirms the first member of this question is bound to be an Arminian; the affirmant of the latter member must, as we suppose, logically be a Calvinist....

Our views of responsibility require us, therefore, to affirm fully and unequivocally the doctrine of *the freedom of the will*. With the limitation which we have already indicated in our axiom, every obligatory and every responsible volitional act is a *free act*; that is, put forth with the adequate power of putting forth a different act instead....

DIVINE SOVEREIGNTY

We hold it to be a doctrine both of natural and revealed religion that God is an omnipotent being, possessed of power for all operations which involve not a contradiction. But any act the expression of which involves a contradiction we consider to be no act at all; so that this exception is not a limitation of divine power, but only a definition of the true idea of omnipotence. God is sovereign over the realm of nature and of free agents; yet in both cases he limits his uniform action by self-circum-scribing laws. The laws of nature are the uniform rules of God's action, imposed by himself upon himself. And these self-imposed laws are nec-essary to the very existence of the kingdom of nature; and they do, in fact, give God his position as sovereign of nature, and therein are neces-sary to his divine sovereignty. In the realm of free agency, also, God finds, as we think, his highest exaltation as sovereign, by so circum-scribing his own modes of action as to leave unviolated the full exercise of the freedom of the agent, so far forth as he is a free and responsible agent. For God to secure absolutely and limitatively the one possible volition of the agent, and yet leave him a free agent, is, in our view, a contradiction; as genuine a contradiction as for God to cause a heavier body to ascend, and yet preserve the law of gravitation. The requirement that God's sovereignty must jealously *cause* and *secure*, as well as limit, every act of the agent in our estimation reduces God from his position as a sovereign to the predicament of a mechanist. He is no longer king of free beings, but a mover of automatons. The highest glory of God as a divine sovereign consists, as we conceive, in his giving the fullest permis-sion for the freest range of responsible agency, though it sweep the scope of half the universe; and yet so taking the wise in their own craftiness, and over-mastering the mighty in their own might, as to accomplish all his own grand designs and produce the best and most glorious possible of ultimate results....

DANIEL D. WHEDON

FOREKNOWLEDGE

It might at first appear fair to say that the reconciliation of foreknowledge with free agency is *the* difficulty of our theology. Yet there seems to be a great difference, of which a theology ought to avail itself, between the admission of simple foreknowledge and the additional admission of predestination. If the term *predestination* has any proper significance, it implies a strict causative relation between the long past predestinating act and the predestined event. If it becomes any thing less than this, it becomes simply *prerecognition*, with non-prevention in view of some collateral good; which is, properly speaking, foreknowledge. The true distinction, in fact, between foreknowledge and predestination is, that the former simply cognizes the act which another cause will put forth, while the latter causatively determines its putting forth, purposely excluding, by necessitative limitation, any other act instead. God may be supposed to *foresee* the act because the agent will put it forth; but God cannot properly be said to *predestinate* the action because the agent will put it forth; on the other hand, the agent must perform the act because it is predestinated. The act of the agent cannot properly be free, because it is antecedently limited and determined....

DOCTRINE OF SIN AND GUILT

Sin is, according to John, *anomia*, or disconformity to the law; and the term, therefore, though primarily applicable to actual transgression, is nevertheless used, both in theology and Scripture, to designate a moral *state* or *condition* of being. Should, however, a being be placed in such a state otherwise than by his own free act, with full power of acting otherwise, for such a state we hold that he could not be strictly responsible, or, with absolute justice, punishable. In such a being there would be *evil, moral evil, sin*, but not responsibility, or desert of penalty. Should such a state of being be brought about by the agent's own free act, the responsibility would, we think, exist in full force; or, should the free being in such a state, possessed of full power to act otherwise, nevertheless sanction and appropriate to himself his depraved condition, making it the controlling power of his life, he thereby contracts the responsibility. Such a depraved state, in our view, has never been produced in any being by God, but always by free secondary agents. All responsible sin, therefore, whether of action or condition, arises from the action of free finite beings, in disconformity to the law, and in abuse of their free agency....

The act of the will, put forth with full power otherwise, in intentional disconformity to the law, is actual or *actional sin*. The resultant ethical quality of *condemnability*, which our moral sense sees as inhering in the personality of the agent in consequence of the commission of such sin, we call *guilt*. And as the moral sense can see this guilt solely in the personality of the committing agent, it is impossible for this guilt to be transferred to another personality. Correlative to this *guilt*, the moral sense sees inhering in the person of the guilty *a desert of just punishment*. These correlations are fundamental and axiomatic. *Punishment*, therefore, is no more transferable, literally, than *guilt*. Neither is any more transferable than is a *past act* personally performed by one agent transferable to another agent. When, therefore, an innocent man is said to suffer in the stead of a guilty man, it is only in figurative conception that the guilt and punishment of the guilty are attributed or imputed to the innocent man; the literal fact is, that the innocent man is still *innocent*, and the endurance by the innocent is simply *suffering*, but not literally, to him, *punishment*.

THE FALL AND DEPRAVATION OF MAN

In the primordial man, Adam, as in every primordial progenitor, a whole posterity is conceptually enfolded. As in the acorn is inclosed, not only the oak, but a whole descending lineage of oaks, so in our first parent was inclosed a whole system of diverging lineages embracing a race. As his primordial nature shall stand higher or lower, so shall the deduced nature of that race be higher or lower. Under this fundamental law, extended through the whole generative system of creation, and based upon reasons of the highest wisdom, man, with his fellow races, animal and vegetable, is placed on earth. That law, that self-limiting law, God cannot wisely change. Upon the first man he bestows a nature of transcendental excellence, yet with a free and plastic power of self-degradation by sin. As man stands or falls, he stands or falls in his typical character; and his whole race, under the universal lineal law, must bear the same physical, intellectual, and moral type. And with this natural law corresponds the theodicic arrangement. Under the same moral and judicial conditions in which man places himself, must, as we believe, his posterity, if born, be born....

Under these conditions, shall he bring a posterity into existence? He can bring them into existence, by the laws of nature, only with his own character, and, apparently, to his own destiny. For conceptionally, as above stated, his whole race is seminally existent in him. The sentence of condemnation is addressed to him individually, indeed, yet to him, containing his whole race within himself. Shall the individuals of that race, by the prosecution of the natural generative law, be brought by him into personal existence? Man, then, by a second procedure, would consummate the terrible evil of his first procedure. He, under the fundamental laws, in the prosecution of second causes, would plunge a race in endless misery, *naturally* resulting from his unholy procedures. There are but two methods, that we can conceive, of arresting man in his full course of evil-doing. By the first method the full force of the sentence may be executed and exhausted upon himself by the infliction of temporal, spiritual, and eternal death immediately interposed, previous to the production of offspring. God's veracity is thus sustained, and the evil of sin is manifested by the abortion of the race. By the second method, a redemptive system may be interposed, by which, on the continued basis of free agency and probation, man, the whole race, or that part of the race which attains the end of its probation, may be restored to even, perhaps, a higher glory than the Adamic race could have attained. . . .

THE REDEMPTION

The introduction of the Redeemer, sequently upon the fall of man, was not a divine afterthought. By a divine predetermination, *conditioned* upon that foreseen apostasy, Christ was the Lamb slain from before the foundation of the world. In view of the compensations by it afforded, expressions of deeper severity toward sin are made than otherwise would have taken place. A Redeemer is introduced who, by a death of infinitely more value than that of Adam and all his race, is entitled to take humanity into his guardianship, and measure out mercy and justice according to the laws of a wise probation: 1. In view of the future atonement, the natural continuity of the human race remains uninterrupted, and a basis is thus afforded for a new system. 2. In view of that same atonement, the Holy Spirit is restored, whereby motives in the direction of spiritual realities may become grounds of action, and their proper improvement may lead to justification and regeneration. Man does not thereby receive any new faculty. He is not even organically *made* to be a free agent; for he never ceased to be such; only spiritual things, and the possibility of pleasing God, are again *brought within the reach* of his free agency. Nor is the Holy Spirit, nor any other influence, normally so brought to bear upon his free agency as to be *irresistible*, or *secured to be unresisted*; since that would be to overwhelm his free agency on the other side. To afford him such aids as render him able to accept salvation without overcoming his ability to reject it, probationarily leaving the decision to his own free-will, is the precise law by which the dealings of God with him are now governed. 3. Though, both in the matter of temporal and eternal death, man still remains under liability, so that, by rejection of the Redeemer, he may come under full execution of the primal sentence, yet by the proper exercise of his free-will, aided by the Spirit graciously bestowed, in accepting and obeying the Redeemer, he may finally attain a glory through Christ, greater, perhaps, than he lost through Adam....

So far as we can see, these statements present the antithesis between our loss through Adam and our gain through Christ, in full accordance with its presentation by Paul in the fifth chapter of Romans. By the sin of the former, we incur death and judgment unto condemnation, and are made sinners. By the righteousness of the latter, we receive life and justification, are made righteous, attaining a grace much more abundant than the previous sin. And inasmuch as we are made sinners antecedently to the atonement, without the power of being other than sinners, we can be held in that case as responsible sinners only by a conceptual imputation of sin. Under the atonement, that conceptual imputation is continued only as the logical antithesis to the conceptual imputation of righteousness to the guilty through the atoning righteousness of Christ.

RIGHTEOUSNESS AND GRACE IN THE REDEMPTION

In regard to parts, if not the whole, of the provisions of the redemption, as thus stated, it will be said that they are but provisions of justice and not of grace. If powers were necessary in order to the fulfillment of requirements, God was bound, in righteousness, to grant them; and, in justice, could not withhold them; and they are therefore not gracious. Nevertheless, we hold that such provisions are none the less by grace because by righteousness. Benevolence is the goodness of God exhibited in nature; grace is the goodness of God exhibited in redemption. And as God could not be justified in the works of nature without appealing to the proofs of benevolence, it might be said that "God is bound to furnish that benevolence; and it is therefore no benevolence, but mere righteousness." Nevertheless, it is none the less benevolence because necessary to justify God's righteousness. The righteousness and the grace are but different views of the same thing.

...Every endowment that man receives, by nature or redemption, even though it be the basis of a duty and a requirement, is none the less a gratuity. God gives the grace, and imposes the requirement, because it is a grace; nor does the requirement abolish the grace.

NATURE AND EXTENT OF THE ATONEMENT

...Christ died for all men, and for every man, and for no one man more than for another. The personal, voluntary reception of the atonement, in its full conditions, by the sinner himself, constitutes the difference between one man and another in the obtainment of its benefits. A fountain stands for the entire inhabitants of a town, for one man no more than for another; and the personal drawing and drinking of the water may constitute the only difference in the enjoyment of its benefits. The atonement itself is universal and irrespective; the personal appropriation, by which the individual sinner secures his share of its benefits, is in each case particular.

JUSTIFICATION BY FAITH

The method by which the sinner appropriates a share of the benefits of the atonement personally to himself is comprehensively said to be *by faith*. By the works of the law, that is, by a Christless morality, can no flesh be justified. The law finds us in sin and in depravity, made responsible by volitional action, and reveals our sin unto us. When its perfectness is comprehended, all hopes of meeting its full demands must die within us. We can, therefore, only hope for salvation by the acceptance of the offered atonement for past sins and future short-comings.

The *faith which justifies* implies the belief of the intellect, the accord of the affections, and the submissive acceptance by the will. By this entire act of the whole soul the sinner surrenders himself to Christ for salvation. The sincerity of this faith implies the full renunciation of sin by repentance, and the full self-commitment to obedience to Christ. This act of the sinner is accepted of God, and is imputed to him for righteousness. By the law of the redemptive kingdom, he stands justified before God for all his sins past; the record of condemnation is blotted out, and his name is enrolled in the Lamb's book of life. In accordance with the conditions of the atonement, the Holy Spirit is now imparted unto him, not merely in its convicting, but in its witnessing, enlightening, strengthening, and sanctifying power....

The gracious influences of the Spirit ever precede our action, working within us both to will and to do, and are ever graciously given more abundantly upon our action; so that in attaining justifying grace God and man previously co-operate.

Though the *convicting* influences of the Spirit are often, for a time, to a degree *irresistible*, measurably awakening the conscience and convincing the reason, in spite of our resistance, yet neither is the influence that results in saving faith, nor the saving grace which follows properly *irresistible* by the will. Justifying faith is voluntary and free. The soul is normally able to withhold it; nor is the operation of the Spirit such as necessitatively to secure it.

We are not saved by the *merit* of faith. Faith may indeed be considered in one sense as a *work*, a good work, a right work, the rightest work which, in the case, the sinner can perform. It has in itself the same sort of *good desert*, or ethical merit, as we ascribe to every act which in its given place is morally right. The contrary act would be morally wrong. And it is because of the meetness and ethical fitness and moral rightness in the case, that faith is selected as the proper medium of reconciliation and acceptance. Yet the *value of this faith is not such as that it merits the salvation* sequently bestowed upon it. Abstractly, God might rightfully drop the being into non-existence at the instant of its accomplished faith. The sinner has presented no equivalent for the salvation he receives, and he is truly saved by the free and abounding grace of God. . . .

POSSIBILITY OF APOSTASY

In full consistency with that doctrine of human freedom and responsibility which pervades our theology, we maintain that, inasmuch as we were free in first performing the conditions of salvation, so we are free in the continuance or cessation of their performance. The volition by which we accepted the terms, we could have withheld; neither our probation nor our freedom on that test-point has ceased at our conversion. Amid the temptations, the unbeliefs, and the backslidings of life, the test-question may again and again recur, whether we shall hold fast our first faith; and there still exists the same freedom for decision for either alternative. . . .

We affirm, indeed, that God grants full enabling grace to persevere. He protects us so that none can snatch us from our Father's hand, nor separate us from the love of God; he keeps, supports, and guards; he confirms us when we are strong, and raises us when we are fallen; but he performs all this for us, not as *things*, but as *agents* from whom the consenting accordance and co-operation are conditionally presumed, both in the promise and performance of all these preserving acts of grace. After all these gracious aids on the part of God, there still remains, by the very nature of free agency, an ultimate element of *selfhood*, which alternately decides whether or not that grace shall be in vain. That free selfhood intrinsically remains, however it may sometimes objectively be circumscribed, through the entire existence of the self....

REGENERATION

We have said that, consequent upon our justification, the Holy Spirit is imparted unto us no longer in its mere convicting power, but in its enlightening, quickening energy; giving us not, indeed, a new organic faculty, but the power and disposition, with our existing faculties, freely to love God with all our heart, and our neighbor as ourselves. This is regeneration. Though always concomitant with justification, it is in the order of nature consequent. So truly *new* is this gift by the Holy Spirit, so new and powerful are the views, feeling, purposes of the man, that it is said he is a new creature; that all things with him are made new; that he is born anew, born of God, regenerated. He is now a child of God—a member of the justified family of God.

We thus hold that regeneration *succeeds* justification. It is the unregenerate who is first convinced of sin by the Holy Spirit, who considers upon his wicked ways and seeks repentance, who examines the law of God and the Gospel of Christ in order to learn the method of escaping the wrath to come, who bows in penitent prayer for the continuing guidance of the Holy Spirit in order to the accomplishment of the work, and who does at successive points receive, in consequence of these his preparatory doings, the gracious aid of God. To the question, can these actions of the unregenerate man be holy, and so acceptable to God, we seem to ourselves to have abundant answer. They are not holy in the absolute sense of the word; and yet in their place they are acceptable and accepted by God, as by him prescribed to the man in his case....

Regeneration is the act of God. It presupposes conditions previously performed by the man; but in the work itself God is the doer, and man the submissive recipient. It presupposes anterior justification, and the performance, by the free-will of the sinner, of all the conditions requisite to the work. The Holy Spirit aids in those conditioned acts, but, except, perhaps, at particular points, never necessitates. The sinner acts as a free, responsible agent, and his free agency, so far forth as it exists and extends, excludes necessitation or predestination as its contradictory. Upon the decision and choice of the man as a free agent it ultimately depends whether the condition be performed and salvation attained, or rejected and eternal death incurred. This is the *great alternative point* of man's free probation. From his own essential and central self is the decision most freely made; upon his own central and essential self must the eternal responsibility rest. And, hereby, though man be condemned, God shall be justified.

WITNESS OF THE SPIRIT

Where God performs directly the work of justification and of regeneration, is it not to be expected that he will as directly give notice of so wonderful a mercy? And this thought suggests the reasonableness of the doctrine of the witness of the Spirit, directly testifying to us that we are born of God.

The *witness of our own spirit* is that self-judgment which we are rationally able to pronounce, in the light of consciousness and Scripture, that we are the children of God. This is a logical inference, drawn from the fruits we find, by self-examination, in our minds and external conduct.

But besides this, is there not felt in every deep religious experience, a simple, firm assurance, like an intuition, by which we are made to feel calmly certain that all is blessedly right between God and our own soul? Does not this assurance seem to come into the heart as from some outer source? Does it not come as in answer to prayer, and in direction, as if from him to whom we pray? Scripture surely makes the assuring and witnessing act of the Spirit to be as immediate and direct as the justifying or regenerating acts. Hereby, then, we have the *witness of God's Spirit*, concurrent with the *witness of our own spirit*, testifying to the work of our justification and adoption. "The Spirit itself beareth witness with our spirit that we are the children of God." Rom. viii, 16....

ENTIRE SANCTIFICATION, OR CHRISTIAN PERFECTION

... Through a maturity of Christian experience and the fullness of the Spirit imparted, the spiritual powers of the faithful Christian may be so strengthened that he may, and often does, maintain, through grace, for a longer or shorter period, a permanent state of the undiminished fullness of his acceptance with God, and under no more actual condemnation than at the moment of his justification.

Every thing which has attained the normal completeness of its own class or kind is rightly called *perfect*. Not after an ideal, but a normal standard, we speak of a *perfect egg*, a *perfect chicken*, a *perfect full-grown fowl*. There may be a perfect child or a perfect man. And every thing which is wanting in none of the normal complement of qualities, in normal degree, is *perfect* in its class. Now the Christian who has attained to the description of our formula, is at the normal standard of a *perfect* man in Christ. We use an abundantly scriptural term in calling this a state of Christian *perfection*. It is a state in which all the normal qualities of the Christian are permanently, or with more or less continuity, possessed in the proper completeness. And as this spiritual strength and power over and against sin, derived from the Holy Spirit, is *sanctification*, so in the completeness which we have described, it is not improperly, perhaps, by us called entire sanctification.

Of this state of sanctification, the actual divine acceptance, in its uncondemning fullness, is, according to our present statement, the actual standard. With how much short-coming from the perfect law this is in any case possible, the Spirit is itself in every case judge. It may, therefore, not be possible to answer this question by antecedent words, especially to a metaphysician, demanding absolute exactness; and in this fact, perhaps, consists the basis of the complaint often made by theologians, that they cannot understand the thing we attempt to describe.

The evangelic law requires love with all our present feeble powers to God, and to our neighbor as ourselves. As we are unable to love God with full Adamic powers, the perfect law even then condemns us. Moral weaknesses contracted by past sinful habits, moral ignorances resulting from our own past fault, prejudices of which we are more or less unconscious, nervous irritabilities and physical idiosyncrasies, may produce condemnation from censorious man, where there is still acceptance from him who "knoweth our frame." So far as the will is concerned, Mr. Wesley excluded from the sanctified state all "voluntary transgressions;" but it is questionable whether under the term "involuntary" he did not really include countless numbers of minuter *volitions*, inevitably escaping from our moral weakness, in spite of our most vigorous tone of spiritual purpose and spiritual activity. With how much of all these "infirmities" the uninterrupted fullness of the divine approbation can consist, it is, as we before remarked, impossible in human words exactly to define, even if we could exactly conceive. Thus much, at any rate, is fully certain, that

Leighton correctly describes it as an "imperfect perfection." Ample work, doubtless, is found from these short-comings for a permanent exercise of the most *perfect* repentance, as well as the most perfect faith in the blood of Christ. Ample reasons will be found for praying, "Forgive us our trespasses." Ample verge there is for all those texts of Scripture which affirm that there is none that "sinneth not;" that is, in the wider sense of the word "sin." Nor is there any difficulty in understanding how the most exalted of our Christian saints, in the light of the pure and perfect law, looking at themselves with the eye of a sanctified conscience, can scarce find words sufficient to express their deep humiliation, not only for the depths of the fall of their own nature, but for their own short-comings and for their sins against infinite purity.

But the law is our school-master to drive us to Christ. And yet when in Christ it is not our duty to keep our shuddering eyes perpetually fixed upon the *school-master*. Greater spiritual power, as well as higher spiritual joy, can be derived from dwelling in Christ, and holding up before ourselves the measure of Christian holiness we can attain through him. A goal is thus set up for our holy ambition; a positive standard for which we may labor. Thence a more cheerful piety arises in him who contemplates what he may gain through Christ than in him who is ever trembling under the lash of the law, and who is ever exclaiming, "I am all sin, and nothing but sin." Hence, as the doctrine of apostasy constitutes a real warning against backsliding and sin, so the doctrine of Christian perfection is a living incitement to progressive holiness.

CONCLUSION

Upon the whole, the writer of this article has doubtless failed in his task if he has not made it conceivable to a candid examiner from the other side that our Arminianism is a well-defined, symmetrical system, which a mind possessed of the broadest logical consistency may reasonably be imagined to accept as the best approximation to a satisfactory solution of the facts of the divine government. It is an attempt to show the reconcilability of the divine sovereignty in the plenitude of its holiness with the freedom and responsibility of man, by a method securing the divine honor, and affording the most powerful motives for human piety....

WILLIAM BURT POPE

W illiam Burt Pope (1822–1903) was the North American continent's first contribution to British Methodist theology. Born in
Nova Scotia, Pope returned to England where he received his
education and entered the Methodist ministry. Shy and retiring by
nature, he was an excellent scholar, prodigious student, and a writer
with a fine literary style; he became theological tutor at Didsbury College,
Manchester, in 1867. Catholic in his religious sensibility and theological
interest, he expressed Methodist theology in a manner which utilized
the resources of the wider Christian tradition while also understanding
himself to be hewn from the rock of Wesleyan Methodism. Among his
books are *The Person of Christ* (1871) and *Sermons, Addresses, and Charges*
(1878). His major theological writing was the three volume *Compendium
of Christian Theology* (1875–76). This major work is the most important
statement of British Wesleyan theology from the last half of the nineteenth century. The following article was included in *The Wesley Memorial
Volume*(1880), a publication that represented an effort to assess Wesley
and the Methodist Movement. "Methodist Doctrine" is taken from *The
Wesley Memorial Volume*, ed. J. O. A. Clark (New York: Phillips & Hunt,
1880), pp. 168–190.

METHODIST DOCTRINE

The term Methodism was, some hundred years since, a watchword of
contempt for a body of fanatics supposed to hold some new religious
doctrines, to profess some strange experiences, and to arrogate to themselves a peculiar commission from Heaven. To many it is a watch-word of
reproach still. But it has, nevertheless, rooted itself firmly in the nomen-
clature of the Christian Church. Evangelical Christendom generally

105

agrees with those who bear it to accept the term as a human designation of a system of thought and action which it has pleased the Head of the Church to take into his plans for the spread of his kingdom in these later days. Its history has produced a very general conviction that the Holy Spirit, the Lord and Giver of life ecclesiastical, has added this to the corporate bodies of our common Christianity. Meanwhile, not solicitous about the judgments of men, it is commending itself to God by doing faithfully the work appointed for it in the world. Its sound—or rather, the sound of the Gospel by its lips—has gone out into all the earth. It is slowly diffusing its leaven through almost every form of corrupt Christianity; it is silently impressing its influence, acknowledged or unacknowledged, upon the uncorrupt Churches of Christendom; while, as an independent and self-contained organization, it is erecting its firm superstructure in many lands.

This last fact implies that the system has its varieties of form. Methodism is a genus of many species. The central term has gathered round it various adjectives or predicates which express more or less important differences. But the term itself remains a bond of union among all these; a bond which will be, as it has been hitherto, permanent and indestructible, if the type of doctrine of which it is the symbol shall be maintained in its integrity. For, though Methodism began as a life, that life was quickened and nourished by its teaching; its teaching has sustained it in vigor; and to its teaching is mainly committed its destiny in the future. The object of the following pages will be to indicate briefly, but sharply, that type of doctrine. It must be premised, however, that there will be no systematic exhibition of its tenets illustrated by definitions, quotations, and historical developments generally. The scope assigned to this paper in the programme of the present volume allows only of a few general remarks.

The subject takes us back to the beginning of the great movement. There are two errors which we have at once to confront: that of assigning a doctrinal origin to the system, and that of making its origin entirely independent of doctrine.

The founders of Methodism—*sit venia verbo*—did not, like the Reformers of the sixteenth century, find themselves face to face with a Christianity penetrated through and through by error. They accepted the doctrinal standards of the English Church; and the subscription both of their hands and of their hearts they never revoked. What is more, they adhered to the emphatic interpretation of these standards as contained in liturgical and other formularies. Nothing was further from their thought than to amend either the one or the other in the dogmatic sense.

Though they clearly perceived that certain truths and certain aspects of truth had been kept too much in the background, and therefore gave them special prominence, they never erected these revived doctrines into a new confession. They did not isolate the truths they so vehemently preached; but preached them as necessary to the integrity of the Christian faith. The strength of their incessant contention was this, that men had ceased to see and feel what they nevertheless professed to believe. It was a widespread delusion concerning the Revival in the last century, and it is not quite exploded in this century, that its promoters pretended to be the recipients and organs of a new dispensation: modern Montanists, as it were, deeming themselves the special instruments of the Holy Ghost, charged to revive apostolic doctrines and usages which had been lost through intervening ages. Neither earlier nor later Methodism has ever constructed a creed or confession of faith. It never believed that any cardinal doctrine has been lost; still less, that its own commission was to restore such forgotten tenets. Its modest and simple revivals of early practice are such as Christian communities in all ages have felt it their privilege to attempt; but these have never touched the hem of the garment of Christian primitive truth. To sum up in one word: Methodism, as the aggregate unity of many bodies of Christian people, is not based upon a confession, essentially and at all points peculiar to itself, which all who adhere to its organization must hold.

On the other hand, it is no less an error to disregard the theological character which was stamped from the very beginning on this branch of the great Revival. Never was there a work wrought by the Holy Ghost in the Christian Church which was not the result of the enforcement of Christian truth; and never was such a work permanent which did not lay the foundations of its durablilty in more or less systematized doctrine. Now it was one of the peculiarities of Methodism that it threw around all its organization, and every department of it, a doctrinal defense. The discourses which produced so wonderful an effect in every corner of England were, as delivered, and are now, as preserved, models of theological precision. There is not one of them which does not pay the utmost homage to dogmatic truth; and it is a fact of profound importance in the history of this community, that the very sermons which, under God, gave the movement its life, still form the standard of its theological profession. No more remarkable tribute to the connection between ecclesiastical life and ecclesiastical doctrine can be found in the history of Christendom. It is customary to ascribe the stability of the new economy to the wonderful organizing genius of its founder; it may be questioned whether his zeal for solid dogma has not a right to be included. Certain it is, that early Methodism had a sound theological training; theology preached in its discourses, sang in its hymns, shaped its terms of communion, and presided in the discussions of its conferences. Hence its stability in comparison of other results of the general awakening. The mystical Pietists of Germany, quickened by the same breath, threw off, to a great extent, the fetters of dogmatic creed; they retired from the external Church, disowned its formularies, gathered themselves within a garden doubly inclosed, cultivated the most spiritual and unworldly personal godliness, but made no provision for permanence and for posterity. Methodism, on the other hand, while steadily aiming at the perfection of the interior life kept a vigilant eye on the construction of its peculiar type of theology. That was always in steady progress. It had not reached its consummation when the old Societies of the eighteenth century were consolidated into the Church of the nineteenth. But all the elements were there: some of them, indeed, indeterminate and confused; some of them involving troublesome inconsistencies; others of them giving latitude for abiding differences of opinion; but on the whole supplying the materials of what may now be called a set type of confessional theology.

For that type no name already current can be found; in default of any other, it must be called the Methodist type. But that term is no sooner written than it demands protection. It may seem at once to suggest the idea of an eclectic system of opinion. But, apart from the discredit into which this word eclectic has fallen, whether in the philosophical or in the theological domain, it is not applicable here. The staple and substance of Methodist theology is essentailly that of the entire Scripture as interpreted by the catholic evangelical tradition of the Christian Church. It holds the three Creeds, the only confessions of the Faith which ever professed to utter the unanimous voice of the body of Christ on earth; and, so far as these three Creeds were ever accepted by universal Christendom, it accepts them, with only such reservations as do not affect doctrine. Among the later confessions—the badges of a divided Christendom—it holds the Articles of the Church from which it sprang: holds them, that is, in their purely doctrinal statements. The eclectic hand has done no more than select for prominence such views of truth as have been neglected; never has it culled from this or that Formulary any spoil to make its own. It has no more borrowed from the Remonstrant Arminians than it has borrowed from the Protestant Lutherans. It agrees with both these so far as they express the faith of the New Testament; but no further. It has had, indeed, in past times a conventional connection with the name Arminian; but its Arminianism is simply the mind of the Catholic Church down to the time of Augustine; and with the historical Arminianism that degenerated in Holland it has no affinity. It might be said, with equal propriety or want of propriety, that it has learned some of its lessons from Calvinism. Certainly it has many secret and blessed relations with that system; not with its hard, logical, deductive semi-fatalism, over which Absolute Sovereignty reigns with such awful despotism, but with its deep appreciation of union with Christ, and of the Christian privileges bound up with that high principle.

But to return. The simple fact is, that any truly catholic confession of faith must seem to be eclectic: for there are no bodies of professed Christians, even to the outskirts of Christendom, which do not hold some portions of the truth; while it may be said that many of them hold some particular truth with a sharper and more consistent definition of it than others. But a really catholic system must embrace all these minor peculiarities; and in proportion as it does so, it will seem to have borrowed them. In this sense, the defenders of Methodist theology admit that it is eclectic. They claim to hold all essential truth; to omit no articles but those which they consider erroneous; and to disparage none but those which they deem unessential. This, of course, is a high pretension, but it is not a vainglorious one; for surely it is the prerogative of every Christian community to glory in holding "the faith once delivered to the saints." And as it is with the doctrines, so it is with the spirit, of Methodist teaching. In this also it is, after a fashion, eclectic, as it sympathizes with those who make it their boast that they know no other theology than the biblical, and is as biblical as they. It also agrees with those who think that divinity is a systematic science, to be grounded and organized as such; while with almost all its heart it joins the company of Mystics, whose supreme theologian is the interior Teacher, and who find all truth in the experimental vision and knowledge of God in Christ.

We have to say a few words upon certain peculiarities in the doctrinal position of Methodism. But it is a pleasant preface to dwell for a moment on the broad expanse of catholic evangelical truth, concerning which it has no peculiarities, or no peculiarities that affect Christian doctrine. To begin where all things have their beginning, with the being, triune essence, and attributes of God; his relation to the universe as its Creator and providential Governor; his revelation of himself in nature: this supreme truth it holds against all atheism, antitheism, pantheism, and materialism. The unity of mankind, created in the image of God; fallen into guilt and depravity in Adam; restored through the intervention of the Son of God, who offered a vicarious atonement for the whole race, and is now carrying on the holy warfare for man, and in man, and with man, against the personal devil and his kingdom of darkness: this it holds against all who deny the incarnation of the divine Son, one Person in two natures forever. The divinity and economical offices of the Eternal Spirit of the Father and the Son, the source of all good in man; the inspirer of all holy Scripture; the administrator of a finished redemption to sinful men convinced by his agency on their minds, justified through faith in the atonement which he reveals to the heart, and sanctified to the uttermost by his energy within the soul, operating through the means of grace established in the Church over which he presides, and revealing its power in all good works done in the imitation of Christ: all this it holds against the Pelagian, Antinomian, and Rationalist dishonor to the Holy Ghost. The solemnities of death, resurrection, and eternal judgment, conducted by the returning Christ, and issuing in the everlasting severance between good and evil, the evil being banished from God's presence forever, and the good blessed eternally with the beatific vision: all this, too, it holds with fear and trembling, but with assured confidence that the Judge will vindicate his righteousness forever. In this general outline we have all the elements of the apostles' doctrine and the truth of God. And with regard to these substantial and eternal verities, the system of doctrine we now consider is one with all communions that may be regarded as holding the Head. . . .

The doctrine of the most Holy Trinity might seem to be one in which there is no room for variety of sentiment among those who hold it: that is, the great bulk of the Christian world. But that doctrine is deeply affected both in itself and in its relation to the universe generally, and the economy of redemption in particular, by the view taken of the eternal Sonship of the second Person. Those who would efface the interior distinctions of generation and procession in the Godhead surrender much for which the earliest champions of orthodoxy fought. They take away from the intercommunion of the divine Persons its most impressive and affecting character; and they go far toward robbing us of the sacred mystery which unites the Son's exinanition in heaven with his humiliation as incarnate on earth. Now, we lay claim to no peculiar fidelity here, nor would this subject be mentioned, were it not the Methodism has had the high honor of vindicating the eternal Sonship in a very marked manner. It has produced some of the ablest defenses of this truth known in modern times; defenses which have shown how thoroughly it is interwoven with the fabric of Scripture, how vital it is to the doctrine of the incarnation, and how it may be protected from any complicity with subordinational Arianism. The transition from this to the person of Christ in the unity of his two natures if obvious. And here two remards only need be made: first, that our doctrine—we may say henceforward our doctrine—is distinguished by its careful abstinence from speculation as to the nature of the Redeemer's self-emptying, simply holding fast the immutable truth that the Divine Son of God could not surrender the essence of his divinity; and, secondly, that is the unity of his Person he was not only sinless but also incapable of sin. Any one who watches the tendencies of modern theology, tendencies which betray themselves in almost all communities, and watches them with an intelligent appreciation of the importance of the issues involved, will acknowledge that this first note of honest glorying is not unjustified.

Turning to the mediatorial work which the Son became incarnate to accomplish, we have to note that the Methodist doctrine lays a special emphasis on its universal relation to the race of man, and deduces the consequences with a precision in some respects peculiar to itself.

For instance, it sees in this the true explanation of the vicarious or substitutionary idea, which is essential to sound evangelical theology, but is very differently held by different schools. There are two extremes that it seeks to avoid by blending the truths perverted by opposite parties. The vague generality of the old Arminian and Grotian theory, which makes the atonement only a rectoral expedient of the righteous God, who sets forth his suffering Son before the universe as the proof that law has been vindicated before grace begins to receive transgressors, was very current in England when Methodism arose. This was and still is confronted by the vigorous doctrine of substitution, which represents Christ to have taken at all points the very place of his elect, actually for them and only them, satisfying the dreadful penalty and holy requirements of the law. Throughout the whole current of Methodist theology there runs a mediating strain, which, however, it would take many pages to illustrate. It accepts the Arminian view that the holiness of God is protected by the atonement; but it insists on bringing in here the vicarious idea. The sin of Adam was expiated as representing the sin of the race as such, or of human nature, or of mankind: a realistic conception which was not borrowed from philosophic realism, and which no nominalism can ever really dislodge from the New Testament. . . .

The blessings of the Christian covenant, administered and imparted by the Holy Ghost, which constitute the state of grace, are so simply set forth in the New Testament that there is not much room for difference of opinion among those whose views of the atonement are sound. We hold them, in common with all who hold the Head, to be one great privilege flowing from union with Christ, in whom we are complete; and that this great privilege of acceptance is administered both externally and internally. But, as we are dwelling on shades of difference, we may observe that the Methodist theology lays more stress than most others upon the fact that in every department of the common blessing there is both an external and an internal administration....

But this leads to the doctrine of the Witness of the Spirit, which has been sometimes regarded as a Methodist peculiarity. By many it is set down as a specimen of what may be called an inductive theology; that is, as a formula for certain experiences enjoyed by the early converts of the system. Now, there can be no question that there is some truth in this. The experiences of multitudes who felt suddenly and most assuredly delivered from the sense of condemnation, enabled to pray to God as a reconciled father, and conscious of their sanctification to his service, may be said to have anticipated the confirmation of the word of God. They first read in their own hearts what they afterward read in their Bibles. For that the induction of experience coincides in this with biblical induction is most certain. That it is the privilege of those who are new creatures in Christ Jesus, and have passed from death unto life, to know the things that are freely given them of God, cannot be denied by any who, with unprejudiced eyes, read the New Testament. In fact, the general principle is admitted in all communions, the differences among them having reference either to certain restrictions in the evidence itself, or to the medium through which it is imparted. A large portion of Christendom unite this witness with sacramental means and ordinances; making personal assurance of salvation dependent on priestly absolution, either with or without a sacrament devised for the purpose. Another, and almost equally large body of Christian teachers, make this high privilege a special blessing vouchsafed to God's elect as the fruit or reward of long discipline and the divine seal upon earnest perseverance; but, when imparted, this assurance includes the future as well as the past, and is the knowledge of an irreversible decree of acceptance which nothing can avail to undermine however much it may be occasionally clouded. The Methodist doctrine is distinguished from these by a few strong points which it has held with deep tenacity from the beginning. It believes that the witness of the Spirit to the spirit in man is direct and clear; distinct from the word, and from the faith that lays hold on the word, though closely connected with both. It is not separated from the testimony which is believed; for, implicitly or explicitly, the promise in Christ must be apprehended by faith. But faith in this matter is rather trust in a Person than belief of a record; and that trust is distinct from the assurance He gives, though that assurance follows so hard upon it that in the supreme blessedness of appropriating confidence they are scarcely to be distinguished. While the faith itself may be always firm, the assur-

112

ance may be sometimes clouded and uncertain. Neither can co-exist with lapse into sin; and therefore the witness may be suspended, or may be indeed finally lost. It is the assurance of faith only for the present; only the assurance of hope for the future. It may be calm in its peace, or may be quickened into rapture. But it must be confirmed by the testimony of a good conscience; while, on the other hand, it is often the silencer of a conscience unduly disturbed. It is, to sum up, in all types of Methodist theology—whatever abuses it may suffer in some Methodist conceptions of it—no other than the soul's consciousness of an indwelling Saviour through the secret and inexplicable influence of his Holy Spirit.

Perhaps the most eminent peculiarity of the type of doctrine called Methodist is its unfaltering assertion of the believer's privilege to be delivered from indwelling sin in the present life. Its unfaltering assertion: for although varying very much on some subordinate matters of statement as to the means of attainment and the accompanying assurance, it has always been faithful to the central truth itself. Its unfaltering assertion: for in the maintenance of this it has met with the most determined hostility, not only from such opponents as deny the doctrines of grace generally, but also from those whose evangelical theology in general and whose high sanctity give their opposition a very painful character and make it very embarrassing.

It cannot be too distinctly impressed that the one element in the Methodist doctrine that may be called distinctive, is the article that the work of the Spirit in sanctifying believers from sin—from all that in the divine estimate is sin—is to be complete in this state of probation. This is the hope it sees set before us in the Gospel, and this, therefore, it presses upon the pursuit and attainment of all who are in Christ. This is, in the judgment of many, its specific heresy; this, in its own judgment, is its specific glory....

Another is the doctrine of the sacraments. Methodist teaching has, from the beginning, mediated here between two extremes which need not be more particularly defined: in that mediation keeping company with the Anglican Formularies, and the Presbyterian Westminster Confession, both of which raise them above mere signs, and lay stress on their being seals or pledges or instruments of the impartation of the grace signified to the prepared recipient. All its old standards, including its hymns, bear witness to this; they abundantly and irresistibly confirm our assertion as to the sacramental idea generally. As to the two ordinances in particular, there can be no doubt that the sentiments of the various Methodist communions run through a wide range. Recoil from exaggerated doctrine has led many toward the opposite extreme; and a large proportion of their ministers put a very free construction upon their standards, and practically regard the two sacraments as badges simply of Christian profession, the Eucharist being to them a special means of grace in the common sense of the phrase. There is a wide discretion allowed in this matter, and the wisdom of this discretion is, on the whole, justified. With that question, however, we have nothing to do here; our only object being to state the case as it is.

But this essay must be closed, leaving untouched many subjects which naturally appeal for consideration. Something ought to be said as to the controversial aspect of this theology. But leaving that for other essays, we have only to commend the general principles of the Methodist theology to any strangers to it who may read these pages. They will find it clear and consistent, on the whole, as a human system, worthy of much more attention than it usually receives from the Christian world; and, what is of far more importance, they will find it pervaded by the "unction from the Holy One," which is the secret of all truth and of all edification.

THOMAS N. RALSTON

T he first American to write a systematic theology in the Wesleyan tradition was Thomas N. Ralston (1806–1891). A native of Kentucky, he was principal of a Methodist school for women in Louisville and a theologian of importance. His major work, *Elements of Divinity*, was published and then enlarged posthumously with his notes by Thomas O. Summers, another southern Methodist theologian. The statements selected on the sacraments are typical of the era and represent the mainstream of Methodist thinking on this subject. The selections are taken from *Elements of Divinity*, ed. T. O. Summers (Nashville: A.H. Redford, 1871), pp. 940–1004.

CHRISTIAN BAPTISM

Christian Baptism is a subject upon which, for centuries past, there has, perhaps, been a greater amount of polemic strife than upon any other theological question. Upon this arena master combatants oft and again have fiercely met, and plied their utmost skill and strength, and left the field with the question no nearer being settled than when they began. Judging from the past, we may reasonably despair of perfect harmony of sentiment in the Church on this trite and much-mooted theme till the second coming of Christ. In the present stage of this controversy we can scarcely hope to present any thing substantially *new;* nor shall we aim at any thing farther than a clear and condensed view of the leading and most important arguments necessary to sustain what we consider the correct and scriptural statement of the doctrine.

I. The first question in connection with this theme naturally presenting itself for our consideration is this: What is the NATURE of *Christian baptism*?

As this is admitted to be what is termed a *positive* institute, it is clear that we are dependent entirely upon the divine record for our information.

The term *baptism* is from the Greek *baptizo*, which is a derivative of *bapto*. This word, according to the lexicographers, means *"to dip, to plunge into water, to wash, to dye,"* etc. It is, however, very clear that the etymology of the word can furnish us no information as to the *nature* or *design* of the ordinance. Upon *this* point, whatever we may conclude as to the *mode* and *subjects* of baptism, no light can be shed by the etymological discussion; and we may also add that, in the question now before us, we have nothing whatever to do with the *mode* or *subjects* of baptism. Those matters must be held in abeyance for after consideration.

As to the *nature* and *design* of baptism, we must rely solely on the history of the subject and the statements concerning it, as recorded in the Bible. It is admitted that our Saviour ingrafted the sacrament of the "Lord's-supper" on the Jewish Passover; and it may be affirmed that "Baptism," the other Christian sacrament, had its origin in a similar way—being substituted for "circumcision." The institution of Christian baptism unquestionably was set up and established in the great commission given to the apostles by the Saviour after his resurrection: "Go ye therefore, and teach all nations, baptizing them in the name of the Father, and of the Son, and of the Holy Ghost; teaching them to observe all things whatsoever I have commanded you; and, lo, I am with you alway, even unto the end of the world." Matt. xxviii. 19,20. Here we date the divine origin of baptism as a standing, obligatory, and perpetual ordinance of the Christian Church. Here is the great charter from which the Christian ministry in all ages derive their divine authority for the administration of this ordinance....

II. We now proceed to examine the OBLIGATION OF CHRISTIAN BAPTISM in the proper sense of that term.

Christian baptism is an ordinance of *universal* and *perpetual obligation*. By this we mean that it is the duty of all who would become Christians to be baptized, and that this obligation was not a temporary requirement, but is to be perpetuated in the Church "alway, even unto the end of the world."

We know of no denomination, "professing and calling themselves Christians," who have denied the perpetuity of this ordinance in the Christian Church, except the Quakers. It is, however, admitted that some among the Socinians, Unitarians, and other classes of sectaries of loose principles and heterodox creed, have lightly esteemed water baptism, contemplating it as possessing no *sacramental* character, but being mainly an external mark of distinction between Pagans and Christians; useful at the introduction of the gospel in Pagan countries, but not necessary as a perpetual ordinance of the Church. It has been well said that "extremes beget extremes;" and, perhaps, the early tendency in the Church to magnify the importance of external rites, and attach a superstitious and unscriptural efficacy to mere forms and ceremonies, has tended to drive some to the opposite extreme of esteeming them too lightly. Indeed, the error, in this respect, of the Mystics, Quakers, Socinians, and all others who have repudiated or undervalued water baptism or other external rites, is but an outbirth from the opposite and more dangerous theories concerning *sacramental salvation, water regeneration,* etc.

That water baptism is an institution of perpetual obligation in the Church, is a clear deduction from the language of the great apostolic commission: "Go ye therefore, and teach *all nations, baptizing them* in the name of the Father, and of the Son, and of the Holy Ghost; *teaching them to observe all things whatsoever I have commanded you*; and, lo, I am with you *alway, even unto the end of the world."* (Matt. xxviii. 19, 20.) Or as it is recorded by St. Mark: "Go ye into *all the world*, and preach the gospel *to every creature*. He that believeth and *is baptized* shall be saved." (Mark xvi. 15, 16.). . . .

III. We have already contemplated baptism, as also the other sacrament—the Lord's-supper—as a *sign* and *seal* of "internal spiritual grace." We now inquire more particularly concerning the *design* and *efficacy* of baptism.

1. The first theory upon this subject which we shall notice, is that of the Roman Catholics. They attribute to this sacrament a *saving efficacy* —teaching that, in some mysterious way, there is directly imparted through this ordinance, when properly administered, spiritual grace, in such sense, that whatever may be the character of the subject (unless he be guilty of some mortal sin), his moral nature is at once regenerated and sanctified; thus attributing to the element of water the efficacy pertaining alone to the blood of Christ, and to the agency of the priest the work of regeneration and sanctification, which can only be effected by the agency of the Holy Spirit.

2. Another theory, somewhat different from the view just presented, though closely allied to it, has been sanctioned by a class of High-church Episcopalians, and very zealously advocated by Alexander Campbell and his followers. This theory, while it rejects the notion that there is any saving efficacy in the sacrament of baptism itself, or any spiritual grace directly imparted through this application of water, independent of the

character or disposition of the subject, yet maintains that baptism, properly administered and received, secures the grace of regeneration, and is the means and pledge of the remission of sins. . . .

It is apparent, from the account just given of the views of Roman Catholics, High-church Episcopalians, and of Alexander Campbell, as to the connection of baptism with regeneration and the remission of sins, that there are several shades of difference in sentiment among them. Yet, so closely are they allied, that a refutation of the position of Mr. Campbell, as just presented in his own language, will comprise a refutation of all the schemes to which we have referred. Therefore, we proceed directly to examine that position.

The position is substantially this: that the remission of sins is imparted only through baptism.

This, which is the theory of Mr. Campbell, we consider but little better than the doctrine of the High-church Episcopalians or of the Roman Catholics. These schemes, we are satisfied, are radically erroneous, substituting, in effect, the element of water and the physical agency of man for the blood of Christ and the divine agency of the Holy Spirit.

Now, if we can show that there is some other condition, separate and distinct from baptism, with which the remission of sins is inseparably connected, and that remission is not thus inseparably connected with baptism, it will follow, of course, that the position we oppose cannot be true.

We appeal, then, "to the law and to the testimony." "He that *believeth* on him *is not condemned.*" (John iii. 18.) "He that *believeth* on the Son *hath everlasting life.*" (John iii. 36.) "Verily, verily I say unto you, he that *believeth* on me *hath everlasting life.*" (John iii. 47.) "Therefore we conclude that a man is justified *by faith* without the deeds of the law." (Rom. iii. 28.) "To him give all the prophets witness, that through his name whosoever *believeth* in him *shall receive remission of sins.*" (Acts x. 43.)

A large portion of Scripture, to the same effect, might be adduced; but to add more is needless. If the above passages do not decide the point that *faith*, and not *baptism*, is the condition on which the "remission of sins" turns, no language could be framed to prove the position. Here we are taught that every *believer* is freed from "condemnation"—"hath everlasting life"—"is justified"—and "shall receive remission of sins." Now, we affirm that no man *can* possess all these things and his sins *not* be remitted. Can a man be "not condemned," "have everlasting life," and be "justified," and his sins not be remitted? The supposition is utterly inadmissible. Can he have *faith* without baptism? Surely he can. Why not? Then it follows that his sins may be remitted without baptism.

Indeed, Mr. Campbell's system not only contradicts the Bible, but fights against itself. Mr. Campbell teaches that a man must have *faith* before he can properly receive baptism; but if he has *faith*, if the Bible be true, "his sins *are* remitted;" and Mr. Campbell correctly tells us that if he has not *faith*, his sins will not be remitted in baptism. Hence it follows that if all who believe (as the Bible teaches) have already received "remission of sins," and if (as Mr. Campbell teaches) they can only receive the "remission of sins" by first believing and then being baptized, it amounts to this: a man must *first* have "his sins remitted" *before* they *can* be remitted —that is, a thing must *be* before it *can be*. The truth is, the theory that "remission of sins" is inseparably connected with baptism flatly contradicts the Bible. The Bible connects remission inseparably with *faith*. Admit the truth of this position (which we cannot deny without flatly contradicting many plain scriptures, as we have shown), then we cannot escape the conclusion, according to Mr. Campbell, that we must *first have* remission before we *can have it*, which is a contradiction.

We take the first text which we quoted above—*"He that believeth on him is not condemned"*—and if there were no other scripture bearing on the subject, this alone contains a proof of the position for which we here contend, that can never be shaken (unless we flatly contradict the Saviour) by all the skill, ingenuity, and sophistry in the world. "He that believeth on him is not condemned." Now, if this text means any thing, it means this: that all who believe on Christ are, *that instant*—*the very moment they first believe on Christ*—free from *condemnation*; and if *free from condemnation*, then they are *pardoned, forgiven*, their *sins are remitted*, they are *justified*, they are *the children of God*, they "shall not come into *condemnation*, but are passed from *death* unto *life*." Can language be plainer, or proof clearer or more direct? If it be, then, a settled Bible maxim that the "remission of sins" is inseparably connected with *faith*, can it, at the same time, be inseparably connected with *baptism*? It is utterly impossible, unless we say that *faith also* is inseparably connected with baptism. We arrive again at the same conclusion—*faith* gives *remission*; but if faith must *first exist* in order to proper baptism, then baptism cannot give remission; for you cannot give a man what he already possesses....

We arrive, then, at the conclusion that although water baptism should not be too lightly esteemed, and either set aside as not necessary under the gospel, or viewed as merely a form of initiation, or as a help to the exercise of faith, neither, on the other hand, should it be exalted too highly, as possessing intrinsic virtue and saving efficacy. The truth is this: it is a *sign* of Christian men's profession, and also of the inward spiritual grace of regeneration and sanctification, and a *seal* of the gracious covenant by which the Church relation and the promise of eternal life are confirmed unto God's people.

But yet, it is but an external ordinance. It is no substitute for the blood of atonement, by which alone sins can be washed away; or for the influence of the Holy Spirit, by which alone the regeneration and sanctification of the soul can be secured.

It is admitted by all who believe in the propriety of water baptism that *believers in Christ*, or all who are "the children of God by faith in Christ Jesus," are proper subjects of baptism; hence we deem it useless to stop a moment to present proof upon that subject. The question we propound is this, Are *believers* the *only* proper subjects of baptism? That the Baptist position upon this question is erroneous, we shall endeavor to show.

I. That the INFANT CHILDREN of believing parents are proper subjects of Christian baptism, is a plain, direct, and necessary inference from *the express statute and appointment of God....*

The argument here presented in favor of infant baptism may be briefly stated thus: The Church of God is essentially the same Church now that it was when God commanded that infants should be admitted into it as members. God has never authorized the repeal of that command; hence it is still in force; consequently, infants are now entitled to membership in the Church. But membership in the Church of God can now only be conferred through the initiatory rite of baptism; therefore, as infants are entitled to Church-membership, they have also a right to baptism.

Again, substantially the same argument may be stated in another form, thus:

The Abrahamic covenant and that of the gospel are the same; God once ordained that all, upon entering upon this covenant relation with him, should receive the *sign* and *seal* of circumcision. What was once confirmed by the sign and seal of circumcision is now by divine appointment confirmed by the sign and seal of baptism; therefore baptism has come in the room of circumcision. Infants by divine appointment had a right to circumcision; but baptism having come in the room of circumcision, therefore they have a right to baptism.

Again, the Church of God is essentially *one* in all ages. God has enacted that infants constitute a part of that one Church, and that enactment has never been repealed; therefore infants are still a part of that Church. All who compose the Church have a right to all its ordinances which they are capable of receiving; but baptism is an ordinance of the Church which infants are capable of receiving; therefore infants have a right to baptism....

We have presented, from Church-history, but a brief outline of the testimony that might be adduced in favor of infant baptism; but to the unprejudiced mind we think it amounts to evidence of the most conclusive and satisfactory character. To our mind it carries irresistible conviction. In three centuries from the apostles' time, many changes had occurred in the Church—many abuses had entered—but that so important and so serious a change as the introduction of infant baptism should have been made so soon, and become the universal practice of the Church, and yet no one ever hear, or read, or speak of the marvelous revolution is utterly incredible.

In the language of an excellent writer (Dr. Miller), we add, that "when Origen, Cyprian, and Chrysostom, declare not only that the baptism of infants was the universal and unopposed practice of the Church in their respective times and places of residence; and when men of so much acquaintance with all preceding writers, and so much knowledge of all Christendom, as Augustin and Pelagius, declared that they *never heard of any one who claimed to be a Christian, either orthodox or heretic, who did not maintain and practice infant baptism*—to suppose, in the face of such testimony, that the practice of infant baptism crept in as an unwarranted innovation between their time and that of the apostles, without the smallest notice of the change having ever reached their ears, I must be allowed to say, of all incredible suppositions, this is one of the most incredible. He who can believe this must, it appears to me, be prepared to make a sacrifice of all historical evidence at the shrine of blind and deaf prejudice."

But infant baptism can well afford to dispense with all this historic testimony, and its foundation remain firm and unshaken. It grounds its authority upon the appointment of God, in connection with the everlasting covenant with "Abraham and his seed," and the explicit law of God, embracing infants as members of his Church. The same Church still exists—the same law was never annulled. But Christ and his apostles fully recognized both the real identity of the Church and the right of infants, under the new dispensation, to share the benefits of the same abiding covenant of grace. The promise and oath of God can never fail; and while these remain unchanged, infants, with their believing parents, shall ever share in all the rights, privileges, and benefits of the glorious kingdom of Him in whom "all the families of the earth shall be blessed."

THE LORD'S SUPPER

Having presented from the several evangelists, Matthew, Mark, and Luke, the inspired record of the origin and appointment of this institution by our Lord himself, and from the First Epistle to the Corinthians the apostolic comment upon the same, we have clearly before us the substance of the teachings of Scripture upon the subject.

The *first* question here demanding our attention is this: In what sense should the phrases, "This is my body," and "This is my blood," be understood? The Roman Catholics interpret these words in the most literal acceptation; and contend that, by the prayer of consecration said over the elements by the priest, the *bread* is no longer *bread*, and the *wine* no longer *wine*, but that they have been converted into the *literal* body and blood of Christ; and thus they originate the absurd figment of transubstantiation. But little need be said to evince to the unbiased mind that their position upon this subject is both unreasonable and unscriptural....

But little better than this error of the Romanists is the doctrine of *consubstantiation*, which teaches that although the bread and the wine are not *literally* the body and blood of Christ, yet that his body and blood are *literally present* with the elements in the Supper, and are *literally* received by the communicants.

Among the leaders of the Lutheran Reformation, some—and Luther himself was one of them—leaned too far toward transubstantiation. They seemed unable to take at once so bold a leap on the subject as to escape entirely the errors of the papists. It is true that consubstantiation, for which they contended, delivered them from the grosser absurdities and the idolatrous tendencies of the system they renounced. They did not place themselves in direct conflict with men's external senses, nor were they led to the idolatrous adoration of the *bread* and the *wine*; but still they leaned too far toward the *literal* interpretation, holding that the communicant did *literally eat* the body and *drink* the blood of Christ, which was always, in a manner inexplicable, present with the elements.

Others, led by Carolostadt and Zuinglius, went to an opposite extreme, attaching no farther import to the words, "This is my body," and "This is my blood," than that the elements were merely *signs*, or *figures*, assisting the faith to apprehend the absent body and blood of the Lord. This view is in close correspondence with that of the modern Socinians.

The true scriptural view of the subject, as we conceive, lies between these two extremes, and was advocated by Calvin, and is now the creed of the Protestant Churches generally. While it rejects the *literal* presence of the body and blood of Christ, as held by Luther and the abettors of consubstantiation, it admits with Carolostadt and Zuinglius that the elements are signs, symbols, or figures, of the literal body and blood of Christ. But it goes one step farther. It considers the elements not only as a *sign*, but also as a *seal* of the new covenant. This idea appears to be implied in the words of Christ, "This cup is the *new covenant in my blood;*" and in the words of Paul, "The cup of blessing which we bless, is it not the communion of the blood of Christ? The bread which we break, is it not the communion of the body of Christ?"

Hence we conclude that, in this ordinance,

1. No change is effected in the elements; the bread and the wine are not *literally the body and blood of Christ.*

2. The body and blood of Christ are not *literally present with the elements,* and received by the communicants.

3. But the elements are *signs,* or *symbols,* of the body and blood of Christ, serving as a memorial of his sufferings on the cross and a boon to the faith of the communicant.

4. The elements also possess a *sacramental* character, being a divinely appointed *seal* of the covenant of redemption. As the blood of the paschal lamb served as a seal of this covenant under the old dispensation, pointing the faith of the Israelite to the coming Redeemer, it was fit that, as the *old* dispensation was now to be superseded by the *new*, the seal of the covenant should be correspondingly changed; hence at the conclusion of the last authorized Passover, the holy supper is instituted, as a *perpetual memorial* and *abiding seal* of the covenanted mercy and grace of God, till the Saviour "shall appear the second time without sin unto salvation." . . .

We next inquire, *Who have a RIGHT to the Supper of the Lord?*

We present it as a Bible position, standing forth prominently to view, that

> All real Christians—that is, all who are "the children of God by faith in Christ Jesus"—have a divine right to membership and communion, embracing full fellowship, with the privilege of the Lord's-supper, in every Church, or congregation of Christians, among whom their lot may be cast.

This proposition will be found to contain the principle according to which the great question of Christian communion now before us may be clearly and satisfactorily settled. Before we bring the proposition to bear directly on the question, and exhibit, in all its important aspects, its connection with the subject of Christian communion, we should weigh the proposition itself in the balances of the sanctuary. We bespeak for it a careful investigation and a fair trial. If it be unsound, let it be at once rejected; but if it be according to the teachings of Heaven and the principles of eternal truth, let us plant ourselves upon it, as on a sure foundation, impregnable and indestructible as the "word of God, which liveth and abideth forever."

We now appeal to the Scripture testimony to learn *who* they are that have a right to the fellowship of the Church, to the immunities and privileges of the house of God, to the communion of the Supper of the Lord. If we trace the entire history of the planting of the Church, as laid down in The Acts of the Apostles, we shall find in the apostolic administration but one invariable practice upon the subject. Such as "gladly received the word," such as "believed," not only on the day of Pentecost, but on all subsequent occasions, were without exception and without delay admitted to the communion and fellowship of the Church. This was done too, not on the ground of their perfect agreement in all their views of Christian doctrine, or ordinances, or Church order, but *solely* on the ground of the *fact* that they were supposed to have been made partakers of the spiritual benefits of Christianity "by faith in Christ Jesus."

It is indeed surprising that there should be thought any plausible ground for diversity of sentiment among Christians as to the true basis of Christian communion, after we have looked upon the clear and unmistakable apostolic platform exhibited upon the subject in the fifteenth chapter of The Acts of the Apostles. Here we find the apostles and elders assembled in solemn council to adjudicate upon the very question we are now discussing. *Their decision*, and *the grounds upon which it was based*, are committed to record. This record remains as an imperishable memorial which should never be overlooked—a light to shine upon the pathway of the Church in all succeeding generations.

The history of the case is this: There arose in the Church of Antioch a dissension on the subject of communion. Certain Judaizing teachers from Jerusalem had visited them, and troubled them much with some of their close communion principles. They had taught them that there was a certain rite, ceremony, or ordinance, which many of them had neglected, that was essential to salvation, and of course that such as had hitherto neglected this ought not to be admitted to the communion and fellowship of the Church. Paul and Barnabas opposed strenuously these close communion teachers, and the sectarian and schismatic principles they were inculcating. But still, for a complete and more authoritative settlement of the matter, it was agreed that Paul and Barnabas, and some other disciples, should go up to Jerusalem, and call the apostles and elders together for the decision of the question. We have the record of their *decision*, and the *reasons of it*. Now we invite special attention to the *grounds* of this decision. It was a question of communion and fellowship, identical with the very question now before us. The question was whether certain Gentiles, claiming to be Christians, though they had neglected a certain ceremony which some contended was essential, should be recognized as Christians, and admitted to communion. The decision is in favor of their admission. But what are the *grounds* of that decision? What are the *specific reasons* upon which it is based? We answer, They are precisely the same that are comprised in the proposition we have laid down as the basis of Christian communion, and which we are now endeavoring to establish by Scripture testimony.

It ought to be strictly noted on this subject that we here have an infallible, an inspired touch-stone, or clue, for the settlement of the communion question, whenever, wherever, or however, it may arise; for if these persons, whose right to Church-communion is contested, are admitted to communion *on certain grounds*, and those grounds are specifically stated, it necessarily follows that in all cases of contested right of communion, whatever may be the ground of the objection, *the same reasons specified in this case would establish a similar right, and require a similar decision.* But what are these reasons? St. Peter, in pleading the right of these Gentiles to communion, declares: "God, which knoweth the hearts, bare them witness, giving them the Holy Ghost, even as he did unto us." Here, God is appealed to as a witness for the Gentiles of their claim to communion, on the ground that *he* had "given them the Holy Ghost"—that is, he had conferred on them the spiritual blessings of Christianity—they had received the converting power of the gospel —"even as he did unto us"—that is, they enjoy the same spiritual religion with us; consequently they are entitled to the same Church privileges. But St. Peter goes on: "And put no difference between us and them, *purifying their hearts by faith."* Here the plain argument of St. Peter is this: these Gentiles are true believers, they are genuine Christians, they are "the children of God by faith in Christ Jesus;" consequently they have a right to the privileges and fellowship of the Church.

Now, we ask, will not the same argument prove the same thing in all similar cases? If *these* have a right to Church-communion *because* "their hearts are purified by faith," must not all whose "hearts are purified by faith," or all who are "the children of God by faith in Christ Jesus," have a right to Church-communion? *Quod erat demonstrandum.*

St. Peter still proceeds: "Now, therefore, why tempt ye God to put a yoke upon the neck of the disciples, which neither our fathers nor we were able to bear? But we believe that through the grace of the Lord Jesus Christ we shall be saved, even as they." Here the argument for their right to communion is grounded upon the fact that all are believed to be heirs of a similar salvation.

After St. Peter had closed his argument, St. Paul and St. Barnabas next spoke on the same side of the question, and using a similar mode of reasoning. They appealed to the fact that God, through their instrumentality, had "wrought miracles and wonders among the Gentiles." In other words, they argued, God has conferred upon the Gentiles the spiritual blessings of Christianity, therefore they have right to the external privileges and ordinances of the Church. Here, let it be remembered, there is not one word about the peculiar notions of these persons concerning doctrines and ordinances, about "baptisms and the laying on of hands" —no, nor about any thing else, but the simple fact of their *conversion to God*. *This*, and *this alone*, was *the ground* upon which their right to communion was affirmed. This fact no man dare deny.

JOHN MILEY

J ohn Miley (1813–1895) reflects the intersection of evangelical faith and scientific sensibility as these found expression in the final decades of the nineteenth century. He maintained that theology explores the data of religious experience and is, in this sense, scientific. Miley attempted to be both a natural and a dogmatic theologian. The immediate experience of God is basic; the Scriptures clarify and provide normative interpretation of that experience.

Miley designated his position "Ethical Arminianism." Utilizing the inheritance shaped by D.D. Whedon and others, Miley made free personal agency the foundational principle of his work. His major theological writing was the two volume *Systematic Theology* (1893). This systematic statement was a well structured, thorough discussion of cardinal theological issues from Miley's perspective. The selections included in this reader are selected from *Systematic Theology* and represent central themes in Miley's thought, namely his basic theistic principles and doctrine of the atonement. In his discussion of the atonement he develops a distinctive form of the governmental theory and argues for the sufficiency of the atonement for all people. Miley is distinct among Methodist theologians of his time in making theism and Christology coordinate themes. These Miley selections are taken from *Systematic Theology* (New York: Hunt and Eaton, Cincinnati: Cranston & Cuttis, 1894), *Library of Biblical and Theological Literature*, vols. V & VI: "Theism," V, pp. 57–66; 68–70; "Sufficiency of the Atonement," VI, pp. 195–202, 218–221.

THEISM

I. THE SENSE OF THEISM

1. *Doctrinal Content of the Term.*—Theism means the existence of a personal God, Creator, Preserver, and Ruler of all things. Deism equally

127

means the personality of God and also his creative work, but denies his providence in the sense of theism. These terms were formerly used in much the same sense, but since early in the last century deism has mostly been used in a sense opposed to the Scriptures as a divine revelation, and to a divine providence. Such is now its distinction from theism. Pantheism differs from theism in the denial of the divine personality. With this denial, pantheism can mean no proper work of creation or providence. The philosophic agnosticism which posits the Infinite as the ground of finite existences, but denies its personality, is in this denial quite at one with pantheism. The distinction of theism from these several opposing terms sets its own meaning in the clearer light. Creation and providence are here presented simply in their relation to the doctrinal content of theism. The methods of the divine agency therein require separate treatment. Nor could this treatment proceed with advantage simply in the light of reason; it requires the fuller light of revelation.

2. *Historic View of the Idea of God.*—Religion is as wide-spread as the human family and pervades the history of the race. But religion carries with it some form of the idea of God or of some order of supernatural existence. There is no place for religion without this idea. This is so thoroughly true that the attempts to found a religion without the notion of some being above us have no claim to recognition in a history of religion. But while religion so widely prevails it presents great varieties of form, especially in the idea of God, or of what takes the supreme place in the religious consciousness. Such differences appear in what are called the ethnic religions, the religions of different races. Of these James Freeman Clarke enumerates ten. Some make the number greater, others less. However, the exact number does not concern our present point. In the instances of Confucianism, Brahmanism, and Buddhism there are wide variations in the conception of God, and equally so in the other ethnic religions. As we look into details these variations are still more manifest. In view of the objects worshiped, the rites and ceremonies of the worship, the sentiments uttered in prayer and praise, we must recognize very wide differences of theistic conception. The case is not really other, because so many of these ideas are void of any adequate truth of theism. They are still ideas of what is divine to the worshiper and have their place in the religious consciousness. We can hardly think that in the low forms of idolatry there is nothing more present to religious thought and feeling than the idol. "Even the stock or stone, the rudest fetich before which the savage bows, is, at least to him, something more than a stock or stone; and the feeling of fear or awe or abject dependence with which he regards it is the reflex of a dim, confused conception of an

128

invisible and spiritual power, of which the material object has become representative."

3. *Account of Perverted Forms of the Idea.*—These perverted forms arise, in part, from speculations which disregard the imperative laws of rational thinking, and, in part—mostly, indeed—from vicious repugnances to the true idea. When God is conceived under the form of pantheism, or as the Absolute in a sense which precludes all predication and specially denies to him all personal attributes, the idea is the result of such speculation as we have just now characterized, or a creation of the imagination. In either form the idea is just as impotent for any rationale of the cosmos as the baldest materialism. Neither has any warrant in rational thought. When God is conceived under the forms of idolatry the conception is from a reaction of the soul against the original idea. The reaction is from a repugnance of the sensibilities to the true idea, not from any discernment of rational thought. This is the account which Paul gives of the source and prevalence of idolatry. His account applies broadly to the heathen world. "When they knew God, they glorified him not as God, neither were thankful; but became vain in their imaginations, and their foolish heart was darkened." Thus closing their eyes to the light of nature in which God was manifest, they "changed the glory of the uncorruptible God into an image made like to corruptible man, and to birds, and four-footed beasts, and creeping things." It was because "they did not like to retain God in their knowledge."

4. *Definitive Idea of God.*—A definition of God that shall be true to the truth of his being and character is a difficult attainment. This must be apparent whether we study definitions as given, or the subject of definition. God is for human thought an incomprehensible Being, existing in absolute soleness, apart from all the categories of genus and species. Hence the difficulty of definition. The true idea cannot be generalized in any abstract or single principle. As the Absolute or Unconditioned, God is simply differentiated from the dependent or related; as the Infinite, from the finite. The essential truths of a definition are not given in any of these terms. As the Unknowable, the agnostic formula is purely negative and without definitive content. Absolute will cannot give the content of a true idea of God. In order to the true idea, will must be joined with intellect and sensibility in the constitution of personality. Some of the divine titles have the form of a definition, but are not such in fact. God is often named the Almighty, but this expresses simply his omnipotence, which is only one of his perfections. Another title is Jehovah, which signifies the eternal, immutable being of God; but while the meaning is profound the plenitude of his being is not

expressed. "God is love." There is profound truth here also; but the words express only what is viewed as supreme in God.

The citation of a few definitions may be useful. "The first ground of all being; the divine spirit which, unmoved itself, moves all; absolute, efficient principle; absolute notion; absolute end." — *Aristotle*. This definition conforms somewhat to the author's four forms of cause. It contains more truth of a definition than some given by professedly Christian philosophers. "The moral order of the universe, actually operative in life." — *Fichte*. Lotze clearly points out the deficiencies of this definition. It gives us an abstract world-order without the divine Orderer. "The absolute Spirit; the pure, essential Being that makes himself object to himself; absolute holiness; absolute power, wisdom, goodness, justice." — *Hegel*. "A Being who, by his understanding and will, is the Cause (and by consequence the Author of nature; a Being who has all rights and no duties; the supreme perfection in substance; the all-obligating Being; Author of a universe under moral law; the moral Author of the world; an Intelligence infinite in every respect." — *Kant*. "*God* is derived incontestably from *good* and means the Good itself in the perfect sense, the absolute Good, the primal Good, on which all other good depends—as it were, the Fountain of good. Hence God has been styled the Being of beings (*ens entium*), the supreme Being (*ens summum*), the most perfect Being (*ens perfectissumum s. realissimum*)." — *Krug*. "The absolute, universal Substance; the real Cause of all and every existence; the alone, actual, and unconditioned Being, not only Cause of all being, but itself all being, of which every special existence is only a modification." — *Spinoza*. This is a pantheistic definition. "The *ens a se*, Spirit independent, in which is embraced the sufficient reason of the existence of things contingent—that is, the universe." — *Wolf*. These citations are found in the useful work of Krauth-Fleming. Some of them contain much truth, particularly Hegel's and Kant's. The serious deficiency is in the omission of any formal assertion of the divine personality as the central reality of a true definition. On the other hand, too much account is made of the divine agency in creation and providence. This agency is very properly included in a definition of theism, particularly in its distinction from deism and pantheism, but is not necessary to a definition of God himself.

We may add a few other definitions. "God is the infinite and personal Being of the good, by and for whom the finite hath existence and consciousness; and it is precisely this threefold definition—God is spirit, is love, is Lord—this infinite personal Good, which answers to the most simple truths of Christianity." Martensen gives the elements of a definition substantially the same. "God is a Spirit, infinite, eternal, and unchangeable, in his being, wisdom, power, holiness, justice, goodness, and truth." Dr. Hodge thinks this probably the best definition ever penned by man. Personality is the deepest truth in the conception of God and should not be omitted from the definition. With this should be combined the perfection of his personal attributes. All the necessary truths of a definition would thus be secured. Hence we define thus: *God is an eternal personal Being, of absolute knowledge, power, and goodness.*

II. ORIGIN OF THE IDEA OF GOD

1. *Possible Sources of the Idea.* — We here mean, not any mere notion of God without respect to its truth, or as it might exist in the thought of an atheist, but the idea as a conviction of the divine existence. How may the mind come into the possession of this idea?

There are faculties of mind which determine the modes of our ideas. Some we obtain through sense-perception. Sense-experience underlies all such perception. We cannot in this mode reach the idea of God. Many of our ideas are obtained through the logical reason. They are warranted inferences from verified facts or deductions from self-evident principles. Through the same faculty we receive many ideas, with a conviction of their truth, on the ground of human testimony. There are also intuitive truths, immediate cognitions of the primary reason. The conviction of truth in these ideas comes with their intuitive cognition. Through what mode may the idea of God be obtained? Not through sense-perception, as previously stated. Beyond this it is not necessarily limited to any one mental mode: not to the intuitive faculty, because it may be a product of the logical reason or a communication or revelation—to the logical reason; nor to this mode, because it may be an immediate truth of the primary reason.

If the existence of God is an immediate cognition of the reason, will it admit the support and affirmation of logical proof? We have assumed that it will. Yet we fully recognize the profound distinction in the several modes of our ideas. The logical and intuitive faculties have their respective functions, and neither can fulfill those of the other. Further, intuitive truths are regarded as self-evident, and as above logical proof. Yet many theists, learned in psychology and skilled in logic, while holding the existence of God to be an intuitive truth, none the less maintain this truth by logical proofs. We may mistake the intuitive content of a primary truth and assume that to be intuitive which is not really so. Many a child learns that two and three are five before the intuitive faculty begins its activity, particularly in this sphere. The knowledge so acquired is not intuitive. Yet that two and three are five is an intuitive truth. But wherein? Not in the simple knowledge which a child acquires, but in the necessity of this truth which the reason affirms, in the cognition that it is, and must be, a truth in all worlds and for all minds. That things equal to the same thing, or weights equal to the same weight, are equal to one another is an axiomatic truth; but it is its necessary truth that is an intuitive cognition, while a practical knowledge of the simple fact of equality may be acquired in an experimental mode. The point made is that some truths, while intuitional in some of their content, may yet be acquired in an experimental or logical mode. So, while the existence of God may be an immediate datum of the moral and religious consciousness, it may also be a legitimate subject for logical proofs. It is a truth in the affirmation of which the intuitive reason and the logical reason combine. Hence in holding the existence of God to be an immediate cognition of the mind we are not dismissing it from the sphere of logical proofs. . . .

SUFFICIENCY OF THE ATONEMENT

The substitution of Christ in suffering answers for an atonement through a revelation of such moral truths as give the highest ruling power to the divine law. It must, therefore, embody such facts as will make the necessary revelation. Only thus can the atonement have sufficiency. It is proper, therefore, that we specially note some of these facts of atoning value. Authors differ somewhat respecting them. This may arise, at least in part, from a difference in the doctrine. The vital facts are clear in the light of Scripture.

I. THE HOLINESS OF CHRIST

1. *A Necessary Element.* — A criminal cannot be a proper mediator. Whoever dishonors himself and the law by his own transgression is thereby disqualified for the office of mediation in behalf of a criminal. If human government does not require moral perfection for such office, still, the mediator must not be amenable to penalty on his own account. And the higher his personal righteousness and moral worth, the more valuable will be his mediation as the ground of forgiveness. As a mediation, so accepted, must inculcate respect for law and enforce obedience to its requirements, so, much depends upon the moral worth of the mediator.

And Christ, in the atonement, must be without sin and clear of all its penal liabilities. He must be personally holy. . . .

II. HIS GREATNESS

1. *An Element of Atoning Value.* —Whoever needs the service of a mediator is concerned to find one of the highest character and rank attainable. The minister of the law vested with the pardoning power is officially concerned therein. For the value of the mediation is not in its personal influence with him, but from its rectoral relations. He may already be personally disposed to clemency, but lacks a proper ground for its exercise, so that law shall not suffer in its honor and authority. Such ground is furnished in the greatness and rank of the mediator. And the higher these qualities, the more complete is the ground of forgiveness, or the more effective the support of law in all its rectoral offices. There is a philosophy in these facts, as manifest in our previous discussions. Beyond this, the case may be appealed to the common judgment. . . .

III. HIS VOLUNTARINESS

1. *A Necessary Fact.* —The injustice of a coerced substitution of one in place of another would deprive it of all benefit in atonement for sin. But when the sacrifice is in the free choice of the substitute, its voluntariness not only gives full place to every other element of atoning value, but is itself such an element.

2. *Christ a Voluntary Substitute.* —On this fact the Scriptures leave us no reason for any question. And the frequency and fullness of their utterances respecting the freedom of Christ in the work of redemption give to that freedom all the certainty and significance which its truth requires. It is true that the Father gave the Son; that he sent him to be the Saviour of the world; that he spared him not, but delivered him up for us all; that he prepared for him a body for his priestly sacrifice in atonement for sin: but it is none the less true that in all this the mind of the Son was at one with the mind of the Father; that he freely and gladly chose the incarnation in order to our redemption; that he loved us and gave himself for us, an offering and a sacrifice to God; that, with full power over his own life, he freely surrendered it in our redemption. And the fact of this freedom is carried back of his incarnation and atoning suffering to the Son in his essential divinity and in his glory with the Father.

3. *The Atoning Value.*—The voluntariness of Christ crowns with its grace all the marvelous facts of his redeeming work. His atoning sacrifice, while in the purest free-willing, was at once in an infinite beneficence toward us, and in an infinite filial love and obedience toward his Father. And the will of the Father, in obedience to which the sacrifice is made, so far from limiting its atoning worth, provides for its highest sufficiency by opening such a sphere for the beneficence and filial obedience of the Son. Both have infinite worth with the Father. So he regards them, not in any commercial valuation, but as intrinsically good. Now forgiveness on such a ground is granted only on account of what is most precious with God, and therefore a vindication of his justice and holiness, of his rectoral honor and authority, in the salvation of repenting souls.

IV. HIS DIVINE SONSHIP

1. *Sense of Atoning Value.*—The nearer a mediator stands in the relations of friendship to an offended person the more persuasive will his intercession be. But this is a matter of more personal influence, not of rectoral service. The person offended is regarded simply in his personal disposition, not as a minister of the law, with the obligations of his office; and, so far, the case has more affinity with the satisfaction theory than with the governmental. According to this theory God needs no vicarious sacrifice for his personal propitiation. His need is for some provision which will render the forgiveness of sin consistent with his own honor and authority as moral Ruler, and with the good of his subjects. Hence, while we find an element of atoning value in the divine Sonship of Christ, we find it not in a matter of personal influence with the Father, but on a principle of rectoral service. This value lies in the moral worth which the Sonship of Christ gives to his redeeming work in the appreciation of the Father. The nature of it will further appear under the next heading.

2. *Measure of Value.*—The divine filiation of the Redeemer furnishes an element of great value in the atonement. This may be illustrated in connection with two facts of his Sonship.

The divine filiation of the Redeemer is original and singular. It is such as to be the ground of the Father's infinite love to his Son. On nothing are the Scriptures more explicit than on the fact of this love. Therein we have the ground of the Father's infinite appreciation of the redeeming work of the Son. And the truth returns, that forgiveness is granted only on the ground of what is most precious with the Father. By all this preciousness, as revealed in the light of the Father's love to the Son, his redemptive mediation, as the only and necessary ground of forgiveness, gives utterance to the authority of the divine law, and the obligation of its maintenance; to the sacredness of moral rights and interests, and the imperative requirement of their protection; to the evil of sin, and the urgency of its restriction. These are the very facts which give the highest and best ruling power to the divine law. And thus we have an element of sufficiency in the atonement.

The redeeming love of God toward us is most clearly seen in the light of his love for his own Son. Only in this view do we read the meaning of its divine utterances. Why did the Father sacrifice the Son of his love in our redemption? It could not have been from any need of personal propitiation toward us. The redeeming sacrifice, itself the fruit of his love to us, is proof to the contrary. He gave his Son to die for us that he might reach us in the grace of forgiveness and salvation. Why then did he so sacrifice the Son of his love? The only reason lies in the moral interests concerned, and which, in the case of forgiveness, required an atonement in their protection. But for his regard for these rights and interests, and, therefore, for the sacredness and authority of his law as the necessary means of their protection, he might have satisfied the yearnings of his compassion toward us in a mere administrative forgiveness. This he could not do consistently with either his goodness or his rectoral obligation. And rather than surrender the interests which his law must protect he delivers up his own Son to suffering and death. Therefore, in this great sacrifice—infinitely great because of his love for his Son, and therein so revealed— in this great sacrifice, and with all the emphasis of its greatness, God makes declaration of an infinite regard for the interests and ends of his moral government, and of an immutable purpose to maintain them. This declaration, in all the force of its divine verities, goes to the support of his government, and gives the highest honor and ruling power to his law, while forgiveness is granted to repenting sinners.

V. HIS HUMAN BROTHERHOOD

1. *Mediation must Express an Interest.* — A stranger to a condemned person, and without reason for any special interest in his case, could not be accepted as a mediator in his behalf. A pardon granted on such ground would, in respect of all ends of government, be the same as one granted on mere sovereignty. The case is clearly different when, on account of intimate relations of friendship, or other special reasons of

interest, the mediation is an expression of profound sympathy. Forgiveness on such an intercession is granted, not for any thing trivial or indifferent, and so evincing an indifference to the law, but only for what is regarded as real, and a sufficient justification of the forgiveness. This gives support to law. It loses nothing of respect in the common judgment, nothing of its ruling force. And the profounder the sympathy of the mediator, the greater is the rectoral service of his mediation as the ground of forgiveness.

2. *The Principle in Atonement.*—Christ appropriates the principle by putting himself into the most intimate relation with us. In the incarnation he clothes himself in our nature, partakes of our flesh and blood, and enters into brotherhood with us. Herein is the reality and the revelation of a profound interest in his mediation. The love and sympathy of this brotherhood he carries into the work of atonement. They are voiced in his tears and sorrows, in the soul agonies of Gethsemane, in the bitter outcryings of Calvary, and are still voiced in his intercessory prayers in heaven. Men and angels, in a spontaneous moral judgment, pronounce such a mediation a sufficient ground of forgiveness, and vindicate the rectitude. The divine law suffers no dishonor nor loss of ruling power. Thus the human brotherhood of Christ gives sufficiency to his atonement....

MILTON S. TERRY

M ilton S. Terry (1846–1914) was a professor of biblical studies at Garrett Biblical Institute. His *Biblical Hermeneutics: A Treatise on the Interpretation of the Old and New Testaments* (1883) was a major contribution to American Methodism's acceptance of the historical-critical study of the Bible. Under the guidance of Terry and others, such as Hinckley G. Mitchell (1846–1920), Episcopal Methodism found the new approach to Scripture an acceptable way of investigating the biblical message. There was resistance in some quarters, but by the First World War Methodist theology was characterized by its utilization of these critical resources. The presentation by Terry indicates some central issues in the discussion during the period of transition. The chief points of controversy were the authority of Scripture, the relation of the Word of God to the words of the Bible, the nature of historical change relative to the unchanging will and Word of God, and the authenticity of human transmission of the biblical text. The selection included is a pamphlet, *Methodism and Biblical Criticism* (New York: Eaton and Mains, Cincinnati: Jennings and Graham, 1905).

METHODISM AND BIBLICAL CRITICISM

The chief characteristic of Methodism, as an epochal religious movement of modern Christianity, is the emphasis it has put upon self-conscious spiritual life. "Our main doctrines, which include all the rest," said John Wesley, "are Repentance, Faith and Holiness. The first of these we account, as it were, the porch of religion; the next is the door; the third is religion itself." At Wesley's first Conference, in 1744, the first two days were devoted to the question of what should be the chief staple of Methodist preaching, and the unanimous conclusion was that they should keep clear of all theological subtlety, and make prominent the doctrines of repentance, faith, justification, sanctification, and the witness of the Spirit. And this has been the glory of Arminian Methodism for over a hundred and fifty years. Wesley's thirteen discourses on the Sermon on the Mount declare that wonderful sermon of our Lord to be "the sum of true religion." And I may add that first, last, fundamental and positive, the source of the life and power of Methodism, is her firm immediate hold on the Supernatural. Her abiding watchword for living and for dying is, "The best of all is, GOD IS WITH US."

Another notable feature of Methodism is the broad, catholic spirit it has shown. Among John Wesley's sermons we find one entitled "A Caution Against Bigotry." It is immediately followed by another on "The Catholic Spirit." This providential founder of Methodism was accustomed to boast of the liberality of Methodism. We do not impose human opinions, he often argued, as a test of membership in our societies. "One condition, and one only, is required, a real desire to save their souls. Where that is, it is enough." In a letter to the Rev. Mr. Venn he says: "I impose my notions upon none. I will be bold to say there is no man living farther from it. I make no opinion the term of union with any man. I think and let think. What I want is holiness of heart and life. They who have this are my brother, sister and mother." In his *Journal* of May, 1778, he writes: "There is no other religious society under heaven which requires of men, in order to their admission into it, nothing but a desire to save their souls. The Methodists alone do not insist on your holding this or that opinion, but they think and let think. I do not know any other religious society, either ancient or modern, wherein such liberty of conscience is now allowed, since the age of the apostles. Here is our glorying; and a glorying peculiar to us."

But it must not be supposed from these utterances that either Wesley or his followers made light of fundamental truths. In his sermon on the "Catholic Spirit" he declares that the true catholic spirit is "not speculative latitudinarianism. It is not an indifference to all opinions: this is the spawn of hell, not the offspring of heaven." It was agreed at the first conference that the great, practical, fundamental doctrines of Christianity should be the main substance of the Methodist preaching and teaching. The simplicity and self-evidencing authority of their principal doctrines, and the conviction that such truths needed only a fair hearing to be generally accepted, made those fathers of Methodism perfectly willing to allow all reasonable liberties of thought.

What I wish here and now to note is that this wide liberty of opinion,—the boast and glory of John Wesley in the organization of his

societies,—*was at that time a new thing under the sun*. The whole world
was publicly challenged to show another religious body like it under the
wide heaven. Other churches had their prescriptive and proscriptive
creeds, and confessions, and dogmatic tests of membership. But Wesley
was gifted with the spiritual discernment to anticipate Neander in con-
tending that "it is the *heart* that makes the theologian." His sole great
question was, "Is thy heart herein as my heart? If it be, give me thy
hand."

From this rapid glance at the fundamental and characteristic position
of Methodism as to spiritual life and catholicity I pass to a notice of the
pre-eminence it has always assigned the Holy Scriptures as the supreme
rule of faith and practice. Originating within the Church of England, it
naturally and most loyally accepted the declaration of the sixth of the
historic 39 Articles, which declares that "the Holy Scriptures contain all
things necessary to salvation; so that whatsoever is not read therein, nor
may be proved thereby, is not to be required of any man that it should be
believed as an article of faith." In his sermon on "God's Vineyard,"
Wesley says that the first four Oxford Methodists were each of them "a
man of one book. God taught them all to make his word a lantern to their
feet and a light in all their paths. They had one, and only one, rule of
judgment with regard to all their tempers, words and actions, namely,
the oracles of God. They were one and all determined to be Bible
Christians." There is, then, and there can be no question as to the high
place the Bible holds in the estimate of Methodism.

But when we ask, Who is the authorized interpreter, or who are the
authorized interpreters, of these scriptures for the Methodist world,
what shall we say? Is John Wesley our Pope to pronounce *ex cathedra*
what critical opinions must be accepted as to the origin and composition
of the different books of the Bible? Are his Notes on the New Testament
and his other expositions a finality for us in exposition? Must we be open
to censure if we decline to accept all he affirms in his sermon on "The
Cause and Cure of Earthquakes?" May one not be a good, loyal
Methodist, sound in doctrine and discipline, and yet reject the teaching
of Wesley in his famous sermon on the brute creation, that by reason of
the sin of Adam the whole animal world has been made subject to pain
and all manner of evils, and even insects and worms lost the high intelligence they previously possessed, but that they are all hereafter to be
delivered from this deplorable condition, and that when man is made
equal to angels, the kid and the cow and the wolf may be made equal to
what we are now?

Now, in the full light of the actual teachings of the founders of Methodism and of the relevant facts of some four generations of Methodist history, we may safely affirm the proposition that, aside from those fundamental truths which formed the staple of Methodist preaching, there exists no prescriptive creed, confession, law, rule or standard of Methodism which defines or determines our liberty of thought and opinion on matters of biblical criticism and interpretation. Accepting the canonical Scriptures, both of the Old Testament and the New, as given by inspiration of God, and profitable for comfort, for teaching, for reproof, for correction and for instruction in righteousness, all questions of higher and of lower criticism are to be treated as matters of personal opinion. Whether it be a question of criticism or interpretation on which all the Methodist fathers agree, or a question on which they differ, no one among us, whether he be minister or layman, is necessarily shut up to any such opinion of the fathers. To contend for the contrary of this statement would seem to be the extreme of presumption. The question of the authorship of any particular book, or set of books, is not a matter of essential doctrine. Every Methodist commentator on the Epistle to the Hebrews, so far as I know, from John Wesley to D. D. Whedon, maintains the Pauline authorship. But must that uniformity of opinion be therefore regarded as a finality of investigation, so that if one, following the steady drift of scholarly opinion for the last forty years, finds that no distinguished commentary on Hebrews, except Whedon's, that has appeared for half a century past, accepts that older view, he is not at liberty to follow the all but unanimous modern opinion because Wesley, and Clarke, and Benson, and Coke, and Watson, and Whedon thought otherwise? Surely on such a question, and with such facts before him, no one is bound even by the unanimous opinion of revered fathers, when upon careful examination he discovers other views and other arguments of more convincing and more satisfactory character.

But if on critical questions in which the fathers were agreed we claim the right of differing from them in opinion, much more may we claim that liberty on matters wherein they differed among themselves. Let us first notice what Wesley says about himself as an expositor of the New Testament. His "Explanatory Notes upon The New Testament" occupy no secondary place among the Methodist standards. If there is anything of the nature of authoritative interpretation of any part of the Bible among the Methodists, it is these "Notes" of Wesley on the New Testament. And yet, in the Preface of his work, the author observes three things which we do well to consider. 1. First he expresses his own deep sense of inability and want of learning, experience, and wisdom for the important task. 2. Then he advises the reader that his *notes* were not principally designed for men of learning, who are provided with many other helps; but he writes for plain, unlettered men. 3. He furthermore informs us that he has appropriated most of his comments from a work of Bengel, a German professor and critic, who had died some three years before the date of his Preface to the "Notes."

Let us now ponder for a moment the significance of these utterances of Wesley as against the supposition that a faithful and loyal Methodist preacher is not at liberty to differ from the views of the founder of Methodism in matters of biblical criticism and interpretation. No matter what new discoveries have been made since 1754, no matter what contributions have been made to biblical science during a hundred and fifty years, no matter how clear and convincing other views than those of Wesley have become to scores and hundreds of "men of long and deep experience in the ways and word of God," at whose feet Wesley says in that same Preface he would like "to sit and to learn," no matter if half or two thirds of the best known scholars of Christendom outside of Methodism offer other critical opinions which they believe better conserve the views of Christ and of Paul, and "justify the ways of God to man;" no matter if all the world think otherwise, no honest Methodist can think otherwise and continue as a consistent member or minister of the Methodist Church! I am slow to believe that we have any among us who would seriously presume to maintain a position so unreasonable. What! After all that we have quoted from Wesley himself, his boast of the liberty of opinion enjoyed in his societies, his emphatic repetition of the phrase "think and let think," and in spite of his disclaimer in the Preface to his New Testament "Notes" of any superior wisdom and ability as an expounder of the Scriptures, shall we rise up in these later days and forbid the liberty which he extolled?

We turn next to examine a few specimens of Wesley's critical opinions. In his first note on the New Testament, speaking of the genealogy of Jesus Christ and its difficulties as compared with that of Luke, he observes that "if there were any difficulties which could not easily be removed, they would rather affect the Jewish tables than the credit of the evangelists." "Nor was it needful that they should correct the mistakes, if there were any." He further argues that, as their chief aim was to show "that Jesus was of the family from which the promised seed was to come," these New Testament genealogies, even if they contained errors, would have "had more weight with the Jews for the purpose than if alterations had been made by inspiration itself." I cannot but imagine what a turmoil would be made in some quarters if only some radical "higher critic" should publish such a statement as this. For this very first comment of John Wesley on the New Testament involves the following propositions: (1) The Jewish Tables of Old Testament genealogy may contain some mistakes. (2) Such mistakes would not invalidate but might even be a help in accomplishing the purpose of the evangelists with Jewish readers. (3) Even divine inspiration itself employed in correcting the records would have been less effectual in influencing the Jews in this matter. (4) Would it not logically follow that, if any errors exist in the Old Testament records, and if they can be made to serve a good purpose, it may be better even for divine inspiration to let them stand for such supposable good uses rather than correct them?

In the textual criticism of the New Testament Wesley did not hesitate to make changes where occasion seemed to him to require it. He tells us in his Preface that he embodied in his text those various readings which Bengel had shown to have a vast majority of ancient copies and translations on their side. But as one noteworthy example of his following the great German critic into error, observe what he says about the text of the "three heavenly witnesses" in John V, 7: "What Bengelius has advanced concerning the authority of the controverted verse will abundantly satisfy any impartial person." The same opinion is in substance repeated in his sermon "On the Trinity," which he bases on this questionable passage. Coke and Benson adopt the view of Wesley, but Adam Clarke, who stands pre-eminent as critic and commentator among the older Methodists, tells us that this famous text "is wanting in every manuscript of this epistle written before the invention of printing, one excepted. It is wanting in both the Syriac, all the Arabic, Ethiopic, Coptic, Sahadic, Armenian, Slavonian; in a word, in all the ancient versions but the Vulgate; and even of this version many of the most ancient and correct manuscripts have it not." In Dr. Whedon's commentary on the passage, published 24 years ago, we read: "Scholars are agreed, at the present day, that this entire verse is not genuine; being a late interpolation and not the words of St. John." In the Revised Version of our Bible this text is omitted, and there is not an intimation even in the margin that it ever existed. . . .

Wesley's comments on the Psalms are comparatively few and meager, but we should make mention of the fact that in his "Sunday Service of the Methodists in North America" he took great liberty in abridging the Psalter, and he wrote in the Preface: "Many psalms are left out, and many parts of others, as being highly improper for the mouths of a Christian congregation." In his Preface to the Psalms he observes that these ancient songs of Israel are not all from David, but by many different authors of various times, some in the time of the Babylonian exile.

142

It is notorious that Adam Clarke was very bold in questioning the Davidic authorship of the 23d and 51st Psalms, which have been all but universally attributed to the great king of Judah. He declares his opinion that the 23d psalm was written after the captivity, and he cites Bishop Horsley and Dr. Kennicott to show that the title to psalm 51 is misplaced, and that it must have been written during the captivity. He is very positive in the conviction that, whether the title be misplaced or not, the last two verses of the psalm do not fit the subject of the preceding verses nor the times of David. They are rather a prayer of some one of the captives in Babylon for the redemption of Zion and the rebuilding of Jerusalem. It is also a noteworthy fact that Clarke questioned the Solomonic authorship of Ecclesiastes, pointing to the fact that the style is that of writers who lived after the exile, and declaring his opinion that the attempts to deny this are often trifling and generally ineffectual. . . .

The foregoing facts have been presented to show the glaring impropriety, not to say the absurdity, of anyone now pretending that we, earnest and loyal Methodists of the twentieth century, are not at liberty to accept the interpretations of Scripture and the critical views prevalent in our time, if they are seen to differ from those of the founders and fathers of Methodism. Observe, it is no question of any of the great practical truths of Arminian Methodist theology that we are here discussing. There has never been in the entire history of our Arminian Methodism any considerable dispute over matters of fundamental doctrine. Our record in this respect is that of a beautiful and glorious unity of faith. No doctrine of religion enunciated in our 25 Articles, or in our General Rules, or in any other recognized standard, is compromised by the differences of opinion among the fathers, or among the sons, on such matters of biblical criticism as we have been presenting. If any one is persuaded in his mind that Adam Clarke's views on a critical question are preferable to those of Wesley, he ought to feel at full liberty to adopt them. He may with equal liberty prefer to abide by the views of Wesley or some other. That is his right as an honest Methodist, and his plain duty as a conscientious Christian. And if we find that on some critical questions the drift of opinion is away from the views universally accepted in Wesley's time, and contrary to those maintained by all the early Methodists, no faithful student of the Holy Scriptures should feel himself tied up to old opinions when he sees or believes them to be superseded by a better exposition. . . .

It is a noteworthy fact that Wesley put the personal experience of the witness of the Spirit above all other evidences of Christianity. He maintained that the conversion of a soul to God is essentially miraculous. "I suppose," he writes, "that all who allow there is any such thing believe it to be supernatural. And what the difference is between a supernatural and a miraculous work, I am yet to learn." It was the prevailing custom of the orthodox apologetics of Wesley's time to lay stress first of all on the "external evidences" so called, especially the historicity of the miracles recorded in the Bible. In fact, the main argument in the Deistic controversies of the eighteenth century rested upon the question of the traditional genuineness and authenticity of the books which recorded the miracles and the prophecies. But nothing in all the writings of John Wesley is more remarkable than what we read in his famous "Letter to Dr. Conyers Middleton," where he argues and insists that the internal witness of the Spirit is of a higher grade than any external and traditional testimony. He boldly declares that what he "experiences in his own breast" is of greater weight than anything which appeals to him merely from without. And so he contrasts the two in the following manner:

1. First, he argues, traditional evidence is weakened by length of time; it must pass through many hands, in a succession of ages. But no length of time can possibly affect the strength of this internal evidence.

2. Traditional evidence is extremely complicated and taxes the brains of men of strong and clear understanding. But the internal experience is so plain and simple that a child may feel all its force.

3. Tradition stands a great way off, and gives account of what happened long ago. The inward evidence is intimately present, at all times, in all places. "It is nigh thee, in thy mouth and in thy heart."

4. Even if it were possible for the historic foundation of Christianity to be shaken (which of course Wesley nowhere concedes), still he contends that the internal evidence would remain firm and unshaken.

5. "I have been sometimes almost inclined to believe," he writes, "that the wisdom of God has, in most later ages, permitted the external evidence of Christianity to be more or less clogged and incumbered for this very end, that men (of reflection especially) might not altogether rest there, but be constrained to look into themselves also, and attend to the light shining in their hearts."

6. "Without this I cannot but doubt whether they can long maintain their cause." More stress, he urges, must be put on the internal evidence. It will be an advantage to the Christian cause, and "perhaps the speediest and the only effectual way of bringing all reasonable Deists to be Christians." Thus he puts his great emphasis on the intrinsic value of the Christian faith, and asks: "What reasonable assurance can you have of things whereof you have no personal experience?"

In all this we cannot but note how remarkably John Wesley anticipated the trend of modern critical thought in placing the internal above the external evidences of Christianity. He thus adopted in substance the same position and argument as the late Professor Bruce, who says: "It must be confessed that miracles cannot be offered as evidences of Christianity now with the confidence with which they were employed for this purpose by the apologists of the past age. Men do not now believe in Christ because of his miracles; they rather believe in the miracles because they have first believed in Christ. For such believers Christ is his own witness, who accredits everything connected with him: scripture, prophecy, miracle. Those who are in this happy position need no help from apologists." . . .

In like manner Wesley maintained the necessity of personal inspiration of every true believer to understand the deep things of God. In his letter to the Rev. Mr. Potter he argues that one must have "a particular and immediate inspiration before he can either understand, or preach, or live the gospel." "But," says Mr. Potter, "the Scriptures are a complete and sufficient rule. Therefore, to what purpose could any further inspiration serve? The supposed need of it is highly injurious to the written word." To which Mr. Wesley replies: "High sounding words! But, blessed be God, they are only *brutum fulmen* (empty sound); they make much noise, but do not wound. 'To what purpose could any further inspiration serve?' Answer yourself: 'To enlighten the understanding and to rectify the will.' Else be the Scriptures ever so complete, they will not save your soul. . . . When you say yourself, 'The Spirit is to teach us all things, and to guide us into all truth,' judge you, whether this is to 'explain, or to supply, the written word.'"

And so, in one way and another, did that good man of God emphasize the truth that the Scriptures are not an end in themselves, but a means to an end. And that end is the cultivation of spiritual life. And this has been the accepted view of our Methodism from the beginning. We must seek the divine illumination of the Spirit in order to a proper and profitable understanding of the Holy Scriptures.

I have not been able to find in Wesley's works any dogma or theory of biblical inspiration. Bengel's note on 2 Tim. III, 16, is: "Scripture was divinely inspired, not merely when it was written, God breathing through the writers, but also while it is being read, God breathing through the Scripture, and the Scripture breathing him." Wesley's note is as follows: "The Spirit of God not only once inspired those who wrote it, but continually inspires, supernaturally assists, those that read it with earnest prayer. Hence it is so profitable for doctrine, for instruction, etc."

There is nothing in our Articles of Religion which so much as names a theory of inspiration, but the fifth article affirms (not the inerrancy, nor the infallibility, but) the SUFFICIENCY of the Holy Scriptures for a knowledge of salvation. . . .

When, now, it is asked what the attitude of modern Methodism should be toward modern biblical criticism, our answer is, That which it has been from the beginning, and that which has been our boast and glory from the time of Wesley until now: "We think and let think." We act according to the apostolic precept: "Prove all things; hold fast that which is good." Among the things now quite generally maintained by biblical scholars are the following opinions touching the various books of the Bible:

1. The Bible is not so much a single book as it is a great library, a collection of books of very different dates and authorship.

2. Of a considerable number of the books the authorship is unknown, and opinions vary as to their origin and relative value.

3. Many of these books are of composite origin. The composite character of the Pentateuch, of Joshua, Judges, Samuel, Kings, Chronicles, Ezra, Nehemiah, the books of Isaiah, Zechariah and Proverbs, is quite generally conceded.

4. The compilation of the Book of Psalms, as it now appears in our Bibles, was the work of the post-exile leaders of the Jewish people.

5. The biblical witers have employed nearly all the forms of literary composition which appear in the other great literatures of the world. We find various styles of prose writing, and also poetry, parable, riddle, symbol, fable and proverb. We also find in these scriptures various types and grades of religious thought.

6. No divine authority, either of Jesus, or of the prophets or apostles, has ever fixed the limits of the biblical canon.

7. The contents of these Scriptures, taken as a whole (whether one accept the Palestinean or the Alexandrian canon of the Old Testament), furnish us with a priceless record of the progressive revelation of God in and through the Jewish people. Therefore we call these holy scriptures "oracles of God;" the things which "God spoke of old time unto the fathers in the prophets by divers portions and in divers manners." . . .

I cannot better close this paper than by citing the words of the Rev. Dr. W. T. Davison, a well known leader among the Wesleyans of England, and late president of the British Conference, in an article which appeared in "The Methodist Times" of February 4, 1904. He therein expressed his general approval of Canon Driver's recent work on the book of Genesis, and declares "that we cannot read these early chapters of the Bible precisely as our fathers did. The literalist who believes that by a miracle the serpent spoke in the garden, and that the deluge covered the whole globe, is apt to assume that it is he alone who accepts the Bible as true, whereas his principles of interpretation are really at fault. . . . Methodism will not be behindhand in this work (of criticism and interpretation). Rashness is not characteristic of us as a community, and rashness in such matters is little short of wickedness. But timidity is not goodness, and obscurantism is not helpful or kind. The Spirit of truth who inspired the writers of the Sacred Scriptures, and who guided our fathers to read and expound them, will still guide us as we seek to know and teach the whole truth, and nothing but the truth. And it is written—the Master himself has said it—'The truth shall make you free.'"

PART III

CHANGING DIRECTION

T he turn of the twentieth century brought a new era in Methodist thought. Protestant liberal emphases became characteristic of Methodist Episcopal theology. The most important person in this transition was Borden Parker Bowne, who provided a generative philosophical foundation for theological construction. Bowne also represented a heightened sensitivity to contemporary culture. He developed his thought in relation to reigning cultural themes such as personality, process, and moral character. Albert C. Knudson's article on Henry C. Sheldon describes some of the major alterations that were taking place. Following the lead of Bowne, along with Sheldon and Knudson, were Olin A. Curtis, Edgar S. Brightman, Harris F. Rall, Georgia Harkness, and L. Harold DeWolf. Deeply rooted in personalistic philosophy, these thinkers combined a rational defense of Christian faith with a devoted service to Christian morality. The readings which follow set forth dominant themes of this theological stream as well as the particular interests of the individual writers.

BORDEN PARKER BOWNE

B orden Parker Bowne (1847–1910) was the most influential Methodist Episcopal theologian at the beginning of the twentieth century. Born into a pious Methodist home in New Jersey, he possessed unusual intellectual ability and graduated as valedictorian of his class at New York University. He stayed on to earn a master's degree then entered the parish ministry. He continued his education through two years of study in Germany and France. In Germany he was primarily influenced by Rudolf H. Lotze and Hermann Ulrici upon whose foundations he developed his philosophical position of personal idealism, or, as he designated it, *personalism*. Bowne always remained a layman. In 1876 he joined the faculty at Boston University and established the most interdisciplinary, inclusive and important school of Methodist theology in North America. Among his more important books are: *The Philosophy of Herbert Spencer* (1874) and *Studies In Theism* (1879).

Bowne attempted to mediate between his Methodist inheritance and his cultural context. He responded positively to critical study in Bible, history and philosophy; he held an optimistic view of human nature and stressed the themes of God's immanence and moral character. He also followed a vision of service to God's earthly kingdom and the goal of moral achievement among human beings. From these perspectives he reinterpreted Methodist theology and set it upon a new course of development. "The Immanence of God" is from *The Immanence of God* (Boston and New York: Houghton, Mifflin and Co., 1905), pp. 1–4, 116–128, 139–153.

THE IMMANENCE OF GOD

The progress of thought is slow, but there is progress nevertheless. In every field of life men have had painfully to find their way. In religion man has always had some sense, more or less dim, of an alliance with the unseen and the eternal, but it has taken ages to organize and clarify it and bring it to clear apprehension and rational expression. As men begin on the plane of the senses, this unseen existence has been mainly conceived in sense terms, and hence has always been exposed to destructive criticism from the side of philosophy. The crude anthropomorphism of early thought invited and compelled the criticism. Again, this vague sense of the unseen has always been confronted by the apparent realities and finalities of the outer world; and in comparison with them it has often seemed unreal and fictitious. Matter we know and things we know; but God and spirit, what and where are they? When thus skeptically accosted by the senses, they sometimes fade away. Hence religious faith has always had a double difficulty to combat, arising from its alliance with sense forms, on the one hand, and from sense dogmatism, on the other. The alliance was perpetually plunging religion into destructive anthropomorphism; and the sense dogmatism led to a frequent rejection of religion as baseless, because spiritual realities lie beyond seeing and hearing. But we are slowly outgrowing this. Religious thought is gradually casting off its coarse anthropomorphism; and philosophic criticism is fast discrediting the shallow dogmatism of sense thinking, with its implication of mechanical and materialistic naturalism. Thus religious thought is progressing; and the result to which all lines of reflection are fast converging is the ancient word of inspiration, that in God we live and move and have our being. This is at once the clear indication of thought and the assured conviction of faith. In this conclusion, moreover, both religion and philosophy find their only sure foundation.

This doctrine we call the divine immanence; by which we mean that God is the omnipresent ground of all finite existence and activity. The world, alike of things and of spirits, is nothing existing and acting on its own account, while God is away in some extra-sidereal region, but it continually depends upon and is ever upheld by the ever-living, ever-present, ever-working God.

This divine immanence has important bearings on both speculative and religious problems, and contains the solution of many traditional difficulties. To trace this doctrine into its implications is the aim of the discussion. The thought will centre on four leading points,—God and Nature, God and History, God and the Bible, and God and Religion. On each of these points naturalistic and deistic dogmatism has long wrought confusion and mischief.

Thus far we have considered the bearing of the divine immanence upon our thought of nature, history, and the Bible. We have seen that it discharges the false or "bald" naturalism of popular thought, and dispels the fears of naturalism which haunt so much religious discussion. Instead of a self-sufficient mechanical nature, it gives us a supernatural natural, that is, a natural which forever depends on the divine will and purpose, and a natural supernatural, that is, a divine causality which proceeds according to orderly methods in the realization of its aims. We have now to consider the significance of this doctrine for the religious life.

And here, too, popular thought has been confused greatly by the traditional misconception of the natural. As God was supposed to be in nature and history only, or at least mainly, in the form of signs and wonders, so he was supposed to be in the soul only, or at least mainly, in the form of manifestations of a somewhat anarchic and prodigy-working type. And as the familiar laws of nature were supposed to represent no divine purpose, but only a mere determination of a blind and unpurposed mechanism, so the familiar laws of life and mind, and all the normal workings of human nature, were supposed to be unrelated to any divine purpose, and were dismissed as "merely natural." Of course, in both cases, by the logic of the situation it was necessary to look for the divine in the extraordinary and anomalous. And the dealers in such things verily thought that they were defending religion, and never suspected that they were really the victims of a shallow philosophy. The uproar over Dr. Bushnell's "Christian Nurture" fifty years ago is a good illustration. Many ark-savers experienced the severest alarms at what seemed to them an ignoring of the supernatural.

Now here again the divine immanence helps us. We are in our Father's house and Father's hands; and though we may not be able always to trace his presence or interpret every feature of his work, yet his will is being done. And this is really what faith seeks for in this matter. The soul longs to find God, to believe that it has not fallen into life headlong, to feel that it is in the hands of him that made it, and that he is ever near. The religious soul fears naturalism because nature seems to be a barrier between God and itself, and to thrust him into a past so distant as to make him doubtful and to put him beyond any real, living, present interest in us. And a naturalism of that sort is to be feared, as in its presence high faith is sure to wither, or cry out in mortal anguish. It is not nature or law that the soul fears, but nature or law without God in it. It is not the burdens and distresses of life that oppress and depress us, but burdens and distresses that spring from nothing and lead to nothing. If they are appointed by our Father for our discipline and development, we can bear them with good courage and unrepining hearts; we break down only when we view them as the blind raging of a storm. Now from this distress the belief in the divine immanence saves us. He is in the darkness as well as in the light, in failure and sorrow as well as in success and joy, in death as well as in life. He is the God of all things, and is God over all things, and is blessed forevermore. This view, we repeat, is what religious thought really desires to reach in its opposition to naturalism and its emphasis on the supernatural. Its real aim is to find God, not prodigies; but it errs and strays from the way because of the crude philosophy which banishes God from the natural and finds him only in the strange, the anomalous, the chaotic. And this illiteracy culminates in the fancy that this is the only religious view.

But after we had driven off false naturalism from the philosophy of nature and history, we found a place for a true naturalism. Similarly here, after we have driven off false naturalism from the spiritual life, we find a place for a true naturalism. In other words, the conviction that we live and move and have our being in God does not decide the form and mode of God's work in us; and to learn this, we must fall back on experience.

The great error of religious thought in this matter is the same as its error at the corresponding point in its thought of God in nature. It has sought to walk by sight rather than by thought and faith. Hence the conception has been almost exclusively thaumaturgic. A changed life, a clean heart, a strengthened will, a deeper moral insight, and a purer devotion would be very poor marks of a divine indwelling in comparison with some psychological exaltation which, by its strangeness or excess, might impress persons of wonder-loving mental habit. Hence, again, there has been a very general tendency in the history of the church to look upon emotional ebulliencies, anarchic raptures, anomalous and spectacular experiences, as the truly classical manifestations of religion, while the interaction of religious feeling, intellect, and moral will has been viewed as a falling away from the highest and only classical form. To guard against this error, we must analyze our problem somewhat at length.

And first of all we must bear in mind that it is not a question of the reality and necessity of God's work in the soul in order that we may attain unto the life of the spirit. Upon occasion we should steadfastly deny any Pelagian self-sufficiency of the human will, and that for both philosophical and religious reasons. It is simply a question respecting the form of this divine co-working. Is it natural or supernatural?

This question at once reveals the fact that these terms have peculiar meanings in religious speech. Natural is often used to mean the sensuous in distinction from the spiritual, as in the text, "That was not first which is spiritual, but that which is natural." Sometimes it means that which is possible to man's unaided powers; and the affirmation of a supernatural means a power from above which reinforces our weakness. And sometimes natural means that in which an order of law can be observed and traced. It is in this last sense that we use it here. We are far enough from affirming that man is sufficient unto himself in the spiritual life. Such a view is a mark of gross philosophic and religious illiteracy. The professional defender of the faith seldom discriminates these widely differing meanings, and thus begins, continues, and ends in confusion.

God's work in nature and history, we have seen, is not against law, but through law. The thaumaturgic element, in any case, is a vanishing factor in comparison. A moment's reflection convinces us that the same must be true of God's work in the soul. It is not against the laws of mind, but through them, that God realizes his purposes in us. This is an absolute condition of our mental and moral sanity. If we are to lead a moral and rational life of any sort, there must be an order of life on which we can depend. If religion is not to be an excuse for indolence, we must work out our own salvation. It is indeed God who worketh in us, but he works according to law, and in such a way as to call for all our effort. He gives us spiritual bread as he gives us daily bread. In the latter case the bread supply does not come by any celestial express, but through the springing corn and the ripening harvest; yet it is from God after all. In like manner spiritual blessing is not conferred in any scenic and unmediated fashion, but by power moving along the lines of normal life, and manifesting itself in its products rather than its abnormal methods. And in the case of both physical and spiritual bread, we have to work for it.

The religious life is the last realm to be brought under the notion of law. Law is now a matter of course in physics, astronomy, meteorology, medicine, hygiene, education, but it is very imperfectly apprehended in its religious bearing. In all those subjects we see that there are conditions to which we must conform if we would accomplish our ends. No one would expect to get a harvest by prayer alone, while neglecting to plow and sow. No one would expect to become educated without appropriate labor. But in religion we have not yet learned this lesson. We expect God to work in the spiritual realm immediately and without reference to law. We are simply to ask and receive. To speak of law is to thrust a barrier between the soul and God. To suggest conditions is an act of unfaith. To work for spiritual blessing through the laws God has made is to lean to our own understanding and have confidence in the flesh. Education is the work of man; as for the work of the Spirit, we cannot tell whence it cometh nor whither it goeth. In all this the false naturalism and false

155

supernaturalism of untrained thought are manifest. God's action is supposed to be above and apart from law, rather than through it, or in accordance with it; and religion is supposed to be something apart from living interests, a thing of frames and retreats and special exercises, rather than a spiritual principle for all living, the abiding inspiration of all work.

Religious thought cannot too soon unlearn this false supernaturalism and learn the lesson of law. We must lay to heart and remember that the fact that God worketh in us in no way vacates the rule that we must work out our own salvation. The wise man proceeds in spiritual things as in physical things. In the latter case, he inquires for the laws which rule and adjusts himself to them. In the former case, he asks for the laws of successful and developing life and adjusts himself to them. He avails himself of all his knowledge and of every means of influence in both cases. This we must all do. We must study the order of life, and avail ourselves of all the normal means of influence for developing character and of all the great institutions evolved by humanity on its upward way. We must look upon the family, the school, the social order, the great industrial and commercial activities, as ordinances of God, or as instruments through which he works as certainly as through the church and formal religious exercises. Pray upon the family, the school, the social order, the great industrial and commercial activities, as ordinances of God, or as instruments through which he works as certainly as through the church and formal religious exercises. Prayer and meditation of course will always have their place and function, but they are by no means the only way of reaching God and securing his aid. We must discern the divine presence and agency in life as a whole, and work with him along the natural lines which he has established, in the full faith that thus we are co-workers with God, and that results thus reached are as divine as they would be if reached by some miraculous fiat. The undivineness of the natural is the great heresy of popular religious thought, and a great source of the weakness of the religious life. Good intentions, zeal, and deep religious desire often come to nought from being left to lose themselves in formless religiosity, instead of being directed into normal lines of effort in accordance with human needs and human nature. And there will be no lasting reform in religion until we return to a true naturalism in this matter, recognizing that only God can give the increase, and also that God will give no increase unless we plant and water, and further recognizing the natural order of things as a part of the divine appointment for our spiritual training, and as the field for our life's work. . . .

In his work, "The Varieties of Religious Experience," p. 200, Professor William James gives an interesting passage from Jonathan Edwards which shows that Edwards already understood the influence that suggestion, expectation, and imitation often have in moulding experience. Edwards says:—

> "A rule received and established by common consent has a very great, though to many persons an insensible influence in forming their notions of the process of their own experience. I know very well how they proceed as to this matter, for I have had frequent opportunities of observing their conduct. Very often their experience at first appears like a confused chaos, but then those parts are selected which bear the nearest resemblance to such particular steps as are insisted on; and these are dwelt upon in their thoughts and spoken of from time to time, till they grow more and more conspicuous in their view, and other parts which are neglected grow more and more obscure. Thus what they have experienced is insensibly strained so as to bring it to an exact conformity to the scheme already established in their minds. And it becomes natural also for ministers who have to deal with those who insist upon distinctness and clearness of method, to do so too."—"Treatise on Religious Affections."

Edwards had not the language of modern psychology, but he had recognized the fact of suggestibility and the influence of expectation in the religious field with all clearness. In his works written after the "Great Awakening," one clearly sees a growing conviction on his part that "manifestations" are very uncertain tests of a work of grace. And the only way out of all these confusions is never to aim at "experience," but to aim at righteousness, and find the essential and only sure mark of the divine presence, in a religious sense, in the fruits of the Spirit. And along with the marked and sudden transitions of character which may occur in mature persons of strenuous type, we must make place for a gradual training of the will under the divine education of life, or for quiet, unreflective growth into the kingdom of heaven. Here too the divine immanence helps us. We are no longer compelled to set nature and grace, the secular and the religious, the human and the divine, in mutually exclusive antithesis; but rather find them in mutual penetration.

If some days were ushered in with a mighty bang, and other days came with the quiet of the dawn, we might conceivably have an astronomical school of bangers and one of anti-bangers; and they might so confine their attention to the bang as to forget that the only point of any real importance is to have the day come, with or without a bang. Compared with this, the bang question is insignificant. We have these schools in religious experience, emphasizing the bang or the non-bang and over-looking the only matter of importance, — the dawn of the spiritual day.

This false supernaturalism in the inner religious life of the subject has led to corresponding error in determining religious duty. The result has often been an abstract religiosity and other-worldliness, which has some-times made sad work of the life that now is. Submission to the will of God is indeed the central thing in religion, and its importance cannot be overestimated. Hence religious thought has occupied itself largely with securing this harmony without inquiring what that will is in its positive contents. The result has been a body of determinations, largely negative, and for the rest mainly concerned with the securing of tempers, dispositions, and aspirations supposed to be peculiarly spiritual. When this result is combined with the disastrous separation of the secular from the religious, it leads straight toward asceticism and monasticism. In the Protestant bodies it has led to fixing attention too exclusively on sin and salvation, abstractly conceived, as the matters of supreme importance in religion.

Now this may be good as far as it goes, but it certainly does not go very far. To be sure, submission to the divine will must be secured, if it be wanting; but what is that will for men? After man has returned from his willful wanderings, he is only at the beginning, not the end. Now he must begin to work the will of God. As worldliness consists less in what is done than in the spirit of the doing, so religion consists less in what is done than in the spirit of the doing. Both the worldling and the Chris-tian have to do largely the same things. But the worldling loses himself in the outward and sense life, and fails to relate it to any divine meaning and purpose. The Christian, on the other hand, is in the same sense life, but he relates it to a divine order, and seeks to glorify that life by filling it with courage and devotion. Religion conceived as a specialty, as a matter of prayers and rites and ceremonies, is a minor matter, and one of no great importance; but religion conceived as a principle which knows no distinction of secular and religious, but pervades all life, and perpetually offers unto God in living sacrifice as its continual spiritual worship the daily round with all its interests and activities sanctified by the filial spirit, — this is the ideal of humanity. So long as we form any lower conception of religion than this, so long will religion be only one interest among many, and life will lack its true unity.

This I conceive to be the deepest aim of Christianity. The forgiveness of sins is essential, but it is only introductory. The forms of worship and the practices of piety are important, but they are only instrumental. They are not the thing, and their significance consists entirely in what they help us to. The thing, the central thing, is the recognition of the divine will in all life, and the loyal, loving effort to make that will prevail in all life: first of all in the hidden life of the spirit, and then in family life, in social life, in political life, in trade, in art, in literature, in every field of human interest and activity. Only thus can religion be saved from unwholesome and baneful subjectivities. Only thus can it gain the healthy objectivity needed to keep it sane and sweet. The religious spirit must have all fields for its own; and at the same time we must remember that all that is normal to man and demanded by his life has its place in the divine purpose and its justifying function in the divine training of men. To think otherwise is atheism.

One of the good signs of the religious times is the growing recognition of this fact. We are outgrowing the conception of religion as a thing of rites and ceremonies, of cloisters and retreats, of holy days and holy places, and are coming to view it as the divine principle for all living, whatever the day or the place or the work. We are coming to deny the distinction between secular and religious work, and to adopt into holy places all the normal and necessary work of the world. All of this is a divine ordinance, and expresses God's will concerning us. Men are tiring of the cloister and the smell of incense. They are tiring equally of the barren inspection of their spiritual states, and of churning up artificial emotions. They need to be taken out of themselves and given some worthy task to perform under some worthy inspiration; and this they find in the realization of the kingdom of God upon earth, and the doing of his will here under the stars as it is done in heaven. It is under the unconscious influence of these impulses, which are really strivings after God, the present God, the immanent God, that men grow dissatisfied with the formal and barren exercises of traditional religion.

The need of the divine help in order to live the life of the spirit is as manifest as it ever was. The sense of a divine presence in our lives is not dying out, but it is taking on a new form in accordance with a more careful psychology and a greater precision of thought. Instead of being something sensuously presentable or emotionally definable, it is rather the assurance of faith and the sense of reality which comes in spiritual living. Along with this has come the insight that it is preeminently in the conscience, the pure heart, the surrendered will, and holy activities that God makes his abode with us. From this we may expect great gain to religion. We shall lay aside our irrational fear of naturalism and also our crude supernaturalism. We shall find God everywhere, not merely in unmediated and miraculous manifestations, but also in the world he has made, in the laws he has ordained, in the great forms of life and society which he has appointed, and in the multitudinous activities which life necessitates. We shall come into communion with God in prayer and meditation, and also in work of all kinds, as we seek to build up his kingdom in the earth. We shall work more definitely along lines of training, culture, education, the improvement of all the conditions of human life in accordance with the laws of our being, yet without closing the spirit to direct contact with the Divine. In so doing we shall manifest ourselves as wise sons of God, and the divine manifestation will correspond. Indeed, there is no telling what God would do for a community thoroughly bent on doing his will and using all the means of influence in their power. Nature is no closed system, but forever becomes that which God wills it to be. Along with a moralized humanity might well go new heavens and a new earth. To them that have shall be given. At this point I more than suspect that I am what Professor James calls himself, "a crass supernaturalist." My "crassitude" is limited, not by any respect for nature as something having metaphysical existence and rights of its own, but solely by the insight into the necessity of an order of experience on which we can depend. Without that, we should be equally at sea in both mind and morals. We must, then, learn the lesson of law and self-help. For some time, at least, the keynote of religious progress must be found, not in vague and illiterate utterances about the supernatural, but rather in the divineness of the natural and the naturalness of the divine. This term supernatural has so many misleading associations, and is still the subject of so many misunderstandings, that we would do well to abandon it altogether and in its place write God; and then, in the assured faith that we are in his world and his hands, resolutely set about our Father's business, looking not for signs and wonders, but for the coming of the kingdom of God in the form of higher and holier living.

Thus we see the deep significance of the divine immanence for religious thought. It dispels that great cloud of difficulties, born of crude naturalistic thinking, that haunt popular religion. This is largely a negative service, but it is important nevertheless. It recalls God from the infinite distance in space and time to which sense thought must banish him, and where we so often lose him, and makes him the omnipresent power by which all things exist and on which all things continually depend. This metaphysical presence does not indeed secure spiritual sympathy and fellowship on our part, but it removes the speculative obstacles thereto that exist in many minds, and thus makes room for the spiritual life of communion and sonship. This life itself can be secured only in devout and faithful living by each for himself, but it is something to have the speculative intimidations removed that sometimes, like Bunyan's lions, frighten pilgrims from the way. It is something to know that this world, however mysterious and even sinister in many of its aspects, is after all God's world; that we are not standing helpless and hopeless in the midst of Strauss's "enormous machine" world with its pitiless wheels and thundering hammers, but we are in a personal world, a moral world, where character is being wrought out and a kingdom of righteousness is being set up. In such a world it is permitted to see visions and dream dreams, and devote ourselves to the service of the highest and best, in the sure faith that they are also the truest and most real, the abiding and essential stuff of the universe.

But we also see the necessity of uniting this thought of the divine immanence with the thought of law. All is law; all is God. All is God; all is law. We read it either way, according to the emphasis demanded by the times and circumstances. For those who have not learned the lesson of law, who are seeking short cuts, and who are not availing themselves of the natural means of growth and influence, we say, All is law. For those, on the other hand, who have lost God in the law, and who have fallen into the paralyzing notion of a self sufficient mechanism, we say, All is God. In both cases alike we say with the apostle: Work out your own salvation with fear and trembling; for it is God who worketh in you, both to will and to work for his good pleasure. For in him we live and move and have our being.

ALBERT C. KNUDSON

Initially as a professor of Old Testament and then as a systematic theologian, Albert C. Knudson (1873–1953) became a prominent Boston personalist. Knudson was born into a parsonage family in Grand Meadow, Minnesota, and received his education at The University of Minnesota. He attended Boston University for graduate work and joined its faculty in 1905. Knudson lived through and was keenly aware of the changes taking place in Methodist Episcopal theology at the turn of the century. Knudson used his article on his predecessor on the Boston faculty, Henry Clay Sheldon (1845–1928), as an occasion for discussing the transition in Methodist theology and revealed as much about himself as about Sheldon. Knudson's most important theological books are *The Doctrine of God* (1930) and *The Doctrine of Redemption* (1933). He also made significant contributions with his *The Philosophy of Personalism* (1927) and *The Validity of Religious Experience* (1937). The selection chosen for inclusion in these readings reflects Knudson's understanding of the alterations in Methodist theology at the turn of the century. While it overstates the failures of Sheldon's predecessors, it accurately describes the Protestant liberal theology which characterized much Methodist Episcopal theology of the first half of the twentieth century. "Henry Clay Sheldon—Theologian" is chosen from *Methodist Review* (March, 1925), Vol. CVIII, 5th series, Vol. XLI, pp.175–192.

HENRY CLAY SHELDON—THEOLOGIAN

This article is not a personal eulogy; it is an historical study. Its occasion is the eightieth birthday of Methodism's most learned and most influential theologian.

Dr. Henry Clay Sheldon was born in Martinsburg, N. Y., March 12,

1845. He graduated from Yale University in 1867 and from Boston University School of Theology in 1871. During the year 1871–72 he served as supply at the Methodist church in Saint Johnsbury, Vt., and in 1872–74 was pastor at Brunswick, Maine. He was admitted into the Maine Conference on trial and also was ordained deacon in 1873, and in 1876 was ordained elder and received into full connection. In 1874–75 he studied at the University of Leipzig. On his return from Germany he became professor of historical theology in Boston University School of Theology, and held that chair for twenty years (1875–1895). He then transferred to the department of systematic theology, and occupied that position until he was granted the *emeritus* relation in 1921. For forty-six consecutive years he was thus actively engaged as a teacher of theology. This is a record unequaled by any other Methodist theological teacher with the exception of Dr. William Fairfield Warren, who, however, during most of his long career as an educator was able to devote only part of his time to the actual work of teaching because of his heavy administrative duties as Dean and President.

In its outward aspects Doctor Sheldon's life has been a comparatively uneventful one. He has not participated to any marked extent in the councils of the church. He has not figured in the sessions of the Annual and General Conferences. With extraordinary steadiness of purpose he has devoted himself to the office of a teacher in the church. No ecclesiastical ambition has seduced him from the path of scholarly research. The lure of administrative position has made no appeal to him. Not even the excitement incident to a charge of heresy has fallen to his lot. To a very unusual degree he has escaped that curse of the scholar's life, the doing of "other things," and has been permitted to keep the even tenor of his way. . . .

But it is not simply the extent of his learning, his productivity and the general soundness and sobriety of his judgment that give to Doctor Sheldon's work its importance. What makes his work of historic significance to the church is that it marks the change from the older to the newer type of Methodist theology. No one who knows Doctor Sheldon would accuse him of being a radical. Not even the crudest theological reactionaries in our church have, so far as I know, assailed his orthodoxy. And yet it is he more than any other systematic theologian in our church who has given to our theology the stamp of what may be called "modernity." The change he introduced had no doubt been prepared for by others. His "theology," when it appeared, did not impress the church as a novelty. But it did stand in sharp contrast with all the earlier systematic treatises, so much so that Doctor Sheldon himself apparently had no idea that it would receive the kind of official recognition that has been accorded it. In 1897, when his class lectures on theology appeared in typewritten form, I urged their publication, but he met the suggestion by saying that it would be fifty years before the Methodist Episcopal Church would be ready to accept his standpoint. It turned out, however, that eleven years from that time not only was there no serious objection in the church to his theological position, but those very lectures were adopted as the textbook of theology in our Conference Course of Study. This fact might perhaps impugn any claim that Doctor Sheldon might make to being a prophet—as he himself facetiously remarked when he was reminded of it—but it does not imply that he was mistaken in the view he held in 1897 of the marked contrast between his own type of theology and that current in the church up to that time. It is no exaggeration to say that he introduced into Methodist theology an abrupt change.

That this change did not cause any particular stir was due to a number of reasons, three of which may be briefly mentioned.

First, the earlier Methodist theology did not express the real genius of Methodism. It was not in the proper sense of the term a native growth; it was rather an exotic, transplanted from other spiritual climes. In the theological field early Methodism was not creative. It took most of its theology second-hand from others, and in it it had no immediate and profound interest. It was, for instance, over eighty years after Methodism was organized before its first "Systematic Theology" was written; and not until fifty years later was the next work of any consequence in the field published. The *Theological Institutes*, by Richard Watson, appeared in 1821–29, and the first edition of William Burt Pope's *Compendium of Christian Theology* in 1875. Both of these works display considerable learning, especially that by Pope, and both were in some respects remarkable productions. But it can hardly be said that the type of theology which they represent, and which held the field throughout the nineteenth century, stood organically related to the life and thought of the Methodist movement. Much of it was traditional in character, and sustained a purely adventitious relation to that vital experience of religion which was the basal emphasis in Methodism. Hence a change in theology did not affect the Methodist Church so seriously as it did some of the other communions.

Second, the Methodist works on systematic theology, written during the twenty-five years preceding the publication of Sheldon's *System of Christian Doctrine*, failed in a marked degree to adjust themselves to the new developments in the field of biblical criticism and of science in general. They distinctly did not keep pace with the times. This is true of Miner Raymond's *Systematic Theology* (1877), of John Miley's *Systematic Theology* (1892, 1894), and of the colossal work, entitled *Studies in Theology*, projected by Randolph S. Foster in his old age and carried through six volumes (1889–1899). Of these six volumes Bowne once said in all kindness that the pathetic thing about them was that they were obsolete before they came from the press. And the same might be said to a large extent of Raymond's and Miley's works. These scholars made no real advance beyond the theological method of Watson and Pope, and they fell noticeably behind the scientific and theological thought of their own day. They thus suffered from a double handicap. Their theology stood in no vital relation to the Methodist emphasis on religious experience, and it was out of accord with modern science. The result was that it became a burden to faith instead of a help; and hence it was with a measure of relief that the church laid it aside, as one would an outworn garment that never had been a fit, and accepted in its stead a more modern type of theology.

A third reason why the transition from Miley to Sheldon was effected with so little difficulty is found in Doctor Sheldon himself, his profound acquaintance and sympathy with historic Christianity. As professor of historical theology he had for twenty years immersed himself in the life and thought of the church. When he came, therefore, to his task as a systematic theologian, it was with a mind and heart rooted deep in Christian history. For him a disturbing radicalism was impossible. However modern he might be, he felt himself at one with the faith of the past. This feeling prevades his entire *System of Christian Doctrine*. The work is ballasted with such a profound knowledge and reverence for history that only the most recalcitrant obscurantist could have any serious doubt as to its safeness. It is this fact especially, a fact manifest in the temper as well as the content of the book, that has saved it to such a large extent from adverse criticism.

Thus far I have spoken of the transition from the older to the newer type of Methodist theology, introduced by Sheldon, without defining the nature of the change. The question now arises as to what the change consisted in. In what respects does Sheldon's theology differ from that of his Methodist predecessors? A detailed answer to this question would call for a small volume. Here I can deal with only a few of the outstanding differences.

The first and most striking difference is found in the field of apologetics, in the method of grounding the Christian faith. The Methodist theologians from Watson to Miley and Foster were authoritarian rationalists. They based the Christian faith on the divine authority of Scripture, and this authority they believed could be established by purely rational considerations. The argument appears in its purest form in Watson, but in its substance it is repeated by the others. Watson distinguishes between "external" and "internal" evidence. The former he regards as primary and fundamental. It consists in an appeal to the fact of miracle and of prophecy. "Miracles," he says, "must be considered as the leading and absolute evidence of a revelation from God" (*Theol. Inst.*, one vol. ed., p.55). The internal evidence, which has to do with the essential rationality and intrinsic excellence of the biblical revelation, is in itself altogether inadequate. "The reason for this," he says, "is evident. A mere impression of truth on the understanding could not by itself be distinguished from a discovery made by the human intellect, and could have no authority, as a declaration of the will of a superior, with the person receiving it; and as to others, it could only pass for the opinion of the individual who might promulge it. An authentication of a system of truth, which professes to be the will, the law of Him who, having made, has the right to command us, *external* to the matter of the doctrine itself, is therefore necessary to give it authority, and to create the obligation of obedience" (p.41). A distinction is thus made by Watson between the truth of Scripture and its authority, and between what he elsewhere calls "rational" and "authenticating" evidence. "Rational evidence," as Raymond says, "shows reasons why the proposition is true, or why it must be true. Authenticating evidence shows reasons why we should believe it is true" (*Syst. Theol.*, I, 119). The latter type of evidence can only be found in miracle. Apart from miracles the teachings of Scripture might, says Watson, "be true, but they are not attested to be divine. We have no guaranty of their infallible truth, because our own rational powers are not infallible, nor those of the most gifted mind" (p.56). Hence "though the rational evidence of a doctrine lies in the doctrine itself, the rational proof of the divine authority of a doctrine must be external to the doctrine" (p.58). But although "external to the doctrine" the authenticating evidence is rational in character. It is an appeal to the intellect. A religious teacher, says Raymond, "claims that what he says, God says; and as evidence that his claim is valid he proposed to do, and does do, what no man can do except God be with him" (I, 48). That is, he performs a miracle, and the miracle is convincing evidence of the truth and divine authority of his message. The inference from miracle to truth and authority is assumed to be logically irresistible; the human reason by its very nature acknowledges its cogency. The whole argument for Christianity thus takes the form of authoritarian rationalism.

Pope, Raymond and Miley, it is true, gave a larger place than did Watson to the self-evidencing power of faith or religious experience. But they did not make this idea an organizing principle in their theology. It remained external to their system; it did not form a structural part of it. While they conceded a certain apologetic value to religious experience, their own standpoint remained essentially rationalistic. Take, for instance, Miley's argument against the view that the Christian consciousness is a source of theology. "To assume," he says, "the religious feelings as first in order, and then to find in them the central truths of theology, is to reverse the logical and necessary order of the facts. Clearly a knowledge of the central truths of Christianity conditions the Christian consciousness and must be first in order. . . . As the Christian consciousness is thus conditioned by the possession of the central truths of Christian theology, it is impossible to deduce these truths from that consciousness. Back of these truths there is no Christian consciousness to begin with" (*Syst. Theol.* I, 21). In these statements an intellectualistic view of religion is manifestly implied. Christianity is represented as a body of doctrines rather than a unique form of experience. At least, experience is secondary; the doctrines come first, and so express the essential nature of the Christian religion.

These doctrines, it is true, are thought of as supernaturally communicated. They did not originate in the human reason, nor do they even necessarily commend themselves to man's reason. In the latter respect a distinction was made between different doctrines of Scripture. Some of them were regarded as standing on the plane of "natural religion" and as having an adequate rational basis. To this group, according to Raymond, "belong the doctrines of the being and attributes of God, moral distinctions, the free agency, moral responsibility, and immortality of man, the fact of sin and need of salvation, probation in the life that now is, and retribution in the life to come" (I, 124). As distinguished from these doctrines, however, there are others that were regarded as the peculiar property of "revealed religion" and as completely transcending human reason. To these, says Raymond, "belong the doctrines of the trinity, divinity of Christ, the hypostatic unity, the personality and divinity of the Holy Ghost, the atonement, justification by faith only, supernatural agency in the regeneration and sanctification of the believer, the witness of the Spirit to adoption and heirship, and the resurrection of the dead" (I, 124f.). Substantially the same list appears also in Watson, except that he puts the atonement in the first group. Of the truth of the doctrines in the second group "we have," says Watson, "no evidence whatsoever" (p.118). They are to be accepted wholly on the authority of Scripture. But this does not mean that they are in and of themselves irrational, or that it is irrational on our part to accept them. There are, we are told, adequate grounds for believing that the Bible is the Word of God; and, if it is such, its contents, no matter how much they transcend human reason, are in the very nature of the case rational. An irrational divine revelation is unthinkable. "Nothing," says Miley, "is accepted with higher reason of its truth than that which God has spoken" (I, 47). The standpoint of the earlier Methodist theologians was thus clearly and explicitly rationalistic. Their ultimate appeal was made to the theoretical reason, not to Christian experience. They thought that religious truth could be presented in the form of assent-compelling knowledge, so that even the non-religious mind would be forced to admit its logical cogency. This was the motive of the so-called "authenticating evidence," the appeal to miracle and prophecy, as well as that of the so-called "rational evidence." Miracle was regarded as an adequate rational ground for accepting the super-rational teaching of Scripture. The entire apologetic structure thus in the last analysis rested on the non-religious reason; and in this sense the whole theological system of the earlier Methodist theologians was, as I have termed it, an authoritarian rationalism, or, what amounts to the same thing, a rationalistic authoritarianism.

When we now turn to Sheldon, we find all this changed. There is no polemic against the older view, but it is quietly set aside. We hear no more about "authenticating" as distinguished from "rational" evidence. Miracle recedes into the background. It is, we are told, "most appropriately regarded as a part of the rounded whole of revelation. Whatever it may have been to the contemporary generation, for us it is adapted to establish conviction in the biblical system only as it fulfills a function of revelation, only as it is harmoniously connected with the process of sacred history, and serves to disclose the character of God or to illustrate his redemptive purpose. Outside of this relation and office, it does not generate faith in the Bible, but rather needs an already existing faith to provide for its acceptance" (p.118f.). Miracle thus becomes a deduction from faith rather than the ground of it. And with the adoption of this standpoint the "external evidence" of the older apologetics completely collapses. The "internal evidence" takes its place. "The proof for the Bible," says Sheldon, "lies in its contents— that is, in the spiritual wealth of the factors which it contains, and in their harmonious relation to each other—rather than in any form of external attestation" (p.118). There is, therefore, no basis for the old distinction between the truth of Scripture and its divine authority. Apart from the convincing and convicting power of the truth it expresses, the Bible has no authority. Its authority consists in its truth. It is the truth of Scripture that proves its inspiration, not the reverse.

Such is the position adopted by Sheldon; and with it we are introduced to a new type of Methodist theology. The old rationalistic authoritarianism, with its assumption of biblical infallibility, is at an end. In its stead we have a theology that is at once more empirical and more rational, truer to the genius of Methodism and more in accord with modern science.

It is more empirical in two respects. First, unlike the older theology, it constructs its theory of inspiration in harmony with the facts instead of with an abstract ideal of perfection, and so rules out the notion of biblical inerrancy. Second, unlike the older theology, it holds that revelation not only finds its ultimate attestation in religious experience, but is also determined in its scope by its power of appeal to the human heart. Revelation is not, then, an objective entity, unrelated to experience. It is conditioned both in its nature and range by faith.

The newer theology, represented by Sheldon, is also more rational than the older in that it tends to limit revelation to the religious realm and denies to it a coercive power over the human reason. It allows to science its full rights and does not attempt in the name of religion to impose upon the modern man the imperfect scientific notions found in the Bible. Thus without being rationalistic it avoids a conflict with the theoretical reason. It does this chiefly by its freer attitude toward Scripture. The older theology was vitiated to an almost incredible degree by a false biblicism. It was led to take up irrelevant issues, wasted its strength in futile attempts to harmonize the Bible with modern science, and as a result failed to bring out, as it ought to have done, the distinctive character and true ground of the Christian faith. Faith stands in its own right; it has a reason of its own. In this sense we may, if we wish, speak of a new religious rationalism, a rationalism based on the autonomous validity of our religious nature instead of on the theoretical reason. Such a rationalism is founded on experience, and furnishes an incomparably firmer basis for the Christian faith than did the older authoritarian rationalism. Indeed, the latter has lost practically all value. It has been rendered obsolete by biblical criticism. The only fundamental and adequate apologetic is to be found in the self-evidencing power of faith. This I have sought to show at some length in my *Present Tendencies in Religious Thought*, recently published; and in developing this idea I have simply brought out the new point of view introduced into Methodist theology by Sheldon's *System of Christian Doctrine.*

A second difference between Sheldon and the earlier Methodist theologians appears in their treatment of the doctrines of the trinity and the subject of christology. The point of special interest in this connection is the divinity of Christ. In his presentation of the evidence in support of this doctrine Sheldon marks a decided advance beyond his Methodist predecessors. The latter made a very uncritical use of Scripture, failing to discriminate between the different strata in it and citing the Old Testament almost as freely as the New. They also laid chief stress on the biblical ascription to Christ of such divine attributes as eternity, omniscience, omnipotence, omnipresence, and immutability. It was his miracle-working power and his participation in the work of creation and providence rather than the ethical and spiritual quality of his life that in their opinion stamped him as divine. In Sheldon, on the other hand, the tendency is to emphasize the ideal character of Christ, his consciousness of oneness with God, his triumph over the world, his fidelity to his divine vocation, and his spiritual lordship over men. It is these qualities that stand out in the Gospel picture, and that make of Christ the true revealer of the Father and the Redeemer of the world. This line of evidence, however, does not lead Sheldon to deny value to the christological theories and affirmations that appear in the New Testament writings. He cites them and apparently accepts them as valid; but the stress falls on the facts of Christ's inner life rather than on speculations concerning his person, no matter how early they may be.

In his construction of the doctrine of the trinity Sheldon concedes a certain value to such analogies as those drawn from the different forms of mental activity, from the social implications of the ethical life, and especially from the idea of the divine immanence in us. In this respect he differs from the earlier Methodist theologians who denied all value to such analogies, and relegated "the trinity and its cognate doctrines" to the realm of absolute mystery. But while holding this view they were certain that "a Person in the Godhead continues his personality in the human nature, which is therefore of necessity itself impersonal or without any personal existence independent of the Divine" (Pope, II, 115). This is also the position taken by Olin A. Curtis, and taken with the utmost emphasis. "All the personality," he says, "of our Lord he brought with him into human existence. He takes on an addition, a human addition, to his individuality, that is all. The mankind is ever impersonal, never anything but a lower coefficient for the abiding person of the Son of God" (*The Christian Faith*, p.235).

In Sheldon, however, we find a different emphasis. He lays no special stress on the full personality of the preexistent Son, nor does he sacrifice the human to the divine element in Christ. He recognizes both, but if anything makes the human factor primary. He represents "the finite psychical nature in Christ" as mediating "the divine content in more or less of a partitive and successive fashion," and speaks of "the divine as fulfilling... the function of an oversoul uniquely related to the humanity of Christ and uniquely contributory to its furnishing for an unexampled mission" (p.356). In these statements we manifestly have a step in the direction of an anthropocentric as distinguished from a theocentric christology, but only a step. Sheldon abides by the traditional recognition of the two natures, but he does so with so much moderation and metaphysical restraint that he may be regarded as leaving the door open to those who feel constrained to move further in the anthropocentric direction than he himself does....

There are two other important developments in Sheldon's theology that call for consideration, but space will permit only a brief reference to them. One appears in his treatment of the atonement, and the other in his idea of the divine immanence.

The older Methodist theologians leaned either to the "satisfaction" or the "governmental" theory of the atonement. Watson and Pope were not satisfied with either, but expressed a preference for the former. Raymond rejected the "satisfaction" theory, and expressed dissatisfaction with the "purely governmental" theory, but his own "declarative" theory was apparently only a modified form of the latter. Miley was a champion of the governmental theory, and contended that this is the true Methodist theory. Sheldon, however, rejects it, at least in the form represented by Miley. He criticizes Miley for distinguishing too sharply between God as Person and as Ruler. "There is," he says, "in truth no occasion for a disjunction between the personal and the governmental in him. In his absolute self-consistency he stands in the same identical plane as Moral Ruler and as Divine Person" (p.400). But while rejecting the traditional governmental as well as the satisfaction theory Sheldon seems reluctant to adopt the Abelardian or moral-influence theory, which sees in the death of Christ the supreme revelation of the love of God. He contends for "an objective element, or Godward bearing, in Christ's work"; but inasmuch as it "in no wise implies a change of attitude in time on the part of God toward the race," and as it consists simply in the demonstration "that the love which is outpoured so lavishly is still *holy* love," I cannot see that his view differs in any essential regard from the "moral theory" advocated by Bowne. It is this theory, if such it may be called, which is rapidly gaining headway in current religious thought; and Sheldon's treatment of the subject really marks the transition to it in Methodist theology.

The idea of the divine immanence, together with the personalistic idealism associated with it, stands opposed to the natural realism held by the earlier Methodist theologians. Realism affirms the extra-mental existence of the material world. However the world originated, it at present is an independent and self-running mechanism. There are thus, from the realistic standpoint, two kinds of being, one spiritual and personal, the other material and impersonal. This dualistic view of the world did not form a specific item in the older theology, but it constituted its background and virtually determined its conclusions on a number of important points. It was this realistic and dualistic philosophy that made the idea of miracle so fundamental and dominant in the older theology. For in an independent and self-running world of nature it is only through miracle that God can make himself directly known and felt; the genuineness of the biblical revelation and the validity of Christian experience imply miracle. A sharp antithesis is thus established between the natural and supernatural; and how on this assumption to think of the divine providence, of answers to prayer, and of the relation of divine grace to human experience becomes an insoluble riddle. Confusion and obscurity in one's fundamental thinking result, and the whole theological situation is bedeviled, so that Curtis was hardly exaggerating when he referred to the crude philosophical realism of Wesley as an "unspeakable curse." Yet it was this type of thought that formed the philosophical background of all the earlier Methodist theologians. Not even Foster transcended it. It was Sheldon who first introduced into Methodist systematic theology the idealistic viewpoint with its conception of the divine immanence. This carried with it a new conception of miracle, of the natural and supernatural, of revelation and inspiration, of Christian experience, and of the general relation of God to the world, and in so doing removed to a large extent the intellectual scandal involved in the old conflict between science and theology. In this philosophical background of his thinking is to be found perhaps as important an aspect of Sheldon's theology as any, though it does not obtrude itself in the pages of his *System of Christian Doctrine....*

Methodism in the past has been too much inclined to look upon theology as a kind of ecclesiastical accessory, necessary perhaps as an adjunct to church activity, but not an essential part of it. The result has been that she has not made adequate provision for the theological training of her ministers, nor has she given adequate encouragement to thorough and original investigation in the field of theology. We have been too complacent in our attitude to our own theology; we have prided ourselves on its being "preachable" or we have tacitly expressed ourselves as being contented with it by taking an indifferent attitude toward theology in general. We have not as a church come to grips with the theological problem as we ought and as we must do, if we are to fulfill our mission in this day and particularly in the day to come. We have been too passive in matters theological, we have accepted too readily leadership from without. For this there no doubt have been historical and perhaps adequate reasons. But a new responsibility for educational work now rests upon our church, a responsibility that she dare not and, I believe, will not shirk. We need to be more creative than we have been in the field of religious thought, we need to construct our theology more in harmony with the distinctive nature and major emphases of the religious movement that we represent. But this we can do only as we throw more of our resources and more of our energy into theological education. We need to make provision for a larger number of such careers as that of Doctor Sheldon. He stands out today as a shining example of the immense service that can be rendered the church by a lifetime of devotion to theological scholarship. . . .

OLIN A. CURTIS

Olin A. Curtis (1850–1918) was a professor of systematic theology at Drew University. He was born in Frankfurt, Maine, the son of a Methodist ministerial family. Educated at Lawrence and Boston Universities, he taught theology at Boston University (1889–1896) and at Drew University (1896–1914). Curtis gained wide respect in Methodist theological circles and was an intellectual leader in both of the Methodist Episcopal churches. His books, *The Christian Faith* (1905) and *Personal Submission to Jesus Christ* (1910), expressed his mature position. Curtis was an independent thinker who utilized biblical foundations and personalistic philosophy in an individual way. He was not easily identified with any school of thought, but with a trenchant style he developed what he would have been pleased to call a biblically based theology. He focused his theology on the theme of salvation. In the following selection Curtis examines the church, a more prominent subject in his thought than in that of most of his contemporaries. His discussion of the church is thought by many to be his most significant contribution to Methodist theology. "The Church of Our Lord," is selected from Christian Faith (New York: The Methodist Book Concern, 1905), pp. 415–424.

THE CHURCH OF OUR LORD

The Kingdom of God. Before stating my own view of the significance of the "kingdom of God" I wish to call your attention to a scholar's protest which has been made by Professor Briggs against the modern Protestant practice of sharply distinguishing between the meaning of *basileia* and the meaning of *ekklesia*, as these terms are used in the Word of God. He says: "Let me say that I have carefully examined all the uses of these and cognate terms in both Testaments, and as a result of my investigations I declare that nothing can be more false than the distinction between 'kingdom' and 'church' asserted by many moderns. These are chiefly men who are displeased with the historic church and seek refuge in the kingdom as taught by Jesus Christ in the conceit that this is something larger and better. In fact, 'church' and 'kingdom' differ only as synonymous terms. There is nothing of importance which can be asserted of the kingdom of god which may not be also asserted of the church of God, if we faithfully use biblical material without speculation and theorizing. Jesus is King of the kingdom, and he reigns over it, subduing all external enemies under his feet, or transforming them by his grace into citizens of his kingdom. He is also the head over all things to his church. The church and the kingdom are coextensive; both are Old Testament institutions and New Testament institutions; both are institutions of this world, and both are eternal institutions of the world to come; both are organizations in the midst of the world and of the universe; both will eventually subdue and absorb the world and also the universe; the one is as spiritual as the other; the one is as external as the other."

The conclusions of Professor Briggs as a biblical scholar have, and should have, great weight with us; still I can but feel that in this instance his entire study of the scripture teaching has been superficial. When, for one example, our Lord says, "Thy kingdom come," can we believe that by *kingdom* he means exactly the *church* which he came to establish and to which he committed the sacrament of baptism? I cannot believe so. It is contrary to the whole tone and drift of his teaching. I am quite ready to admit that now and again the two Greek words, as we see them in the New Testament, slip into each other's province, and that a line of absolute consistency in usage it is impossible to trace through all the various writings; but I hold that there are plain indications of facts which are not the same; and that these facts should not be confused in our thinking, if we are ever fully to understand the Word of God and all Christian history.

My own view I can give economically as follows:

1. Let us start with God's unrealized plan to have an ultimate kingdom. Most comprehensively considered, the kingdom of God is the final, universal, absolute, everlasting dominion of God. All persons, all events, all creation will express the one fact—*God rules*. This is the sublime ideal toward which the universe struggles. But there is another sense in which the kingdom of God is a present reality. It has already *begun* in the hearts of angels and saints. And all its great spiritual laws are in operation— "the world of invisible laws by which God is ruling and blessing his creatures." The entire movement in the moral government is in an important sense expressive of the kingdom of God.

175

2. In this ultimate kingdom of God there is to be a *cosmic sweep*. The final universe—everything as formed and placed and used—every person in either his character or his condition—will manifest the sovereign holiness of God. I mean that in God's ultimate kingdom the entire cosmos will not merely conform to his will, but will show forth his nature. The obedience will reveal something more than power, it will reveal the perfect divine holiness.

3. Within this cosmic kingdom, there is to be "the kingdom of heaven." This inner kingdom will be made up of all holy persons, all those having "the vision of God," and experiencing the ineffable felicity of the divine fellowship. The *beginning* of this kingdom of heaven is in the present life of the angels of God; but the kingdom will be fully realized only after the general resurrection.

4. Within this kingdom of heaven there is to be "the kingdom of Christ." This is a very definite matter, even that new race of men redeemed by the death of our Lord, and organized in him, and glorified in bodily conformity to him. This kingdom of Christ is also now in existence in an incomplete way, and comprehends all those persons who are by saving faith actually joined to Jesus Christ. The test is this actual union with Christ and not whether the persons are members of the Christian church or not.

5. These three, the cosmic kingdom, the kingdom of heaven, and the kingdom of Christ, are to be conceived under the figure of three concentric circles (recall our discussion of the moral government); so that the kingdom of heaven is the inner dominion of the cosmic kingdom, and the kingdom of Christ is the inner dominion of the kingdom of heaven, and also the innermost dominion of the cosmic kingdom, and all three constitute the kingdom of God.

6. This kingdom of God, taken in its entirety, is the kingdom of God the Father, which is the kingdom referred to in the Lord's Prayer. The full consummation of this kingly dominion of God the Father is to take place when our Saviour "shall deliver up the kingdom to God, even the Father, . . . that God may be all in all" (1 Cor. 15. 24–28). This does not mean that Christ is to become anything less to his own people whom he hath redeemed, but merely that Christ and his kingdom are to become an integrant feature of the larger kingdom of God over which only the Father is to be the absolute and everlasting Ruler. It is the last extreme emphasis of that idea of the inherent subordination of the Son of God which is a fundamental idea in the whole system of Christian doctrine.

7. What, then, is the church of our Lord? It is the concrete exponent of the kingdom of Christ. It is a formal organization of men which stands

for the kingdom of Christ while that kingdom is in the process of formation. Not exactly, as Kahnis said, "an aeon of the kingdom"; but rather, as Draseke said, "the workshop of the kingdom"; or, as Neander most beautifully said, "the seminary for the heavenly community." I am willing to allow just this much: The church of our Lord *belongs* to his tentative kingdom; but it is not coextensive with that kingdom (even as that kingdom exists to-day), and cannot be coextensive with it until, anyway, there is what Saint Paul terms "a glorious church, not having spot or wrinkle or any such thing" (Eph. 5. 27). But even this admission is somewhat misleading, for to many it will suggest that the difference between the kingdom and the church is merely that one is perfect and the other is imperfect. That, though, is not the fundamental difference. The fundamental difference is one of essential structure. The kingdom is a simple personal and spiritual organism. The church is a formal and complex organism. The kingdom is a life of fellowship mediated only through Jesus Christ. The church is a machine; at its best a machine full of life and expressing life, and yet a machine. In its worship and in all its service the church has, and must have, some sort of outward instrument —forms, symbols, creeds, what not; but the kingdom needs only the complete man. If, as some believe, the Christian church itself is to be purified, completed, glorified, and then taken into eternity for ever-lasting worship and service, even then it will not be, strictly speaking, the kingdom of our Lord, but merely the formal instrument of that kingdom. It will be, perhaps, to the kingdom as a whole what the glorified body will be to the one moral person—the instrumental means of perfect objective manifestation. The kingdom of Christ may, so to speak, show its life to the entire universe through a glorified church —Saint Paul's *endoksos ekklesia*.

The Holy Catholic Church. As Protestants we cannot afford to surrender this great historic phrase. Nor should we transform its original meaning into that of "the invisible church of Christ." The holy catholic church is precisely the visible church of our Lord, that is, the entire body of persons who are in actual organization about the two points, the gospel and the sacraments. Whenever a company of men unite, in any way whatsoever, to maintain the preaching of the gospel of redemption, and to secure the administration of the sacrament of baptism, and to have Christian communion in the sacrament of the Lord's Supper, that company of men constitutes a Christian church; and the sum total of such churches is the holy catholic church. Forms of ecclesiastical government, and preferences in ceremony, and peculiarities of denominational belief, have no large significance; the essential points of organization are simply the two sacraments and the preaching of the gospel. This church of our Lord is *holy*, not in the sense that every member is now entirely holy in personal life, but in the sense that the church is our Lord's own instrument in building up a holy kingdom. The whole plan and movement of the church are unto holiness. This holy church is *catholic* in the sense that it is *for all men*. In it there is no ethnic limitation. Its ambition is for world-wide conquest. Catholicity is to the church just what the racial plan is to the kingdom of Christ. It is the humanity-note. In this holy catholic church there are three kinds of membership: First, there is *formal* membership. In many situations there are men who submit to all the tests used, and become members of an organized church, and yet do not have any redemptional relation to Jesus Christ. Of course the question soon arises, "Are these formal members really members of the church of our Lord at all?" I myself find it best to regard them as in the holy catholic church, but not members of the kingdom of Christ. This view renders possible large emphasis upon the absolute need of having a Christian experience; and yet, with this emphasis, a certain practical wisdom in pastoral work. And, further, the view is helpful when we try fairly to estimate the situation in any of the great national churches, or when we try to understand the condition of the whole Christian world. Second, there is *dynamic* membership. I mean by this more than any one term can denote. The power of the holy catholic church is due to the Holy Spirit. But his action is (not wholly conditioned) largely related to those members of the church who are also members of the kingdom of redemption. They may be called the dynamic personal points of his action. For example, the force of a sermon, or the influence of a sacrament, depends, in quite a measure, upon the reality and vitality of the Christian experience of the congregation. And so every member of the church who actually lives in Christ Jesus adds a veritable dynamic to the church. Third, there is membership by *Christian claim*. The church of our Lord has the right and the duty to claim the helpless. She should take into her atmosphere and association and (if possible) service all people who are unable to make a choice for themselves—not only all irresponsible children, but all the feeble-minded, and all those unfortunate souls who have been mentally wrecked by woes too terrible for human fortitude. Of course, there are involved here serious questions in church economy, but they all can be met and mastered, if we are determined to make the church of Christ a worthy instrument of the kingdom of Christ.

But surely you will not misunderstand me here—you will not think that I intend to teach the possibility of a mechanical salvation. No human being is saved, or can be saved, by membership in the holy catholic church—salvation is only by *personal* union with Jesus Christ.

The Organism of the Church. To appreciate the philosophy of the organism of the holy catholic church, we need to remember that, as the concrete exponent of the kingdom of Christ or the new race, the church is also designed to be a brotherhood of moral persons dominated by Jesus Christ. Thus there are three features to be protected and emphasized in the church-organism: 1. The personal. 2. The societary. 3. The spiritual, in fellowship with Christ. I can get at these three features most lucidly, I think, by comparing the organism of the church to the structure of an ellipse, with its two *foci* and a major axis.

First, in the church, there is *the personal focus*. This is the preaching of the gospel. Not merely the Christian sermon, but all personal testimony, everything which is done in the church to show what the gospel means to separate persons. The purpose is to bring about the conquest of the world by the church through this personal feature of preaching. And how wonderful it all is, this giving to the world the entire message of redemption through the experience of men! The most effective Christian sermon is really nothing other than a chapter of the inner life of a person who lives in our Lord Jesus Christ. The moment the sermon loses that personal quality, that moment the sermon ceases to be effective. Do you not begin to apprehend the philosophy—one might almost say the strategy—of this personal focus? Why, we reach the great Christian verities through each other, our very apprehension of the finalities of the gospel is only by entering the living personal experience of Christian men. And so every time you grasp a Christian truth it prepares you to understand better the life of Christian men; and to live—helpfully, joyously, to live with them forever. Thus, the whole Christian brotherhood comes to its mighty certainties of faith in one great entanglement of personal experience, the very emphasis upon personality making a contribution to ultimate fellowship.

Second, *the societary focus*. But it is not enough to preach the gospel through persons; the Christian society, as an organized body, must have a chance to express itself. Hence the second focus, which is the focus of the Christian sacraments. Not now are we to consider the significance of each sacrament; I merely wish you to note the fact and worth of the sacramental idea in the organism of the church. This focus is a perfect balance to the other. As the aim of preaching is to stir up personality, to make men think, to keep the personal life from stagnation, so the sacramental aim is to fill consciousness with the sense of Christian companionship, to make the person realize that he is only a part of the large

Christian community. In both sacraments it is the holy catholic church which dominates the scene. The person is there surely, but he is there for submission and fellowship. His very meditation and confession and consecration are *in the midst*.

Third, there is (to keep our ellipse in mind) *a major axis*. This major feature in the organism of the church is, some would insist, the Holy Spirit. Such insistence is a mistake. Indeed, there is, I fear, in our day, and emphasis placed upon the Holy Spirit which is not quite true to the New Testament. To protect with words every side of the matter is extremely difficult; but I will say this: *No emphasis is ever to be given to the Holy Spirit which, in any moment or in any degree, shuts our Lord out from the Christian consciousness*. The real work of the Spirit always exalts Christ; *that* is his mission. As to the church, the Holy Spirit is the very life of it all. The preaching, the sacraments, the service, are literally nothing without his presence and power. But the major axis is only Jesus Christ our Redeemer. And just what do I mean by this? I mean that the spiritual organism of the church requires actual fellowship with Christ. You have a complete organism to just the extent that in the sacraments and in the preaching and in all the work the people are in conscious union with Jesus Christ. This implies, you easily perceive, that it is only dynamic membership which contributes to the spiritual organism of the church. O, if we all could only feel this; if every Christian preacher could only realize that *size* is not what the organism requires for its completeness and efficiency, but fellowship, actual fellowship with Jesus Christ. If you say that conversions are the test of church efficiency, I will say that conversions will follow if the church is in living union with our Lord.

A further word of caution is necessary in this connection, owing to certain widespread tendencies: Fellowship with Christ cannot normally be secured in the church by exalting his person at the expense of his atonement. It verily seems as if the whole realm of Christian scholarship were trying to minimize the death of the Son of God. The tendency is not only wrong, but even pernicious. Fully to enter into the life of Christ, one needs to be overwhelmed by his death as Saint Paul was over-whelmed by it until he could hardly think a thought which was not colored by its sacrificial meaning.

Christian Unity. At this point I cannot speak an effective word; for I am out of sympathy with every effort to crush out the denominational churches in the name of Christian unity. I believe in uniting all those churches where the fundamental interpretation of the Christian faith is the same; but I do not believe in asking any church to yield any real conviction. In the present state of things there is more Christian vitality in these denominational convictions than in all the superficial combinations of forced external conformity. Solidarity is the ultimate, is the Christian ideal; but real Christian solidarity cannot come by sacrificing personality to machinery. I fully appreciate the dreadful fact of waste; but a waste of life is better than any artificial economy.

EDGAR SHEFFIELD BRIGHTMAN

E dgar S. Brightman (1884–1953) was born in Holbrook, Massachusetts. He attended Brown and Boston Universities and then taught at Nebraska Wesleyan University and at Boston University as the Borden Parker Bowne Professor of Philosophy. He developed the historical and contemporary connections of Bowne's philosophy, especially in his own concentration on the metaphysical statement of personality. Brightman was the most eminent philosophical theologian in the Boston Personalist school after Bowne. He wrote on a full range of issues in philosophy of religion but was especially influential for his discussion of the problem of evil and his idea of God as limited. Among his more important books are *An Introduction to Philosophy* (1925) and *Finding of God* (1932). He also wrote on biblical topics and the spiritual life. Brightman built his philosophy upon the bases of experience and intended to construct an empirically defined philosophy. His position is acknowledgedly Christian in perspective, and his effort to explore the nature and power of God was germane to his total work. Religious experience, he argues, leads to an understanding of God as finite, as a Person limited by givens that contain principles of delay and suffering. These dimensions of his thought are discussed in the selection which follows: "The Resultant Idea of God" is taken from *The Problem of God* (New York: The Abingdon Press, 1930), pp. 107–138.

THE RESULTANT IDEA OF GOD

We have found that the tendency of history, accentuated by many aspects of modern thought, is toward a broadening and enlargement of the idea of God. We have seen that the broadening in one direction usually also involves a narrowing in another. This, in many instances, is a logically necessary result. On the other hand, the broadening involves a loss in meaning. There is some danger that our ideas may become so broad as to be meaningless. Thus we seem to move back and forth between an expanded and a contracted idea of God without finding a resting place.

A cynically minded conservative might be tempted to comment that, if for every plus that is added to our conception of God a corresponding minus must be subtracted, we always have the same quantity on our hands with which we started, and we therefore retain the traditional idea of God unchanged. But such a view is hopelessly wooden. Surely none of our ideas can escape change as the race advances. Even the simplest and most certain facts, the observations made by sense or the elementary processes of arithmetic, come to acquire a new meaning when seen in the light of the advancing interpretations of science. Red always looks red to the normal eye; but it conveys vastly different meanings to the railroad man, the socialist, and the physicist. Eight plus eight will always be sixteen in the sphere of arithmetical integers; but the moral law and the beauty of holiness can never be understood by a mere process of counting. Thus our thought must always move on to a fuller and more complete understanding and even to a transformation of the meaning of the most commonplace and apparently obvious facts of life. Otherwise we become dogmatists, life stagnates, self-content renders further growth impossible. In every field stagnation and smug self-satisfaction are deadly, but nowhere more so than in the field of religion. When religion reaches the stage where it says to itself, "I now know all that I need to know. I am perfectly right, and I expect no further light either from man or from God," then religion needs no foes from among the ranks of skeptics or atheists to attack it; it has already poisoned itself from within. Dogmatic self-complacency is the suicide of religion.

It is one of the anomalies of history that anyone who has believed in God could have been satisfied that his belief was in need of no essential improvement or revision. Since the idea of God is the idea of a being supremely good and just, it would naturally follow that such a being would not leave the human race without any clew to his purposes. Hence many have supposed that there has been revealed in Scripture a complete and adequate idea of God. Yet this seems to be a radically mistaken view. God is, indeed, revealed in his world, in human experience everywhere, in the life of all genuine religions, and especially in the development of Judaism and Christianity. But there are two contrasting views of how a God might reveal himself. Revelation, whatever form it takes, may be regarded as a stopping place for thought and life, a point of rest; or it may be regarded as a stimulus to further thought and life, a starting point of motion. On the former view, revelation is dogmatic; it imparts fixed and unchangeable truths. On the latter view, it is teleological or functional; it serves the purpose of leading men to move nearer the real God, and this may be accomplished even when the ideas believed to be true are not wholly correct. If we accept the second view, the most devout Christian believer will be as open-minded as the experimental scientist, and far more so than the dogmatic skeptic. He will not only welcome investigation, being aware that fear of investigation is a mark of the guilty rather than of the innocent, but he will also be among the first to perceive that no understanding of God which we have yet attained can come anywhere near to exhausting the whole truth about the divine nature. From every point of view, then, we must acknowledge both the need and the possibility of learning more about God, if there is any God at all....

Sooner or later everyone who cares about honest dealings in religion comes to the point where he must state plainly his conception of God. If there is no other value in his statement, it will at least enable others to avoid his errors; and if there is any real truth in his idea, they may profit by it. It is in this spirit that I shall now formulate a definition of God in which I have come to believe as a result of my investigations. I shall state it at first, in a rather detailed way, as follows:

> God is a conscious Person of perfect good will. He is the source of all value and so is worthy of worship and devotion. He is the creator of all other persons and gives them the power of free choice. Therefore his purpose controls the outcome of the universe. His purpose and his nature must be inferred from the way in which experience reveals them, namely, as being gradually attained through effort, difficulty, and suffering. Hence there is in God's very nature something which makes the effort and pain of life necessary. There is within him, in addition to his reason and his active creative will, a passive element which enters into every one of his conscious states, as sensation, instinct, and impulse enter into ours, and constitutes a problem for him. This element we call The Given. The evils of life and the delays in the attainment of value, in so far as they come from God and not from human freedom, are thus due to his nature, yet not wholly to his deliberate choice. His will and reason acting on The Given produce the world and achieve value in it.

This definition may be put more concisely in the following terms:

> God is a Person supremely conscious, supremely valuable, and supremely creative, yet limited both by the free choices of other persons and by restrictions within his own nature.

This definition makes God much more limited than does traditional theism, yet much less limited than does any form of dualism which contrasts God with matter or with any being in the universe which originated independently of God. Let us now consider this definition in its background and development....

One who asserts that God is a spiritual personality and who is conscious of the limitations of human reason is likely to be impressed by the counter assertion that God is suprapersonal. To say that God is personal sounds much like saying that God is human. Yet this is not intended. Of course the being that originates and controls the universe is far above the human plane, and must have powers and properties of which we know nothing. Yet, if we are not to talk nonsense, we must not ascribe to God any attributes which contradict the best we know. It is highly probable that the good, the true, and the beautiful for God are so far beyond the best truth and goodness and beauty of our experience that we may well be said to be playing on the shores of an infinite ocean of goodness, truth, and beauty. Nevertheless, if God is God, his truth cannot contradict any real truth we possess; likewise his goodness and beauty cannot contradict experienced truth and beauty. Hence, if we wish to call God suprapersonal, there is no objection to doing it, provided by suprapersonal we mean only superhuman. Who can deny that God's experiences transcend man's? But if we mean, as some do mean, to deny that God is a conscious spirit, then we are moving off into the dark. To deny that God is conscious is to assign to him a state of unconsciousness; it is to deny that he can love or know or will or purpose, for all of these are conscious processes. If there is a God at all, a being worthy of our worship, he must be conscious. A blind force might be feared, but could not be worshiped; an unconscious spirit might be pitied, but could not be adored. To be a God is to be conscious. To try to improve on consciousness is to go beyond the evidence of experience and the powers of imagination. If we seek for something which is not consciousness, we find only the unconscious. An unconscious being is not a being more than human; it is far less than human. In this sense, the suprapersonal turns into the subpersonal. But there remains the truth in the idea of the suprapersonal that there is always more to learn about God. Yet as soon as we grant the possibility that more may turn out to be utterly irrational, so soon we have taken away the ground of all rational thought whatever.

We have been discussing the first trait of God in the concise definition given above, namely, that he is supremely conscious. Now let us turn to the second, namely, that he is supremely valuable. The goodness of God is his most essential attribute. We could feel much more religious in the presence of an impersonal and unconscious power that was making for goodness in the world than we could in the presence of a conscious person who was evil or indifferent to values. While this is abstractly true, it does not render the idea of an impersonal or unconscious God any more reasonable. Moreover, goodness and all other values are meaningless except as conscious experiences. If the universe has any value beyond man's enjoyment of value, it is because there is a cosmic consciousness that realizes that value. Goodness that is nobody's goodness is no goodness at all. A reason that is unconscious and impersonal is not reason until a mind understands it. Beauty which is no one's enjoyment is only a possibility of beauty, but not real beauty. Value does not belong to impersonal things; it dwells only in minds.

Religion has always been concerned with value. It has faced the evils of life with the confidence that there is a good power behind them, just as science has faced the unsolved problems of experience with the confidence that they have a cause. As Hoffding says, religion rests on the axiom of the conservation of value as science has rested on the axiom of the conservation of energy. The critics of religion have always made much of the facts of evil; but no more than has religion itself. Sin and suffering have been the central problem of most great religions. On the other hand, critics of religion have evaded the problem of good. By the problem of good I mean the explanation of how there comes to be any good at all in the universe. Evil is a problem only because there is some good which we are not now attaining and which the evil prevents our attaining. "Where did all this evil come from?" asks the doubter. "Where did all this good come from?" asks the believer. We need, it is true, a conception of God which will account for both good and evil in the world. However, almost any conception of God has the advantage over atheism of at least attempting a fundamental explanation of both good and evil; whereas atheism assumes that the whole range of value experience arises in man from a source that neither knows nor cares anything about value. In the next chapter we shall consider value experience as evidence for God. But whether this God of ours exists or not, the only reasonable way to conceive him, even as a possibility, is as supreme value.

This conception of God means that we think of him as the one who can bring good out of evil. If he is supreme value, he cannot allow any evil that will permanently frustrate his purpose. He may delay, but he cannot fail. Whatever the origin of evil may be, and however awful it may be, God is the one who is never baffled by any evil. It may be that many goods are possible only through a co-operation of God's will and man's will, and it may be that man may fail to co-operate. Yet, in any given situation, we may suppose, God can achieve certain goods through man's co-operation; if man does not co-operate, then different goods will have to be achieved by God in a different way. But no situation is finally evil. Beyond every obstacle there lies a possible achievement, out of every evil a possible good may grow. This is the meaning of faith in God.

The third point in our definition of God was that God is supremely creative. To speak of creativity is to mention God's most mysterious attribute. Yet this particular mystery is no product of religious thought; somehow, in some way, some power has originated the energy of the universe and has brought the worlds into being. The mystery of creation is inherent in the nature of things, and, strangely enough, this particular attribute of God is one that is most easily and most widely believed. Yet if anything were to justify us in regarding God as suprapersonal, it is his creative power. For God to create means for him to bring into being by an act of will. Human wills cannot create; they can only select from that which has already been created or combine factors in such a manner that powers beyond their control will create something new. Pure creation is indeed superhuman and mysterious. But mysterious as is the thought of creation, it is far less so than those theories which would account for the origin of all things apart from purpose and will and would try to explain all of the actual facts of purpose and will in the world as products of unconscious and impersonal forces. There must be some source of the vast cosmic energies. To regard that source as a will is to make creation less miraculous than to regard it as a mindless source of mind or an unconscious source of consciousness.

To call God creative involves several points. It means that the entire universe is dependent on his will for its existence. The idea that creation occurred at some one point in time, long ago, is untenable in the light of the expansion of the idea of God. The constant conservation of the energy of the universe points to a will that is eternally creating. Hence, creation implies the immanence of God in all things. In particular, it means that the law of evolution is God's method of creation. It is coming to be generally recognized that evolution is not merely a recombination of pre-existing elements, but is the scene of the arrival of new qualities which could not possibly be explained merely as forms of what had been there before. Consciousness, for example, when it arises in the course of evolution, is plainly no combination of atoms, no matter how subtle or complex the atoms are. It is a genuine novelty. Similarly, evolution could not progress at all unless novel variations were to occur which are fit to survive. Thus evolution reveals with especial vividness the creative activity of God, and, by its teaching of the relatedness of all life, adds much to the force of the argument for one divine creator. Furthermore, God is creative in a special sense when he produces other persons. There seems to be no reason for regarding physical nature as anything other than the conscious will of God in action. There is no ground, or very little ground, to suppose that physical nature has any inner life of its own apart from the God who controls it. The case is different with persons. We know by experience that a person has an inner life, or, rather, is an inner life; and we have seen in connection with our study of pantheism how unreasonable it is to suppose that any imperfect or incomplete person is literally a part of God. Therefore, when God creates persons, he wills that there shall be consciousness in the world other than his own; that there shall be wills which are self-determining; and so, in this supreme act of his creative power, he limits his control over the universe. Thus we have found that a supreme act of divine expansion produces a supreme contraction.

We have now reached the fourth and last of the elements in the definition, namely, that God is limited both by the free choices of other persons and by restrictions due to The Given within his own nature. That he is limited by the free choices of other persons is generally conceded by all who believe in God, in accordance with the point of view which we have just expressed. If we find God a problem, it is not impossible that he also finds us a problem. Supreme reason may find the strange uses we make of our freedom far less intelligible than human reason finds God. Yet the limitation due to human freedom is, in the last analysis, founded in the will of God, and so is not to be regarded as a serious threat to the traditional attribute of omnipotence.

The new part of my definition is the suggestion that there are real limitations within the divine nature. The idea seems at first abhorrent. But, as we have said before, the evidence for God lies in experience, and we must think God, if we are to think truly, in such manner as to make experience intelligible. At this point we have to consider the mass of evidence which pointed toward what we have called the contraction of God. On the one side is God, the glorious and expanded one, supreme in goodness and power; on the other, the facts of evil in the world. It may be that we can ascribe all sin to human wills; but we certainly cannot impute to man the blame for the slow and painful processes of life, or for the presence of earthquakes, cyclones, and disease germs in the world. It is difficult for the mind to refrain from two judgments on nature: that it is the work of a power which aims at ends and achieves them, and also that this power is working under great difficulties. Indeed, so great are the difficulties that some observers can see nothing but them. H. M. Kallen says that "a surd lurks under every law of nature, a flaw in every design of God," and General Smuts speaks of "the dark opaque character" of the universe—ethically and rationally. But our view frankly sees these dark factors as elements within the life of a good God.

Four main types of evidence have contributed to my conviction that God is limited. They are based respectively on the facts of evolution, the nature of consciousness, the principle of dialectic, and religious experience. Let us consider these separately.

In the long sweep of evolution, Mother Nature (a name we use when we wish to avoid saying God) seems to display prodigality and wastefulness. Many species die an untimely death, entire species perish and are known only through their fossil remains, many forms of life are seemingly trivial, and others, such as disease germs and parasites, are destructive and exclusively harmful. In the light of these facts, it is impossible for me to say honestly that I can regard all this as the deliberate purpose of an all-powerful and good God. On the other hand, the law and the progress evident in evolution, the adaptations of life to environment and of environment to life, the origination of higher and higher forms, all make it evident that evolution is purposive. Putting these two aspects together, we are led to say that nature is the work of a power that is achieving its ends in the face of what seems to be opposition. There is evidence of design in nature; there is also evidence of frustration of design and of delay in its achievement.

There are at least three possible explanations of this situation, if we are to assume a God at all: first, that this element of opposition is a product of the creative will of God, chosen as the best means of attaining his ends (this is the view of traditional theism); secondly, that this element is something external to God (this is the view of Manicheism, Zoroastrianism, and some forms of modern dualism); and, thirdly, that it is due to factors within God himself, which are eternal aspects of his nature, but not products of his will or choice. The last-named view is the one which I have become convinced is nearest to the truth, and I shall undertake to show why I regard it as the best attainable idea of God at the present stage of thought. It holds that God is eternal reason and eternal will, dealing with what I have called The Given in his eternal experience. God's will is the creative aspect of the universe, but that will is limited by the laws of eternal reason and by the facts of The Eternally Given. That there is an eternal reason must be evident to anyone who has studied elementary mathematics or logic; Plato knew that God geometrizes. That there is eternal will follows from the purposive ongoing of things. That there is an eternal Given element in divine experience which is not a product of divine will is evident from the difficulties under which the divine will evidently labors in expressing perfection in the world. . . .

Another consideration growing out of evolution points to the idea of a finite God. Evolution plainly means that time and change are of fundamental importance in the universe. Now the traditional faith has laid great stress on the immutability of God, his absolute eternal unchangeability. Doubtless the universe must be guided by certain unchanging laws; but our whole experience is that of a world changing and evolving in time. Religion has sung of the day when "the trumpet of the Lord shall sound and time shall be no more"; but if there is such a day, thought cannot avoid asking about the day after that. In short, any view of God which elevates him entirely above time and process and renders him an eternal *nunc stans*—a standing present—pays tribute to his excellence without relating his being to the actual facts. The only God worth believing in, however, in the light of the evidence, is a God in living relation to the facts of cosmic and human history. He is a God into whose very being time enters; we need a temporalistic rather than a purely eternalistic view of God. God is one who works; one to whom the passage of time means something; to whom the events of a progressive creative evolution are significant; for whom change is profoundly important—such changes as occur in human character, as well as those more sublime changes in his revelation of himself to man in the course of history. Indeed, taking evolution in the largest sense, it may be that the development of the entire physical universe as we know it is but an insignificant episode in the eternally active history of God. For to call God temporal is not to deny that he is eternal; it is only to deny he is timeless, or that he is not intimately related to and concerned with events in time. . . . Thus our finite God is not one of a finished perfection; his perfection and the perfection of his world consist in their perfectibility. This does not mean that God is ever ignorant or evil in his will; he always knows all that can be known and his will is always guided by perfect devotion to the ideal of love. Yet it does mean that he confronts within his own experience genuine difficulties, out of which arise the apparent defects of the physical world. On this view, God does not deliberately choose the cruelties of evolution and the sufferings of creation; they represent, rather, the necessary outcome of his own eternal Given nature, out of which he is always bringing a higher good.

Evolution, the first type of evidence for the belief in a finite God, has been discussed. The second type, as we stated, is based on the nature of consciousness. Assuming, again, that there is a personal God, I wish to show from the nature of consciousness that he must be finite. It is true that some have used similar considerations to disprove God's existence, or at least his personality. I use them to disprove the conception of a God so infinite that he cannot be personal. We shall reflect on human freedom and its relation to the divine foreknowledge, on the relation between will and "nature," and on the presence of active and passive factors in consciousness.

First, then, let us examine the bearing of human freedom on our conception of God. That every human consciousness is largely determined by factors beyond its control is manifest. The past and the environment exercise an unescapable influence on us. One who holds to freedom does not deny these facts or belittle them. Freedom, indeed, can be rationally defined only by reference to them, for it consists in the choice or selection of elements from a total field of experience which is determined by a power beyond our control. The effects of our choice are beyond our direct control too, in a sense, although not beyond our powers of prediction and indirect control. If this is the nature of human freedom, it is not impossible that there is something analogous in the divine freedom, although only remotely so. With all the creative power of God there may be something Given in his nature as subject matter for his choice. I offer this particular argument very diffidently. More confidently I express the view that if man is truly free, God must be finite as regards his knowledge. At least, if our temporalistic view of God be true, and God is not utterly above and beyond all time, he cannot be thought of as knowing in advance what a free person will choose. This we have discussed already in another context. Man's freedom is an actual limitation on the foreknowledge of God. A thinker no less than John Locke said: "I cannot make freedom in man consistent with omnipotence and omniscience in God, though I am as fully persuaded of both as of any truths I most firmly assent to." We have here the calamitous consequences of the influence of a one-sided devotion to the expansion of God. Even when the expansive ideas lead to contradiction, they are held to tenaciously. Why not be consistent and acknowledge that God is limited in his foreknowledge? His power and wisdom would still be amply sufficient to bring good out of any situation that could arise.

Next, in our examination of consciousness, we note that there is an inseparable relation between the will and the nature of any conscious being. Every conscious being, or every being of any sort whatever, must have a nature; that is, it must have a definite structure, definite properties and qualities. In the nature of a conscious being it is possible for it to make choices; this fact we call its will. But its will is not a separate faculty or power; it is, rather, the act of a whole self possessing a specific nature. Traditionally God has been thought of as self-caused (*causa sui*) and as pure actuality (*actus purus*)—a being completely self-determined with no potentiality for further development. These abstractions, an inheritance from the great Aristotle, have been entirely on the side of expansion and have blinded the eyes of theists to the empirical difficulties of the view. If God be regarded as a wholly self-caused will, we are brought into serious difficulties. Can God choose whether his nature shall be in time or not? Can he choose whether the laws of reason shall be true or not? The old questions haunt us: Can he make a round triangle, a two which multiplied by two will produce six, a time prior to his own existence? Manifestly not! Rather his eternal nature includes reason, never-ending activity in time, and the rich realm of The Given with which his will has to cope in the task of world building and development. His nature as a conscious being sets limits to his will; God must be finite. . . .

The third main argument for the finiteness of God may be stated briefly, although it may be taken as a surprising twist of thought. Hegel is the one thinker of all in the history of philosophy who would be most radically opposed to the finiteness of God. He believes that God is the infinite and absolute. Yet he developed an important principle of thought which plays right into the hands of our conception, namely, the principle of dialectic. Stated simply, this means that all reality is full of opposition and contrast; everything that is stands in contrast with something else; every thesis implies some sort of antithesis. This means that the nature of God is to contain opposition and tension. But every opposition leads on to a higher level of life; every struggle points to a higher meaning or synthesis. Thus, for Hegel, as for our view, the divine life consists essentially of struggle and victory over opposition, a victory for which a price has always to be paid even by God himself. The traditional view almost inevitably engenders the idea that God's task is an easy one; that he stands apart from the struggle in spotless white. Our view sees him as the greatest sufferer in the universe and through this the greatest victor; his nature is not merely goodness but also dialectic struggle, or, rather, his goodness is not merely an abstract quality but the constant victory of constant effort.

The fourth main argument is derived from religious experience. Religious life demands that full weight be given to the contraction of God. Sometimes this demand is crude; God is thought of as having a human form, as being capricious and lawless, as feeling angry or as being opposed by devils and powers of darkness. But these beliefs are not the heart of religion; they are its excrescences. Some hold, indeed, that any finite God is of no worth. This is the view of McTaggart, who knew very little about religion, save as a body of beliefs; it is also the view of Hocking, who is one of the most sympathetic interpreters of religion in modern philosophy. Yet the testimony of most religious experience points to something like the finiteness we assert. It worships a God who is, on the one hand, reasonable and good, and, on the other, mysterious and above our comprehension. His ways are not our ways. He is one to whom the believer prays knowing that he will be heard justly and reasonably; yet he is also one who has hidden counsels which lead him often to answer in the negative. It seems to be the voice of religion that there is something above and beyond reason in the reasonable God. This is a hard saying, against which I have often rebelled. Yet I wonder whether it is not an intuitive recognition of the depths of the eternal divine experience, which our view has led us to recognize as Something Given, which his reason and will do not create, but with which they have to deal. Jakob Boehme speaks of a "bitter torment," a "fire of anger" within God; Rudolph Otto describes the irrational element in the divine nature as "the numinous." This dark aspect of religion points to a tragic reality in God. God is not simply a happy, loving Father; he is the struggle and the mysterious pain at the heart of life. He is indeed love; but a suffering love that redeems through a Cross.

It might seem that the resultant idea, as we have been describing it, surrenders too much of the expansion of God to his contraction. But this is not the case. Rather, we accept the expansion in so far as it refers to the divine goodness and the range of his experience, and assign the contraction to the divine power. The advance of modern thought has compelled us to modify our faith either in God's character or in his omnipotence. We believe that it is far more reasonable to deny the absolute omnipotence of the power manifesting itself in the world than to deny its goodness. On our view, God is perfect in will, but not in achievement; perfect in power to derive good from all situations, but not in power to determine in detail what those situations will be. It is not a question of the kind of God we should like to have. It is a question of the kind of God required by the facts.

HARRIS FRANKLIN RALL

arris Franklin Rall (1870–1964) was the son of a German itinerant preacher in the Evangelical Association. Reared in Iowa and Nebraska, he received his education at the University of Iowa, at Yale, and in Germany. Rall served as President of the Iliff School of Theology but spent most of his life as professor of theology at Garrett Biblical Institute. Rall was a deeply devout, adventurous man who sought to enrich and broaden the personal and social dimensions of Christian faith and life. Rall's theology was centered on the theme of salvation, and his task, as he conceived it, was to defend the validity of Christian interpretation of human existence. His defense against the intruding secularization of modern life was intended to convince people outside the faith and to support those inside. Rall also had a strong ethical sensitivity and was involved in social causes because, for him, Christian truth was always a truth for life with decisive personal and social moral implications. Rall was a prolific writer and among his more important books are *A Faith for Today* (1936), *The Christian Faith and Way* (1947), and *Religion as Salvation* (1953). The selection which follows represents the beginning point of his theological construction. "The Finality of the Christian Religion" is chosen from *Christianity: An Inquiry into its Nature and Truth*, pp. 68–81. Copyright 1940 by The Trustees of Lake Forest University: copyright renewed 1968 by Harris Franklin Rall. Reprinted with the permission of Charles Scribner's Sons.

THE FINALITY OF THE CHRISTIAN RELIGION

Christianity claims to rest upon a divine revelation. Its followers have declared that it is original, absolute, and final. We need to consider these claims, ask their meaning, and inquire whether Christianity can assert uniqueness among the many religions of the world and finality in a universe of constant change.

For traditional theology the problem of the absoluteness of Christianity is very simple. The transcendent and almighty God works his will by direct action. When he gives men the Bible or establishes the Church, the result is absolute and inerrant. Christianity is thus lifted above the stream of time, above the conditioned and relative. What is overlooked here is the fact that God cannot enter the stream of time except in definite and conditioned relation to history, and that truth can come to man only as an element in conscious experience and as related to human life. For Christian faith Jesus Christ is God's supreme word of revelation. But Jesus passed through the stages of physical, mental, and spiritual growth, confessed limitations of knowledge, and voiced truth in the thought forms of his age. The divine is not a tangible, thing-like substance, thrust down from some upper level; it is the life of the Spirit realized in human experience, that is, in human insight and thought, in ideal and devotion. The divine, therefore, must always be relative for us, relative to man's apprehension, to his stage of development, to his response. So the New Testament speaks of our seeing through a glass darkly, of growing up, of not yet having attained, of being guided into further truth. Absoluteness in this sense is not a demand of religion or an implication of Christian faith.

In another sense, however, religion does demand the absolute, and that is because it demands the divine. It does not think of its ideas or attainments as absolute; only the epigones feel the need of making this claim, and it is with them that the theories of verbal inspiration and infallible Church arise. But faith does demand God, and that means the absolute. One may even say, where there is no absolute there is no religion, for religion is man's conviction that there is a final power on which he depends, a final good for which he must strive, a highest to which he owes utter loyalty if he is not to be wholly untrue. Other demands of life are relative, a matter of less or more; religion means all or nothing, "the utmost for the highest." The authentic note of religion speaks clearly here in Jesus. Men may call it arrogance or delusion, as Nietzsche did, but Jesus could do no less. He made on men an absolute demand because he brought absolute reality. He brought the highest, and he summoned men to leave all and give all.

The issue is clear when we turn to the opposing position, with its pure relativism and humanism. There are in this position elements of truth that we must recognize. There is Kant's insight that all knowing is a human activity, man's own ordering perception and shaping reason.

There is the fact of the functional significance of religion, that religion springs from human need and maintains itself as a minister to human life. But relativism leaves out of account or flatly denies the other member of this relation, that higher world of spiritual reality the belief in which is at the heart of religion. A consistent expression of this position is to be found in *The Philosophy of the As If*, by Hans Vaihinger, where God is one of various useful fictions whose assumption is justified by the practical needs of life. When this stage is reached we have come not merely to the twilight of the gods, but to the twilight of all religion.

For traditional theology the answer to this second question was likewise very simple: Christianity is true, other religions are false; Christianity is original and unique because it came direct and perfect from the hand of God. This answer, too, is untenable. The Old Testament itself reveals a larger point of view, especially in the prophetic writings. It sees the one God of all the earth, concerned with righteousness and not with differences of nationality, interested in all peoples and moving in all history. The New Testament points even more clearly the same way. Christian thought must hold not only to the one God of all men, but to the one indwelling and illuminating and redeeming Spirit of love and truth that has everywhere and always wrought in men. As God is one, so truth is one and righteousness is one. Wherever they are found, there men may see God.

Further we must recognize the continuity and interrelation of all man's cultural life, including religion. The stream of history is one; there is no one current that we can separate from the rest and call sacred, or supernatural. Christianity confessedly roots deeply in the religion of Israel. Israel herself throughout her history had been under many and varied influences and mediated these to Christianity. The latter, even in its earlier development, not merely took terms but inevitably ideas and forms from the Graeco-Roman world in which it lived, and has been similarly affected ever since. If God be one, everywhere seeking to reveal and give himself to men, and if man be one, everywhere the same in his fundamental needs, then we should expect analogies in all religions, common ideas such as those of revelation, salvation, sacrifice, and communion with the divine.

1. In our earlier discussion we found the distinctive nature of Christianity not in its institutional forms, in doctrine or organization or code or cultus, but rather in a conviction concerning God and the way of life which had its abiding inspiration and direction in the person of Jesus. Our question then is as to the significance and originality of Jesus.

The whole matter has been put in the wrong light by being turned into a dispute as to whether Jesus set forth any doctrines that were strictly new. History does not move in that way; her first principle is continuity. No advance is ever made except as related to what went before; Jesus stood definitely upon the faith of his race and especially upon the teachings of the prophets. Just as erroneous is the assumption that religion can be summed up in ideas. Jesus' avowed purpose was not to give a new teaching but to summon men to repentance and faith and to bring in a new life on earth. Irenaeus gave the right answer back in the second century: "He brought all newness in bringing himself." The modern theory of emergent evolution offers a suggestive idea here. What it shows us is a process which we can describe but cannot really explain. The whole development of life depends upon this process of making new wholes, in which elements are joined together to form a new unity not by way of mere addition, but in such manner that a new and higher life appears with qualities that the closest study of the individual parts would not have suggested. We have been told again and again that Christianity is a syncretistic religion, and we have had pointed out to us the origin of this sacrament and that doctrine. If we look at it as a whole, however, we see rather a great creative synthesis and the personality of Jesus as its beginning and its abiding center. The first Christian century was an age of deep religious interest and great religious confusion. The most diverse elements had been brought together in the Roman world. Universalism and syncretism marked the time. It was their refusal of this easy-going tolerance that brought suspicion and enmity to the Christians. The facts seem contradictory, the explanation is simple. Jesus was the creative center of this new movement. Christianity was no sum of addition, no chance confluence of diverse tides of religious thought and life, any more than it was the product of a given social milieu. With that insight which is the final secret of his own being, Jesus saw for himself the truth of God and life and used the rich heritage of his people's past. And all this came to a new creative expression, first in his own life, then in his teaching, then in that life which he was able to create in others. Even a slight acquaintance makes plain, first the unity of his message, then the unity of word and life in himself. He is neither a quoter of authority nor a collector of wisdom.

2. If now we look at the heritage which he left, we see how all the old truths gain power and meaning becaues of what he chose, what he omitted, and what he made central.

(1) We note first what he did to the idea of religion. (a) He gave humanity a religion of the spirit. He found religion identified with the externals of ceremonial and rules of behavior. He called men to see the

significance of the inner spirit, the higher righteousness. Yet the spirit, the reverent trust which he emphasized, the loyalty to the highest, the absolute good will, did not mean mere subjectivism or passivity; it summoned men to the highest activity. (b) He gave men a religion that was ethical through and through. His God was ethical, not abstract essence or sheer power or even highest sovereignty first of all, but righteousness and love. Fellowship with this God was ethical; its supreme demand was that men should share the Father's spirit of good will. The test of religion for him was not observance of ritual, or feeling, or correct ideas. And his idea of salvation was ethical; it was the life and help that came to men as they turned, repentant and trustful, to fellowship with such a God. No salvation without repentance and obedience and moral likeness! (c) He made religion universal. It had always belonged to some given place and people. Nationalism was both the strength and the limitation of Judaism. The religion of Jesus is for man as man.

(2) If we turn to the great concepts that underlie his teaching, we shall see again their simplicity, unity, thorough-going ethical character, and universality of appeal. One conclusion is made clear by the centuries that have passed: if any spiritual faith can maintain itself in man, it will be this faith. The heart of it is his idea of God. It is no conclusion of philosophy, to be overturned some time when its premises are shown false. it is no inheritance of tradition unthinkingly accepted. It is a faith that dares to believe that the highest that man knows is supreme in the universe, and that man must live in the light of that highest. His God is transcendent in power and goodness, calling men to reverence and awe; he is immanent as the ever-working God of redeeming love, calling men to trust and surrender. He is personal and man may have fellowship with him; yet the center of religion is never man but always God, always the God that is above man, the power to be trusted, the good that summons to obedience and calls to achievement. Supremely significant is his idea of God as redemptive good will. "The rabbis," says Montefiore, "attached no less value to repentance than Jesus. . . . They too welcomed the sinner in his repentance. But to *seek out* the sinner, and, instead of avoiding the bad companion, to choose him as your friend in order to work out his moral redemption, this was, I fancy, something new in the religious history of Israel." And Jesus regarded this attitude and activity on his part as representing the spirit and deed of his Father.

Equally significant is his idea of man. Stoicism offered the highest conception of man in the Graeco-Roman world; it transcended the limits of race and even of sex, and called for an equal regard for all. Yet it drew its lines in another way. It was intellectualistic and aristocratic; it could recognize the wise man in a slave, but for the mass of men, not wise, not strong, but unfortunate and wretched, it had no word. The eye of Jesus was just as keen for the realities of life. He was no sentimentalist, but he did see more deeply than the noblest of the Stoics; he saw the inner motive and ultimate possibilities. He condoned no evil but he believed in the power of the good. For him every man in his truest nature and in God's intention was a son of God; therefore every man was sacred as man. And he believed in men; in his reverence for humanity, in his passion for justice, in his faith in men, in his summons to a common service for a common weal, Jesus is the deepest spring of the best that we mean by democracy. The teaching of Jesus is the foundation of the highest social idealism of our day.

Of vital importance in his teaching is the goal of human life, set forth in threefold aspect. He offers fulfillment for all the needs and hopes of men, recognizing the individual in his own right; he holds up a social hope, a kingdom of God which means a new humanity; he includes the life beyond. His word for all three is life, and in them he presents a lofty and inclusive hope as well as a commanding summons.

3. So far we have considered simply the teaching of Jesus. But neither the nature of Christianity nor the significance of Jesus can be rightly determined unless we take account of his influence upon others, the forces that he released in the world, and the experiences and insights of his followers, especially of the first generation.

It has been repeatedly urged in recent years, in denial of the originality and uniqueness of early Christianity, that it was simply one of the many mystery cults of that age, and that it is to be interpreted in the light of these religious movements which were so characteristic of that time. Our knowledge of the mystery cults is meager; their special lore and peculiar rites were restricted to initiates and little has come down to us from this period. Common is a deep sense of the evils of life, a longing for deliverance, the faith in some deity, or hero-god, the belief that a certain mystical-emotional communion with this god is possible, and the stress upon rites of purification and sacrament through which this union with the god is achieved and by which immortality is assured. Very common is the thought of this hero-god as one who died and rose to life again.

There are obvious points of likeness not only with later Christianity but with Paul: the sense of evil, the concern with redemption, the idea of a dying and risen Lord (kyrios), the belief in mystical communion, the use of sacraments, a certain dualism of world-view, and the union of followers in cult groups as against religions which included whole peoples. But such analogies of form are common in religon; the crucial

199

matter is as to the content. It is sufficient here to state certain main contrasts. (a) Early Christianity held, with Judaism, to a thorough-going monotheism; Jesus was not a hero-god, but one through whom the living God had come to men. The concern of the mystery cults was not with God but with this or that divine hero. (b) Jesus was a historical figure, whose spirit, teaching, and life stand forth in clear and unmistakable individuality. The central figures of the mystery cults are vague in outline and either mythical or of unknown origin. (c) Ethical elements, though distinctly subordinate, are not lacking in the mystery religions, especially in the later stages; rites of purification and discrimination in choice of candidates are in point. Celsus, indeed, suggested their ethical superiority to Christianity which, he said, receives "every one who is a sinner, who is devoid of understanding, who is a child." But it is at this very point that the superiority of Christianity appears. In it the ethical is not preliminary or incidental but a central and constant demand; and the redemption that it offers is no mere deliverance from such natural ills as change and death, but the power of a new life by which to meet these high demands. Hence it dares to invite, not the selected few, but the many, not just the wise and virtuous, but the simple and sinful.

Can we regard Christianity as the final religion? The objections lie at hand: If Christianity as we actually have it in Scripture and creed and Church is always something relative to the historical and human, to man's apprehension in thought and realization in life, then must it not be partial and imperfect? If it be something here in time, must it not show constant change? Does not the history of Christianity reveal such change from the beginning, and is not such progress what we desire? Does not the final mean the static, and so mean death? Are not the open mind and loyalty to truth at the very heart of high religion, so that we must repudiate the claim to finality in the very name of religion? In answer we must examine more closely what is involved in the Christian position.

1. It has been a common mistake to seek finality for Christianity in the wrong place, that is, in its institutional forms of expression, in creeds, moral codes, organization, and ritual; this would, indeed, mean a static finality and a closed mind. But these are all interpretations and expressions of religion. For Christianity as a prophetic religion, however, the dominant category is personal and vital, not institutional. It knows how imperfect its life is, how faulty the empirical Church, how far its formulae are from expressing the truth of the infinite God. But its conviction is that the personal and living God, infinite and eternal, has spoken

to men in Jesus Christ. Our knowledge about this God is not absolute, but we do know this absolute God. In Jesus Christ we have heard his word to us, have found the way of living fellowship with him, and have seen his will for our lives.

2. It is a mistake to think of development, whether in nature or history, as merely ceaseless change. The law of life is rather a double one, that of change on the one hand, of continuity and conservation on the other. An age-long movement reaches a definite achievement with a certain finality. There is still movement, but it is along other lines; the achievement becomes a permanent gain and the stage is set free for other needed work. Thus, as has been suggested by H. F. Osborn and others, man came to the end of his development as a psycho-physical organism with the Cro-Magnons, perhaps two score thousand years ago. In his natural endowment the man of today is no whit his superior; human advance since then has been in the cultural field through social heritage. In the apprehension and creation of beauty the Greeks reached certain goals that have not been passed. There are insights in the field of ethics which, though age-old, retain their place; we still recognize the value and authority of truth and justice and mercy. Despite opposing forces the monogamic family, reached long since in human development, will remain an abiding social institution.

In like manner Christianity represents definite and final insights in religion. Jesus made religion through and through ethical and supplied to ethics the motive force of religion. "It is the distinction of Jesus," writes Havelock Ellis, "that he has, for us, permanently expanded the bounds of individuality. What a supreme work of art we already possess in the Gospels! So that now when I open and turn over with reverent joy the leaves of the Gospels, I feel that here is enshrined the highest achievement of Man the Artist, a creation to which nothing can be added, from which nothing can be taken away." So if we turn to his conception of God, his idea of man, or to the ideal of life as seen in his own spirit, we find again what seem like final insights. "The finality of Christ and of what he imparts," says H. R. Mackintosh, "can justly be called in question only when a loftier fact than holy love has come into view." When we look at the movement of thought of the last nineteen centuries in relation to these basic ideals, the trend is forward toward the position of Jesus rather than beyond him.

3. Such finality does not exclude growth but demands it. No religion can be final which is not a growing religion. The finality of Christianity lies in a life of fellowship with God by faith and with men in love. As

such it is a great creative experience, and advance in knowledge and insight are of its very essence. Here quiet confidence and daring venture go together.

Historically the Christian religion has approved itself as final by this very capacity for growth. It has constantly taken over and assimilated new truth while at the same time maintaining its identity. The cynical saying, *Plus ça change, plus c'est la meme chose*, may be used here in tribute instead of criticism. As Archbishop Temple has said: "This is one of the distinctive characteristics of Christianity, that whereas all other religions have tended to stereotype the conditions in which they originated, because only in those conditions could their requirements be obeyed, Christianity has been a fermenting principle of change in every society into which it has come. This is primarily because it is centered not upon a formula but upon a Person, and its regulative principle is not a code but a Spirit." What is needed for progress, he says, is change with constancy of direction. "This is the constancy that the Gospel gives us. Our starting-point is fixed: it is the creative love of God. Our goal is fixed: it is the realized Kingdom of God. And our way is fixed: it is found in Him who said, 'I am the Way.' " Christianity has always kept a forward look. It believes in an indwelling Spirit who is to guide into larger truth. Despite recurrent lapses, it has made loyalty to truth central in the religious attitude. It has believed in a living God, continually working in the world. And the truths that it has taken up have not only found room in the Christian faith but have gained in that faith their richest expression. We may agree with Bishop F. J. McConnell that the uniqueness of Christianity includes a unique power to use everything that is usable. "Everything of the true and good and beautiful will get a better chance to show truth and goodness and beauty after it has been converted to Christianity than it ever had before."

It is in this connection that we can best consider the problem that has been raised for many by the apocalyptic element in early Christianity. It is not so easy to determine the actual teaching of Jesus at this point. The longer apocalyptic discourses attributed to him furnish an outstanding illustration of the influence upon the gospel account of the thought and life of the later community out of which these writings came. But that he expected in the immediate future the end of the age and the saving deed of God by which his rule was to be established on earth, that this expectation was shared by the early Church, and that primitive Christian thought and life were profoundly influenced by this hope, this is hardly to be disputed. Can we then accept as valid and final a religion whose central hope was not fulfilled, and whose ethical teaching seems to have been an *ad interim* affair designed for the brief time before the end?

But here again we have an illustration of Christianity's unique significance. Within that apocalyptic framework was the belief in the one living God and his saving purpose of love, and the summons to repent of sin and live in the spirit of this God. "The ethical teaching of Jesus," says C. H. Dodd, "is 'interim ethics' for those who expect that the world will shortly come to an end, but it is absolute ethics for those who have experienced for themselves the end of the world and the coming of the Kingdom." It springs "from its roots in the very constitution of the Kingdom of God, as determined by the nature and character of God himself, the loving God and our Father. The one universal ethical principle is that which is revealed in God's free grace to underserving men in offering them the blessings of his Kingdom. The finality of Christianity is seen here once more in the validity of its central faith and its capacity to receive new truth and make the needed change in the form of its expression.

GEORGIA HARKNESS

Georgia Harkness (1891–1974), a native of New York state, was educated at Cornell and Boston Universities. After teaching at Elmira and Mount Holyoke colleges, she taught at Garrett Biblical Institute and at the Pacific School of Religion for twenty-two years. Harkness was the first woman to become a major professional theologian in the United States in the twentieth century. She wrote some thirty-six books along with numerous articles, pamphlets and occasional pieces. In both her personal life and social concern she impressively exemplified basic qualities of Christian character. Harkness' theology worked out themes derived from Boston personalism such as the Fatherhood of God, the Bible as witness to Christian experience, Jesus as Lord and example for Christian living, and the Holy Spirit as the sustaining presence of God. Among her most important publications are: *Conflicts in Religious Thought* (1929, 1949), *Christian Ethics* (1957), *Foundations of Christian Knowledge* (1955), *Understanding the Christian Faith* (1947), and *Grace Abounding* (1969). The following selection continues the traditional Wesleyan emphasis on the role of the Holy Spirit in personal and corporate life. "The Work of the Holy Spirit" is taken from *The Fellowship of the Holy Spirit* (Nashville/New York: Abingdon, 1966), pp. 82–99.

THE WORK OF THE HOLY SPIRIT

In the preceding chapters, and particularly in the three devoted to a biblical survey, we have had occasion repeatedly to note the effects of the Spirit in human life. There has been no systematic discussion of these effects, but it is impossible to consider properly what the Holy Spirit is without recognition of what the Spirit *does*. This is inevitable, for the Holy Spirit is no inert entity or metaphysical essence, but the living God

204

himself as he imparts grace and power to the human spirit.

In the chapter which follows this one, we shall move into a difficult, but from a Christian standpoint an unavoidable, question, the doctrine of the Trinity. There we shall discover that the Trinity makes sense if it is grounded in Christian experience. If it is not, the problems multiply until irrationality breeds despair.

The present chapter, standing midway between the biblical survey and the theological issue soon to be examined, has a dual purpose. It aims to lay further groundwork for the declaration that the Trinity makes sense if it is rooted in Christian experience. Further than that, it aims to suggest from a biblical base how the works of the Spirit, manifold but discernible as certain continuing types, are vitally relevant to life at all times. Far from being simply an historical legacy from long ago, the Holy Spirit is still "God present and God acting."

Where shall we begin? As we saw in noting Paul's contributions, he recognized that the work of the Holy Spirit relates to the whole of life. The whole of life is many-sided, and thus every angle is related to every other. Yet there can be no system without a beginning somewhere, and this involves a selection of categories and their arrangement in a sequence.

The rubrics I shall adopt are historical and biblical, but they are also contemporary in meaning if not in terminology. Let us, then, think of the work of the Holy Spirit as the Life-giver, as Source of power, as Sanctifier, and as Revealer of truth.

In the Nicene Creed, repeated times without number in services of Christian worship since the end of the fourth century of our era, stand the words, "I believe in the Holy Ghost, the Lord, the giver of life." That the Holy Spirit is the Lord, even though not the only manifestation of the Lord, is clearly evident in the New Testament and especially in the words of both Paul and John. But what does it mean to say that he is also the giver of life?

To retrace some ground, though from a new perspective, even before the Old Testament and its people and times emerged, there was a belief in spirit as the giver of everything important. Whether as many spirits in animism, as *mana* in a semi-pantheistic monism, or personalized in some such fashion as in Longfellow's

> Gitche Manito, the mighty,
> The Great Spirit, the creator,

both nature and human life were more than themselves, and owed their existence to a Power beyond themselves. This mysterious Power—this "something more"—was spirit, not material substance, and Spirit was the life-giver.

This primitive faith was, of course, transcended in both Hebrew and Christian thought. It must be affirmed beyond possible misunderstanding that origins do not determine or define the subsequent stages of development. A higher stage was reached when in the words of the Jahwist writer (the "J" narrative of creation) we find in Genesis 2:7, "Then the Lord God formed man of dust from the ground, and breathed into his nostrils the breath of life; and man became a living being." Still later the author of the priestly, post-exilic story of creation suggests that the Spirit of God not only gives life to man but order to nature, "The earth was without form and void, and darkness was upon the face of the deep; and the Spirit of God was moving over the face of the waters" (Gen. 1:2).

It would not be profitable to restate here all that was said in chapter two about the work of the Spirit as it is found in the Old Testament. However, Ezekiel's vision of the revivification in the valley of dry bones is especially pertinent. Israel was alive biologically; it was almost dead spiritually. . . .

Not until the coming of Christ did this vision find fulfillment. Then it was not the nation, but individuals, that "came alive" with a great new faith and hope. This occurred again and again as Jesus brought healing, cleansing, and renewal of life to those whose lives he touched. We have seen that this was a major note in the coming of the Holy Spirit at Pentecost. Such new life in the Spirit is evidenced in the courage to witness to the faith and to spread the gospel to ever-widening areas that shines through the pages of the book of Acts and Paul's letters. For Paul such new life in the Spirit begins, continues, and ends in the living Christ, and his major message is its availability through God's grace to any who will claim it in penitence, faith, and love. . . .

Thus far, we have thought of the Holy Spirit as life-giver to the individual. This, indeed, is what the Bible for the most part does. Yet the work of the Spirit is by no means limited to solitary selves, or even to persons in their immediate, face-to-face relations.

The Church came into being through the life-giving work of the Holy Spirit. That is what Pentecost is all about. Probably not all of the initial 120 Christians in that company, and certainly not all of the ensuing 3000, knew each other by face and name. Yet all were quickened to new life both individually and in their corporate relations, and the Church was born.

So it has remained to the present insofar as the Church has been

Christ-centered, life-renewing in its service, and renewed in its own life as changes have taken place from age to age. There have been arid stretches, and as institutions took shape and form tended to replace spirit, the glow of Pentecost faded. Administrators replaced prophets, and the sacraments became functional elements in ecclesiastical control. Yet never wholly, and the institutions and sacraments may themselves be regarded as the vehicle of the Holy Spirit to the extent that they are genuine channels of grace. Without them the Church, if it continued to exist, would be much weakened in its endeavors for the glory of God and the service of the world. . . .

Some would stop at this point, and regard the life-giving work of the Holy Spirit as limited to the Christian experience of the individual believer and the corporate fellowship of the Church. Here we must be careful in our use of terms. We have seen that the Holy Spirit, as two words with one meaning, is found only in the New Testament, and as a designation for the living Christ still present in the lives of his followers, it is limited to a Christian context. Nevertheless, the Holy Spirit is the Spirit of God, and the divine Creator Spirit is not thus limited. The "living God who made the heaven and the earth and the sea and all that is in them...did not leave himself without witness" (Acts 14:15–17) among any people.

From this far-reaching fact it is legitimate to infer that the Spirit of God is present in the spiritual strivings, insights, and achievements of people who seek him through other paths than the Christian. Furthermore, he is present in the life-giving forces of nature. The passage just quoted continues with evidence of this, "For he did good and gave you from heaven rains and fruitful seasons, satisfying your hearts with food and gladness" (vs. 17). Need we hesitate to say that the Spirit is present and active in man's utilization of these gifts for human good? If we may, then the life-giving eternal Spirit is present also in man's eternal quest for goodness, truth, and beauty; for government "with liberty and justice for all"; for spiritual foundations in other high religions. This is not to say that any of these channels of the Spirit can be a substitute for the Christian way; it is to say that "God is greater than our hearts" (I John 3:20), and it is unbecoming for us to fence in the life-giving work of his Spirit.

An ancient prayer, spoken in services of worship for many centuries and still in use in the more liturgical churches, is *"Veni, Creator Spiritus!"* *"Come, Creator Spirit!"* This may well be our prayer today.

If there is one thing that all persons may be said to possess, it is a desire for power. Even the ever-present fact of human sin is not more pervasive, for it is in the longing for or the exercise of power to be, to do, or to have what one wants, regardless of obligation to God or man, that the sinning lies.

There are, of course, many kinds of power. As power to survive, the instinctual urge to self-preservation is shared with man by the animal world, and to this is linked in varying degrees the power to possess and to dominate. It characterizes nations, races, economic, cultural, and even ecclesiastical groups as well as individuals. No society could exist without it, yet from this fact stem some of the greatest perversions of justice. Obviously, the Holy Spirit may not be regarded as the source of the manifold perversions of power which are visible to anyone who reads his newspaper or listens to the radio or television.

It is power of a different sort, centering in self-mastery, concern for others, and obedience to the divine will that the Holy Spirit imparts. It is epitomized in the power of love and the reconciliation of man to God and to one another through love. Yet the power of the Spirit is no vague emotion dignified with the name of love; it is a dynamic, energizing force.

To glance again at the biblical sources, wherever the Spirit of God appears in the Old Testament there is an imparting of power, whether of physical strength to Samson, ecstatic utterance to the early bands of prophets, inspiration to the great prophets, or revivification to Israel. In the Gospels the Holy Spirit is to come upon Mary by the power of the Most High (Luke 1:35); Jesus returns from the wilderness temptation in the power of the Spirit (Luke 4:14); he undertakes his life's mission in the conviction that the Spirit of the Lord is upon him (vs. 18). Nowhere in the Gospels is the relation between the Holy Spirit and the earthly ministry of Jesus more clearly stated than in Peter's words to Cornelius in the tenth chapter of Acts, "You know . . . how God anointed Jesus of Nazareth with the Holy Spirit and with power; how he went about doing good and healing all that were oppressed by the devil, for God was with him" (Acts 10:36–38).

It is, of course, in the book of Acts and in the letters that one sees the tremendous increments of power that came into the lives of ordinary persons when they were Spirit-filled and Spirit-led. It is significant that in the post-resurrection promise of the coming of the Holy Spirit as this is recorded in Acts, power is the one specific gift mentioned (Acts 1:8). This gift was bountifully imparted and gloriously used. The records of courage under difficulty, forthright and inspired witness in speech, and fidelity in Christian living under tremendous odds ought never to leave us unmoved. Further healings of the infirmities of the body are recorded,

208

but most of all, the healing power of the Spirit. Like a cleansing wind—to revert to the original meaning of the term—the Holy Spirit blows away the mists and impurities of the human spirit to give new life and new power....

It was this emancipation of spirit that Paul found in Christ through the Holy Spirit. Thereafter he did not feel himself a slave to other men or to old traditions, but to Christ alone. Obligations there still were, more binding than before, but they were obligations accepted with a new zest. They could be accepted seriously but joyously, by men who found themselves no longer slaves to legalism or to passion but sons of God....

Familiar as we are today with the disorders that send people to psychiatrists and mental hospitals, with family quarrels terminating in broken homes, with bitter strife between racial, economic, and national groups, who can say that such counsel is irrelevant to the times? If such freedom is possible through ordered and disciplined living in the power of the Spirit, we had better find it!

Sanctification with its correlative term "holiness," as applied to Christian experience, is in bad odor today. Those of an older generation (and possibly not so old) who have heard those of the "holiness" sects talk about their "entire sanctification," claiming a self-righteous superiority in the victory over sin which others fail to see manifest in their living, will have no truck with either term. Recent theology with its stress on the holiness of God but the sinfulness and unworthiness of man moves in the same direction. If we add to "sanctification" and "holiness" a third term, "Christian perfection," the rout is apt to be complete.

With the rejection of what these terms are commonly taken to mean, I have great sympathy. However sincere the belief that one has reached the point of no return in his sinning, sin remains, and the Christian must fight an ongoing battle with it. To repent, to ask forgiveness of God and usually of the human person sinned against, and to go forward humbly by God's grace, is the continuing experience of the Christian.

Yet in a deeper sense, the Holy Spirit remains the Sanctifier that the Christian tradition has long conceived him to be. The Latin "sanctus" is the English "holy," and the Holy Spirit does impart what John Wesley called "scriptural holiness." God's design in raising up the people called Methodists, he said, was not to form a new sect but "to reform the nation, particularly the Church, and to spread scriptural holiness over the land." It need hardly be said that this task is not the exclusive prerogative of Methodists.

Such scriptural holiness with the Christian perfection which is its goal would arouse less confusion and dissent if it were understood to mean growth in Christian experience and in moral victory through Christ. It means, in short, "growing in grace," and there is no finer statement of its meaning than in the injunction found in II Peter 3:18, "But grow in the grace and knowledge of our Lord and Savior Jesus Christ. To him be the glory both now and to the day of eternity." The New English Bible further accents Christian maturity by suggesting an alternative reading, "But grow up, by the grace of our Lord and Savior Jesus Christ, and by knowing him."

John Wesley may have had more confidence in the possibility of Christian perfection, or of being "made perfect in love in this life," than do most Christians today. Yet what he was above all concerned about was the actual difference it makes to become a Christian and to continue going forward in the Christian way. And on this point, and on the work of the Holy Spirit in the daily demands of Christian living, the New Testament is completely clear. . . .

Since in traditional terminology a sharp distinction is sometimes drawn between justification and sanctification, a further word at this point may be in order. There is certainly a difference between the initial act of decision for Christ, which may be accompanied by a great emotional glow though it need not be, and the humdrum and difficult processes of daily Christian living. Yet there is no absolute line of demarcation. What the Holy Spirit does in bringing us to Christian commitment, whether suddenly or gradually, is also what the Holy Spirit does in the years of growth to greater Christian maturity. What is different is that "every one to whom much is given, of him will much be required" (Luke 12:48). As the gifts and the requirements increase, so does the sense of the undergirding presence and power of the Holy Spirit. There may be less of an ecstatic glow about it; what matters is that the light still shines and the fire burns.

The New Testament abounds in passages which indicate the difference the Holy Spirit makes in the life of the Christian. Perhaps the greatest, and certainly the most familiar, is "the more excellent way" set forth in I Corinthians 13. Yet for a summary of the gifts and graces imparted by the Spirit, nothing excels Galatians 5:22: "But the fruit of the Spirit is love, joy, peace, patience, kindness, goodness, faithfulness, gentleness, self-control; against such there is no law." Nor, we may add, is there any insuperable barrier to such fruit in those who will let the Spirit have his way within us.

One cannot read the account of the promise of the coming of the Holy Spirit as found in the Last Supper discourse in John's Gospel without discovering the prominence given to the work of the Holy Spirit as the revealer of truth. Yet it is truth projected forward from the revelation already given in Christ. In the words Jesus is quoted as speaking to his disciples the Counselor, the Holy Spirit, will "bring to your remembrance all that I have said to you" (14:26); the Counselor "will bear witness to me" (15:26); the Spirit of truth "will take what is mine and declare it to you" (16:14). It is clear that to the author of this Gospel the Spirit's revelation of truth was to be no independent witness dissociated from the truth already disclosed. Yet it is equally clear that the entire mood of these passages is open-ended and oriented toward the future. This is implied throughout but epitomized in the words, "I have yet many things to say to you, but you cannot bear them now. When the Spirit of truth comes, he will guide you into all the truth" (16:12–13). . . .

The term "inspiration" is often bandied about today, whether in reference to the Bible or to some kind of human experience which may or may not be religious. Without attempting to give an extended analysis of its meaning it may be pointed out that there is a direct connection between the Holy Spirit and a Christian understanding of inspiration. In the field of Christian faith and life, the possibility of new insights depends not only on long and rigorous search but on the illumination of the Spirit. In fact, the word inspiration means "inbreathing"—a cognate term to the original meaning of "spirit." This readily suggests that the breath of God continues to blow upon the human spirit from the supreme and decisive revelation in God's Son. . . .

The possibility of the discovery of new truth and a fresh understanding of the will of God amid changing circumstances is a great boon. Yet it is beset with perils. No communication is given except to and through human minds, and these are always susceptible to sin and error. Ever in the offing is the danger lest human presumption replace divine leading. That this can happen unconsciously even in sincere Christians, and perhaps most often in persons of such inflexible conviction that a sense of dogmatic certainty replaces humble quest, should put us all on guard.

To know when we are hearing the voice of the Holy Spirit, and when we are listening to our own unhallowed subconscious impulses, is not an easy matter. There are indices and channels of discovery in an unbiased and comprehensive survey of the total situation, in corporate worship that is deep and genuine, in interchange of thought with other wise and well-grounded Christians, in prayer and commitment that carries with it a willingness to go where the Spirit leads. Yet there is one safeguard that is indispensable to all others. It is what Paul calls the mind of Christ. Whatever carries forward our understanding of God and of his will as this has been revealed to us in Jesus *is* the work of the Holy Spirit; all else is suspect. . . .

L. HAROLD DEWOLF

L Harold DeWolf (b. 1905), a Nebraskan, completed his college work at Nebraska Wesleyan University. He did his graduate study at Boston University where he studied under Knudson. He later became professor of systematic theology at Boston University. In 1965 he became dean of the faculty and professor of systematic theology at Wesley Theological Seminary in Washington, D. C. The most important works of this productive scholar are: *The Religious Revolt Against Reason* (1949), *A Theology of the Living Church* (1955, 1960), *Present Trends in Christian Theology* (1960), and *Responsible Freedom* (1971). DeWolf's early theology is a continuation of Boston personalistic interests, such as a basic trust in rationality and the promise of human fulfillment in the Kingdom of God. Later he shifted his emphasis in this context to a more thorough recognition of the affliction of sin in human life. Throughout his writings the power of God's redemptive grace remains central. The selection included in these readings indicates DeWolf's view of the nature of God's actions and the nature of human faith. "The God who Speaks" is selected from *The Case for Theology in a Liberal Perspective* (Philadelphia: The Westminster Press, 1959), pp. 85–103.

THE GOD WHO SPEAKS

The God who reveals himself to us is One who is and must remain for us veiled in mystery. We are accustomed to thinking and talking of things and persons capable of identification in terms of spatiotemporal perception. God, on the other hand, is unseen. Of his presence, as of his Kingdom, we are unable to say, " 'Lo, here. . . !' or 'There!' " (Luke 17:21). He is always out of sight and beyond comprehension.

The Athenians erected an altar "To an unknown God" (Acts 17:23). He

212

is not so to Christians or to men of the Old Covenant. Yet throughout the Bible his hiddenness is often emphasized. Although Moses can see his glory when he has passed by, God tells him, "You cannot see my face; for man shall not see me and live" (Ex. 33:20). Not only to sense perception is he hidden, but also to understanding, especially in our darkest hours of suffering and grief. Job speaks for the many when he complains:

> "Behold, I go forward, but he is not there;
>   and backward, but I cannot perceive him;
> on the left hand I seek him, but I cannot behold him;
>   I turn to the right hand, but I cannot see him."
> (Job 23:8–9.)

Truly, "clouds and thick darkness are round about him" (Ps. 97:2), even in the hours when we are gratefully conscious of his reign.

In the midst of eternity, we have lived but a few years since birth, and even the history of all mankind is only a moment in astronomical time. How should we understand the darkness from which we came and into which we soon go at death? The mystery is too great for us. Out of the mystery God has spoken to us, and so by his will we know him. Yet even as we know him the mystery remains. Some *men* are largely beyond my comprehension. The composer-conductor of a great symphony, carrying in his mind, indeed constructing there, all that complex score and all the intricate tonal tapestry woven by one hundred instruments, is quite beyond my ability to imagine. One such musical genius has tried to tell me about the experience of composing. Yet, though such self-disclosure tells me much, the composer remains to me mostly a mystery. How infinitely more the Creator of the universe—composers and all!—must remain always heavily veiled in unfathomable distance for our limited minds.

This inherent, overwhelming hiddenness of God must not be forgotten as we stand in wonder before his self-disclosure. Only as we remember the depth and darkness of the mystery shall we with sufficient awe and gratitude receive the revelation. Only thus shall we be possessed by that fear of the Lord which is the beginning of wisdom. However well known, the one God, when truly encountered, is confronted as the *mysterium* and *tremendum*, never as one comprehensible, clearly definable, and comfortably familiar.

The wonderful truth is that the God who surpasses our understanding has revealed himself to us, even to our understanding, in many ways. The "unknown God" is the self-revealed God who can be proclaimed with confidence to all men. (Cf. Acts 17:23.)

He has disclosed himself "in the things that have been made" (Rom. 1:20); in the norms of truth, beauty, and goodness engraved in the human heart, however disfigured; in the mighty acts of revelation to which the Bible testifies; and in those encounters with us in the depths of our own hearts which we call religious experience. He "did not leave himself without witness" (Acts 14:17) among any people. There is no nature nor human nature without grace. The stamp of the Creator and Sustainer is upon all things and all men, however much else may obscure it. . . .

God has also disclosed his own nature in all that cumulative body of revelation to which men have borne witness in the Bible. Here, too, he is revealed as reason and will, a personal Being most like man at his best, but much more specific meaning is given to the divine character and purpose for man. He is the God of righteous judgment and love. Indeed, his judgments, which sometimes appear to men in the guise of wrathful severity, are expressions of his love. (See Hos., *passim*; also Heb. 12:5–11.)

It is strange that in recent Christian theology there is doubt expressed, not uncommonly, about the propriety of describing God as personal. Of course for many centuries various philosophers have thought the world-ground to be impersonal and sometimes they have spoken of an impersonal universal substance or world-ground as "God." However, the Christian Scriptures, liturgies, and practice of prayer so plainly imply that God is personal that it is incongruous to find among Christian theologians reluctance to affirm that he is personal. . . .

When it is declared that God is personal, it is affirmed that, *whatever other attributes he may have*, he is *at least* able to know and to will. Granted that we cannot imagine what it would be like to be aware of all events everywhere, to sustain the whole world-process, and to have power to act without limitations of space, it is apparent that such awareness and will are like powers of our own spirits heightened to the nth power and completely free from limitations imposed by any such bodies as ours. If God were not a purposive, willing being who knows what is going on, he would be less than we, and not the God who creates and acts upon his creation according to his loving purpose. The modes of his perception, reason, love, and will are doubtless unimaginably more than ours. But they *are* more and not less than ours. With all his vast powers, known and unknown to us, he is *at least* personal. In the same sense we may speak of him as the divine Person, not for a moment implying that he is *limited* to the attributes of a personal being such as we know in the human spirit. When some writers deny that God is personal, on the ground that to be personal is to be limited as God is not, the effect is to declare him impersonal, which is to say subpersonal. A force that is blind, purposeless, unknowing, is plainly of no value to itself. There can be meaning and value only to mind. To believe that man is the only being capable of thought and appreciation is to make all meaning and value anthropocentric. Theocentrism requires the belief that God is personal, though without limitation to the attributes of human persons....

To the Christian, God is known not only as personal but also as the particular loving Father who acts in history on our behalf, and especially as the love incarnate in Jesus Christ. God is no abstract universal, whether the Platonic Good or a generalized spirit of love. He is the particular loving Person who, as Creator, is the ground of all being and source of all meaning. Hence the validity and relevance of all abstract universals that truly represent reality are rooted in him. He is the Particular ontologically prior to all universals.

Jesus speaks truly as the experiential faith of the believer in the words, "He who has seen me has seen the Father" (John 14:9). The words, deeds, and life of Jesus in history are the Word of God disclosing himself in his particular character, purpose, and power. In Jesus the character of God is seen as love. His purpose is to love and so to redeem his children. His power is the power of love.

To declare that "God is love" is to affirm a mysterious and wonderful faith. There is much in the world that seems to contradict it. The sufferings of children dying of cancer, the wasted life of idiots, the devastations wrought by earthquakes, hurricanes, and floods, do not look like the work of a loving God. Youth who in adolescence become estranged from themselves and lash out in desperation against those who love them, men and women whose lust seeks to use each other's bodies with wanton disregard for the dignity of selfhood, races and classes of people who deny their common humanity in divisive injustice and fear, and nations of men who devastate the earth and threaten total mutual annihilation in war—these do not look like the children of a loving Father....

Although there is much in our experience that remains mystery, even when our best thought has been long devoted to it, it does not follow that we should declare our faith irrational or nonrational. Despite the evils that remain unexplained, the view that God is good, that his goodness is love, and that his is the supreme power, is, on the whole, the most adequate of the explanatory doctrines that men have conceived.

All the evidence that God is love is immeasurably heightened in Jesus and his church. In Jesus the most wretched errors, religious fanaticism, cruelty, and hate met the most sublime love. Although Jesus faced all this evil in terrible human solitude and went to death before his enemies who were armed with the power of the mighty Roman Empire, yet the power of his love outmatched all. This power which he declared and his disciples believed to be the power of God in him, was vindicated when he was raised from the dead. The vindication continues in the life of the faithful Christian community. His disciples continue to testify that when they are weak, yet in him they are strong, for he has overcome the world.

The sciences, the common experience of mankind and the ancient writers of the Scriptures, alike acknowledge that the universe in which we have been placed is, on the whole, an orderly system. The inorganic processes, from the movements of the stars to changes within the atom, lend themselves remarkably to mechanistic description. Living things require further principles of description, so that biology cannot be fully reduced to physics and chemistry. Yet the biological realm, too, has its orderly regularities of reproduction, growth, and death. Neither biological mutations nor electronic indeterminacies obscure the overarching and dominant regularity of the world.

In all this vast order God makes himself known to us as the dependable and faithful Governor of the world, which he has created. We ourselves are of this world, as well as in it, and with all the rest of God's creation we are subject to his orderly government.

Spiritually, as well as physically, we are subject to this orderly rule. Our subjection is made evident in two different ways: First, there are causal laws in the realm of our mental processes as well as in the physical order. Psychology and psychiatry confront greater difficulties and narrower limitations than biology and medicine, but their achievements and further possibilities are admissible only because they, too, are working in a realm of causal order. Secondly, our wills are subject to obligations that are not, like causal law, coercive, but that are morally inescapable. We are not *compelled* to be honest, loyal to our ideals, or generous toward our neighbors, but we *ought* to be....

Many conservative Christians recognize as God's own acts only those events which appear to violate or to transcend the regular order of nature. To such persons God is the miracle-worker who breaks into this world on special occasions rather than the constant, orderly Governor.

It is well that most thoughtful Christians have come to know, with Tennyson, that though "He thunder by law the thunder is yet His voice."

Now, however, much religious thought has moved to an opposite distortion of the truth. Accepting gladly the doctrine that God is orderly Governor, whose action we see continually in the regular causal order of nature, many people have ceased to believe that God can act and does act at particular times, in particular places, in behalf of particular people.

God has been so thoroughly identified with law that in much thought he has become nearly indistinguishable from it. . . .

The God in whom we believe as Christians is no mere system of law nor yet a helpless prisoner of the structure he has created. He is a Person who chooses to maintain an orderly system but who is also free to act within that system. It would be ironical, indeed, if, in a world where his humble creatures are free to express their wills within limits broad enough so that they can make quite perceptible differences on the face of the earth, the Creator were incapable of any such free expression of his purpose. The idea that he is powerful in the creating and sustaining of the world system, but powerless to act now upon any particular life, comes from loss of full faith in the personal God and Father revealed in Christ. The God who in particular times and places spoke by the prophets and supremely revealed his eternal Word in Jesus ministers also today in particular ways both to and through men and women of faith.

In Christian history theological thought has swung back and forth between emphasis on the transcendence of God and on the immanence of God. Some writers have represented God as so utterly different from man and so completely separated from this world of trouble and sin as to be altogether veiled in mystery. Others have stressed his never-failing faithful activity within the world and his presence to the human spirit.

Both emphases are indigenous to the Christian faith. When we accept the testimony of Scripture and experience in full perspective, we acknowledge that God is both transcendent and immanent.

In his holiness God so far surpasses us that he is altogether beyond the bounds of our sense perception, imagination, or adequate conception. The ancient Hebrews represented in many ways the awful gulf of difference that separated them from God. They taught that no man could see God and live. Where his presence was concentrated, as at the Ark of the Covenant or in the Holy of Holies, no approach could be safely made excepting by certain designated persons and by them only after solemn preparation and on rare occasions. Even the self-revealing God remained also the hidden God of mystery. . . .

The transcendent God disclosed in the Bible is not represented as unconcerned or unrelated. To be sure, he is represented as not requiring to be "served by human hands, as though he needed anything," but the next clause shows that he is not regarded as unrelated: "since he himself gives to all men life and breath and everything" (Acts 17:25). The relations between God and man are never denied, but are irreversible. He

217

does not depend upon men for his own being; we do depend upon him for ours. . . .

Indeed, a striking fact of Biblical teaching is that the doctrine of divine immanence is there made ontologically dependent upon the doctrine of divine transcendence. Hence, affirmations of God's immanence in the world testify to his transcendence. The very teaching that "he himself gives to all men life and breath and everything" is proof that he "does not live in shrines made by man, nor is he served by human hands, as though he needed anything" (Acts 17:24–25). The psalmist tells of God's immanent activity as he says,

> "For thou didst form my inward parts,
> thou didst knit me together in my mother's womb" (Ps. 139:13).

But this acknowledgment leads him immediately to declare,

> "I praise thee, for thou art fearful and wonderful" (Ps. 139:14). . . .

It is precisely because God is infinitely secure and strong that he is able to love so purely and involve himself so humbly with us in our sin and suffering. Only the God whose ways of knowing and caring unimaginably transcend our own could know each one of his earthly children in tender concern. Only the omnipotent God who is mysterious to our weakness could be omnipresent. Only he who transcends all bounds could be he of whom it can be said, that "he is not far from each one of us, for

> 'In him we live and move and have our being'" (Acts 17:27–28).

The transcendence of God passes all our understanding. Yet it does not pass our understanding that only a God of just such transcendent greatness, so far removed from our own limitations, could be always so near, so aware of our innermost thoughts, and so sensitive of our every need as faith affirms God to be in his immanence.

PART IV

RESTATING DOCTRINES

The development of Methodist theology in the decades of the 1930's and 1940's was not in a single stream. The strength of Protestant liberalism as particularly expressed in Boston personalism was obvious, but there were also other influences and changing directions. Many of the assumptions of the liberal position, such as the immanence of God, the amelioristic possibility of human life—both personal and social—and the confidence in human rationality, were reevaluated. Those decades were also a time of reassessment of John Wesley's theology and reaffirmation of some of his basic interests. Important in this reaffirmation was Edwin Lewis, who was the first to challenge the regnant liberal presuppositions. Others joined the effort to re-envision the interpretation of Christian doctrine; among these were Edward T. Ramsdell, Robert E. Cushman, Albert C. Outler, and Carl Michalson. The diversity of positions among these theologians was typical of the variety of theological options in Methodism. The readings that follow indicate some of the theological streams that developed during those twenty years.

Concluding our historical survey of individual contributors at this point is necessitated by space limitations. Many significant contemporary United Methodist theologians are reworking inherited positions and charting new directions, and it would be a disservice to select the contributions of only two or three. As this current work is well-known and available it is not represented in this source book.

EDWIN LEWIS

E dwin Lewis (1881–1959) was born in England, emigrated to
Newfoundland, Canada, and then came to the United States. He
was educated in Canada and the United States, completing his
work at Drew University in 1918. He joined the faculty of Drew in 1920
and served there until his retirement. Originally an exponent of a liberal
Protestant position in theology, he wrote several books of importance:
Jesus and the Human Quest (1924), *A Manual of Christian Beliefs* (1927), and
God and Ourselves (1931). He was co-editor of the *Abingdon Bible Commentary* (1929), and it was this work that precipitated a change. In the 1930's
he shifted to a more traditional position and in *A Christian Manifesto*
(1934) challenged the assumptions of liberalism and stated a case for a
new appreciation of biblical authority, the two natures of Jesus Christ
and human sinfulness. Upon this new ground he built his mature theology as expressed in *The Faith We Declare* (1939), *A Philosophy of the
Christian Revelation* (1940), and *The Creator and the Adversary* (1948). "A
Christian Manifesto" comes from "The Fatal Apostasy of the Modern
Church," *Religion in Life* (Autumn, 1933), Vol. II, No. 4, pp. 483–92.

A CHRISTIAN MANIFESTO

Modern theological liberalism undoubtedly rendered the church an
important service. It helped to break the strangle-hold of terms and
phrases which had become in all too many cases merely empty
shibboleths. It re-established, after the fashion of the thirteenth century,
the rights of the intellect in the evaluation of the things of the spirit. It
garnered for the use of the church the rich harvest of scholarship in
many fields—biblical, historical, sociological, psychological. It served
notice to a world too often skeptical that a man could believe in Jesus and

at the same time be fully aware of all the amazing kaleidoscopic changes occurring in contemporary life. For such a service we cannot but be grateful. Nevertheless, all is not well with us. Liberalism has not brought us to the Promised Land. We may have gained a battle, but the campaign is still on, and there is more than a suspicion that the gain made at one point involved a serious loss elsewhere. We yielded positions whose strategic significance is becoming more and more manifest. We so stressed the Bible as coming to us in "the words of men" that the sense in which it is also "the word of God" has become increasingly vague. We so freely allowed the influence of contemporary forces in the development of doctrine as to have endangered the continuity of that living core of truth and reality for which contemporary forces were but the *milieu*. We exposed all the delicate nuances of spiritual experience to the cold dispassionate gaze of psychology, until it has become a question whether psychology of religion is not in danger of destroying the very thing it lives by. And in particular we were so determined to recover for the church "the human Jesus" that we lost sight of the fact that the church is the creation of "the divine Christ," or at least of faith in Christ as divine. Have we sown the wind, and is the whirlwind now upon us?

The *Hibbert Journal* symposium of a generation ago, "Jesus, or Christ?" was a sign of the times. It showed very clearly the results of the "Jesus-study" of the latter part of the nineteenth century. It prophesied an increasing emphasis on "the religion of Jesus," a prophecy which has been abundantly fulfilled. In many quarters of the modern church it is now taken for granted that "the Jesus of the Gospels" is the primary datum for Christianity. This would not be disturbing if Jesus were given his complete significance, but before he can become a datum he must be passed through the alembic of critical investigation. By that time, he has become a hardly recognizable Figure, as Schweitzer himself—notwithstanding his own arbitrary construction—so vigorously contends. But such as he is, he is given to us. We are asked to suppose that one who may have been anything from the energetic "go-getter" of Bruce Barton to "the Man of Genius" in the Middleton Murry sense, is the adequate explanation—plus certain "tendencies" in the time—of the genesis of Christianity and of its historical growth. Let us therefore "return to Jesus." Let us eliminate from Christianity everything not agreeable to the "Portrait" we have had re-constructed for us. Let us be done with the majestic Figure of the Epistles. Let us admit that the Prologue of the Fourth Gospel, and the Kenosis passage in Philippians, and the daring flights of Colossians, and the introduction to Hebrews, represent simply so much mythologizing—understandable enough in the circumstances, but corresponding to nothing in the world of actual reality. Having thus arrived at "the essence of Christianity"—Harnack's familiar grouping, "the Fatherhood of God, the value of the soul, the righteousness of the heart, and the commandment of love"—let us "re-think" the whole Christian enterprise in the appropriate terms. Let us be realistic. Let us frankly change our direction. Let us abandon definitely and forever the whole concept of the supernatural; and as men who will tolerate no illusions, comforting and inspiring though they may be, let us set ourselves anew to the church's unfinished task. Which is—*what?*

But perhaps the case is not so simple as it seems. Say what we will, the stubborn fact remains that the Gospels are themselves the product of a community which already had "seated Christ at the right hand of God," and that, failing that audacious act of their mind and heart, we had had no Gospels at all. If the dangerous expression may be permitted, it was "Christ" who saved "Jesus" to us. That is to say, although Jesus was saved to posterity by "the Christian community," that community organized itself not around the fact that a man named Jesus had lived and taught and wrought and died, but around the belief that in that same Jesus had "dwelt all the fullness of the Godhead bodily." But for that belief, Jesus would have disappeared from human ken, for not one single unimpeachable reference to Jesus of any independent value do we possess from the first century outside of the Christian literature. We may object to the faith of that early community. We cannot but admit, however, that it is to this community that we owe the Synoptic Gospels. They produced for us and saved to us the very documents by which we propose to discredit their dynamic faith! They produced them, used them, loved them, circulated them, at the same time that they were integrating their Lord with the very being of the Godhead, saying of him that he *is* the Spirit, that he *is* the Ever-living One, that by him the invisible God is apprehended, and nowhere is there the least evidence that they felt any incongruity in doing this. By the Gospels they accounted for their historical origin and justified their claims, but the community preceded the Gospels. There was a Church of the Living Christ before there was any attempt made to collate the traditions respecting Jesus. Apply to the Gospel Portrait all the historicism and psychologism you will: you cannot thereby get rid of that confident faith in a Redeemer-God which is the sole reason why we have the Portrait at all. Take the Synoptic Gospels, discriminate their sources, lay bare their inconsistencies and contradictions, explain away their mighty works, find the Rabbinic parallels of their teachings, "reduce" Jesus to what level you will—and you have not destroyed Christianity thereby, because Christianity was born not of these documents but of contact with the Personality whom the documents attempt to describe. And be it added that although in the order of *time* the contact with him was "in the flesh" first and "in the spirit" second, nevertheless the *fundamental* contact was the second because it was through that that the first came to its full understanding and appreciation. . . .

The Christian "facts" are not to be limited to what fell between Bethlehem and Calvary. What was then said and done was but part of a larger whole—of a movement taking place within the very being of God. Men believed that this was implied in the indubitable historical and experiential facts. They therefore wrought out the idea of "pre-existence" as applied to their Lord, identified him as the permanently active occasion of that life of fellowship in which the church as they knew it was constituted, and from this were led on step by step to formulate finally the doctrine of the Trinity. It is easy enough to complain that this was to transform "the simple Gospel" into a *Weltanschauung*, yet we have no evidence that the so-called simple Gospel was ever preached, even at the beginning, apart from at least some of the elements of this philosophy. Not that unlettered apostles suddenly found themselves possessed of a full-blown philosophy that answered all questions in the world and out of it. But they were making affirmations of such an astounding characteof this philosophy. Not that unlettered apostles suddenly found themselves possessed of a full-blown philosophy that answered all questions in the world and out of it. But they were making affirmations of such an astounding character as that inevitably before long took to themselves coherence, and the original Christocentric religion became a Christocentric philosophy.

As to this, the New Testament is the evidence, and the New Testament reflects the life and faith of the primitive church. Here we read of a God who had an eternal purpose respecting mankind, a purpose that had to do specifically with delivering men from the power of sin and bringing them to holiness. We read that such a deliverance could not be an arbitrary act upon the part of God, since in all that he does he must be true to the demand of his own holy nature. We read that God himself was so constituted that he could enter in the most intimate and personal way into the stream of human life both to experience all its limitations and struggles and to establish within the stream the principle of its purification, and that the point of this entry was the man Jesus, who would never have existed at all but for the eternal purpose of God. We read that the ensuing intimacy of relationship between the Eternal God and this human life was such that the experience of the man thereupon became the experience of God—which makes it actually true to say that the Infinite knows finitude, that the All-Holy knows moral trial, that the Creator knows creatureliness, that the Deathless knows death. We read that therefore something has "happened to" God which makes his relation to men different from what it would have been had this *not* "happened." And we read that henceforth in speaking of God men may speak of him as One who was in Christ reconciling the world unto himself: therefore the Christian God is God suffused with all the qualities men saw in Jesus, and a God so suffused and transformed is also that divine Christ who is the very source and center of the life of the redeemed.

What then is the object of Christian faith? Not a man who once lived and died, but a Contemporary Reality, a God whose awful holiness is "covered" by one who is both our representative and his, so that it is "our flesh that we see in the Godhead," that "flesh" which was historically Jesus of Nazareth but is eternally the divine Christ whose disclosure and apprehension Jesus lived and died to make possible. I do not deny for a single moment that this overwhelming conception lent itself to all sorts of crudities of expression, impossible analogies, and gross materialisms. But he is blind indeed who cannot see what the New Testament is trying to say. Though language were not adequate to the thought, we can see what the thought aimed to be. It was that thought that created and sustained the church, and the church languishes to-day because it has substituted that thought with one of lesser power as it is of lesser truth.

Many reasons are alleged for the modern turning away from Christianity as thus understood. Not one of these reasons can touch its intrinsic credibility. A philosophical view that precludes it is quite possible. A philosophical view that allows for it is equally possible. Why is the first view so generally accepted? Because Christianity, with the view of things it necessarily calls for, makes such a terrific onslaught upon human pride. We would fain be self-sufficient, and this means that we are not. We would fain be the masters of our fate and the captains of our souls, and this says that our fate is in another's hands and that our souls are not our own but have been bought with a price. We do not like Christianity, not because it is intrinsically incredible but because it is so vastly humiliating. We do not *want* it to be true that "the Son of Man came to give himself a ransom for many," and so we find "critical" reasons for doubting that the words were ever spoken— as though by proving that Jesus did not say them we should prove that they were not

225

true! We do not *want* it to be true that "the Word became flesh and dwelt among us": therefore we get rid of one of the most profound, heart-searching, and revolutionary truths ever uttered—the truth which must always be the touch-stone of any proposed Christology—by the simple device of labeling it "Platonism." We do not *want* it to be true that "through one act of righteousness the free gift came unto all men to justification of life": this being so, we ask by what right Paul "distorted" the simple Gospel of brotherhood and service and good will by introducing into it misleading analogies from temple and law-court.

No; we do not like Christianity. We do not like its cosmic audacity. We do not like its moral pessimism. We do not like the way it smashes the beautiful orderliness of our metaphysical systems. We do not like its uncompromising insistence on the possibility of our being damned souls, whose only hope is in the sovereign grace of God—a God who voluntarily endured self-immolation as the cost of his own graciousness. We be *men*—men whose prerogative it is to stand before God, face him without a tremor, and *demand*; not slaves whose duty it is to kneel before him with covered face, humbly and reverently and gratefully to *accept*. Away with this doctrine of grace! Away with this whole mythology of Incarnation! Away with this outworn notion of Atonement! Make way for emancipated man!

But in this pride lies our shame, our weakness, and our defeat. What has it done for us? What has it done for the church—at least, for evangelical Protestantism? How far have we gotten with our various substitutes? Look over our churches: they are full of people who, brought up on these substitutes, are strangers to those deeper experiences without which there had been no New Testament and no Church of Christ. Thousands of clergymen will go into their pulpits next Sunday morning, but not as prophets. There will be no burning fire shut up in their bones, by reason of which they cannot forbear to speak. Those who come to listen will not be brought face to face with eternal verities. Hungry sheep will look up, but will not be fed. Men harassed with a thousand problems and seeking not inexpert advice on how to solve them but the sense of another world in whose light they can see this one and find strength to cope with it and remold it nearer to the heart's desire, will go away as impotent as they came for anything the preacher has to say. Grievous is the hurt of the daughter of God's people, and slight is the proffered healing. They go to Gilead, and there is no balm. They go to the fountain of waters, and they find there a broken cistern. They cry for bread, and behold a stone.

And to a large extent, this plight of the church is traceable to a weakening of its dogmatic basis. Whether the phrase, "humanitarian Christology," is defensible or not is a question. Unless Christ is conceived as one who "stands on the divine side of causality in effecting redemption," it is difficult to see why we need a doctrine of him at all. If Jesus is not specifically related to God's eternal purpose to enter sacrificially the stream of our humanity, to the end that he might thereby change its direction and set it flowing toward himself, then we no more need a doctrine of Jesus than we need a doctrine of Jeremiah or a doctrine of Paul. There is no permanent resting-place between *some form* of the Logos Christology and a "humanitarian Christology" (allowing the phrase) which in effect surrenders the whole idea of direct divine sacrificial saving activity. And what we mean theologically by a Logos Christology we mean practically by a Christ-centered religion rather than a "religion of Jesus." If the emulation of "the religion of Jesus" were presented as the possible end of a Christ-centered faith, that would be different. What we are actually doing, however, is supposing that unregenerate men can be "like Jesus"! Even a casual acquaintance with great sections of modern Protestantism makes it evident that it has departed very widely from the Christocentric emphasis. We must recover that emphasis, or perish. The divine Christ saved the human Jesus from disappearing, and if the human Jesus is to continue to mean for men all that he should, it must still be through the divine Christ. Christ must continue to save Jesus!

It is not the men cannot live "the good life" without faith in the divine Christ. It is not that there cannot be a profound appreciation of the character of Jesus without it. But Christianity does not consist simply in the good life and in moral appreciation and endeavor. It *is* this, of course. One of the incredible suppositions of our day is that the only persons who are interested in the wellbeing of their fellows are the so-called "humanists." No one who really knows what Christianity has done for the world could possibly make that supposition. . . .

Yes; Christocentric religion means human devotion carried to its ultimate issue—say a Damien with a crucifix on his breast the while he dresses the rotting stumps of a leper, a Damien who, as R. L. Stevenson says in his noble defense of the man, "shut to with his own hand the doors of his own sepulcher." But it means an "experience" as well—an experience falling within that "unleaguerable fortress" of the innermost soul "whose keys are at the cincture hung of God," and which is something one can better know for oneself than describe to another. And this experience, whence comes it? It comes of *belief*. If we are going to psychologize religion, well and good; but by what imaginable psychological process can there be "spiritual experience" completely independent of all intellectual assent? It were absurd to say that Christianity is *only* credal; to say that it is in no sense credal would be equally false. And to say that "it does not matter what one believes" so long as one "lives the good life" and "has a religious experience" reveals rather an amazing *naivete* than any profound insight into the life-movement.

But what *does* the modern church believe? The church is becoming creedless as rapidly as the innovators can have their way. The "Confession of Faith"—what is happening to it? Or what about the "new" confessions that one sees and hears— suitable enough, one imagines, for, say, a fraternal order. And as for the Apostles' Creed—"our people will not say it any more": which means, apparently, that "our people," having some difficulties over the Virgin Birth and the resurrection of the body, have elected the easy way of believing in nothing at all— certainly not in "the Holy Catholic Church." So we are going to allow them to be satisfied with "The Social Creed of the Churches," quite forgetful of the fact that unless the church has a "religious" creed besides a "social" creed the church as such will cease to exist long before it has had time to make its "social" creed effective in the life of the world. "But the social creed *is* religious." Yes; but has its religion proved dynamic enough, impelling enough, to maintain itself at the high point—the Himalayanly high point—necessary to make its creed effective? The church has set itself to do more at the very time that it is lessening its power to do anything.

The church, especially the American evangelical churches, must re-enthrone Christ, the divine Christ, in the life and thought of the people, or cease to exist. Not that the church merely as an institution is the necessary desideratum. But the church in the high New Testament sense of "the body of Christ"—this *must* be saved for the sake of the world. Here is the world's one redeeming force because here is the world's one redeeming message—if the message be *complete*. It is that completeness whose lack is the secret of our impotence. Can we recover it? Nay rather, do we here highly resolve that we *will* recover it? Let us be done with compromise, and let us affirm—affirm magnificently, affirm audaciously. Let us affirm God—his unchanging love for men, his unchanging hatred of sin, his sacrificial presence in all the life and work of Jesus. Let us affirm Christ—Christ as the meaning of God, Christ as what God *is* in virtue of the mysterious "kenosis" by which he made himself one with a human life, and at the same time that he was doing the utmost he could do for men endured the worst—a Cross—that men could do against him. Let us affirm the Spirit—the divine concern to bring to bear upon the hearts and consciences of men the impact of what God in Christ has done and is forever doing on their behalf, to the end that they may be moved to repentance, to that faith which ensures forgiveness, to that love which brings moral empowerment, and to that surrender of the will which makes God's purposes their purposes. Let us affirm the church — the community of the redeemed, those who in all their life seek the regnancy of the spirit of Jesus, carrying on and extending the mystery of the Incarnation against that day when God, the Christ-God, shall be all in all. Let us affirm the Kingdom — the Christianizing of life everywhere, children with straight backs and happy faces, women released from drudgery and set free for creative living, industry conducted for the good of all, war and kindred evils done away, racial antipathies lost in a universal brotherhood, the rich heritage of culture made available to the last man. O there is no limit to the affirmations, and, better still, no limit to the dynamic needful to make them effective, once we grasp the profound structural coherence of Christianity, the wide sweep of its thought, the absoluteness of its demands, the revolutionary results of its consistent application. "That in all things he, who is the image of the invisible God, might have the pre-eminence."

EDWARD T. RAMSDELL

E dward T. Ramsdell (1902–1957) was born into a Methodist ministerial family in Michigan. He attended the University of Michigan
and Boston University and then was professor of systematic theology at the Divinity School of Vanderbilt University and at Garrett
Biblical Institute. His one book, *The Christian Perspective*, was important
because it indicated an interaction of his personalist position with neo-
orthodox and biblical theological influences. The sovereignty of God was
his primary theme, followed by his stress upon the significance of the
Bible as the vehicle of God's decisive disclosure of divine love in Jesus
Christ. With his personalist philosophy, he continued to express confidence in human rationality as well as the reality of a personal God of
ultimate goodness. In reshaping that position he stressed the vision
of faith as establishing the perspective from which reason operates,
the fallen and marred human condition, and the new creative act of
God in Jesus Christ. The following selection represents Ramsdell's theological foundations. "The Rational Predicament" is taken from *The Christian Perspective* (New York/Nashville: Abingdon-Cokesbury Press, 1950),
pp. 31–43.

THE RATIONAL PREDICAMENT

That the evaluation of significance is inevitably personal is the compli-
cating factor in man's rational life. Reasoning never occurs in the abstract.
It is always the activity of an individual mind. It can never be separated
from the crucial experience of a particular living person. To be sure a
thinker may abstract from his experience what he regards as universally
significant and ignore the rest, but it is just such a judgment that is
inescapably personal. To decide that only certain aspects of his experi-

ence are significant is to evaluate, at the same time, all other aspects as unimportant for understanding. What we evaluate as meaningful is inextricably bound up with our total life as persons. It shows what we are really interested in. It discloses our personal understanding of value. It indicates the level at which we seek personal integration. It points to the object of our worship—that is, to the focus of meaning in which we seek unity. When one seeks his unity at a level which he does not regard as significant for his understanding of the world, he remains unavoidably divided against himself. His deepest potential creativity is blocked.

Any evaluation of significance is an expression of faith that our experience is, in some real sense, objective. It is our confidence that our humanity has, at some points at least, universal meaning. If our experience as persons were not objectively meaningful, we should indeed be shut up in hopeless subjectivity. Those who regard the presuppositions of reason as altogether arbitrary and irrational would be right, except that, like the ancient skeptics, they would give us this much hope: they would want us to accept their judgment against reason as itself reasonable!

Granted, then, that our reason is controlled by the understanding of meaning to which we appeal, our freedom lies in our capacity to recognize and define our presuppositions and critically to compare them with the presuppositions of another perspective. Any effective critical comparison of perspectives must, however, be undertaken by the whole self. To contrast two points of view merely as intellectual concepts in unavoidably superficial. At such a level of comparison one never transcends the dynamic understanding of meaning that constitutes his own controlling perspective. A person can genuinely understand the presuppositions of meaning of another mind only by projecting himself sympathetically and imaginatively into the life experience of that other mind. Only when the whole self moves into the "position" of another mind, feeling so far as possible what it feels as crucially significant, can some degree of effective comparison become possible. When he thus enters personally into another perspective, he may ask whether its understanding of meaning comprehends his own experience—in integration with the total structure of scientific and critical knowledge—more fully than his own point of view. Does this other perspective reveal and illuminate the deeper levels of his own experience? Thus he can compare another evaluation of significance with his own—indeed, he can choose between them. Here lies the elemental freedom of the human mind. Each person can, to this extent, determine his own evaluation of significance. He can choose the object of his worship. It is just this that is the philosophic import of Joshua's challenge: "Choose you this day whom ye will serve" (Josh. 24:15). Whatever a man worships as *the supremely important* defines his perspective.

But does not such a choice between possible evaluations of significance appeal, in the nature of the case, to the greatest possible coherence? In the final analysis there is no other possibility. A person enters into a new evaluation of significance because his earlier categories have not been able to comprehend all the levels of his experience. He turns to the new because it illuminates his total world more deeply and permits a surer and more creative integration of his life. The norm which any mind chooses must finally justify itself in the experience of that mind as a living self. As Borden Parker Bowne put it, "The standard is the mind itself—the living mind in contact with the facts." The life of the mind, in all of its knowledge and experience, must be coherent. The requirement is vital and psychological quite as much as it is logical. Coherence in the sense of a comprehensive unity is the last line of defense for any understanding of meaning.

Logically, however, the appeal to coherence is chiefly a matter of defense. It is not very useful for critical attack against a divergent perspective. The theist, for example, judges that his world view is more coherent than that of the naturalist; but his judgment means very little to the naturalist, who is perfectly sure of the comprehensive unity of his own interpretation. Part of our rational predicament is just that every philosophy appears coherent to itself. The grounds which any philosopher adduces for his beliefs seem to him "good grounds." As Karl Heim has rightly observed, one does not overthrow another perspective by amassing facts against it, for it already comprehends all facts as it reads them. The reason that coherence cannot be an effective criterion for logical attack is simple enough: Each thinker necessarily judges coherence with reference to what he himself has experienced as crucially significant. It is intimately tied to the life which he himself has lived. It is inseparable from the critic as a living person. None the less, we cannot avoid the appeal to coherence. No thoughtful person could be content with a point of view that did not comprehensively unify for him the total structure of his knowledge and experience. Certainly those who presume to reject the criterion of coherence do not mean to claim thereby that their philosophies are incoherent.

A plea for greater coherence can only mean the invitation to deeper levels of meaning. Put merely in logical terms such a plea would not be likely to move a critical mind from one evaluation of significance to another. A person must feel the inadequacy of his established limit-notion before he can feel the promise of a new perspective. He must feel the deeper meanings of human experience breaking out of the partial categories in which he has sought to confine them.

One may, it is true, show the logical positivist that his evaluation of meaning cannot itself be sensuously or scientifically established, but one cannot logically induce a logical positivist to evaluate mind and value as more important for understanding than sense experience. Only life can do that. One may ask the naturalist whether uniformities and predictable sequences can comprehend the meaning of human freedom and worth, but not until he discovers in personal and cultural experience that the freedom and dignity of human life cannot be sustained by the worship of impersonal process is he likely to sense the inadequacy of his established evaluation. One may ask the value-relativist whether his own moral experience does not belie his theory, but not until he discovers in life itself the emptiness and tragedy of his subjectivism is he likely to sense the deeper meanings of the moral struggle. One may ask the "natural man," as Paul designated the man who lives apart from faith in God, whether his truest freedom does not lie in an acknowledged dependence, but not until he discovers the self-defeating character of his assumed self-sufficiency is he likely to trust a goodness which transcends his own. The man who dreams "that he has no need of ruler or guide, but rather is competent himself to guide others," says Plato, seems "to many, indeed, . . . to be some great one, but after no long time he payeth the penalty, not unmerited, to Justice, when he bringeth to total ruin himself, his house, and his country." Plato is right; it is crisis, personal and social, that often brings the *final* argument to those who deny the significance of man's spiritual life, or who gloss over man's capacity for evil and demonic destruction.

Crisis is the kind of fact that decisively tests every perspective. It is the rock against which every superficial understanding of meaning is sooner or later broken. Crisis literally sifts out (*krinein*) our presuppositions and condemns (*krinein*) them in the measure of their inadequacy. It literally judges (*krinein*) our philosophies even as they seek to understand it. It is the kind of fact which operates to move our spiritual center of gravity. It is the predicament which reminds us that we are creatures and not the Creator, that the ultimate laws of life are legislated for us, not by us. Crisis mocks our attempts to "write our own ten commandments." It reveals the thinness of egocentricity as an implicit norm of meaning and value. It articulates the importance of the personal and the good for understanding and points unmistakably to the need of a divine content for both. It makes clear that there can be no final separation of life and thought; what is important for understanding is important for life, and what is important for life is important for thought.

The task of mutual understanding is at once one of the most difficult and one of the most important of human responsibilities. Chasmal differences separate the minds of men. Some of those differences are ideological; that is, they are rooted, not in any desire to understand, but in the purpose to realize a particular social or economic goal. An ideological perspective is controlled by an evaluation of what is important for action. Its philosophic interpretations serve chiefly to rationalize the goal and the program for reaching it. On the other hand some of the great differences among men are genuinely philosophical; that is, the primary motive is the desire to understand. Here the decisive factor—the factor that defines the rational perspective—is the evaluation of what is important for understanding.

That science and phenomenology provide a fundamental common ground for the minds of men is clear. In any particular problem situation one must first know the denotable facts. But then he must go on to ask: What is the totality of relations in which this set of facts is involved? If he assumes that the scientific account is the final account, either he is overlooking the metaphysical reference of all judgments of meaning and value, or he is taking for granted a naturalistic perspective.

When we understand that our evaluations of significance determine our perspectives, we recognize that different perspectives are indeed possible. Then we can free ourselves from the uncritical assumption that any one perspective is obviously the only rational one. This realization has often been vigorously voiced within our democratic tradition; indeed, without it there can be no real democracy. This does not mean that one perspective is as adequate as another. It should be clear that one perspective may reveal depths of meaning unrecognizable from another. Plato was very confident in his trust of reason, but quite evidently saw the import of rational perspectives when, after counseling us to "grasp the truth as a whole," he added that we ought to grasp it "in the right way."

Further, when we understand that our world view is always a point of view, we will not attempt to storm the citadel of a conflicting perspective by any frontal attack of logic. Every perspective is defined by an evaluation of significance, not by any mere marshaling of facts. Our understanding of the world is never merely an inductive conclusion; it is always an integration of our knowledge in the light of what we believe to be supremely important. In contrasting metaphysics and religion Anders Nygren suggests that metaphysics assumes that it begins with the question of what is real and moves toward its answer, while religion frankly recognizes that it begins with the answer. Actually, however, as Nygren recognizes, metaphysics too begins with its answer; that is, it begins with an evaluation of significance that controls its entire investigation.

Certainly an appreciation of rational perspectives ought to keep us from supposing that we can refute another philosophy simply by exhibiting the same facts within our own perspective. Yet just this is one of the most common and curious fallacies of the contemporary naturalist—to assume that he can refute an idealistic or theistic philosophy by exhibiting the facts of mind and value within a naturalistic frame of reference. This, in substance, is the whole force of the criticisms of the illusionists. With great confidence Leuba and Freud, and many others, have shown that the facts of religious experience can be interpreted within a naturalistic perspective! To be sure they can, and they can similarly be interpreted within an absolutistic or a theistic framework. The only critical question here is: Which perspective generates religious attitudes most creatively, and comprehends the facts of religious experience most deeply?

To recognize the impossibility of an absolute rational perspective is not to deny the legitimacy of metaphysics. For one thing we cannot avoid metaphysical interpretation even if we want to do so. We cannot help taking fundamental attitudes, involving belief, toward persons, values, knowledge, physical nature, and reality as a whole. One may be positivistic in theory, but no one can be positivistic in the attitudes and conduct of his life. The evaluation of significance which reason presupposes always has its metaphysical reference. And it is in such evaluation that we find the ground of our psychic unity as well as of our understanding of experience. The legitimate function of metaphysics is to exhibit the implications of a particular evaluation of significance and its usefulness in comprehensively unifying experience.

Nor is anyone kept by the perspectival character of his own position from using phenomenological knowledge gained within another perspective. Socrates' discovery of the unity of the good life, Plotinus' analysis of consciousness, Marx's insight into the economic motivation in history, Freud's recognition of the nonrational character of most human motivation and of the pervasive influence of the sex drive in the total life of man, Einstein's perception of the relativity of space and time—such are familiar examples both of the fruitfulness of different metaphysical points of view and of the availability, within certain limits, of important factual analyses across perspective lines. Indeed, co-operation across perspective lines is imperative for a democratic society.

It is our obligation to think critically about the meaning of our total experience. With integrity and thoroughness we can analyze the various kinds of fact from our acknowledged vantage point. With a Socratic awareness of our own perspectival limitation we can accept the metaphysical task for what it is. Certainly we can find in our predicament no warrant for intellectual surrender. Challenged we can find in our predicament no warrant for intellectual surrender. Challenged by the irrationalist proposal of Meno, Socrates replied:

> Some things I have said of which I am not altogether confident. But that we shall be better and braver and less helpless if we think that we ought to inquire, than we should have been if we indulged the idle fancy that there was no knowing and no use in searching after what we know not;—that is a theme upon which I am ready to fight, in word and deed, to the utmost of my power.

Changes in perspective never occur easily. Often they are acutely difficult and painful. And the reason is clear: meaningful evaluation involves the whole self. No matter how promising a new appraisal of significance, to change is to abandon the understanding upon which the life of the self has been previously built. It is never any merely intellectual matter but a shift in one's elemental and dynamic moorings. At times it involves terrific struggle and soul-searching. It is true that changes in perspective often occur with very little critical appreciation of the full implications of a new limit-notion of significance; one simply becomes preoccupied with a new interest and allows it to determine for him his evaluation of importance. But whether critical or uncritical, a shift in meaningful evaluation is a movement of the whole self. It is literally conversion, whether in one direction or another.

One becomes a Christian as he opens the motivating center of his life to the healing and light mediated through the life and work of Jesus Christ—as he sees that what is important for understanding is inseparable from what is important for life. Often it is crisis, personal or social, which calls attention to the perspective of mature Christian faith. But in crisis or out of it, it is the preaching of God's Word that opens up the understanding of significance that defines the Christian perspective. "How are men to call upon him in whom they have not believed? And how are they to believe in him of whom they have never heard? And how are they to hear without a preacher? . . . So faith comes from what is heard, and what is heard comes by the preaching of Christ." (Rom. 10: 14, 17.) From the assumed ultimacy of natural process, or of mind, or of indeterminate being, the believer turns to the revealed ultimacy of God's Word Incarnate.

Christian faith, then, is a way of looking at the whole of experience, including crisis, that grows out of the acceptance of Jesus Christ as the climactically and literally crucial fact within that whole. In Him faith intuits the Word which God is speaking to that whole. Sharing with idealistic and theistic philosophies the evaluation of the personal and the good as decisive for understanding, Christian faith is the confession that the full content of both is found in the Incarnation and the Atonement. In Christ, as Son of God and Saviour, the formal categories of meaning and value find their ultimate and concrete content. He is the supremely significant datum for the Christian mind. Faith in Him as the dynamic vehicle of God's Word to man both conditions and completes the rationality of the mind which responds to Him. To see in Him the Incarnation of the Word is to see man in his essential humanity as a child of God, and nature as the divine work. It is to know one's self as creature and God as creator. It is to know one's sin and God as judge. It is to realize the healing and wholeness and creativity which come from God as redeemer. In Christ the nature of every crisis is illuminated. It is seen for what it is—a condition of the spiritual life of man. The Christian stands within a perspective that makes it possible to deal at once realistically and creatively with the critical problems of our world. He says, with Augustine, "If thou art not able to understand, believe that thou mayest understand."

Christian faith could not stand as a philosophy of life if it did not bring to experience and the ordering of life a profound coherence. Peter could counsel: "Always be prepared to make a defense to any one who calls you to account for the hope that is in you" (I Pet. 3:15). Faith has always had its reasons, whether they be identified, as with Pascal, with the "heart" or with the whole self. Christian faith never negates reason; rather, as Richard Niebuhr strikingly puts it, faith brings "the discovery of rational pattern" in our life. Faith knows the gift of God and is grateful; reason sees that by that gift life is made whole. It is this sense of gratitude to God that brings the self to the profoundest levels of its experience and its greatest spiritual dynamic. Yet it is just this sense which the naturalist as naturalist or the neutralist as neutralist can never have. To be sure, no mind creates the ultimate object of its trust, whether that object be nature, or mind, or being, or race, or self, or Word of God. But one responds with the deep gratitude of one's whole person alone to God.

Christian faith, then, is a perspective of reason like any other in so far as it is constituted by an evaluation of significance. It differs most sharply in the following respects: First, it finds decisive significance, not in an abstract universal, but in the concrete goodness which Jesus Christ lived and further revealed on the Cross. Second, it believes that man's deepest freedom and creativity are realized in the acknowledgment of utter dependence upon a transcendant Goodness in whose judgment we always stand and by whose grace we are made whole. It sees God, not simply as a logical postulate of the practical reason, as in the philosophy of Kant, but as a dynamic condition of goodness. Third, recognizing that any rational perspective is limited, never absolute, it believes that man's most comprehensive perspective is provided by faith in the Word which transcends history as well as speaks within it. Fourth, it acknowledges paradox as a possible tool of understanding. We shall look to this latter characteristic of Christian faith in the next chapter.

When one sees that rationality is inseparable from the object of one's worship, it is no longer necessary to speak of faith as supra-rational, as Reinhold Niebuhr often does, or to say that the Christian way of life cannot be comprehended rationally, as Brunner puts it. It is not a matter of rationality but of the perspective of rationality. It is never, at bottom, a matter of opposition between faith and reason but rather between the faiths which define the divergent perspectives of reason. The natural man is no less certainly a man of faith than the spiritual, but his faith is in the ultimacy of something other than the Word of God. The spiritual man is no less certainly a man of reason than the natural, but his reason, like that of every man, functions within the perspective of his faith.

"The Christian faith represents deeper sources of insight into the meaning of life and, therefore, also greater sources of power for the fulfillment of life than has been assumed in the main currents of modern culture." With this judgment Reinhold Niebuhr reflects the thought of an increasingly large number of Christian minds. But how, it may be asked, can Christian faith speak of the greater reach of its perspective? Is not one perspective as inclusive of all the facts of experience as another? Is there any fact that cannot be dealt with within every perspective? True, every fact can be read within any perspective, but the readings are not equally searching. No perspective can read any level of meaning not comprehended by its limit-notion. In his attempt to probe human experience the logical positivist is restricted by his limit-notion of sensuous verification, the naturalist by his limit-notion of impersonal process, and the idealist by his limit-notion of rational autonomy. Perspectives therefore may be the same in horizontal inclusiveness, but not in depth. They may be equally broad in denotation, but dimensionally different, to use the valuable term of Karl Heim. It is because it can illuminate the moral and spiritual tensions of human life that Christian faith claims to read more deeply. Its dimensional advantage lies in its possibility of probing to the core of life—in "having the eyes of your hearts enlightened" (Eph. 1:18).

It is obvious that the Christian perspective never comes to one as any merely intellectual formulation of meaning and truth. Rather it emerges out of response of the whole self to the Word of God. As such it is as deeply subjective as it is objective. To ask concerning the meaning of the facts of human motivation becomes finally the question: "What must *I* do to be saved?" It is to ask: What must *I* do to understand my essential humanity and to realize the potential goodness of life? And to ask what mankind must do to realize the creativity of genuine community is to ask what mankind must do to be saved. Christian faith reveals the perennial crisis of human life—the temptation to worship self and things rather than God. It reveals man's deepest need as salvation from himself. It points to motivation as the profoundest problem in human experience and to the dynamic relevance of faith in the Son of God to it. It exhibits every problem in our modern world, for all of its economic, political, and social complexities, as fundamentally spiritual. It offers to us the means of our healing and creativity, our freedom and community, because it brings us back to the goodness which is God.

ALBERT C. OUTLER

A lbert C. Outler (b. 1908), a native of Georgia, was educated at Wofford College, Emory and Yale Universities and taught at Duke and Yale Universities. The major part of his career has been spent on the faculty of the Perkins School of Theology at Southern Methodist University. A specialist in the history of doctrine and in the theology of John Wesley, Outler has made significant contributions to the history of Christian thought and has been a leader in contemporary ecumenical activities. Among his important works are *Tradition and the Unity We Seek* (1957), *That the World May Believe* (1966), *Who Trusts in God* (1968), and *Theology in the Wesleyan Spirit* (1975). In his writings Outler has attempted to reinterpret the inner life of Wesley's theology in order to make a contemporary statement of the Christian gospel. Outler was the principal author of the statement on doctrine which appeared in the 1972 *Discipline* and which continues to represent United Methodism's theological position. "Holiness of Heart and Life" is from *Theology in the Wesleyan Spirit*, pp. 65–78, 84–88. Copyright 1975 by Discipleship Resources-Tidings. Used by permission of Discipleship Resources.

HOLINESS OF HEART AND LIFE

Most non-Methodists, and not a few Methodists, would be startled by some of the questions a Methodist ordinand is asked in the course of his "being received into full connection" (i.e., membership) in an Annual Conference. The present list is a curious conflation of various examinations that Wesley devised for "admitting" his own preachers into "connexion." When one recalls that these men were all laymen, it is obvious that these queries are also applicable, in principle, to any and all baptized/confirmed Christians. Their being reserved now for ordinands

240

does not alter the fact that, for Wesley, they were appropriate clues for the examination (*self*-examination!) of all earnest Christians, to be asked and answered with unflinching seriousness.

The first one is commonplace enough. But then come three real "stickers," certainly for sensitive and knowledgeable young men and women nowadays—and for the generality of Christians of any age and station:

1. Have you faith in Christ?
2. Are you going on to perfection?
3. Do you expect to be made perfect in love in this life?
4. Are you earnestly striving after it?

The requisite answer, in each case, is affirmative!

All too often, in actual current circumstances (as Methodists will know from experience), these probes into the very heart of a person's Christian self-understanding are dealt with in a way that appeals to the individual interpretation of the several ordinands, few of whom have puzzled their way deeply enough into the Wesleyan doctrine of perfection to have clear and responsible commitments to what they are professing ritually. Nor is it always and altogether clear to their elders in the Conference!

There are at least two reasons for this pious confusion. The first, of course, is a widespread consensus in modern culture (instructed as we have been by depth psychology, together with an inbred cynicism) that rejects any notion of "perfection" simply out of hand and would, therefore, assess anybody's serious expectation of being "made perfect in love *in this life*" as symptomatic of a psychotic delusion. The second reason is historical and is related to the greatest tragedy in Methodist history: the nineteenth century conflicts that swirled around Wesley's emphasis upon "holiness of heart and life" and its alterations and distortions at the hands of men and women who were seeking to be faithful Wesleyans (on both sides!) without having experienced anything close to the theological and spiritual struggles out of which his own original synthesis had emerged. The ironic outcome of this process (especially in America) was that the keystone in the arch of Wesley's own theological "system" came to be a pebble in the shoes of standard-brand Methodists, even as a distorted version of Wesley's doctrine of sanctification (as "a second and separate work of grace *subsequent* to regeneration") was becoming a shibboleth of self-righteousness amongst a pious minority of Methodists who professed themselves holier than the rest. That conflict and its abrasions had the effect of leaving the average Methodist (and many much above that average) alienated even by the bare terms— "holiness," "Christian perfection," "sanctification"—not to speak of an aversion toward those persons who actually profess such spiritual attainments. . . .

But I take comfort and courage in such a venture from the undeniable fact that John Wesley believed and taught an explicit doctrine of "holiness" as the goal and crown of the Christian life, and if this gives you trouble, the burden of proof shifts over onto your side (if, that is, you profess to be a Wesleyan at all) to explain why you are prepared to reject or ignore what he regarded as not only essential but climactic. His irreducible minimum of Christian fundamentals were, as we have seen, three: (1) sin and repentance (i.e., self-knowledge), (2) justification and pardon (i.e., assurance) and (3) "holiness of heart and life." "Sanctification," "perfect love," "Christian perfection" were various synonyms, in his vocabulary, for "holiness," and he rang the changes on this theme throughout his whole evangelistic career, insisting that it was the special mission of the Methodists to hold "and to spread [this doctrine of] scriptural holiness over the land."

It is important, therefore, always to start with Wesley's first conversion (1725), a conversion to the ideal of holy living, and to remember that he never thereafter abandoned this ideal even when further conversions (and other experiences) complicated his interpretation of it by a good deal. The seed of the idea had been planted in his mind in the Epworth parsonage by Susanna, one of whose favorite devotional texts was Lorenzo Scupoli's (or, as was then thought, Juan de Castaniza's) *Spiritual Struggle*. The seed had flowered under the stimulus of Jeremy Taylor, Thomas a Kempis, William Law and others. But the idea of perfection as a dynamic *process* with a flying goal did not take its mature form until, finally, Wesley found his way back to the great devotional traditions of Eastern Orthodoxy—Clement of Alexandria, Gregory of Nyssa, Macarius of Egypt, and others. The first fruits of these discoveries may be seen in the only great sermon of his of which we have any record before 1738. This was "The Circumcision of the Heart" (written in December of 1732 and preached in St. Mary's on January 1, 1733 [which was not New Year's Day on the then current calendar]). Too little attention has been paid to the implications of the fact that Wesley never discarded this sermon or even recast it. It turns up, in its original text but out of its chronological order, as No. XIII in *Sermons on Several Occasions*, Vol. II, 1748.

It is true, that in those years, 1725–1738, he consistently misplaced "holiness" (or pure intentions) *before* justification, as preparatory to it. Bishop George Bull and most other Anglicans from Bull to Tillotson had done the same thing—and Wesley would berate them for it later on.

One of the decisive shifts in his 1738 transformation was the reversal of this order. Thereafter, justification always stands first, without any antecedent "holiness" or merit of any kind as a *necessary* precondition to human salvation. Our natural sinful state can be dealt with only by God's sheer gratuitous mercy, based upon Christ's freely offered mediatorial merit. Then, and only then, can anything like new birth and Christian nurture *begin* to restore the power not to sin intentionally which may then be developed further in a nurturing process toward the goal of sanctification: "the mature man in Christ." This relation of justification to sanctification was the critical issue that had first been raised for Wesley in his encounters with the Herrnhuters and Salzburgers in Georgia. It was the main issue that divided Wesley and Whitefield almost as soon as the Revival began. It was the issue on which Wesley and Count von Zinzendorf soon clashed and finally parted.

It is easy for us to miss the originality of this Wesleyan view of faith alone and holy living *held together*. Here was a great evangelist preaching up *sola fide* and, at the very same time, teaching his converts to go on to perfection and to expect it *in this life!* His critics were quick to notice this strange move and to seize upon it as proof of Wesley's inconsistency. Actually, it was yet another of Wesley's characteristic "third alternatives" —maybe his most original one. In this view, the stages of the unfolding Christian life may be laid out in something like the following sequence (a psychological sequence which was more nearly concurrent than spaced out): (1) contrition and repentance (true self-knowledge); (2) justification by faith alone (with Christ's atonement as the *meritorious* but not the *formal* cause—for, remember, this was the crux of his quarrel with the Calvinists!); (3) regeneration ("new birth") issuing in (4) Christian nurture in intensive small encounter groups (with no carpets and no nonsense!); looking toward (5) maturation into "holiness," always in its twin dimensions ("internal holiness" [our *love of God* and neighbor] and "external holiness" [our love of God *and of neighbor!*]). All this was aimed at a climax (6) "perfect love" of God and neighbor as the Spirit's greatest *gift* (which means that, in Wesley's mind, sanctification *by faith alone* was as self-evident as justification ever was, never a moral achievement). And yet, as Wesley never ceased to insist, none of these "stages" is static, none of them so fully completed that one may not lapse from it by unbelief or willful sin—hence his rejection of "final perseverance." What mattered most was that "going on to perfection" has a consistent character and a clear end in view: (1) *love* (of God and neighbor), (2) *trust* (in Christ and the sufficiency of *his* grace) and (3) *joy* (joy upwelling in the heart from the "prevenience" of the indwelling Spirit). This *is* "holy living": to love God and neighbor with all your heart, to trust securely in Christ's merits, and to live joyously "in the Spirit"!

But this vital linkage between faith alone and holy living was forever being misconstrued and Wesley was forever being baffled by its misconstructions. Somehow, he could never grasp the fact that people formed by the traditions of Latin Christianity were bound to understand "perfection" as *perfectus* (perfec*ted*)—i.e., as a finished state of completed growth, *ne plus ultra!* For him, certainly since his own discoveries of the early fathers, "perfection" meant "perfec*ting*" (*teleiosis*), with further horizons of love and of participation in God always opening up *beyond* any given level of spiritual progress. This seemed so *obvious* to him that he allowed himself a swig of smug triumphalism:

> It has been frequently observed, that [in the Reformation time] very few were clear in their judgment both with regard to justification and sanctification. Many who have spoken and written admirably well concerning justification had no clear conception, nay, were totally ignorant of the doctrine of sanctification. Who has wrote more ably than Martin Luther on justification by faith alone? And who was more ignorant of the doctrine of sanctification, or more confused in his conceptions of it?... On the other hand, how many writers of the Romish Church (as Francis Sales and Juan de Castaniza) have wrote strongly and scripturally on sanctification, who, nevertheless, were entirely unacquainted with the nature of justification! insomuch that the whole body of their Divines at the Council of Trent totally confound sanctification and justification together. But it has pleased God to give the Methodists a full and clear knowledge of each, and the wide difference between them.

Regeneration ("new birth," "change of heart") is a concurrent effect alongside justification. The sense of God's unmerited favor prompts an inner transformation, a new disposition toward God and neighbor, a new *self*-understanding, a new outlook and hope. Even so, "this is only the threshold of sanctification...." The Christian life goes on from here, in a dynamic process of nurture, piety, activity—and of *expectation:* that what is imputed in justification will be *imparted* in the Christian life and its fulfillment. *This* is "Christian perfection"—"to be made perfect in love in this life," even if only in the hour of death (which was Wesley's normal "calendar" for it).

> It is, then, a great blessing given to this people, that as they do not think or speak of justification so as to supersede sanctification, so neither do they think or speak of sanctification so as to supersede justification. They take care to keep each in its own place, laying equal

stress on one and the other. They know God has joined these together, and it is not for man to put down asunder. Therefore, they maintain, with equal zeal and diligence, the doctrine of free, full, present justification, on the one hand, and of entire sanctification both of heart and life, on the other; being as tenacious of *inward* holiness as any mystic, and of *outward* [holiness] as any Pharisee.

Who then is a Christian, according to the light which God hath vouchsafed to this [Methodist] people? He that, being "justified by faith, hath peace with God through our Lord Jesus Christ," and, at the same time, is "born again," "born from above," "born of the Spirit"; inwardly changed from the image of the devil, to that "image of God wherein he was created"; he that finds the love of God shed abroad in his heart by the Holy Ghost which is given unto him, and whom this love sweetly constrains to love his neighbor (i.e., every man) as himself; he that has learned of his Lord to be meek and lowly in heart, and in every state to be content; he in whom is that whole mind, all those tempers, which are also in Christ Jesus; he that abstains from all appearance of evil in his actions, and that offends not with his tongue; he that walks in all the commandments of God, and in all his ordinances, blameless; he that, in all his intercourse with men, does to others as he would they should do to him; and in his whole life and conversation, whether he eats or drinks, or whatsoever he doeth, doeth all to the glory of God.

This is an important version of Wesley's doctrine of "holiness of heart and life" in his own words. Its development (apart from *this* statement) is marked out in a series of six landmark sermons over the six-decade span of his ministry. (1) "The Circumcision of the Heart" which, as we have already seen, was his first full definition of the holy-living tradition. (2) "Christian Perfection" is a sermonic essay never preached, but published first in 1741 with the express encouragement of Bishop Edmund Gibson of London—who could tell an authentic version of the holy-living motif when he saw one. (3) "Sin in Believers" is something of an afterthought, added (in 1763) to correct mistaken interpretations of "Christian Perfection," as if it implied *sinless* perfection. It doesn't, and never did, for Wesley. (4) "The Lord Our Righteousness" (1765) marks the decisive parting of the ways between Wesley and the Calvinists—which is to say, a majority of the evangelicals in the Church of England and most Nonconformists, too. The issue, as we have seen, is between "formal cause" and "meritorious cause." This may sound like a quibble until you probe it more closely (like reading the debates at Trent and Bellarmine and Davenant!). Actually, it's the same issue as between imputation and impartation, between predestination and prevenience. "Formal cause" (to the Calvinists) implied predestination; "meritorious cause" implied

God's prevenience and human synergism. The first is "protestant," the second is "catholic." And Wesley, after a full generation of evangelical preaching of justification, continues to insist that Christ's death is the *meritorious* cause of our justification but not the *formal* cause (which he takes to be God's primordial covenant that those who believe shall be saved and those who refuse shall not).

Sermon No. 5 would have to be "On Working Out Our Own Salvation" (1785), a remarkable statement of Wesley's "synergism" and, maybe, his most carefully nuanced exposition of "faith alone" and "holy living." Our last sermon (6), and a fitting climax for the series, is also the last sermon published in Wesley's lifetime. Its theme is "The Wedding Garment." I had never realized until recently (after all these years of poking around, too) that this particular parable had been a sort of shibboleth between the partisans of *sola fide* and of "holy living." What *does* "the wedding garment" signify? To the Calvinists it meant the spotless robe of Christ's righteousness flung as a cover over the "filthy rags" of our *un*righteousness. To the Anglicans generally it had signified holiness itself—i.e., that Christian moral character that is attained by God's *gift* of grace and his *demand* for holy living. With death only months away, Wesley restates his basic conviction, first fixed in 1725: that "the wedding garment signifies holiness, neither more nor less"—the holiness specified in Hebrews 12:14, "without which no man shall see the Lord." Have you ever preached on this parable or heard it preached on? Have you ever considered how much this issue matters to us *today?*

Holiness as a vision of the human potential is an easily distorted notion, and you can see Wesley struggling with its misunderstandings in his *Plain Account of Christian Perfection as Believed and Taught by the Rev. Mr. John Wesley from the Year 1725 to 1765* and thereafter (six editions from 1766 to 1789). There is also that wonderful little pamphlet of 1762 entitled *Cautions and Directions Given to the Greatest Professors in the Methodist Societies*, where the "professors" (i.e., of perfection) are given six highly relevant advices: (1) against pride and self-righteousness; (2) against pride's daughter, *enthusiasm* (defined as grasping for happiness without submitting oneself to its necessary preconditions); (3) against *antinomianism* (doing your own thing, regardless); (4) against sins of *omission* (getting tired and supposing that what you've already done is plenty—or at least enough); (5) against desiring anything above God, and (6) against *schism* (which, as Wesley saw it, was something like pious cantankerousness!). Obviously, these "cautions and directions" were timely—prompted by more than a few rare cases of self-righteousness and spiritual elitism. Indeed, it was just this syndrome of self-righteousness amongst the holiness people that led "mainstream" Methodists finally to throw the Wesleyan baby of true holiness out with the "second blessing" bath water!...

To love God is not merely a friendly feeling toward the ground of being, nor a mood of prayer and piety toward "The Man Upstairs." It is, rather, an awareness of our radical dependence upon God's grace and our gladness that this is the truth about our lives. It means a sense of Holy Presence and of security and warmth in that Presence. It means our recognition of God's upholding love and our gratitude for his love. It means serenity in the face of death because of our confidence that God's love cannot be conquered or cancelled by death. And, most of all, it means having no other gods of our own, since the *First* Commandment is also the *last*!

But overreaching humans cannot "obey" the command to love God as simple acts of choice or even as a life program aimed at self-salvation and happiness. This is why there's so much confusion nowadays about all these self-help programs, mystical exaltations ("religious highs" and things like that), as if this sort of thing could ever be equated with authentic Christian faith and love. This is why holy living is not, strictly speaking, a human achievement or any part of sinful humanity's "natural capacity" to initiate. It is not, at bottom, part of the human potential, save in the carefully guarded sense that God's prevenient grace stimulates and enables us to respond, positively and gratefully. "We love *him* because he first loved *us*." It is God's *initiative* that makes possible our *response*; it is his *self*-presentation in Christ that frees us to accept his acceptance of us. It is his saving work in our justification that liberates us for valid ethical endeavor: in our personal maturations in grace and in our involvements in all effective transformations of society under the aegis of the Kingdom of God.

Thus "faith alone" remains as the threshold of all true holiness in heart and life—and of human happiness—here and hereafter. Wesley analyzes this in a remarkable trio of sermons on "The Law Established Through Faith." Faith stands first (*sola fide*) but not as an end in itself. Nor is it a meritorious *act*, as many fundamentalists seem to insist. Rather, faith is a means in order to *love* just as love is in order to *goodness*, just as goodness is in order to *happiness*—which is what God made us for, in this world—and the next. *This* is "holy living."

Likewise, our love of neighbor (if it ever becomes more than benevolent feeling) follows from our love of God. Love of neighbor is a function of our concern to hallow *all* of life, in all of its occasions, great and small. It is our part in answering the Lord's prayer, "Thy Kingdom come, thy will *be done on earth....*" [Why *can't* we ever get that punctuation right? The comma belongs after *"on earth,"* not before!] In any case, I'd feel easier with my pietist friends if their neighborly love were not so self-selective of their own kind. I'd feel easier about my activist colleagues if their neighborly love weren't so often ruthless. The only love I've ever known that I've trusted and felt sustained by was *from* God, *through* men and women whose love was unselfish—i.e., people who have loved me grace-fully. This indeed is what I *mean* by love—and all of us have been blessed by it, most of us far beyond our deservings or gratitude. It is grace-filled love that helps us become human and that nourishes our humanity.

This is why there was so much *joy* in Wesley (and in the best Wesleyan traditions of holiness of heart and life)—so much happiness in a man who had been taught from infancy to hold his emotions in check and whose temperament was remarkably cool (even amidst the violent emotions he managed to stir up). He was not an exuberant type and he deplored all flippancy and small talk. This is one reason why he has been easier for me to study than he would have been to live and work with. And yet, there *is* this strange, insistent reality of cheerfulness and high spirits that keeps breaking through this knit-browed earnestness. He was, I've come finally to realize, a happy man, in his own sense of "happiness": the human affects of loving God and serving others. And this joyousness of his (and of his brother Charles even more) was infectious. It became a part of the Methodist tradition, its hymnody, its distinctive lifestyle. Some of it still continues in our current tradition—sometimes trivialized, often faked. But what a wonder it would be if we could recover such a tradition's inner springs: viz., the grace of our Lord Jesus Christ who is the Father's redemptive love making life holy and happy, in and by the power of the Holy Spirit in our hearts! *Then*, we'd have no more trouble with those questions about going on to perfection, etc.! *Are* you? Yes, by God's grace! Then, right on! Praise the Lord!

Wesley died happy—singing and praying. The particular hymn that came to him on that last day was already a favorite with all those people in that little room in the house on City Road. It was by Isaac Watts—a sort of poetic comment on the "art of holy *dying*" that Wesley had so long taught his people as the converse of "the art of holy *living*." "I'll praise my Maker while I've breath...." What we can see now, I hope, is that this was a reiteration, *in extremis*, of what Wesley had always said the breath of life is for—and what it had been for, for him, throughout his whole incredible career. God *has* made us for himself. Our first and last end *is* to love him, and to *enjoy him* forever. This *is* holiness of heart and life, and it was Wesley's witness in life *and* death. It was, therefore, a last reprise of the theme of that first conversion, long ago:

I'll praise my Maker while I've breath
And, when my voice is lost in death,
Praise shall employ my *nobler* powers.
My days of praise shall *ne'er* be past,
While life *and* thought *and* being last,
And immortality endures.
                              Amen!

ROBERT E. CUSHMAN

Robert E. Cushman (b. 1913) is an American United Methodist minister, teacher, administrator and theologian. Born to a Methodist parsonage family in Fall River, Massachusetts, he was educated at Wesleyan University, Connecticut, and Yale University. After teaching at Yale University and the University of Oregon, he became professor of systematic theology at the Divinity School, Duke University in 1945. From 1958–1971 he served as Dean of the Divinity School and then returned to teaching until his retirement. Involved in ecumenical activities, he is well-known for his writings, especially *Therapeia: Plato's Conception of Philosophy* (1958) and *Faith Seeking Understanding* (1980).

Cushman's theology carries on the re-assessment of basic theological themes that was taking place in mid-twentieth century North America. He is responsive to the revival of Wesleyan theology, to the renewed recognition of human sinfulness, and to the uniqueness of God's redemptive action in Jesus Christ. The article that is included in these readings sets forth his theological position in sharply defined contours. "The Shape of Christian Faith—a Platform" was published in *The Iliff Review* (March, 1956), pp. 31–40. Used by permission of *The Iliff Review*. The author has added material to the end of the article to bring it up to date.

THE SHAPE OF CHRISTIAN FAITH—A PLATFORM

If we are to talk about "the meaning of our religion," I would naturally suppose that the religion in question is none other than our Christian religion. If this can be agreed upon without straining, then the question becomes somewhat more precise; namely, what is the meaning of our Christian faith?...

I premise as a beginning-point that our Christian faith is seated in and is responsible to a continuous living tradition. In this respect, it cannot be confused with a philosophy. A philosophy is prompted by a concern for intelligibility of the world. It undertakes to interpret reality in terms of some key-category of meaning which commends itself to a thinker or school of thinkers. The privileged category actually rests upon some acknowledged or unacknowledged criterion of meaningfulness, doubtless a judgment of value. Usually, however, the category is assumed to commend itself to all rational men universally. On the strength of this supposition, philosophy presumes to be independent of all tradition and to stand upon grounds of something called reason alone. This is what, in part, distinguishes philosophy fundamentally from the Christian faith and from any religious standpoint which defers to divine Grace in the attainment of religious knowledge. Religious faith is regularly convinced that man does not go it alone.

Christian faith neither can nor desires to claim this kind of independence and self-sufficiency. Christian faith neither was nor is thought out in the study by a cloistered and self-sufficient intellect. Such a conception of Christian faith would be fundamentally Pelagian. It would be human self-help directed to the end of attaining an intelligible world view. As such, it would be in essence an extension of scientific interest. It could be, as Aristotle long ago indicated that branch of "science" which comes after physics—that is, metaphysics, even though most practitioners of philosophy today prefer to call it ontology, if they concede its possibility at all. My own view is that metaphysics is a permissible and necessary undertaking but that it is never to be confounded with Christian faith and that it can, in no sense, exhaust or contain the meaning of our religion.

Return then to the statement that our Christian faith neither can claim nor desires to claim the independence that characterizes the method of philosophy. This is not because faith scorns human rationality as such. Such a notion is entirely mistaken. The fundamental reason is that Christian faith is not primarily a quest for intelligibility. It is, rather, a life which has already found integrity and redemption in and through the mediating power of a particular history (that of the people Israel), which culminated in and was climaxed by the ministry of Jesus Christ. Christian faith is not, in the first instance—though it may be in the end—an interpretation of reality. It is, rather, a doctrine of redemption. More exactly, Christian faith is not doctrine at all. It is a line of witness, a succession of witness, to restoration of life in Christ. Doctrine is the systematic representation of this witness, as well as interpretation and reapplication of it. This witness may properly be followed by an interpretation of all reality in terms of the key-category of meaning, namely Jesus Christ. Such an effort finds tentative beginnings in St. John's "Prologue" and in Philippians 2:5–11. . . .

Instead of trying to define it abstractly, I shall give you a signal instance of it in the history of our religion. I refer to Isaiah's classical account of his experience in the Temple. We are to recognize the symbolic nature of this account. Isaiah did not see the Lord high and lifted up within the precincts of the Temple, but he beheld the Lord. The seraphim did not literally cry out "Holy, Holy, Holy is the Lord of hosts, the whole earth is full of his glory." Isaiah was suddenly overwhelmed by the aweful majesty and absolute sanctity of the wholly Other by whose presence he was confronted. Here is, indeed, as Rudolph Otto long ago pointed out, something like the nouminous awareness of the Mysterium Tremendum. It is a kind of experience which stands in its own right. It is unique and sui generis like the consciousness of beauty. If you have no participation in it, no amount of argument will convince of its reality; but with it the Divine is given. And the human subject is precipitated into crisis.

What is the crisis? Again Isaiah supplies the answer: "Woe is me! For I am undone; because I am a man of unclean lips, and I dwell in the midst of a people of unclean lips; for mine eyes have seen the King, the Lord of Hosts."

To be in the presence of the wholly Other who is also the Holy Other is a fearful experience, because it is to be personally and totally called into question. The absolute sanctity of the Divine renders everything in its presence profane and unworthy. Hence, the prophet cries out, "Woe is me. I am undone." All pretentious righteousness is negated. The absolute contrast between the altogether Holy and human profaneness registers itself in the consciousness of sinfulness and alienation. Yet, the converse side of the same experience is absolute reverence. Reverence for the Holy One together with awareness of absolute responsibility toward the sacred righteousness disclosed—"Ye shall be Holy as I am Holy." Thus, the authentic moment of religious apprehension embraces two antithetical phases: On the one hand, man finds himself presently contrary in his whole being to the holiness of the Divine Presence. This is his profanity, his wrongness of being. On the other side, he is drawn to the Holy One in relation to whom he is presently the negation. Moreover, he knows himself as unconditionally obligated not to do, merely, but to be assimilated to the sacred righteousness of the Divine. The crisis is intense: Man is not only presently contrary to the Divine Presence, but also there is, as a result, a self-destroying cleavage within his own personal life. It is the contradiction between two inertias. Man at once is inclined away from and toward the Divine. He is divided in the middle, and is the battle ground of contrary powers. . . .

By way of summary and by way of drawing out the implications of the foregoing, certain generalizations offer themselves:

First, according to the Hebraic-Christian tradition, which is our heritage, religion is not man seeking God, fundamentally, but rather God having found and confronted man. This is to say that the religious situation is not one of questing but of having been found. Everything depends upon discovering that one is discovered.

Second, religion is human life in crisis calling for solution through reconciliation. It is the whole and entire man— intellect, affection, and volition—who is engaged and involved in the supremely significant moment of his existence.

Third, in the religious situation the primary desideratum is not the solution of an intellectual problem but the urgent problem of life in disruption. The issue is not what is the intelligible structure of the world, but "what must I do to be saved?"

Fourth, the "meaning and truth of our religion," using E. W. Lyman's phrase, cannot possibly be understood apart from participating personally in its two major moments, that of alienation and that of reconciliation.

Fifth, the problem of Christian apologetic is not that of vindicating the truth of theism or the reality of God, but that of discovering man's condition to himself, that is, his condition as he is approached by God. This was the method of Socrates, of the Prophets, of Augustine, of Pascal, of Luther, of Wesley, and many more.

Sixth, it is notoriously true that men may be blind to the fundamental nature of their plight. From Isaiah to Jesus there is the recurring complaint: "Ye have eyes but ye do not see." Religious blindness is a species of self-ignorance on account of which there is eo ipso blindness to God.

Seventh, the Christian faith testifies to the overwhelming of this blindness through the person and work of Jesus Christ in that, as St. Paul affirms, "God was in Christ reconciling the world unto himself."

The meaning of our Christian faith is that through the reconciling ministry of Jesus Christ our estrangement from God is overborne and the divisive self-disagreement within us is replaced by a new integrity of life. This manifests itself in having God as Father and men as brothers. This is justification and reconciliation on both dimensions of our existence.

. . . To come to the positive standpoint of this section, I revert to the implications of the first section. The implications were that religious faith is not prompted by the effort to solve an intellectual problem; neither does faith exist by being the solution of one, except incidentally. Religious faith does not rest upon a crisis of the understanding threatened with the unintelligibility of the world. It is precisely because this has been the prevailing problem and the prevailing perspective of a post-rationalistic epoch, that people find it so hard to participate in the actual standpoint in which the religious problem is engendered and finds its solution.

This standpoint is precisely that of the "prophetic consciousness" described above. While the prophetic consciousness was actually a minority consciousness in ancient Israel and encountered heavy going, nevertheless it was this consciousness which became the core and gave shape to the history of Israel the history of rebellion and reconciliation.

The prophetic consciousness is not represented simply by ethical criticism which the prophets one and all leveled at iniquitous personal, social, political and ecclesiastical arrangements. This was only a by-product; and concentration upon it has obscured the deeper level. The prophetic conscousness is an overwhelming awareness of the aweful sanctity of the Holy Other whereby everything human is laid under judgment and called to accounting. The profanity of man is laid bare in the dazzling light of the Divine sanctity. Man is not confronted by titanic power of external dimension. He is confronted by power transcending or irrelevant to physical magnitude but qualified in such a way as to startle man, powerfully convict, and render him aghast at his unworthiness....

From this comes a practical observation, namely, that Christian proclamation is essentially and always has been a vigorous effort to get men to examine themselves. It is based on the assurance that, as men see and concede the fundamental distortion in their total nature, they know themselves to be standing under a norm by which they are called to account. But the norm is not a principle; it is a claim of a claimant. That is why Jesus begins with the words: "Repent and believe!" Faith follows on repentance, for faith is reconciliation with God, and there can be no reconciliation without repentance. To treat the reality of God as something to be proved is to approach Divine Reality as if it were of the same order as all other objects. This is to step completely outside the circle of the true religious situation; for when a man is in the circle, he discerns that his first business is not demonstration but obedience.

How then do we commend God to men? Very much, I think, in the way we have described: by inducing them to see where they stand. "Blessed are they that mourn, for they shall be comforted."

The salvation we seek will depend on how we construe our plight. The plight of 20th century man is many-sided. The literature of diagnosis is vast, and proposed therapies are about as numerous. Every department of the social sciences as well as philosophy, religion and belles lettres has made contribution. So the testimony among the intellectuals is well-nigh universal that something is radically wrong with man and society. . . .

There is no panacea for this predicament. But our Christian faith is relevant to it and it to Christian faith; so at least we are not left speechless. In the first place, it is historic fact that great Christian faith, that of St. Paul, of Augustine, of Luther, and of Wesley was triumph out of despair. It was admittedly a different sort of despair because under different auspices. But there is an element of identity—man at the end of his rope. As Wesley himself frequently noted, man, totally disabused of his own capacities, is just fit for the kingdom of God. Salvation happens, if we may trust the Hebraic-Christian tradition, when man is so reduced in his own resources that he is shorn of the will longer to resist divine Grace. "Thus a man who is cast down by fear of the commandments of God, and so has reached knowledge of Him, is justified and exalted by faith in the divine word." (The Reformation Writings of Martin Luther, London: 1952, p. 375). If the Christian message is to have any relevance to the modern spiritual situation, it must cease caricaturing itself by exhorting men to godly works and recover sola gratia as its essential word of salvation. Man does not need to do something more, but to be something else. Pelagian Christianity may have sufficed for the 19th century; for the 20th it is trifling irrelevancy. When the children cry for bread, it is giving a stone. This is the first and more obvious point.

The second is more difficult to convey. I can only sketch it. Everything depends upon man's recovery of his sense of dignity and his escape from isolation.

Paradoxically, the common man of the West—and well into the 19th Century—was in large part possessed of his sense of dignity in the measure that he shared with and in the Hebraic-Christian consciousness such a condition as the General Confession of the Liturgy gives voice to. He was, however haltingly, a self-acknowledged sinner inasmuch as he knew himself the subject of a Divine address that laid him under obligation more compelling than his immediate interests. In that variously acknowledged Divine mandate his status and dignity, as a responsible subject of the Divine notice, was conferred upon him. On the one hand, and in the overarching presence of the Holy Other, he was relieved of his isolation; on the other hand, he was discomfitted by "the infinite qualitative difference" between his culpable humanity and the Divine Sanctity. Thus, while, from time to time, he might be disquieted by awareness of dreadful estrangement from God, yet, in the same moment of consciousness, he was also aware of an exalting destiny in his call to be found faithful in the sight of that same Being. As he was laid under judgment before God, so also, was he aware of an injunction coupled with invitation to be conformed to the image of God and as a candidate for inclusion in the Kingdom. Because, meanwhile, secular man has become progressively unaware of himself in the sight of God, he has become proportionately unaware of himself as sinner, and conversely.

Thus is disclosed the paradox insuppressibly resonant in the prophetic consciousness of the Scriptures but muted and falling to near silence for modern sensibility. For the prophetic consciousness, two seeming incompatibles are inseparable: man's dignity and his awareness of the gap, the shameful disparity, between his *Is* and his *Ought-to-be* that, now and again, would sound in his confession of sin or acknowledged contrariety respecting an imperious mandate other than his own. For the consciousness of sin—according to Isaiah and colleagues—is the initial and insuppressible notice to humanity of the ultimate relationship in which it stands as human, namely, to God. Nevertheless, for the prophetic consciousness, the awareness of sin is not attended by simple negation, for, with it and at one time, we are, by our Maker, affirmed in and with the very negation. The vexing burden of indefectible obligation is man's ultimate privilege, his conferred dignity and pending Divine destiny. Luther's rediscovery in Romans 3:21 of the *justitia Dei* as the promise of God in the "righteousness of God" opened doors to a reformation of Christendom. His despair of estrangement is surmounted by the grace of God, it is true, "through Jesus Christ our Lord." But Luther found that we lay hold of the grace of God by faith, first, by conceding the existing alienation in which we stand after the manner of Isaiah and, thereby discover our destiny manifest in Jesus Christ and, therewith, our conferred dignity as human beings—*all* as a gift of divine grace.

From these things comes the judgment that the principal task of Christian teaching and proclamation today, as also yesterday and tomorrow, is —along with Isaiah and Jesus—the opening of willfully deaf ears and blinded eyes. Hope for our humanity is rightly to discern and distinguish between the seeming and the real causes of man's ageless disquiet, alienation from his Ground of Being, and its present-day agony verging on despair. Such teaching will include unabashed, tireless, candid, yet winsome, invitation to honest self-understanding before God—this under the aegis of the now age-old and ecumenical Christian experience of human redemption through Christ the Lord.

Wherever, and in the measure this nurture of the Spirit advances to some realization, there the *prime datum,* or first principle, for any authentic Christian interpretation of "the misery and possible glory of man" (Pascal) may emerge clearly enough to become self-authenticating to searching human understanding. As to that prime datum, I refer flatly to what St. Paul describes as "the light of the knowledge of the glory of God in the face of Christ" (2 Cor. 4:6). The onset of this traumatic insight is called "faith" in both Scripture and tradition. When it comes to pass, this same Jesus Christ, commends himself age by age, as the One in whom all alienation from the Holy Other is transcended by being overcome. Whence it is the witness of faith in all ages that, in this One and through Him, the righteousness of God (which terrified Luther, the honest man!) becomes, not God's just condemnation of the sinner, but, in Jesus Christ's victory over temptation, Abba, Father. So that St. John declares: "And from his fulness we have all received, grace upon grace" (Jn. 1:16. Cf. Rom. 5:15, 17).

It may be that faith awaits such honesty as that of the truly contrite heart which, may yet, be thunder-struck by the *given* historical mystery of Jesus Christ; for it is only at that given point in our human history that the standing and insuppressible paradox afflicting the prophetic consciousness is answered or is answerable. For it is answerable only *by the kind of actual human life that resolves it.* For the Apostolic church it was so resolved in that reconciliation of opposites which was, as Paul saw, Jesus Christ and his Cross. In this Jesus of history the implicit Divine *affirmation* of all humanity without limit (i.e., God's Grace) is actually mated with God's timeless and universal demand for obedience. Given, however, what we are, the latter leaves us all sinners before God, i.e., original sin. Whereas, by contrast, in the mystery of Jesus' historical presence, as Paul saw and said, the standing Divine-human alienation is resolved in a now restored fellowship (*koinonia*) of man with God and of God with man. With this, the kingdom of God is actualized in history. Here was the "new creation" for Paul, and a new humanity rooted in Christ becomes the expectancy of the whole New Testament.

What has been said must, here, suffice to indicate something of what is intended by the statement that Jesus Christ is the *primary datum* of the Christian religion and the first principle for all Christian reflection as faith moves always onwards toward understanding. Of that primary datum we may say, again, it is Jesus Christ because he is the actual occasion in our human history in whose word-deed the resident paradox of the prophetic consciousness of both Testaments finds its redemptive resolution.

Stated once more the paradox may be objectively described in this: that human beings, created to be conformed to the image of God, decline to espouse their given and exalted calling. Their dignity consists, however in their call-declined which, at the same time, is their sinful disobedience. In a word, man is paradoxical in that he can be a sinner because he is called to be a son, that is, a "saint." His misery is at once his half-awareness of that fact while he often spares little to evade its acknowledgement. By contrast, Jesus Christ is first principle of Christian thought because in him the misery of man's self-alienation from God is resolved and, with it, estrangement of man from God and human beings from one another. This, in a word, is why and how the twofold Great Commandment of Mark 12:29–31 encompasses the twofold way of the Kingdom. As the entire love of God restores community as between humanity and God the Father, so from that restored fellowship shared derives alone the sufficient motivating and sustaining good will of any and all human community of persons with one another in this world. In the twofold Great Commandment we are advised by Jesus that, until we are at home with God in this world, we are ill-equipped to be at home with the neighbor, or he or she with us, that is, for long.

CARL MICHALSON

C arl Michalson (1915–1965), an American United Methodist theologian, was born in Waverly, Minnesota and educated at John Fletcher College, Drew and Yale Universities. He joined the faculty of Drew University in 1943 and remained with that institution until his death. An exponent of existentialist philosophy as an interpretative tool for Christian theology, he wrote several important books: *Faith for Personal Crises* (1958), *The Hinge of History* (1959), and *The Rationality of Faith* (1963). Michalson was tragically killed in a plane accident in 1965, and in 1967 *Worldly Theology—The Hermeneutical Focus of an Historical Faith* was posthumously published. "Jesus of Nazareth and the Word of Faith" is selected from *Worldly Theology* (New York: Charles Scribner's Sons, 1967), pp. 159–180.

JESUS OF NAZARETH AND THE WORD OF FAITH

The appearance of Jesus of Nazareth in human history has radically called in question the form which man's existence tends to take in the world. Everything in the apostolic testimony to his life and work, from his humblest acts to his climactic resurrection, witnesses to a single theme: God has chosen Jesus of Nazareth as the one in whom he calls the world to obedience. By virtue of that call the new age has come, the age in which men may live in the world with reference to God and not with reference to the world. Sin, death, the devil, and all other threats of meaninglessness which the world poses are overcome by the dramatic obedience of Jesus who endures death to claim the world for God.

Why God would do this is a mystery. Why God would join his purpose for mankind with Jesus of Nazareth is a secret which the Christian faith continues to conceal successfully under the vocabulary of love. How

Christians believe that this is what Jesus is about, however, is no mystery. Jesus is there, as any datum of history is there, bidding to animate existence with the meaning intended in his occurrence. A man may possess Christ's eventfulness as he possesses any datum of history, through the witness of a faithful community. There is one important respect, however, in which the history of Jesus differs from all other events. Jesus of Nazareth is the one in whom God has chosen to call history to obedience to himself. Therefore, ultimate meaning can now be found in history there. How a man can bring himself to think such a thing and even to live where he thinks is the story of how one becomes a Christian. Becoming a Christian is a possibility existing somewhere between the irreducible mystery of God's selective love and the aggressive unmasking of the enigmas which parade in history in the absence of that mystery.

I

The history of Jesus of Nazareth reveals that Jesus conducts the struggle for his vocation at three levels. First, as the one in whom God is calling the world to obedience, he eats and drinks with publicans and sinners, washes the feet of the disciples, and at last empties himself in death on the cross. These events interpret each other. They mean that Jesus chose to obey God's call to act on God's behalf. On God's behalf he extended mercy to sinners. Apart from that reconciling act, life in the world has promised nothing for sinners but a drama of flight from the infernal flatness of "the wrath to come."

Second, Jesus stands against all organized attempts to thwart the continued disclosure of God's call to obedience. How is it Jesus acts with mercy towards sinners yet with severity toward the religious? The answer lies in his single-mindedness. To preach himself as the one in whom God is calling the world to obedience requires him at one and the same time to embrace the sinner with mercy and to annihilate with judgment all calculated resistance to the coming of this new age.

Third, Jesus decides what warrant there is for a carpenter and rabbi to act for God. The parable of the pearl of great price, the reading of Isaiah 61 in the synagogue with his own epilogue of self-identification, the temptations in the wilderness, the confession of Peter at Caesarea Philippi, the hesitation in the Garden of Gethsemane and eventual resoluteness concerning death—all interpret each other. That is to say, Jesus had no built-in certainty about his vocation. Spiritual things being spiritually discerned, his vocation occurred in freedom, without coercion by the evident. Albert Camus has said, "Between history and the eternal I have chosen history because I like certainties." That is one way to resolve the ambiguity of vocation. Jesus, however, surrendered certainty in the world for the uncertain pearl of obedience to God's call. Christians have sometimes believed that the resurrection is God's vindication of Jesus' vocation, as if the church now possessed a certainty not permitted to Jesus himself. However, one who takes up the ministry which the resurrected Jesus has made the ministry of the church does so at the peril of affectation bordering on the histrionic if he does so without passing through to personal history of temptation, Gethsemane, and cross. It is now possible to understand as a Christian that the resurrection is for the church what the cross was for Jesus—the risk of faith, the confidence that God is exalted in Christ's obedience to his mission to call the world to obedience. The reason faith is a risk is not that, unlike nature, is is unverifiable, but that in faith *all* forms of worldly security are surrendered in exchange for the righteousness of God. The Christian dies with Christ—yielding up his own claims—in order to rise with Christ in the new life of righteousness which is based upon trust in God alone. The parable of the pearl of great price was Jesus' rationale to his disciples for adopting the call of God as the basis of his mission. The same parable becomes the church's rationale for making Jesus of Nazareth the Lord of our history, the beginning of the new age. . . .

II

Jesus' evident humanity mystified his observers because the intention of his existence was not evidently human. While his humanity was fully as human as anyone else's, it was so with quite a different significance. In Jesus' case, the humanity subsisted by virtue of God's word. That means Jesus had his *raison d'etre* in his vocation as word of God. Early Protestant theologians chose to document this truth with one verse in particular: "There is one God, and there is one mediator between God and men, *the man Christ Jesus*." (1 Tim. 2:5) This passage meant to them that the personality of "the man Christ Jesus" is not comprehensible in itself (*anhypostasia*) but in the word of God which he mediates (*enhypostasia*). To behold Jesus, therefore, is not to understand him as a man, nor as a God, nor even as a man in the presence of God. To behold Jesus is to understand oneself as a man in the presence of God. The theology of the Gospel of John is the most familiar exposition of that theme. Jesus

261

is the word of God become flesh. To discern him is to discern God. To hear him is to hear God. He and the father are one in an auditory moment.

The "more historical" theology of the synoptic gospels expresses the same meaning. The synoptics are called "more historical" than the Fourth Gospel because it is now fairly well established that the self-understanding of Jesus which is recorded there originated with Jesus and not in the post-resurrection faith of his followers. *He* is the father of the prodigal son, and *he* is the sower of the seed. *He* is the light which his hearers must realize cannot remain under a bushel, for he is the light of the world, the light that must light every man who comes into the world. *He* is also the seed (cf. John 12:24) that sprouts and grows, one knows not how. He is the importunate widow whose undeviating petition brings God's kingdom into the present. Through this testimony to himself, Jesus made it known that he had the authority to speak and act for God. When he spoke, sinners were forgiven and God's rule began to germinate. Because of him men may now "sleep and rise night and day" (Mark 4:27) with no more care than the lilies of the field and the birds of the air. That, then, is the evangelical scandal. Not the metaphysical scandal of how one person can be in two natures, but the historical scandal of how a carpenter can substitute for God. When Jesus spoke of himself he said the things that pertain to God. The scandal is obverted when one emphasizes Jesus' role as substitute for man in the presence of God. In the "more historical" faith of the New Testament he is mainly substitute for God in the presence of man.

This singular event is known to theology today as a "speech event." The formulation reflects the primitive Christian understanding of Jesus as a word-become-flesh event as well as Jesus' understanding of himself as a verily-I-say-unto-you event. By "speech event" is not meant a verbal pointing to some otherwise dumb objective occurrence nor even an event from which words can be abstracted as surrogates for the event. A speech event is a mode of existence inherently verbal. As an event it radiates its own interpretation because in that existence acts and words fuse in such a way as to precipitate and constitute meaningful events. Hence, Jesus believed the rule of God would arrive because he announces it. When he announces it, it arrives. When it arrives, its essence is that Jesus is "Lord," that is, the speech which brings the rule of God to pass....

III

When one chooses Jesus of Nazareth as the beginning of his history, he undergoes an ascent from the old age to the new. This transition is experienced as freedom. The experience is roughly analogous to what occurs when a traveler transfers from a bus to a jet, or when the son of a blacksmith succeeds as a wood-carver. World history has its parallel when an epoch like the middle ages gives way to a new spirit and the modern age arises. The philosophical experience of movement from the theoretical reason to the practical reason was called "freedom" by Immanuel Kant and in that sense it was a secular parallel to what Christians have meant by transcendence from the old age to the new. The movement in which synagogues became churches and classical dearth was assuaged by "the bread of life" is the Christian meaning of freedom. Obviously, therefore, when Christians talk about freedom they are not talking about just any ability to choose (*velle*). They are witnessing to a new context which places choice on a radically different level of possibility (*posse*).

Contemporary intellectuals like Nicolas Berdyaev and Ortega y Gasset make a significant point when they say the Greeks did not know history because they did not know freedom. What is customarily meant by that is that the Greeks knew free choice (*proairesis*), which is the selection among alternate ways of doing what one must necessarily do. But they did not know freedom of the spirit (*eleutheros*). Freedom of the spirit is the ability to say yes or no to a destiny and thus to make a choice which sets the whole course of one's life, one's very history. Freedom in that sense is not a psychological state but an event, a decision which is at the same time a way of life. Such decisions are the very possibility of history. Therefore, as is being said, one who does not know freedom does not know history.

The distinctive dimension of Christian freedom, however, is not the freedom with which one chooses, not even when that choice is a destiny-determining choice. Christian freedom is the freedom one experiences when the entire volitional facility of the human spirit is mobilized at the new and unanticipated level of the history invoked by Jesus of Nazareth. The new age initiated in Jesus has to do mainly with the issue of human freedom because it sets up the conditions which force upon the past the very possibility of a new authenticity.

Let me test the sense of the Christian meaning of freedom through a series of illustrations. The Japanese daughter of a Samurai was once sent to a mission school where she was given a plot of ground a yard square with which to do entirely as she chose. It was called a "do as you please" garden. She planted it according to her own design and afterward exclaimed it was the first time in her life she had known what it meant to be free. Christian freedom is like that, to be sure, but it is more.

Radhakrishnan, the Indian philosopher and statesman, has likened freedom to being dealt a hand of cards and being allowed to play out the game, but strictly within the limits of the cards in hand. Christian freedom also includes this sense of a certain latitude within prescribed limits.

Pascal's analogy of the wager comes even closer to what Christians mean by freedom. It recapitulates the others but adds still another element. The coin is tossed. One is free to do as he pleases with his decision. But he can only choose "heads" or "tails"; he must play out the game within those limits. What is added by Pascal, however, is urgency. One *must* call out before the coin has fallen. That is to say, man is not free not to choose. He is not free to filibuster with destiny beyond the deadline for authentic resolution. The Roumanian playwright Ionesco has recently called our attention to a new metaphor for freedom emerging from the space age. In outer space one has a sense of weightlessness which he experiences as a sense of infinite possibility. That is the terrifying burden of human freedom. Is there no springboard, no point of purchase, no clearing or focus within which to set in motion what man feels to be the power of his freedom?

Choice, limitation, urgency, and burdensomeness—that is the progressive movement toward a realistic Christian view of freedom. But what of liberation, which is the promise implicit in the new age? The main ingredient in the Christian view of freedom is left untouched by implications in the foregoing analogies, however right and important they may be. For Christian freedom is not so much concerned with psychology, with the residual potentialities of the human spirit. Christian freedom is a reality primarily historical, an attribute of life in the new age. If the human spirit occupies the old age, and the "old" by definition has not "been formed anew by the spirit of God," nothing of final authenticity is possible to it. For that matter, how do you appeal to freedom of choice in a man who does not even know his name, who is dying of thirst, who sees only his light dying, who is seeking determinedly and listening but is greeted in his universe only by an "immaculate silence" (Samuel Beckett), whose thoughts about existence resemble more the transcription of his fever chart than a work on ethics or logic! Actually, the Christian faith does not simply call upon the capacities of man. Christianity is a redemptive faith which in some sense confers what it requires, such as the focus of understanding which makes choice possible. Freedom is therefore in some sense a gift before it is a task.

One final analogy, then. A young Irish couple was reported to have come to the very brink of marital disaster while failing to agree on the name of their expected son. He wanted the son named "Patrick" after the grandfather; she wanted the baby named "Noel" because his birth was about to occur at Christmas time. Consider the effect on the problem of choice when the doctor announced, "They're twins." Or, even better for the analogy to Christian freedom, if the doctor could have added, "And they're both girls!" Christian freedom closely parallels this sense of a shift in the whole context of choice. When God inaugurates the new age he puts all prior history in question. But he does so by mercifully setting up the framework for a wholly new basis for life, an entirely new history. The introduction of new possibility by the movement from one level of life to another, from the old to the new age, is what the Christian experiences as freedom.

What, then, is the content of Christian freedom? In what form does the transition to the new age express itself in Christians? What is the significance for human behavior in this "freedom wherewith Christ hath made us free?" Four realms predominate in which deliverance from the old age is specifiable.

First, there is *freedom from the world*. In Biblical faith "world" has two connotations. There is the neutral world which provides the stage upon which our lives are acted out, and there is the *hostile* world which is life in a stage of siege against God. Life in the old age draws its inspiration from the world, sets up the world as an object of devotion, hence obscures the world's neutrality by surrendering to it. The world unwittingly becomes man's captor. The freedom of the Christian man is liberation from such bondage and the restoration to man of the world as a stage for the expression of stewardship toward God. To say it as Gogarten does, the Creator has given us the world as the locus of our responsibility to him. But we have worshipped the creature rather than the Creator, perverting our responsibility *for* the world into responsibility *to* the world. The effect of the advent of Jesus is to restore to us the proper relationship by reintroducing obedience to God as the new possibility for life in the world. In the new age, we must be in the world while not of it. We must live in the world "as if not" in the world. We must buy the things of the world "as if not" possessing them and have our wives "as if not" having them.

This paradox of Christian existence is inherent in the transition from the old age to the new. In the world we "surrender to Christ and for the rest be uncommitted" (Herbert Butterfield). We must live in the world "as in a house sold for the breaking-up" (Albert Schweitzer). "He who when he has the world is as one who does not have it, then he has the world, otherwise the world has him" (Soren Kierkegaard). Freedom is the meaning of being a new creature. With it the oldness of bondage to the world has passed away.

Does not this promise crack with incredulity? Behind the confident mask of the minister who says it, is there not some pallor of skepticism? What woman would marry a man who loves her "as if not"? What business man can survive who holds his piece of the world "as if not"?

Yet, one who does not see its cogency may have settled for what the young minister in de Vries' *Mackerel Plaza* calls a "woolly mamma bear *Reader's Digest* optimism." A wrong orientation to the world can be ruinous in any relation. It is possible to lose one's soul even within such elevated relations as human love. Can one love another in any other way than "as if not" in a world in which there is only one God? To confuse human love with acts of worship is not simply romantic; it is demonic. Alternatives to the freedom of Christian love border on vampire acts which tend to bankrupt love by draughts upon it which disregard transcendent claims. Not even the institution of marriage was meant to bear such strains. The *Tristan and Isolde* myth relates this problem. "Two lovers destined solely for each other are already dead: they die of ennui, of the slow agony of a love that feeds on itself" (Simone de Beauvoir). That is why marriage is a rite of the church in which one openly acknowledges that he receives his love "as if not," that is, before God. Marriage is a relation of absolute fidelity because one receives his partner before God, not because one gives himself wholly to another. The same structure which makes of human love a marriage makes of business a vocation. Life in the world is a stewardship for those who live in the new age of obedience to God in Christ. That obedience lifts us out of the age of exclusive investment in the world where lives inevitably depreciate. The Spanish philosopher Unamuno knew of a farmer who died without the final blessing of the church because the priest could not pry open his hand to pour the sacramental oil in his palm. He was clenching three dirty yellow coins. The pathos of the incident is not that the farmer missed the blessing of the church but that he had probably lived as he died, holding so tightly to the world that he was "turned away from the eternal."

A second aspect of Christian freedom in the new age is *freedom from the law*. The structure of a Christian's relation to law is similar to the structure of his relation to the world. Law like love and work becomes demonic when nothing is allowed to transcend it. Moses knew as Kierkegaard did that the law he received was subject to "teleological suspension." Therefore he veiled his face to hide the embarrassment of handing down something which could be superseded. Paul saw clearly what was only dimly implicit in Moses' receiving the law from God. He saw that "Christ is the end (*telos*) of the law." For Paul that meant "all things are lawful."

Does the freedom of the Christian man really border so closely upon license? Actually, license is not the conclusion to be drawn from freedom from the law. The peculiar feature of the law in the old age was the fact that its lack of finality and its oppressiveness were tied up together. Therefore when Christ becomes the law's end, teleologically suspending it by the inauguration of the new age, it is not license he introduces. It is freedom from the oppressiveness of requirements which had no inherent finality, hence no genuine ability to confer authenticity....

A third realization of freedom in the new age is the *freedom from sin*. The concept of sin in the Biblical faith represents a significant contrast to non-Biblical points of view. Sin in the Bible is primarily a religious and not a moral concept. Every instance of sin is reducible to a single dynamic: rebellion against God. Even in the system of legalism where sins are morally specifiable, the root sin is known to be the disobedience to God implicit in the violation.

In the new age which Christ's appearing has inaugurated, however, the content of sin undergoes an important revision. Sin is no longer simply rebellion against God, but rebellion against the particular form in which God has chosen to call men to obedience. Disobedience to God is now defined as refusal to accept Jesus of Nazareth as the source of one's history. In the old age there was only one sin: rebellion against God. All sins were exemplifications of that basic infidelity. In the new age there is only one sin: anachronism. One who lives after the appearance of the new age by the framework and standards of the old age is not living "up to date." Confidence in circumcision, sacred festivals, and laws which no longer have authority is a breach of faith in the new age God has wrought in Jesus of Nazareth. Hereafter, "that which is not of faith is sin." Sin is to turn one's history into mere pastness....

Finally, *freedom from death* is promised in the new age. That would surely be freedom in its least equivocal sense, for any freedom which was finally cut across by death would be a hopeless sort. A man could submit his freedom to spatial limits and even to intermittent deadlines without violation of the sense of authenticity in freedom. But if a man must die at last, where is the *freedom*? If one's space is ultimately reducible to nothing and if one's time is ultimately running out, all talk of freedom is a hoax, like "fishing in a bathtub knowing nothing will come of it" (Camus). Sartre is right, therefore, to reject Heidegger's definition of man as a being-toward-death. For it is impossible to be fully a man where the whole enterprise called humanity is terminated in death. Not that Sartre denies all men are mortal. It is simply that for him mortality is not what defines a man. For Sartre, freedom-notwithstanding-mortality is what defines a man. So he asserts his freedom in deliberate disregard of death. Yet, while his existentialism may be more defiant than Heidegger's, it is scarcely more free as long as the threat of death is not removed.

Freedom from mortality, however, does define the Christian man. The ultimate choice is the decision which the new age precipitates. To make Christ the source of one's history implies the beginning of a being-toward-life and thus a final vindication of all one's freedoms. Now freedom from death is the most extravagant aspect of a Christian's consciousness in the new age. The clue to it has come with the resurrection of Jesus, which is the sign of the new age. The logic of it is that death is the wage of sin, so that with freedom from sin there follows freedom from death. Death is "the last enemy" only in a chronological sense. Its power over life is overcome when Jesus acts on behalf of God in reconciling sinners. Jesus' own resurrection is already implicit in his atoning deeds. Therefore, he could say, "I am the life; he that believeth in me hath eternal life already." Man's victory over death is likewise implicit in his participation in the new age which Christ's deeds precipitate....

The contemporary theologian most influential in my delineation of this view of worldly faith has been Friedrich Gogarten. While details in my presentation vary from him, the main lines are instructed by his view. Let me summarize it as it is stated in his recent volume, *The Reality of Faith*.

What is the nature of the reality in which Christians participate when they have faith? How does this reality differ from the reality of the world in general, or from sheer human invention? Gogarten's answer is that the Christian faith involves a relation to the man Jesus Christ, who experiences the nothingness of the world. Acting in complete obedience toward God, Christ takes the nothingness of the world upon himself and thus introduces into history a new kind of reality, the reality of freedom from bondage to the world. The freedom *from* the world and *for* God is the reality of faith.

The Christian understanding of faith as freedom is held by Gogarten to be the source of modern man's self-consciousness. In the modern world man for the first time can assume responsibility for the world because he knows he is not in bondage to it. This rejection of the world as a basis for one's self-understanding ought not be confused with Gnosticism's dualistic repudiation of the world. For when God makes man his son and heir, he gives man the world as an inheritance. The very responsibility for the inheritance supplies man with the conditions for his freedom as a son. Forfeiture of this responsibility, however, is not an innocent thing. It results in worship of the world rather than worship of the creator, and worship of the world turns the nothingness of the world into a fate, a law which enslaves man. To say Christ frees us from the law is to say he frees us from the religious worship of the world.

The Reformation expressed this position in its doctrine of justification by faith. God did not require men to perform the works of the law in order to justify themselves. Man was justified by the very freedom in Christ by which God sets him free from the world and its laws. Modern science is a twin phenomenon with the Reformation because it defines man's relation to the world in similar terms. In both modern science and Reformation Christianity man is responsible *for* the world, not *to* it. By liberating man from the worship of the world, Protestant Christianity effected a kind of demythologizing of the world, called secularization, setting science free for unrestricted experimentation with the world.

Subjectivism emerged at the point at which modern science confused its freedom from the world with lordship over it. Subjectivism is a world view which binds modern science as a fate in the same way the law bound the pre-Christian man, for it bases man's independence from the world upon man himself, making man the source of meaning for all reality.

Faith, on the other hand, is the reality which has the task of liberating man from just such bondage to the world. In the preaching of Jesus, man is summoned to a new existence of freedom for God. In the preaching of Paul, Christ is proposed as the one in whom bondage to the nothingness of the world is overcome in such a way as to restore man's freedom for God. For Luther, this word of preaching creates faith as man's obedient existence, a condition of reality prior to all man's acts. Luther's strictures against free will can be regarded as his warning that a man is not free to liberate himself on the basis of his own acts. Even his acts of right belief presuppose Christ's act of granting man selfhood in freedom for God.

The discussion with subjectivism, which is the man focus of Gogarten's volume *The Reality of Faith*, must be carried on at the source, at the point where man has chosen to worship the creature rather than the creator. While it is the legitimate task of modern man to assume responsibility

269

for the world, it should be understood that this responsibility is the very form in which modern man is now encountering the law. The responsibility for the world burdens man as a fate when man lacks the freedom for God from whence that responsibility originally arises. Modern man is right to feel responsible for the world. The preaching of the church makes it possible for man to remain free for that responsibility by receiving it from God....

PART V

DOCTRINE AND DOCTRINAL STATEMENT

In recent United Methodist theology the central official document is the statement on "Doctrine and Doctrinal Standards and the General Rules" in *The Book of Discipline of the United Methodist Church*. Understanding this statement—its origin, and its implications—is significant for ongoing Methodist theology. Appropriate preparation for this section is a reading of this section of the *Discipline*. To help interpret this theological presentation the following selections are included. Albert C. Outler chaired the committee which prepared the disciplinary statement. His remarks made at the presentation of the statement to General Conference lead into the discussion. One critical commentary by Robert E. Cushman indicates an important reaction to the formulation. Also included in this part are two papers resulting from bilateral conversations between Methodist and Lutheran theologians on baptism and Methodist and Roman Catholic theologians on ministry. With these papers the ecumenical dimension of contemporary United Methodist theology is represented. These selections set some of the directions for the continuing task of constructive theology in United Methodism.

271

ALBERT C. OUTLER

This selection is the introductory statement made by Albert C. Outler to the General Conference of 1972 as he presented the report of the committee that prepared the "Doctrine and Doctrinal Statements and the General Rules." The report was adopted and now appears in *The Book of Discipline of the United Methodist Church*. This section from the *Discipline* should be read along with these selections. This statement by Outler is taken from the *Daily Christian Advocate*, Atlanta, Georgia, Wednesday, April 19, 1972, pp. 218–221. For biographical information on Outler see the introduction to his earlier selection.

INTRODUCTION OF THE DISCIPLINARY STATEMENT

The most obvious feature of this Report is what it is not. It is not a new creed, nor a new set of Articles of Religion, nor a Confession of Faith, nor a new set of General Rules. The old ones are still retained, in the middle of our text, in their original versions. This is by design, of course—for the next most obvious thing about the Report is that it is not a simple reaffirmation of the old Part II, either. The old Articles, and Confession and Rules have been set in a new context of interpretation, and this means a decisive change in their role in the theological enterprise in The United Methodist Church.

Now this calls for an explanation and any such explanation would have to begin with a reference to our mandate from the General Conference of 1968 (P. 1419):

> . . . to bring to the General Conference of 1972 a progress report concerning "Doctrine and Doctrinal Standards" in the United Methodist Church. If the Commission deems it advisable [said that mandate] it

273

may undertake the preparation of a contemporary formulation of doctrine and belief, in supplementation to all antecedent formulations....

To many in that Conference and throughout the church, this meant a new "creed," or something like that. In the beginning, we were sometimes referred to as "the new Creedal Commission." And, of course, we did consider that possibility: a new creed, a new confession of faith, a new doctrinal summary and affirmation. In fact, one of the general work-assignments for the Commission as a whole was the production of experimental forms of creeds and liturgical affirmation and doctrinal summary—not one but many— and this turned up three or four texts of truly high quality that deserve to be published and used throughout the church.

We are certainly, therefore, not against creed-making. Our concern however is not with a single creed but with the guidelines that should be followed in any given case of creed-making and the claims that any given creed or summary might be able to make to have authority in The United Methodist Church or among United Methodist people. But one of the earliest decisions that emerged in our exploratory discussions was that a single creed, displacing the two that we have now, whatever its form or quality that claimed any sort of official monopoly in the church, would not really serve the cause of theological renewal, or for that matter of theological clarity.

Doctrinal confusion cannot be overcome by official dogmatic pronouncement. There is something profoundly self-deceiving in the assumption that valid authority in disputed question can ever flow from the majority vote in the General Conferences. Such majorities weaken rather than strengthen a church's real authority. A better way, we came to realize, was to strike for a new understanding of the problems of the norms and the normative in theology and ethics and then to seek for a clearer vision of our doctrinal heritage as a resource for solving these problems of norms and the normative. This is not a cop out. It is instead the acknowledgement of three decisive factors affecting our current situation in The United Methodist Church and in the Christian world everywhere....

Somewhere in The United Methodist Church there is somebody urging every kind of theology still alive and not a few that are dead, but your commission came to realize that this apparent bedlam is, at least in part, the perversion of an older, profounder principle of positive importance, that is to say, of doctrinal pluralism, doctrinal diversity-in-Christological-unity. Far from being a license to doctrinal recklessness or indifferentism,

274

the Wesleyan principle of pluralism holds in dynamic balance both the biblical focus of all Christian doctrine and also the responsible freedom that all Christians must have in their theological reflections and public teaching.

"We Methodists think and let think" and there was never any doubt for [Wesley that] the taproot of Christianity was the Scriptural mystery of God in Christ and not much else, really. It is simply a fact that United Methodist doctrinal standards have always had a pluralistic cast to them. Wesley's Sermons and Notes and behind them the Book of Common Prayer, the Angelican Homilies and Articles and the Evangelical and United Brethren Articles and Confessions never were understood as merely judicial statutes. Rather, they were so many varied witnesses to the truth of Scripture and then to the negative limits of allowable public teaching. What then happened of course, was that all too many Methodists found it all too easy to slide off the high plane of doctrinal pluralism as a positive virtue into the slough of doctrinal indifferentism and chaos.

In my own judgment, the most important single achievement of this report by its intention at least, is our attempted reversal of this trend toward indifferentism, by pointing, especially in Part III, to the central core of common Christian teaching that we share with other Christians, and yet also to our own distinctive guidelines for responsible theologizing in the Wesley, Albright, Otterbein tradition. How well we have succeeded is, of course, for this Conference and the wider theological forum outside this church . . . to judge.

In any case, to have come to you with a doctrinal creed or summary that would have pretended to monopolize the doctrinal enterprise would have been profoundly unwise, and misleading to boot! Moreover in the second place, we were very soon and very deeply impressed by the vitality and the relevance of the various new protestant theologies, protesting Theologies, emerging in this epoch of radical change: "black theology," "Women's liberation theology," "third-world theology," etc.

While rejecting their exclusivistic claims—as we have also rejected all doctrinal monopolies, on principle—we are still very eager for all Christians to hear what the Spirit is saying to the churches through them—their protests against injustice and indignity to any of God's children, their protests for the paramount rights of the human person, at every level of interpersonal and social relationships, regardless of race, sex, nationality or life-style.

We are also prepared to take seriously and urge you to take seriously all the various emergent theological viewpoints that are bidding for dominance, or at least a hearing, nowadays: "process theology," "development theology," "linguistic analysis," "existentialism," the "new transcendentalisms" of various sorts, — as well as the veritable kaleido-scope of special-interest theologies of "hope", "ecology" (and, over on the other side, the new "pentecostalisms," the "Jesus Movement," "the Children of God," etc., etc.).

Taken all together, these various "Protestant" and "special-interest" theologies point to the rich diversity that the Christian mind can, and ought to, make room for. But by the very same token, they also suggest that the official sponsorship of any one of these theologies by The United Methodist Church, to the derogation of any of the others, would be wildly imprudent in practice and wrong in principle. Besides, we must never forget that the question of doctrinal standards in The United Methodist Church is closely related to our long standing commitment to the larger cause of Christian unity.

The prime imperative in all serious ecumenical dialogue is that each tradition be prepared to interpret itself to all the others, honestly and openly, without triumphalism or apology, without misleading claims and fruitless polemics. For United Methodists this plainly means, not only to confess, but to expose our doctrinal pluralism. Our concern for pluralism as a positive theological virtue — has been reinforced by a third distinctive feature of our epoch and this may be the most important one of all: the rise and spread of what John Courtney Murray (and Wilhelm Dilthey before him) spoke of as "the historical consciousness," by con-trast with the older "classical consciousness" that dominated the Chris-tian understanding of doctrine and dogma since Constantine.

In the European State Churches, and even in America up to our own time, there has been a tendency to regard creeds and confessions much in the same way that the secular states construe their legislative statutes: that is, as juridical enactments, enforceable by punitive sanctions against all violators, or else let simply slide into the oblivion of the dead letter, which in fact happens to our Articles in our Discipline. But whereas positive law has gone on changing, dogmatic formularies tend to resist change — and in one sense rightly so, since Christian truth, if it ever could be fully stated in propositional form, would then be the creed to end all creeds, the doctrine to end all doctrinal formulations and only have to be repeated thereafter till people understood it properly.

In the past, the appearance of new creeds has always meant displace-ment of the last one you had with the normal implication that the last one had some sort of insufficiency (or maybe error!). But once you con-fess the past creed had an error, that your forefathers and some others could not see, . . . what may be lurking in our creed that our children may see? This juridical mindset was as typical of "classical Protestantism" as of Roman Catholicism up till Vatican II.

Now, our emerging historical consciousness that all of us in this room share, one way or another, has altered this static view of dogma beyond all recognition and control. Nowadays we ask, as if by instinct, about the historical context of any document or pronouncement.

This sense of context and perspective has made modern history possible, and modern Biblical study, too, as one of its byproducts. It allows us to appreciate the ancient creeds and confessions afresh and then to repossess their living truth in the light of radically new experience. This holds true for the Apostle's Creed, the Augsburg Confession, the Westminster Catechism. It holds for Wesley's Sermons. It holds for his Notes, and especially it holds for our Articles and Confession.

Time was when these landmark documents were "contemporary" and the interesting thing is that the most "contemporary" thing about them when they were first formulated are the things that are now most clearly "dated" about them in our own eyes. But each one of them also enshrines perennial Christian truth; and in that sense they are still "contemporary"! Old articles don't have to be discarded. They don't have to be reiterated, either. Thus, we have felt ourselves quite free to retain our historical landmarks without embarrassment or apology. But, then, quite deliberately, to set them in a new twin perspective of interpretation—of our heritage, on the one hand, and that's part one, and our contemporary crisis on the other. And that's what part two is talking about.

We hope that you have noticed that we have tried to clarify the contextual relationships between the Articles, the Confession, and Wesley's Sermons and Notes and Rules—in order to clarify the reference in the First Restrictive Rule about "our present existing and established standards of doctrines." We have not altered these standards, as such, but we have proposed a genuinely new principle for doctrinal self-understanding in The United Methodist Church. Thus, we have tried to reaffirm our share in the Christian tradition, as a whole, even as we have also tried to accent, once again, the distinctive Wesleyan guidelines (Scripture, tradition, experience, reason); and it is these guidelines that we propose to you as our best safe-guard against doctrinal indifferentism!

Now, Mr. Chairman, we would not wish to claim too much for this Report. It bears the blemishes of haste and the inelegancies of committee-English. There is at least one misspelling that I apologize for, and one split infinitive that proves that the Committee got the best of the Chairman more than once. It is, as some of you say, "too long." To this, one might respond, without any disrespect and with all-loving friendship, that in a Discipline that has 268 pages devoted to "Administrative Order" and 53 pages to "Property," less than 40 pages for "Doctrinal Statements and the General Rules" is not wildly disproportionate, (applause) especially when you look at our early Doctrines, where they, so to say, had gotten the "hang of it."

If this Report could be put to fruitful use in promoting theological reflection amongst United Methodists and if it could also serve the urgent cause of helping our theological identity in the eyes of other Christians, the extra print and paper would be as well justified as most of the wood pulp we use up daily.

And yet, for all its faults, there are three bold claims I make for the report, without any personal immodesty or misgiving. The first is that it is a truly corporate product of this Commission as a whole—an unstinted, cumulative, cooperative effort by a wonderfully representative, which is also to say "hard-headed" and difficult, group of United Methodists, all working on marginal time and within a very frugal budget! . . .

Now, my second claim is that minimally, at least, the Report faithfully represents the best in the traditions of the Wesleys, of Albright, and Otterbein, not by replication, but by re-presentation and re-interpretation. As such, it is offered as a useful guide for those who wish to repossess those traditions and to renew them for further service in Christian mission. This is crucially important if the United Methodist Church is to have any sustainable revival of the Gospel in a contemporary version of John Wesley's catholic spirit.

My third claim is that, however crudely, this Report lays the foundations for the still further development of a stable theory of doctrinal interpretation in the United Methodist Church. It is offered less as a legislative statute than as an act of encouragement and enablement. We have tried to open the way for the widest possible participation of United Methodists in the mutual task of the teaching church. Instead of presuming to tell our people what to think, theologically, we have tried to offer basic guidance as to how we may all do theology together, faithful to our rich and yet very diverse heritage, and yet also relevant to our present ideological confusion. If it is adopted and taken seriously enough, which would also mean critically enough, it could quite conceivably become something of a landmark in itself. It could also, of course, serve this Conference and the church to a barely stifled yawn and go down as yet another of our high-minded but largely wasted efforts. Our fears go one way; our hopes and prayers go the other. . . .

ROBERT E. CUSHMAN

The discussion of the doctrinal statements in the *Discipline* is an ongoing opportunity for and responsibility of United Methodists. Consideration of the theological process outlined in the disciplinary statement is in an initial stage, but this stage of the discussion has set forth a challenge that can issue in renewal in the life of this church. Among those who have participated in the discussion and have helped set some agenda items is Robert E. Cushman. A brief biography and selection from his works appears in Section IV. The article, "Church Doctrinal Standards Today," appeared in *Religion In Life* (Winter, 1975), Vol. XLIV, No. 4, pp. 401–411.

In view of critique by this essay of "theological pluralism" as a "principle" for doctrinal formulation, it may be noted that, by action of the General Conference of 1980, the following sentence of Para. 69, p. 72 of *The Discipline* was replaced: "In this task of reappraising and applying the Gospel, theological pluralism should be recognized as a principle" by "In this task of reappraising and applying the Gospel according to the conciliar principle, we recognize the presence of theological pluralism." Apparently, "theological pluralism" was dethroned as a norm for doctrinal reformulation and accepted simply as a fact of life.

CHURCH DOCTRINAL STANDARDS TODAY

In Methodism the concept of doctrinal standards is as old as John Wesley himself and, in the church organized in America in 1784, has as old an official status as the First Restrictive Rule of *The Doctrines and Discipline* of 1808: "The General Conference shall not revoke, alter or change our Articles of Religion or establish any new standards or rules of doctrine contrary to our present existing and established standards of doctrine."

Coincident with unification of The Methodist Church with the Evangelical United Brethren, the General Conference of 1968 established a Commission on Doctrine and Doctrinal Standards for study and report. The Commission undertook a quadrennial task and in 1972 submitted its unanimous findings for legislative action to the General Conference, with the stipulation of the chairman that "we do not regard it [the document moved for adoption] as in violation of the First, Second, or Fifth restrictive rules." In accord with the motion, the report was adopted in place of its disciplinary antecedent (1968) and was published as Part II of *The Book of Discipline*, 1972. The stipulation, on presentation to the General Conference, that the legislation before the supreme law-making body did not invoke or infringe upon the Restrictive Rules was sustained by Decision No. 358 of the church's Judicial Council.

Of Part II of *The Book of Discipline* there are three sections: (1) Historical Background, (2) Landmark Documents, and (3) Our Theological Task. In principle and fact, Section 2 republishes undoubted historic doctrinal standards of the former churches, now The United Methodist Church. These include the Twenty-five Articles of Religion (1784), the Confession of Faith of the former EUB Church (1962), and the General Rules (1784).

When, in these times, a major Protestant church not only aspires but ventures to risk reexamination of its doctrinal heritage with a view to assessing where indeed it stands with reference to historic norms, present internal uncertainties, and relentless worldly metamorphosis, the result should command the attention of serious churchmen almost anywhere. Not only what is essayed but also what is accomplished may be revealing, or at least symptomatic, of what mainline Protestant Christianity in general may undergo in attempting to give an account of itself doctrinally in an era almost incomparably secularized and markedly pluralized. Nor can we deny that the climate of the age so invades some Protestant communions as that an intramural *consensus fidelium* is hardly to be looked for.

It is primarily the want of this consensus, however, which constitutes, at one and the same time, both the risk of such an undertaking and also its imperative. Herewith the churches confront an agonizing dillemma not unlike that of Pope John XXIII in proclaiming *aggiornamento*. Moreover, derivative of this situation is an inherent, attendant twofold problem: (1) On the one hand, how can a secularized church arrive at a *consensus fidelium*, *i.e.*, viable doctrinal unanimity faithful to the tradition? (2) And conversely, how can practicing theologians function if the churches are doctrinally incoherent or unable for want of consensus to clarify doctrinal standards, either by reaffirmation or by reformulation? With whom or what lies the norm?

UNITED METHODIST CONCILIARISM
AND PROCESS THEOLOGY

As I study Part II, one feature fully merits our attention. It is everywhere implicit and recurrently explicit that doctrinal standards and, indeed, Christian theologizing are taken to be a proper task and responsibility of the whole church, and there is conspicuous absence of any mention of theologians. Thus, a frankly conciliar conception of the source of doctrinal standards is affirmed while, at the same time and somewhat shockingly, it is also affirmed that "in this task of reappraising and applying the gospel, theological pluralism should be recognized as a principle."

In Section 3 this conciliar stress is emphatic in such words as: "The United Methodist Church expects all its members to accept the challenge of responsible theological reflection." If this expectancy is exorbitant, the risk is somewhat curtailed by the definition of "doctrinal guidelines" (*i.e.*, the norms of Scripture, tradition, experience, and reason) and by explicit delimitation of theological initiatives according to a twofold rule, *viz.*, "careful regard to our heritage and fourfold guidelines, and the double test of acceptability and edification in corporate worship and common life."

In sum, Part II, Section 3 commits itself to something very close to corporate ecclesial responsibility for the authorization and development of doctrinal standards. The move seems to be in the direction of a kind of collegial *magisterium*, of which there are no elders or bishops as guardians of the faith once delivered to the saints. Indeed, it is denied that doctrinal statements are the special province of "any single body, board, or agency," and none others are dignified by so much as mention.

We have, then, I would think, a most emphatic commitment to a species of intramural conciliarism as the source and authorization of doctrinal standards. Procedurally this may not entirely accord with the tradition of historic Methodism, which, in fact, early made the Conference the prime judicatory for both faith and order. To this, Section 1, "Historical Background," itself gives prominence without, however, noting that Wesley's Conference was composed of preachers and was itself something of a catechetical school. Yet it is now daringly proposed that the whole church become, as it were, a catechetical school writ large for the crossing of what are called "theological frontiers" and in "new directions." Then, rather distinguishing the church from its pilgrim people, it is declared: "The Church's role in this tenuous process is to provide a stable and sustaining environment in which theological conflict can be constructive and productive."

From such a statement a question emerges as to what stability may be expected of a church possessed, for doctrinal standards, of little more than "landmark documents" and for whose pilgrim people doctrine is spoken of most nearly as a continuing process of "informed theological experimentation" and "our never-ending tasks of theologizing." This conception of doctrine as process is to be sure not unchecked by the already noted twofold condition: "careful regard for our heritage and fourfold guidelines." We shall, then, have to examine more closely what is allowed respecting the normativeness of our acknowledged doctrinal heritage.

OUR DOCTRINAL HERITAGE: STATUS AND FUNCTION

The authors of Part II are aware that they are faced with the question "as to the status and function of 'doctrinal standards' in The United Methodist Church" as an inherited issue. Both Sections 1 and 3 manifest conspicuous effort to attain firm dialectical balance between the norm of tradition with loyalty to our heritage on the one side and to make way for timely doctrinal restatement on the other. I would wish to acknowledge the earnestness with which our document faces the treacherous task of attempting to balance the reciprocal counterclaims of loyalty and freedom. We can consider only briefly these contraries in tension, the principle of freedom first.

One has the impression that operative in favor of the principle of freedom are certain prepossessions of thought as various as: Wesley's important sermon, "The Catholic Spirit"; John Henry Newman's theory of the development of dogma; the *aggiornamento* of Vatican II; American process theology; and a wee bit of existential openness for the future. All these leave their mark, but preeminently does Wesley's denigration of what he called "opinion" in matters religious—a concept popularly misunderstood but not, I think, misused in our document.

Disregarding these presumed prepossessions, certain working principles favoring flexibility in doctrinal standards and hospitable to "yet further unfoldings of history" in continuing doctrinal developments

282

are worth noting. They fall into the following groups: (1) judgments of historical fact as interpreted, (2) principles of historical interpretation, (3) axiomatical theological postulates, and (4) pragmatic-prudential considerations.

Among a dozen historical judgments precedential for the principle of freedom and development are such debatable assertions as: that among the fathers of Methodism "doctrinal pluralism" already was acknowledged; that they declined to adopt the "classical forms of the confessional principle"; that a conciliar principle in "collegial formula" was manifest in the Model Deed; that the role of the Articles was ambiguous early in nineteenth-century Methodism. It is judged that the collegial formula "committed the Methodist people to the biblical revelation as primary without proposing a literal summary of that revelation in any propositional form." This last seems right-headed enough save for the objectionable confusion of creedal symbol with a literal proposition.

Finally, and of large import, is the dubious historical judgment rendered upon the longstanding Articles and the Confession that they "are not to be regarded as positive, juridical norms of doctrine," although it is not clear whether this is meant to characterize their past status by alleged longstanding consensus or their future standing. In response to this judgment, one is disposed to inquire earnestly by what rationale the First Restrictive Rule was first instituted in 1808 and with what purpose it has survived in the intervening wisdom of the church. What was the function of such a rule if indeed the confessional principle was as much a matter of indifference to the mind of the church as is represented?

As to principles of historical interpretation there is space to mention but two or three: Emphatically conciliar in import is the hermeneutical principle that "Scripture is rightly read and understood *within* the believing community." This also is anticipated and affirmed in Wesley's way of interpreting biblical language—another question of fact. Secondly, the "new historical consciousness" justifies the historical interpretation of all historical documents and thus also the Methodist Articles or Confession—meaning that they are relative to their given context and so without finality. On this ground, there emerges the third and decisive principle, that all doctrinal standards of the past, present, or future are "landmark documents." They may be pointers to the truth, never finalities. And, finally, the infinite qualitative difference between time and eternity is illustrated in the self-evident proposition that "God's eternal Word never has been, nor can be exhaustively expressed in any single form of words." In consequence, it is perhaps in order to be informed, as historical *fact*, that the founding fathers did not invest "summaries of Christian truth...with final authority or set them apart as absolute standards for doctrinal truth and error."

One outcome of this hermeneutic is surely expressed in the following summation: "But, since they are not accorded any status of finality, either in content or rhetoric, there is no objection in principle to the continued development of still other doctrinal summaries and liturgical creeds that may gain acceptance and use in the Church—without displacing those we already have. This principle of the historical interpretation of all doctrinal statements, past and present, is crucial."

The express denial of any status of finality, of course, imperils the very conception of doctrinal standards and would seem to require positive attention to the question of such surviving normativeness they might yet command. The final quoted sentence strikes me as a remarkable understatement. Depending on how it is hereafter to be used, it is momentous in implication for all doctrinal standards whatsoever (*i.e.*, norms)—and not only those past or present, but, on the same principle of historical interpretation, *those of any conceivable future.* Accordingly, it is not out of keeping that Section 3, whether intentionally or not, tends to replace *all* past, present, or future doctrine or dogma with an unlimited *process* of "theologizing."

In this perspective, is it something like the case that the church is now to live perpetually on theological credit? In reflection one is inclined to wonder whether the authors of this document either did not fully understand their own logic as a committee, or that some did, and because they had relinquished any possibility of standards had resort to collective "theologizing" as a permanent substitute for doctrine. Yet this seems to be the outcome of the logic employed, however awkward the new day in which the church is obliged to rely mainly for truths to live by upon the ever-receding promise of the future.

PRIMARY THEOLOGICAL POSTULATES AND
THE CORE OF DOCTRINE

By examining some theological postulates of our document— mainly set forth in Section 3, "Our Theological Task"—we may be better informed respecting the unanswered question as to what normativeness the "landmark documents" may yet possess, deprived, as they are said to be, of any status of finality. At the same time, we may be better positioned to judge the success of our document in achieving a balance between loyalty and freedom toward the heritage of doctrinal standards. That Part II aspires to such a balance is a note variously sounded, as, for example, with reference to emerging ecumenical theology which seeks to "provide a constructive alternative" to the confessional tradition or in the expressed view in retrospect that Part II has been seeking to chart "a course between doctrinal dogmatism on the one hand and doctrinal indifferentism on the other."

Methodologically speaking, this disavowal of indifferentism in doctrine does operate as a theological postulate whether vindicated or not. It has explicit antecedence in Wesley's pervasive teaching on "the catholic spirit," which rejects speculative or practical latitudinarianism and excludes, therefore, indifferentism in either doctrine or ecclesiology. Whether the contrasting phrase "doctrinal dogmatism" is unduly denigrative of "doctrinal standards" we leave unattended. It suffices here to note that on its face our document allies itself with Wesley in rejecting indifferentism and sets aside as erroneous "the notion that there are no essential doctrines and that differences in theology, when sincerely held, need no further discussion." To this extent, then, we must acknowledge that theological pluralism considered as a principle suffers some modification.

A second primary postulate prefaces Section 3: "Both our heritage in doctrine and our present theological task share common aims: the continuously renewed grasp of the gospel of God's love in Christ and its application in the ceaseless crises of human existence." Herewith, it is plainly indicated that the doctrinal process proceeds both with a core inheritance and is undertaken in context. Our theological task, then, is always contextual and, for that reason, must appropriately take the form of an answering process if it is to be living or relevant. This undergirds the postulate of theological development as an inescapable requirement, which is yet a third.

But let us consider the postulate of the "core" of Christian truth as a fourth postulate, although it deserves to be regarded, and does function, as primary in Section 3. I think it is not misleading to say that the core of any surviving doctrinal standard is intended to be encapsuled in the already quoted phrase, "the gospel of God's love in Christ." The key paragraph is the first under the heading "United Methodists and the Christian Tradition." There it is said that Methodist theologizing does not begin *de novo*, but shares a "common heritage with all other Christians everywhere and in all ages." It is affirmed that there "is a core of doctrine which informs in greater or less degree our widely divergent interpretations." It is not clear whether "divergent interpretations" refers to the *oikoumene* or to Methodists themselves, but we may safely assume to both.

But here one thing becomes very clear: the well-known scene of ecumenical diversity is being applied by analogy to a single denomination—the Methodist—and that, partly on this analogy, the factual diversity *without*—as among denominations *inter alia*—is affirmed to obtain *within* Methodism as a fact but also as a norm. This is, I think, misuse of analogy, but it becomes another basic and unexamined postulate which contributes its unannounced support for the presiding thesis of "theological pluralism as a principle." An appropriate rejoinder may well be the question, With what right is factual doctrinal diversity among a plurality of separate churches taken to be a standard model in assessing the role and status of doctrinal standards in any *one* denomination? To assume that it is or may be modular or normative begs the question on an issue of maximum importance.

What, then, is "core of doctrine," and what is its status for "doctrinal standards" in The United Methodist Church? It is at this point that the assessment of the issue of loyalty will have to be played down to the wire. The core in our document is delineated under two aspects: (1) The first succinctly relates the principal doctrinal content of the universally shared Christian tradition on pages 71–72. This is the "common faith in the mystery of salvation in and through Jesus Christ," which includes overcoming our willful alienation through God's pardoning love in Christ and states that through faith, enabled by the Holy Spirit, we receive "the gift of reconciliation and justification." (2) The second aspect of the core of doctrine, presuming the common Christian tradition as above, singles out distinctive emphases or particular traditions of the Methodist heritage. These, with right, may be viewed as truly embedded in that tradition and as rooted in both the *Standard Sermons* of John Wesley and in the liturgy and hymnody, and exemplified in the Social Creed of American Methodism. Since they are readily available, and for economy of space, I pass over their substance.

Such, then, is the "common," together with the "distinctive," core of the doctrinal heritage by which it is indicated our loyalty ought rightly to be claimed as a wholesome guide and check upon freedom in theologizing. This doctrinal core is, then, a norm claiming our respect, but evidently not our adherence. However, as we scrutinize the language of our document respecting the normativeness of the core of doctrine, a resilient ambiguity persists.

ROBERT E. CUSHMAN

FOUR SUCCESSIVE POSTULATES AND
THEOLOGICAL PLURALISM

On further examination, the ambiguity appears to rest upon a succession of mutually supportive unexplicated theological postulates that, collectively, reinforce the thesis of "theological pluralism...as a principle." This may indicate that the ambiguity is intentional or at least unavoidable in view of the premises.

The first postulate takes the form of a tacit definition of the nature and the status of the doctrinal heritage represented by the core in the following proposition: "From our response in faith to the wondrous mystery of God's love in Jesus Christ as recorded in Scripture, all valid Christian doctrine is born." Doctrine, then, is always faith's response to the mystery. Its nature and status are that it is *our response*. Such a status is also that of the traditions of doctrine which are later described as "the residue of corporate experience of earlier Christian communities." Actually, the postulate simply reiterates the earlier declaration of Section 1: "that God's eternal Word never has been, nor can be, exhaustively expressed in any single form of words." Here, then, the limit to finality—and now with respect, not simply to the Confessions but to the core of tradition—is not the historical relativity of any response of faith; it is, rather, the ineffability of the eternal Word or the wondrous mystery that is symbolized.

The seconding postulate occurs earlier in our document and is used to retire the older "confessional tradition" in favor of "our newer experiments in ecumenical theology." Apparently, there is here further unargued dependency on analogy earlier noted. Thereafter, the passing of the confessional tradition in favor of the ecumenical method in doctrine is justified by the seconding postulate: "The transcendent mystery of divine truth allows us in good conscience to acknowledge the positive virtues of doctrinal pluralism even within the same community of believers, not merely because such an attitude is realistic." Immediately thereafter, it is stated: "The invitation to theological reflection is open to all."

The third consummating postulate is, then, invoked in the paragraph just mentioned, although carried over from its earlier formulation "as the principle of the historical interpretation of all doctrinal statements" —self-styled as crucial, as already discussed. It is this hermeneutical principle that banishes any status of finality for standards and opens the door to horizons unlimited in theological development. And it is this that justifies not only the thesis of theological pluralism as a principle but does so by way of the final postulate.

The fourth postulate functions as the conclusion of the series. It first appeared and offered itself as a judgment of alleged historical fact, *viz.*, that the Methodist fathers "declined to adopt the classical forms of the confessional principle." It now appears in the succession of scantily supported theological postulates as the conclusion: "No creed or doctrinal summary can adequately serve the needs and intentions of United Methodists in confessing their faith or in celebrating their Christian experience" (p. 79). This is, indeed, far reaching in import and amply supplies the rationale for the view that our doctrinal standards are merely landmark documents. It also appropriately justifies the exordium, *viz.*, "The United Methodist Church expects all its members to accept the challenge of responsible theological reflection." If there is no finally reliable past in standards, perhaps hope may yet make a future! So be it, but the concluding postulate, standing as an unsupported *ipse dixit*, smacks rather more of academic sophistication than of the living piety of generations of Christians who have found in the venerable language of the Liturgy and the Creed more than enough light to illumine their darkness, indeed more than they used.

A BRIEF PROVISIONAL ASSESSMENT

This critical analysis must be abruptly terminated without further needed scrutiny of certain of the working postulates, consideration of the role of "experience" in the Wesleyan tradition, or perhaps adequate attention to a defined method for doctrinal development which does set some bounds to conciliar "theologizing" that is otherwise enthusiastically enthroned. This methodology is developed under the heading "Doctrinal Guidelines in The United Methodist Church."

The treatment of guidelines is knowledgeable and skillfully executed. It invokes a fourfold reference to Scripture, tradition, experience, and reason as guidelines in theological reflection. It finds them in Wesley and attributes their centrality to the founding fathers. The method is briefly stated very early in Section 1. There it is allowed that the fathers did acknowledge a marrow of true doctrine, and states: "This living core, as they believed, stands revealed in Scripture, illumined by tradition, vivified in personal experience, and confirmed by reason."

In this viewpoint, attributed to the Methodist fathers, we seem to be within reach of some yardstick to measure loyalty to doctrinal standards.

It may be inadvertent as it is, I believe, unfortunate that the later, more expansive treatment of "guidelines" does not recapture the centrality of Scripture or vindicate its primacy. On the contrary, it vitiates the greater decisiveness of the earlier passage in which tradition, experience, and reason are recognized, in that order, and are subsumed to the primacy of Scripture. Such a viewpoint might well have clarified the dialectic balance of loyalty and freedom, and likewise qualified the outcome, by way of appropriating faith, to be what Wesley did describe, among his sermons, as "Scriptural Christianity." Yet under "Doctrinal Guidelines," faith, though possibly presupposed, has no mention as requisite for operation of the guidelines. In fact, justifying faith has scant treatment in the entire document and is scarcely conceived as the presupposition of Christian theology.

This, too, contributes to the vitiation of the standpoint justly attributed to the fathers respecting the primacy of Scripture, but of course for faith. But the decisive vitiation of the admirable earlier statement quoted above and the resurgence of ambiguity ensues again with the following two sentences in summation of the Guidelines: "There is a primacy that goes with Scripture, as the constitutive witness to biblical wellsprings of our faith. In practice, however, theological reflection may find its point of departure in tradition, 'experience,' or rational analysis."

This statement takes back, it seems, with the left hand what it gives with the right. Moreover, the extraordinary second sentence in this binary formulation quite evidently gives covey to every species of theological partridge except one bred in the Reformation tradition or cognizant of the Pauline gospel. Allowing for whatever the qualifier, "in practice," may mean to the authors, the latter sentence allows to Scripture only par value with the other three norms. But, altogether astonishing, it gives back all that Part II has striven to deny, namely, the confessional principle or tradition, as a starting point in doctrinal formulation. Finally, it is an understatement to observe that *Christian* doctrine, of whatever provenance, has not often found its starting point in "rational analysis." This is a fatal sentence, but perhaps it illustrates a pervasive claim of the document that all theological reflection is historically conditioned.

So far as this analysis has taken us, ambiguity respecting the status of doctrinal standards remains largely unrelieved and the vindication of a true dialectical balance of loyalty and freedom seems unattained. Among things accomplished is a rather fervent postulation of fully liberated conciliarism conceived in virtual equivalence with twentieth-century ongoing interchurch ecumenical dialogue. Without adequate representation of the case, this is unhesitatingly proposed as the timely model for intramural doctrinal standards, both in status and in function. In addition to installing intramural theological pluralism on principle, Part II is correspondingly bent upon the eradication of what it recognizes as "classical forms of the confessional principle." Perhaps it has won favor because in The United Methodist Church, as doubtless elsewhere, theological "indifferentism" has for long been nurturing a favorable climate.

BI-LATERAL DIALOGUES

The recent history of ecumenical theological conversation has included bi-lateral conversations among different denominations and world confessional families. Both the World Methodist Council and the United Methodist Church have entered into dialogues with Roman Catholics and Lutherans. These conversations have furthered the effort for self-definition and mutual affirmation. Because of the importance of the achievement of these discussions and the indications they provide for future theological understanding, two of the documents are included in this collection. The document on baptism prepared by the United Methodist/Lutheran meetings and the document on the ministry prepared by the United Methodist/Roman Catholic meetings represent achievement and challenge in ongoing theological conversation.

A LUTHERAN-UNITED METHODIST STATEMENT ON BAPTISM

developed by
MEMBERS OF THE LUTHERAN-UNITED METHODIST
Bilateral Dialogue Team
Adopted December 11, 1979

I. INTRODUCTION

1. As participants in the Lutheran-United Methodist bilateral consultation, which has met six times since 1977 and has now concluded its work, we report with gratitude to our churches the pastoral, liturgical,

and evangelical concord and concern which we have discovered in our discussions.

2. It is fundamental to this report to note that our Lutheran and United Methodist churches acknowledge Scripture as the source and the norm of Christian faith and life and share with the whole catholic Church in that Christology and that Trinitarian faith which are set forth in the ecumenical Apostles' and Nicene Creeds. We also share the biblical Reformation doctrine of justification by grace through faith. We are agreed that we are justified by the grace of God for Christ's sake, through faith alone and not by the works demanded of us by God's law. We also recognize the common emphasis on sanctification as a divinely promised consequence of justification. We affirm that God acts to use the sacraments as means of grace. As heirs of the Reformation, we share a heritage of scriptural preaching and biblical scholarship. We also share a hymnic tradition, care for theological education, and concern for evangelical outreach.

3. We have continually recognized the validity of the acts of Baptism administered in accord with Scripture in our churches. While this recognition testifies to our considerable agreement in doctrine and practice, it rests finally upon the shared acknowledgment of Baptism as an effective sign of God's grace. First and foremost, Baptism is God's gift, act, and promise of faithfulness. The entire life of faith and even our attempts to articulate a common understanding of God's prior act of grace are but a response of praise and thanksgiving.

4. The acknowledgment of God's gift as validly bestowed in the acts of Baptism administered in United Methodist and Lutheran churches entails the recognition of the shared benefit of the work of the Holy Spirit among us. Thus we are called to confess the scandal of whatever disunity or party spirit may still exist among us and between us lest we are found to despise God's gift. Our unity in Christ and in one Spirit is the unity of those who have been washed and forgiven, incorporated into Christ's death and resurrection, and called together for witness and service in his world until he comes again. This unity made manifest in Baptism is an inauguration and foretaste of the rule of God in all of life.

Thus we are offering to our churches the following Affirmations, Implications, and Recommendations as tangible expressions of our hope that our churches and congregations will seek further means for achieving a fuller manifestation of our God-given unity in Christ, of our sharing in one Spirit and one Baptism.

II. AFFIRMATIONS

5. We accept as valid all acts of Baptism in the Name of the Trinity using water according to Christ's command and promise (Matt. 28:18–20).

6. We affirm that Baptism is the sacrament of entrance into the holy catholic Church, not simply a rite of entrance into a particular denomination. Baptism is therefore a sacrament which proclaims the profound unity of the Church (I Cor. 12:13; Gal. 3:27–28). Baptism is a gift of God for the upbuilding of the Christian community.

7. We affirm that grateful obedience to the divine invitation obligates all believers to be baptized and to share the responsibility for baptizing.

8. We affirm that Baptism is intended for all persons, including infants. No person should be excluded from Baptism for reasons of age or mental capacity.

9. We affirm with Scripture that God gives the Holy Spirit in Baptism:
—to unite us with Jesus Christ in his death, burial and resurrection (Rom. 6:1–11; Col. 2–12);
—to effect new birth, new creation, newness of life (John 3:5; Titus 3:5);
—to offer, give, and assure us of the forgiveness of sins in both cleansing and life-giving aspects (Acts 2:38);
—to enable our continual repentance and daily reception of forgiveness, and our growing in grace.
—to create unity and equality in Christ (I Cor. 12:13; Gal. 3:27–28);
—to make us participants in the new age initiated by the saving act of God in Jesus Christ (John 3:5);
—to place us into the Body of Christ where the benefits of the Holy Spirit are shared within a visible community of faith (Acts 2:38; I Cor. 12:13).

10. We affirm that in claiming us in Baptism, God enables the Christian to rely upon this gift, promise, and assurance throughout all of life. Such faithful reliance is necessary and sufficient for the reception of the benefits of Baptism.

11. We affirm that Baptism is both the prior gift of God's grace and the believer's commitment of faith. Baptism looks toward a growth into the measure of the stature of the fullness of Christ (Eph. 4:13). By this growth, baptized believers should manifest to the world the new race of a redeemed humanity which puts an end to all human estrangement based, for example, on race, sex, age, class, nationality, and disabling conditions. In faith and obedience, the baptized live for the sake of Christ, of his Church, and of the world which he loves. Baptism is a way in which the Church witnesses to the faith and proclaims to the world

the Lordship of Jesus Christ. (See World Council of Churches Statement, "One Baptism, One Eucharist, and a Mutually Recognized Ministry.")

III. IMPLICATIONS AND RECOMMENDATIONS

12. *Baptism is related to a Christian community and (except in unusual circumstances) should be administered by an ordained minister in the service of public worship of the congregation.*

> We agree that Baptism should not be a private act. In communities where United Methodist and Lutheran congregations exist, they can support one another as they resist pressure for private, family baptisms. Normally, for reasons of good order, the ordained officiate at Baptisms, but any person may administer the sacrament in unusual circumstances.

13. *Lutherans and United Methodists agree that pre-baptismal instruction of candidates or their parents (or surrogate parents) is of crucial importance.*

> Therefore we encourage ministers and congregations to take this instruction seriously and to support one another as they resist pressure to minimize such instruction.

14. *The Christian community has the responsibility to receive and nurture the baptized. When infants or children are baptized we regard it as essential that at least one parent, surrogate parent, or other responsible adult make an act of Christian commitment to nurture them in the Christian faith and life.*

> There may be circumstances in which the refusal of Baptism is appropriate because this condition has not been met. Both United Methodist and Lutheran pastors can support one another by respecting and interpreting the action of one of them who has refused to administer Baptism.
> Sponsors (or Godparents) may support the parent, surrogate parent, or other responsible adult in this act of commitment, but are not substitutes for such a committed individual.

15. *When a Christian family is partly Lutheran and partly United Methodist, the nurture of the baptized child is of primary importance. Here an opportunity also exists to display Christian unity in the midst of diversity.*

> It is important for one congregation to assume primary responsibility to nurture the child in the Christian life.
> Where one parent is more active than the other, it is recommended that the sponsoring congregation be the congregation of the more active parent.

It is recommended that the pre-baptismal instruction be given by the pastor of the sponsoring congregation; or joint instruction under both pastors can take place, as this will enrich both traditions.

16. *We believe Baptism is not repeatable.*

Because we understand Baptism as entrance into the Church, we do not condone rebaptism of persons on any grounds, including new Christian experience or change of denominational membership.

Since United Methodists and Lutherans recognize one another's Baptism, we violate the integrity of our faith, pervert the meaning of Baptism, and impair our relation with other baptized Christians if we rebaptize.

17. *When instructed persons have made their profession of faith for themselves in the act of Baptism, their Christian initiation requires no separate rite of confirmation.*

Baptism is sacramentally complete even though the baptized Christian looks forward to a lifetime of Christian instruction and growth regular reaffirmations or renewals of the baptismal covenant.

18. *We respect each other's practice of confirmation.*

We rejoice that both communities have an appreciation for the life-long need for a pastoral and educational ministry. The baptized should be given frequent opportunity to reflect upon the meaning of their covenant through confirmation, sermons, curricula, and other such means.

While orientation to the history, liturgy, and practice of the denomination and a particular congregation is appropriate for persons who transfer from one of our denominations to the other, a further confirmation rite should not be required.

19. *Baptism witnesses to Christian unity, and therefore it enables transfer between our denominations.*

Because we believe that Baptism is the fundamental initiation into the Church, we affirm our oneness in Jesus Christ as taking precedence over our denominational divisions.

When persons transfer their membership between our denominations, they should not feel that they have thereby broken their earlier baptismal and confirmation promises. Pastors should provide opportunity for those transferring to make public reaffirmation of their baptism with the new congregation and denomination in an appropriate manner.

Each denomination affirms the pastoral and nurturing minis try of the other denomination and gladly commits members to the care of the other denomination when its own denomination does not provide an adequate congregational family for those members.

Because we are baptized not into a denomination nor into a particular congregation only, but into the one Church of Jesus Christ, therefore in communities where both Lutheran and United Methodist congregations exist, efforts may be made to share mutually in baptismal celebrations, thereby showing forth our essential unity.

20. *United Methodist and Lutheran theology and practice allow Baptism to be administered in various modes, including immersion, pouring and sprinkling.*

We agree that whatever mode is used, Baptism is an act in which the use of water is an outward and visible sign of the grace of God. The water of baptism, therefore, should be administered generously so that its sign value will be most effectively perceived by the congregation.

21. *The celebration of Baptism should reflect the unity of the Church which Baptism proclaims.*

Because in Baptism the contemporary Church is united to the historic Church, baptismal rites should draw upon the ancient traditions of the Church and also should serve to illustrate the catholicity of the Church in our time. In addition to the normative Trinitarian Baptismal formula in accordance with Matthew 28:19, the renunciation, the Apostles' Creed, and the prayer of thanksgiving over the water are also recommended.

We urge the common development of liturgical formulations for the rite of Baptism by the liturgical agencies of our respective churches.

IV. CONCLUSION

22. This document represents the consensus of the undersigned members of the dialogue team after three years of intense discussion and prayerful deliberation. We commend it to our churches for their study and action. We hope it will serve as an impetus and resource for dialogue among Lutherans and United Methodists in local communities and throughout our churches.

HOLINESS AND SPIRITUALITY OF
THE ORDAINED MINISTRY

I. National bilateral conversations sponsored by committees of The United Methodist Church and the National Conference of Catholic

Bishops have been in progress since 1966. Over the years these have dealt with a wide variety of subjects of mutual interest and concern. In 1971, the decision was reached to focus the dialogue for a time on an issue of special interest to both churches, namely, "Spirituality in the Ministry." The findings of our sustained study of this subject are the concern of this report.

Several reasons dictated the choice of this particular theme for this dialogue. Both our communions emphasize the importance of a life style which authentically derives from relationship with the Spirit of Christ. This emphasis is not in contradiction to others, such as a confessional emphasis on the faith, but can be perceived as a dimension of Christianity, the importance of which is distinctively underscored in our respective traditions. The subject seemed all the more fruitful as it touches our common emphasis on holiness and spirituality as well as our noticeably different ways of expressing this in life and conduct. It has been experienced by Catholics and United Methodists as a source of sympathetic contact and, at times, of puzzlement or uncertainty with respect to one another. Questions have been raised as to whether distorting pietism, individualism, clericalism, cultic ritualism or triumphalism might lurk in our traditions under the guise of holiness. These questions needed to be explored—and, we hope, resolved—in order to set aside one barrier, real even when only subliminally perceived, to further Roman Catholic-United Methodist understanding and the quest for a more profound reconciliation between us.

Another key reason for our emphasis was the supposition that it would open the way to wider reflections on the life of our churches, and so indeed it has. By focusing on the theme of holiness and spirituality with reference to the ministry, and especially to the ordained ministry, the dialogue did not seek to bypass the even more fundamental question of holiness as lived by the whole church. While our churches may have given more concentrated attention to the holiness and spirituality expected of those ordained in the service of the people, we could see that what has been said and encouraged in regard to ordained persons is illustrative of the holiness to which all members of the church are called.

At the same time, the theme is pertinent to an area in which both of our churches have evidenced the need to achieve new perceptions in our time. The concurrent concerns in both churches suggested that the subject was more than merely timely. It indicated as well a vigorous search for ways of life which are in accord with the values of our traditions and in keeping with the shape of society and the needs of changing cultures.

Finally, we observed that our concerns in this dialogue are equally felt in the larger framework of the ecumenical movement as a whole. By concentrating on the complexities of spirituality in relationship to the ministry, we hoped to contribute a new element to the very rich discussion in other ecumenical forums of other aspects of the ministry.

Among the specific questions our consultation has had to face and has sought to answer in the following report are these:

—Is the holiness and spirituality to which the ordained ministers are called different in either kind or degree from that to which all Christians are called?

—What is the source of the efficacy of the ordained ministry as it is exercised in our communions?

—Are new spiritual disciplines, in some ways different from those followed by priests and ministers in the past, needed today to express and support more clearly the holiness and spirituality of the ministers of the church?

As Roman Catholics and United Methodists, we face together the changing needs of people to whom the ministry seeks to respond. We recognize that just as there is no genuine ecumenism, so there can be no effective ministry, without a willingness for changes of heart. Our report comes out of some experience of warmth and insight into such changes.

II. The vocation of the Christian community as a whole and of each person is to accept the gift of holiness and to employ it as God intends. The requirement of Christian spirituality is conformity of the church and its members to the holiness of God. Each person is to celebrate the coming of the new age in the dying and rising Christ, and to receive his Spirit. Becoming a new creation, they are selected by God to be holy before him. Ministers, therefore, stand among the people of God as men and women who serve and who thereby exemplify the call of all to servanthood. Whether we refer to God as Father, Son, or Spirit, we are speaking equally of the One Whose divine holiness is communicated to our human condition. The holiness of the triune God is known and conceived by us through His gracious revelation.

First, God is the eternal Creator and Sustainer of all that is. Thus, our most appropriate attitude toward Him is one of reverence, awe and love.

Second, God makes himself known as the Holy One of Israel (Isaiah 6; 9; 54:5; 55:5), the Maker and Redeemer of all people and all creation (Isaiah 40:25–26; 41:20; Acts 17:24–26). He chose the People Israel to be a holy community, priestly and prophetic, and bound to himself by a lasting covenant (Exodus 19:5–6). Through the incarnation, ministry, death and resurrection of Jesus Christ, God constituted the universal church as the first fruit of the new creation which he is still bringing to reality (II Cor. 5:17).

Third, God communicates to us that mystery of his holiness and makes us heirs of Israel's faith and joint-heirs with Christ (Rom. 8:17). Three dimensions of God's holiness bear upon our own holiness:

a) Separateness

The Holy God is one; he alone is God (Deuteronomy 5:7 and 6:4). He is not to be confused with any divinities, ideologies or value systems of human devising. The church, too, is to avoid those destructive temptations of the world which distract it from the vocation of holiness: not for fear of pollution of a holy life but of dilution of a holy mission (II Cor. 6:16–18). That is to say, the derived holiness of the church is not to be regarded as the basis for a moral superiority over other human beings; it is the holiness of divine intention, the instrumentality of God's own saving mission in history to all people (Mt. 28:19; Acts 1:8; Jn. 17:18).

b) Love

The Holy God is love (I Jn. 4:8); the highest gift of God, the Holy Spirit, is love (I Cor. 13:13). God's love which became incarnate in Jesus Christ, bridges the separation between God and humanity, heals the estrangement caused by sin and achieves reconciliation. The church and its members who received the gift are not only summoned to love as He loves; as both Roman Catholic and Methodist traditions emphasize, they are made holy in love by the Holy Spirit working amongst us. By sanctification we mean that the grace and power of divine love are displacing the sin of pride and faithlessness in our hearts and minds.

c) Righteousness

The Holy God is righteous (Isaiah 6). God's holiness is manifested in Jesus Christ who is our righteousness and sanctification and who calls us to obedience in grace (I Cor. 1:30). Persons and communities that delight in experiencing and expressing the love of God must likewise delight in the righteous law of the Lord (Ps. 1:2) or else fear the consequences of deliberate disregard of it (Mt. 7:21–23). Love without law is sentimental; law without love is tyrannical. The holiness which the Church receives from God includes both law and love. (Rom. 8:2–4)

III. The church's holiness is a *gift* derived from and dependent on God. It has been accented by our two traditions in different ways. While United Methodists and Catholics are at one in their confession that the church is holy, there is divergence both within and between the two traditions regarding the meaning of the church's holiness and its realization in practice. Such divergence can be partially explained by the respective emphases on different models of the church within the two traditions. For example, in the United Methodist tradition, the church is frequently seen as the herald of God's word; accordingly, the holiness of the church is seen as the personal response to the preaching of the Gospel. For example, in the Catholic tradition, the church is frequently seen as a sacrament, a visible sign conveying God's grace; accordingly, emphasis is given to the necessity of visible signs as means of grace and holiness.

Both these (and other) models of the church are necessary in a comprehensive ecclesiology, which views the different emphases regarding the church's holiness as complementary, not incompatible. Nonetheless, it should be candidly acknowledged that it is not always obvious how the divergent aspects of ecclesiological models can be harmonized either in theory or in practice.

Both Catholics and United Methodists agree that God's holiness is communicated to the church. While the Incarnation is the primary reality of this communication, Biblical sources and Christian history indicate that God communicates himself through a variety of channels. The variety and plurality of God's gifts overwhelm us; particularly so when it comes to theoretical appreciation of them. We do agree that manifold persons and events have been used by the Holy Spirit to actualize God's holiness in the life of the Christian community. If the two traditions sometimes diverge in their respective views of the nature of these gifts and its relation to the individual Christian's holiness, nevertheless it should be recognized that this divergence is not pervasive, since each tradition has shared elements of the other.

Both the Catholic and the United Methodist traditions recognize that the Church's holiness is general and the means of holiness in particular challenge individual Christians to a personal appropriation and manifestation of holiness in their daily lives. Both the wide-ranging diversity of gifts as well as the individuality of each Christian imply that the quest for holiness is uniquely personal. Although the holiness of Christians is quite diverse in practice, it is possible to recognize a number of trends or "schools" in the practice of holiness, in Christian life style, in spirituality. While such diversity is both legitimate and desirable as a personal appropriation and manifestation of God's holiness in Christ through the church, it should not be allowed to cloud, much less to negate, the common quest for holiness that is characteristic of both traditions.

IV. The church's holiness is also a *task*. In the design of God, the church's members are called to serve. In the power of the Spirit, Christians are called to offer themselves to God in praise and worship, always giving thanks for his glory. They likewise devote their energies to sharing with the human family the fruits of redemption. They served God by their life of prayer and surrender to divine grace, and by their compassionate attention to the needs of all their brothers and sisters. Guided by the Word of God, they witness to the liberating action of Christ and bring hope to humanity in its struggle for true freedom.

V. The Lord of the church calls his people to be holy in the totality of their lives. The people of God are assisted in their response to this call by their ordained ministers (priests). Our discussions revealed to us that the basic functions of our clergy are the same, namely, to announce the good news of Christ, to interpret the Scriptures, to exhort the faithful to live in *agape*, to lead the people in prayer, to invite the faithful to meet the Lord in the sacraments, to preside at the eucharistic worship, to exercise pastoral care, to develop Christian education, and to administer the parish. Furthermore, the ordained attempt, in ecumenical dialogue, to arrive at a vision of Christian truth which will establish the authority of this truth within the whole fellowship of the disciples of Christ. They must give special attention to the specific needs of our day: the promotion of peace and reconciliation within and among families, races, classes and nations. Often at the cost of their own comfort they must show compassion for those who suffer, provide assistance to the needy, defend the victims of oppression, and participate in the struggle to achieve political, social and economic justice.

VI. The responsibilities of the ordained ministers have been performed in multiform ways through the centuries, but the fundamental purpose has remained the same: to be instruments of the Spirit in symbolizing and actualizing the community's holiness, apostolicity, catholicity and unity. No one of these four notes of the church can be understood apart from the others. The church's holiness must be seen in relation to its apostolicity, for it stands in continuity with the new age first experienced in the apostolic church. Nor can it be understood apart from its catholicity and unity. Within the church, the Spirit seeks to transform and unify Christians with one another. Through the church the Spirit reaches out to transform and unify the whole human family and all realms of society by his gracious power: the collegial exercise of ministerial oversight of the church's holiness should thus be a reminder and a symbol of the church's unity in the service of the Gospel.

VII. Ordination is a sacramental act by which the church recognizes and authenticates the Spirit's call of certain persons to fulfill the particular functions enumerated above. Accordingly, the church prays that the Spirit impart the gift of grace for the fulfilling of its ministers' apostolic stewardship. The Spirit holds up the ministry, death and resurrection of Jesus Christ as the source and norm of ministerial service and contemplation. As High Priest, he sanctifies them and their actions by his continued empowering presence. We agree that there is no difference between the holiness of the ordained and that of the whole people of God. The minister's manner of being and acting should, from that fact, be in harmony with his or her high calling to be a symbol of the church's holiness, apostolicity, catholicity, and unity. The clergy knows its own frailty and dependence upon the whole company of the faithful. Its members can therefore live out their call to holiness in fellowship with one another and with the people whom they serve.

VIII. The Catholic and United Methodist traditions, in different ways and with different stresses, have both insisted upon the ordained minister's duty to lead a holy life in the service of the Lord. The minister of the word and sacraments, in addition to directing prayer and preaching about it, must be a person of prayer whose life is marked by simplicity and humility.

In the Catholic tradition, celebrating the eucharist usually has been identified as the chief source of spiritual strength for bishops and presbyters. Their mode of access to the means of Christian holiness, however, should not set them apart from the people they serve. Also, a commitment to lifelong celibacy as a means to service has been regarded as a means to holiness, although it is not cited as an absolute in recent official reports to the National Conference of Catholic Bishops. Deacons, bishops and presbyters are committed to approachability, not aloofness or privilege.

In the United Methodist tradition, ordained ministers are required to make an earnest and visible commitment to the pursuit of Christian perfection, in the expectation that the Spirit would empower their growth into holiness of life. In its finest expression this love for God and neighbor has taken the form of challenging the evils of one's time and of meeting the pressing needs of one's contemporaries. If this pattern has sometimes tended to degenerate into a legalizing moralism replacing the disciplined freedom of the Christian individual, it has in general served to remind United Methodist Christians of God's sovereign, sanctifying purpose. Personal restraint has been a constant characteristic. This ministry is open to men and women, married and single persons. The means to Christian holiness in the life of a United Methodist minister are not as specified as those of a Catholic minister, although some daily life of prayer and devotion is assumed. In the past it has often had an individual character and is only now becoming identified as communal or ecclesial.

These examples of holiness patterns so briefly provided are not intended as counters to play one against another. While the means of Christian holiness are or have been quite different in the two traditions, the end for both is that perfection which is love for God and neighbor. We join in seeking new modes of expression to that end.

IX. The forms of Christian holiness have necessarily been influenced by the diverse cultures in the many places in which the church has taken root. Today, various African and Asian religious traditions are making claims on the modes of expressing Christian faith and life. Along with other Christians who live in these places, Catholics and United Methodists are seeing that adaptations to indigenous cultures are indispensable if faith in Christ is to be a religious reality for all peoples. Likewise, in both hemispheres the rapid changes occurring in technological societies create new problems for persons seeking authentic holiness of life. Ministers need the gift to discern in their situations the signs of the Spirit's direction of the human quest for a more spiritually abundant and holy life.

X. The ministers and members of the church should take a positive interest in all contemporary paths to Christian holiness. The spiritual realm, in traditional Christian speech, relates to God's Spirit and his action on the human community and the individual human spirit. The present age is marked by many characteristics not always easily reconcilable. Among them are a widespread search for personal authenticity, a return to simple ways of living, the investigation in depth of human motives, and the adoption of practices like fasting and meditation, often without any reference to Christianity. Such manifestations of the power of the human spirit are to be viewed positively so long as the danger of bondage to the elements of this world is discerned. Christian ministers should be alert to the human potential for good (as for evil) and should share in the struggle for justice against poverty and oppression, as well as for the liberation and full equality of both sexes. In no case may a thing that is good for humanity be impugned by those serving in Christian ministry or preparing for it. At the same time, every striving of the human spirit must be subjected to God's Spirit if it is to prosper as contributing to the reign of God.

XI. Ministerial authority needs to be conceived and practiced as service, not as dominion. Its chief characteristic will be an evident solidarity between ministers and those to whom they minister. For example, the poor and other oppressed should be joined in the struggle against the evils of an oppressive society. Frequently, the need is to identify and attack corporate evil: the demonic spirit of power embedded in institutions, such as the unbridled amassing of wealth and its concomitants of war and economic exploitation. The holiness of the individual, whether minister or lay person, is no sufficient answer to the evil operating in institutions.

XII. A simple way of life best befits Christian ministers, who cannot escape completely the social or individual evils they are bound by. Simplicity may go to the extreme of poverty; poverty, however, is creative only when it is voluntarily chosen or accepted. Ministry, after all, is a service, not a servitude. Therefore, neither ostentatious consumption nor an inequitable return for services fittingly characterizes the minister of the gospel.

XIII. The commitment of our traditions to the holiness of the church and of its ministers carries with it the danger of falling into hypocrisy or arrogance. Much of the modern world reacts negatively to the assertion of the holiness of the church because of its apparent hypocrisy. Hence, the need to emphasize that real compassion and true humility are an integral part of holiness. If they are honest, the church's ministers will acknowledge that they share the anguish of men and women who, like them, are unable to live up to the Gospel and to achieve in themselves the holiness to which they aspire.

XIV. There is great urgency in today's world for mankind's needs and awesome earthly powers to be challenged by moral and humane values. A central part of the church's mission is to facilitate that process. Ministers should be at the forefront of this movement, helping to allow the realities of this world to be directed and transformed by placing them at the service of Christ. In a world marked by growing separation of the secular and the religious and by the conflict of peoples against peoples and class against class, the ordained ministry should be an example of wholeness. Essential to this wholeness is the recognition of the importance of the role of women in the church. Such concern encompasses the need of the two churches to work toward full utilization of and respect for women in all forms of ministry.

XV. As it is only in Christ that the church is holy, ministers will manifest the church's holiness in their own spirituality only if they live their lives as a gift from Christ and as a task for Christ. As they discover the Lord deeper in their own lives, they will find new strength for their service and new joy in their calling.

XVI. In the course of our dialogue we have become keenly aware that our two churches share much common ground. We have attempted to articulate afresh those common elements and convictions about the role the ordained ministry plays in the service of the holiness to which God calls his people. Our report is offered to the many persons in our two churches—as well as to the many beyond them—who sense a need to formulate and to live a spirituality that is both faithful to the gospel and appropriate to our time.

INDEX

Anglicanism, 29, 69, 70, 72, 106, 113,
    117–118, 139, 242, 246
Antinomianism, 26, 32, 37, 38, 39,
    110, 246
Apologetics, 165–169
Apostasy, 49, 92, 100–101, 104
Arianism, 13, 108, 110
Arminianism, 30, 92, 94, 104–105,
    111, 127
Atonement, 6, 15, 28, 36, 92, 97,
    98, 99, 109, 110, 111, 127, 132–
    136, 167, 171, 226, 237, 243
Authority, 166, 168, 169

Baptism, 115–121, 291–296
———, infant, 120–121, 294
Bible, 13, 32, 61, 110, 139–140,
    145–147, 166, 167, 168–169, 221,
    230, 277, 283, 288–289, 292
Biblical criticism, 140, 141–144, 146,
    151, 164, 169
Bishops. *See* Episcopacy

Calvinism, 21, 23, 29, 62, 63, 92, 93,
    94, 109, 243, 245, 246
Christianity, 194–203, 224–226, 228,
    236–239, 251–258, 264–265
Church, the, 74, 120–121, 174–175,
    176–181, 206–207, 225, 228,
    229, 293, 299–301, 304
Church governance, 68–69, 71–73,
    76, 83, 84
Consciousness, 167, 190–192
Conviction, 55, 87, 100

Creation, 128, 187–188, 206
Creeds, 108, 274, 276–277, 288, 292

Damnation, 31, 32, 33, 48–49
Deacons, 75, 79
Death, 4, 27, 36–37, 50–51, 53, 55,
    110, 244, 247, 267–268
Deism, 127–128, 130
Depravity, 25, 30, 62, 109
Doctrine, 13, 106–107, 274–275,
    279–287, 289

Ecumenism, 92, 180–181, 276, 289, 298
Education, 73–74, 80, 84, 173
Elders. *See* Presbyters
Election, 29, 45–50, 92
Episcopacy, 68–76, 78–79, 82, 84
Eucharist, 81, 115, 116, 117, 122–
    126, 302
Evil, 30, 60, 95, 110, 182, 186–187,
    233
Evolution, 189, 190, 197
Experience, religious, 157, 167, 169,
    172, 178, 182, 192–193, 205,
    214, 235, 277, 288–289

Faith, 2–9, 14, 15, 23, 25, 26, 31, 36,
    43, 46, 88, 99–100, 104, 112–113,
    118–119, 137, 138, 152, 154, 167,
    168, 169, 201, 230, 237–238,
    243, 244, 247, 254, 256, 257, 268,
    269, 287, 297
Fall, the, 25, 30, 33, 62, 96–97, 98,
    109, 139

Foreknowledge, 92, 95, 191
Forgiveness of sin, 26, 43, 117–119,
    134–135, 158, 242, 293
Freedom, 263–270, 282, 289, 301

God, 2–3, 14–17, 29, 31, 37–38,
    41, 42, 46, 61, 93, 94, 98–99, 109,
    128–132, 134–135, 155–156,
    160, 170, 171, 174, 176, 182–193,
    195, 196, 198, 200–201, 203,
    212–218, 224–225, 230, 247, 252,
    253, 254, 258, 260, 261–262,
    298–299
———, definitions of, 129–131, 184
———, immanence of, 152–154, 156,
    157, 159–161, 172, 217–218
———, righteousness of, 4, 8, 256,
    257, 299
Gospel, the, 29, 33, 178, 179, 202,
    224, 305
Grace, 2, 4, 5, 9, 27, 28, 31, 33, 37, 38,
    39, 41, 46, 49, 52, 53, 62–63,
    64, 88, 92, 98–99, 100, 111, 113,
    157, 172, 212, 214, 226, 256,
    257, 292, 299, 300
———, prevenient, 7, 21, 25, 30,
    56, 91, 247
Guilt, 4, 6, 26, 28, 36, 96

Heart, 14, 16, 38, 112, 138, 139,
    169, 237
Holiness, 6, 14, 19, 26, 27, 37,
    38, 86–90, 104, 111, 137, 138,
    209–210, 224, 241–248, 297–305
Holy Spirit, 14, 27, 33, 39–44, 62–63,
    64, 97, 99–100, 101, 103, 110,
    111, 118, 155, 167, 178, 180,
    204–211, 228–229, 286
———, witness of, 5, 8, 26, 40–43, 92,
    102, 112–113, 138, 143, 144, 167
Hopkinsianism, 46, 48–49

Incarnation, the, 37, 110, 133, 226,
    229, 237, 300

Jesus Christ, 3–5, 8, 13, 15, 25, 26,
    27, 28–29, 31, 33, 36–37, 38–39,
    49–50, 51–52, 54, 97–98, 110–111,
    132–136, 167, 170–171, 175, 176,

180, 195, 196–199, 200–201,
    206, 208, 215–216, 217, 221, 222,
    223, 224–226, 227, 228, 236–238,
    243, 253, 257–258, 259–263, 267,
    268, 286, 298–299, 302
———, blood of, 4, 6, 15, 25, 26, 28,
    33, 36, 39, 50–51, 88, 104, 117,
    118, 120, 123
Justice, 63, 97, 98
Justification, 6–7, 15, 21, 33, 35–39, 55,
    101, 103, 110, 138, 210, 242,
    243, 244–246, 286
———, by faith, 6, 7, 36, 46–47,
    99–100, 118, 167, 243, 244,
    269, 292

Kingdom of God, the, 159, 160,
    174–176, 202–203, 212, 229,
    256, 262

Law, 4, 6, 9, 14, 26, 36, 37, 39, 51,
    52–53, 59–61, 62, 94, 95, 99, 104,
    153, 155, 161, 217, 266–267,
    299
———, civil, 57–58
Liberalism, 221–223
Location, 68, 84
Lord's Supper. *See* Eucharist
Love, 5, 14, 16, 17, 18, 19, 27, 28, 43,
    46, 51, 101, 103, 134–135, 171,
    190, 198, 201, 202, 208, 214, 215,
    242, 243–244, 245, 247–248,
    258, 266, 286, 299
Lutheranism, 108, 122

Man, 2, 25, 30, 57–62, 63, 91, 96–97,
    186–187, 198–199, 215, 255–256,
    268–269
Mercy, 7, 8, 33, 36, 37, 49, 97, 260
Merit, 100, 243
Methodism, 13–19, 67–85 *passim*,
    92, 93, 105–114, 137–140,
    141, 143, 164–165, 169, 274–281,
    285–286, 288–289, 300, 302
Ministry, 69, 73–78, 80, 82, 296–298,
    301–305
Miracles, 144, 145, 166, 168, 172, 216
Morality, 2, 31–32, 56–62, 167

INDEX

Nature, 109, 153, 154, 156, 157, 160, 188–189, 214, 216

Ordination, 70, 73, 82–83, 301–302

Pantheism, 128, 129, 130
Pelagianism, 25, 110, 251, 255
Perfection, 21, 27, 33, 50–55, 86, 102–104, 209, 210, 241, 242, 243, 244, 245
Pietism, 108
Prayer, 15–16, 81, 102, 156, 160, 172, 214
Preaching, 179, 180, 236
Predestination, 48, 49, 92, 95, 102
Presbyterianism, 83, 84, 113
Presbyters, 68, 73, 76, 79
Pride, 6–7, 16, 226, 246, 299
Prophecy, 254

Quakerism, 116, 117

Rationalism, 110, 166–167, 168, 169
Reason, 128, 129, 131–132, 166, 167, 168, 169, 189, 192, 193, 212, 230–238, 251, 277, 288–289
Reconciliation, 208, 254, 286, 301
Redemption, 4, 8, 15, 36, 88, 97–99, 110, 111, 200, 227, 251, 257
———, general, 28–30, 31, 33, 99
Regeneration, 97, 101–102, 117, 118, 119–120, 167, 241, 243, 244
Religion, 14, 128, 154, 155, 156, 157–158, 159, 183, 186, 193, 195–196, 197–198, 251, 254
Repentance, 7, 137, 138, 242, 243
Responsibility, 62, 92–93, 94, 95, 100, 104, 167
Revelation, 19, 60–62, 109, 128, 166, 167, 168, 169, 172, 183–184, 194
Righteousness, 2, 8, 9, 17, 19, 26, 27, 98, 132, 157, 198
———, imputed, 36, 37, 38, 39, 98, 99
Romanism, 9, 13, 23, 117, 118, 122, 244, 300, 302

Sacraments, 113–114, 178, 179–180, 207, 292
Salvation, 2–10, 14, 21, 25, 26, 31, 32, 33, 36, 37, 39, 55, 64, 92, 99–100, 102, 155, 156, 158, 161, 174, 178–179, 198, 243, 255
Sanctification, 21, 26, 27, 32, 33, 36, 50, 55, 86, 92, 102–104, 110, 117, 119–120, 138, 167, 209, 210, 241, 242, 243, 244–245, 299
Scripture. *See* Bible
Sin, 4, 5, 7, 26, 27, 36, 37, 38, 39, 49–50, 51, 53–54, 55, 95–96, 97, 104, 113, 158, 167, 188, 207–208, 209, 221, 224, 242, 256, 267, 268. *See also* Forgiveness
———, original, 25, 26, 33, 98, 111
Socinianism, 13, 116, 117, 122
Substitutionism, 111, 132

Theism, 127–128, 130
Theology, 172–173, 274, 275–276, 279, 281–290
Trinity, 33, 109, 110, 167, 170, 205, 224, 292

Wesley, John, 1, 21, 23–34, 68, 69, 70–71, 103, 137, 138–139, 140–142, 143–145, 172, 209, 210, 240–241, 242–246, 247, 248, 277, 278, 282, 285, 286, 288
Will, 5, 25, 154, 187, 189, 192
———, free, 30, 92, 93–94, 95, 97–98, 100, 101, 188, 191, 217, 269
Works, 2, 6–7, 23, 38, 46, 100
Worship, 81, 158, 301

Publisher, The Labyrinth Press
Design, Arie Verploegh
Typography, Carolina Academic Press
Typeface, Palatino
Printer, Thomson-Shore
Paper, 60 lb. Glatfelter B-31